# The Enjoyment of Food

Jane Grigson was brought up in the north-east of England, where there is a strong tradition of good eating, but it was not until many years later, when she began to spend three months of each year working in France, that she became really interested in food. *Charcuterie and French Pork Cookery* was the result, exploring the wonderful range of cooked meat products on sale in even the smallest market towns. This book has also been translated into French, a singular honour for an English cookery writer.

After taking an English degree at Cambridge in 1949, Jane Grigson worked in art galleries and publishers' offices and then as a translator. In 1966 she shared the John Florio prize (with Father Kenelm Foster) for her translation of Beccaria's *Of Crime and Punishment*. From 1968 she wrote cookery articles for the *Observer* Colour Magazine; *Good Things* and *Food with the Famous* are based on these highly successful series. In 1973, *Fish Cookery* was published by the Wine and Food Society, followed by *The Mushroom Feast* (1975), a collection of recipes for cultivated, woodland, field and dried mushrooms. She received both the Glenfiddich Writer of the Year Award and the André Simon Memorial Fund Book Award for her *Vegetable Book* (1978) and for her *Fruit Book* (1982), and was voted Cookery Writer of the Year in 1977 for *English Food*. All of these are published in Penguin.

Jane Grigson died in March 1990. In her obituary for the *Independent*, Alan Davidson wrote that 'Jane Grigson left to the English-speaking world a legacy of fine writing on food and cookery for which no exact parallel exists . . . She won to herself this wide audience because she was above all a friendly writer . . . the most companionable presence in the kitchen; often catching the imagination with a deftly chosen fragment of history or poetry, but never failing to explain the "why" as well as the "how" of cookery.' Jane Grigson was married to the late Geoffrey Grigson, poet and critic.

D1342364

*The Enjoyment of Food*

THE BEST OF

# JANE GRIGSON

JANE GRIGSON
Compiled by Roy Fullick

*Illustrated by Yvonne Skargon*

PENGUIN BOOKS

PENGUIN BOOKS

Published by the Penguin Group
Penguin Books Ltd, 27 Wrights Lane, London W8 5TZ, England
Penguin Books USA Inc., 375 Hudson Street, New York, New York 10014, USA
Penguin Books Australia Ltd, Ringwood, Victoria, Australia
Penguin Books Canada Ltd, 10 Alcorn Avenue, Toronto, Ontario, Canada M4V 3B2
Penguin Books (NZ) Ltd, 182–190 Wairau Road, Auckland 10, New Zealand

Penguin Books Ltd, Registered Offices: Harmondsworth, Middlesex, England

First published in Great Britain by Michael Joseph 1992
Published in Penguin Books 1993
1 3 5 7 9 10 8 6 4 2

Copyright © Sophie Grigson, 1992
Illustrations copyright © Yvonne Skargon, 1992
All rights reserved

The moral right of the author has been asserted

Printed in England by Clays Ltd, St Ives plc
Set in Baskerville

# Contents

# Note by the Compiler: Roy Fullick

Jane Grigson died in 1990 at the height of her culinary and literary powers, leaving behind a considerable body of published work on food and cooking, and a reputation in her field of the highest order. Inspired by Elizabeth David, she disseminated their shared belief that it was possible for people in this country to eat better, more excitingly and more enjoyably than ever before if they were open to the real pleasures of the table and were willing to experiment.

This book is intended both as a tribute to Jane Grigson's culinary skills and scholarship and as a practical cookery book. It is divided into eight chapters, broadly comparable in layout, which illustrate her personal interests and give a glimpse of Jane the person. All of the early recipes have now been metricated; a note after each extract or recipe shows the book or magazine from which it was taken.

As Jane herself wrote in the Introduction to *Good Things*: 'Anyone who likes to eat can soon learn to cook well.' Her books and articles provide an invaluable guide to achieving that culinary success.

# Introduction by Elizabeth David

The first I ever knew of Jane Grigson was a typescript sent to me by Anthea Joseph of Michael Joseph, my own publishers.

For us in England, Jane's *Charcuterie and French Pork Cookery*, published in 1967, was a real novelty, and a wonderfully welcome one. Now that the book has long since passed into the realm of kitchen classics we take it for granted, but for British readers and cooks in the late 1960s its contents, the clarity of the writing, and the confident knowledge of its subject and its history displayed by this young author were new treats for all of us.

The subject had been little dealt with in English culinary textbooks – and for that matter it was, and remains, one seldom written about by the French – but here was a writer who could combine a delightful quote from Chaucer on the subject of a pike galantine with a careful recipe for a modern chicken and pork version of the same ancient dish, and who could do so without pedantry or a hint of preciousness. Jane was always entertaining as well as informative.

Living half the year in France, the other half in their small Wiltshire farmhouse, provided Geoffrey and Jane with unusual opportunities for driving about the country, searching out interesting food markets and small restaurants where local specialities were likely to be on offer.

The Grigsons didn't frequent expensive establishments. They couldn't afford to. Indeed, I remember Jane telling me that for many years they couldn't even afford a fridge. So, for her, fresh food and good-quality produce never lost their importance or their impact. I think that was one of the essential points which made her articles and her books on English food so worthwhile, to herself as well as to her readers. Those were truly brave undertakings, and they were handsomely rewarded.

When, back in 1967, I read that typescript of Jane's first book, I hadn't met her. It was only later, while the book was already in production, that Anthea Joseph invited us both out to lunch. After lunch I took Jane back to my Pimlico shop so that she could see the glazed stoneware salting jars and rillette pots and earthenware terrines we were at that time importing from France.

Jane found those traditional farmhouse and charcuterie preserving pots and jars as beautiful and beguiling as I did myself and of course they were very relevant to her book. We shared many tastes and convictions, so it was hardly surprising that we soon became firm friends, conducting long Sunday morning telephone conversations, corresponding on subjects of mutual interest – anything from medieval English bread laws to eighteenth-century French ice creams – and every now and again meeting for lunch or dinner in London.

On one memorable Sunday morning, when I had arranged for a Pakistani friend to take me, with Jane, to the big food market at Southall and to lunch afterwards in a local Indian restaurant, both Jane and my friend Nayab arrived to find my house in chaos.

Thanks to the ministrations of an inept plumber, who had, of course, quickly vanished, water from my bathroom was cascading through the living-room ceiling. Rugs, parquet floor, furniture, and my own sanity were all in jeopardy. It was inevitably Jane who took charge, fetching bowls from the kitchen, moving vulnerable furniture and piles of books out of the path of the deluge and generally restoring calm in what had threatened to become a disaster area.

It was a reassuring performance. Indeed, Jane was at all times a reassuring person. I loved her dearly. The cruel cancer which took her from us, so soon after the loss of her beloved Geoffrey, was met by her with the most marvellous courage and good humour. She even laughed at what she knew was her fatal illness.

This varied yet balanced compilation of Jane's work will, whilst reminding us all of the loss of a major creative force in the cookery world, surely persuade everyone to acquire any of Jane's books that are missing from their shelves. Hers are books which can be read in the comfort of one's sitting room as well as used in the kitchen.

# AT HOME IN ENGLAND

JANE GRIGSON'S ENTHUSIASM for English food and cooking stemmed back to her childhood in the north-east of England. 'We lived in Sunderland, in a tall house, with taller, much grander houses across the back lane which had become slum tenements. We spent holidays near Whitby, at the seaside or on farms with ducks and chickens in the yard, peas and gooseberries in the garden.'

She was a relentless champion of the fine tradition of English cooking and of the quality of ingredients produced in these islands. Throughout her career, whether in articles for the *Observer* or in her books, she showed, time and again, that not only does Britain have a culinary heritage to be proud of, but that it is one that is still extremely active. *English Food* was a celebration of that heritage. Ten years later, in *The Observer Guide to British Cookery*, Jane explored the current state of food production and preparation; she gave support and encouragement to the new generation of chefs, producers and retailers who shared her vision.

Her optimism, however, did not blind her to the considerable culinary inadequacies of the country. She was tireless in her condemnation of falling standards, limitation of choice and the sacrifice of flavour and texture in the interests of appearance and profit. The following piece, which is taken from *English Food*, shows this clearly.

The English are a very adaptive people. English cooking – both historically and in the mouth – is a great deal more varied and delectable than our masochistic temper in this matter allows. There's an extra special confusion nowadays in talking of good and bad national cooking. The plain fact is that much commercial cooking is bad or mediocre in any country – it's easy enough to get a thoroughly disappointing meal even in France where there exists an almost sacred devotion to kitchen and table. The food we get publicly in England isn't so often bad English cooking as a pretentious and inferior imitation of French cooking or Italian cooking.

It is also true that a good many things in our marketing system now fight against simple and delicate food. Tomatoes have no taste. The finest flavoured potatoes are not available in shops. Vegetables and fruit are seldom fresh. Milk comes out of Friesians. Cheeses are subdivided and imprisoned in plastic wrapping. 'Farm fresh' means eggs which are no more than ten, fourteen or twenty days old. Words such as 'fresh' and 'home-made' have been borrowed by commerce to tell lies.

In spite of all this, the English cook has a wonderful inheritance if she cares to make use of it. It's a question of picking and choosing, and that exactly is what I have done for this book. My aim has been to put in obvious dishes on a basis of quality: even more, I have tried to show how many surprises there are. I have also included a number of Welsh dishes because I like them, and because they are linked closely with much English food, while retaining a rustic elegance which we have tended to lose.

No cookery belongs exclusively to its country, or its region. Cooks borrow – and always have borrowed – and adapt through the centuries. Though the scale in either case isn't exactly the same, this is as true, for example, of French cooking as of English cooking. We have borrowed from France. France borrowed from Italy direct, and by way of Provence. The Romans borrowed from the Greeks, and the Greeks borrowed from the Egyptians and Persians.

What each individual country does do is to give all the elements, borrowed or otherwise, something of a national character. The history of cooking is in some ways like the history of language, though perhaps it's harder to unravel, or like the history of folk music. The first mention of a dish, the first known recipe for it, can seldom be taken as a record of its first appearance. As far as origins go, there's seldom much point in supposing that a dish belongs to Yorkshire, or Devonshire, or Shropshire because it has survived in those places and may bear their names. What goes for counties goes for countries. Who is to say whether *Pain Perdu* or Poor Knights of Windsor is really English or French; both in France and England it was a dish of the medieval court. Did the English call it payn pur-dew out of the kind of snobbery we can still recognize, or because they took it from France? And if they took it from France, where did the French take it from? It's a marvellous way of using up stale bread, especially good bread, and who is to say that earlier still the Romans, or the Greeks before the Romans, didn't see the point of frying up bread and serving it with something sweet? In England today *Pain Perdu* has been anglicized into a nursery or homely dish, Poor Knights of Windsor. In France with brioche to hand, or the light *pain de mie*, *Pain Perdu* remains a select dish gracefully adorned with brandied fruit and dollops of cream under such names as *Croûte aux Abricots*.

There is no avoiding the fact that the best cooking has come down from the top. Or if you don't like the word 'top', from the skilled, employed by those who could pay and had the time to appreciate quality. In England on the whole the food descends less from a courtly tradition than from the manor houses and rectories and homes of well-to-do merchants – latterly from a Jane Austen world. It hands down the impression of the social life of families in which the wives and daughters weren't too grand to go into the kitchen and to keep a close eye on the vegetable garden and dairy. This was the world in which the great amateur horticulturalist Thomas Andrew Knight in his Herefordshire manor house diversified and improved so many fruits and vegetables in the late years of the eighteenth century and the early years of the nineteenth.

One thing to note is that the great English cookery writers from Hannah Glasse to Elizabeth David have always been women, in contrast to the French tradition of cookery writing by male chefs. Our classical tradition has been domestic, with the domestic virtues of quiet enjoyment and generosity. Whatever happened when the great mass centres developed in the nineteenth century, English cookery books of the eighteenth century to early Victorian times had been written from an understanding of good food and good eating, a concern for quality. Mrs Beeton had her great qualities, and gave many marvellous recipes. But from the first edition of her book in 1859, you can see the anxiety of the new middle class, balanced between wealth and insolvency, and always at pains to keep up appearances. And keeping up appearances remains the *leitmotiv* of much modern food advertising. Showy photographs in what is called 'full' colour and the message 'Impress your Friends' or 'Impress his Boss' suggest that without taking any trouble or thought at all, marvellous food will fall out of the packet on to the plate. We need to renew and develop the old tradition of Hannah Glasse, Elizabeth Raffald, Maria Rundell and Eliza Acton as far as we can in our changed circumstances. It is no accident, I hope, that these early writers are being reprinted, often in facsimile, and that their dishes appear on the menus of some of our best restaurants as well as in an increasing number of homes.

[*English Food*]

# SOUPS AND STARTERS

## ALMOND SOUP

A beautifully white soup which goes back to the cookery of the
Middle Ages, the courtly cookery of England and France (the French
name is *soupe à la reine*). Almonds then played an even larger part in
fine dishes than they do today. As well as its flavour, this soup has the
advantage of being made from the kind of ingredients that most
people have in the house in summer or winter: perhaps this is another
reason why it has survived so many centuries, not just in palaces but
in the homes of people of moderate prosperity.

Serves 6

*60 g (2 oz) ground almonds*
*2¼ litres (4 pt) chicken or light veal stock*
*freshly ground white pepper*
*1 bay leaf*
*300 ml (½ pt) milk*
*1 tablespoon cornflour*
*150 ml (¼ pt) single or double cream*
*1 tablespoon lightly salted butter*
*salt*
*60 g (2 oz) toasted or fried almonds to garnish, or croûtons of fried*
   *bread*

Simmer the first four ingredients for 30 minutes. Remove the bay leaf.
Add the milk, and liquidize the soup to extract maximum flavour and
texture from the almonds (in the old days it was a question of sieving
repeatedly). Mix the cornflour with the cream and use to thicken the
reheated soup, without allowing it to boil (if you do, the almonds will
tend to separate from the liquid and turn gritty). Stir in the butter.
Taste and correct seasoning. Pour through a fine sieve into the heated
soup tureen. Float the almonds on top and serve. If you have chosen
croûtons, put two or three in with the soup and serve the rest in a
bowl. With this kind of fine delicate flavour, it is most important that
the almonds or croûtons should have been fried in butter.

*[English Food]*

# CAWL

Pronounced 'cowl' this is the great nourishing dish of Wales. Like a French *potée* or Scottish cock-a-leekie, it is soup, meat and vegetables in one, a heartening cauldronful when people had only a fire to cook on. To give a recipe with stated quantities is an artificial thing to do. Each cook used what there was to hand, following the general principles. Cawl varied. At the end of the winter, it tasted a bit dead; when new potatoes arrived, it cheered up.

In *First Catch Your Peacock*, Bobby Freeman – who introduced me to cawl – notes that in summer, the tops of young leeks may be cut as they come through the ground and added to the soup. She also points out that the modern style of browning the meat and vegetables was impossible in earlier days: everything had to go into the pot willy-nilly, to cook with the water. One thing I did not know was that in Brecon, cheese and rough brown bread are eaten with cawl, with the liquid I take it, meat and vegetables coming as a second course. Any broth left over was reheated next day and revived with new vegetables, and the next day, and the next. The fat that sets on top was used for other cooking.

There is no doubt that the mixture of two meats improves the flavour, and that 500 g (1 lb) of shin of beef works wonders with 1 kg (2 lb) of best end of neck of lamb, or 500 g (1 lb) smoked ham or gammon or bacon or a hock end goes well with 1 kg (2 lb) of brisket. Extra leeks can take the place of onion: use the white part for the long cooking, the green for the final garnish.

Serves 8–10

> *about 1½ kg (3 lb) boiling cut of beef and best end of neck of lamb, not*
> *cut up, or brisket and smoked gammon etc. (see above for proportions)*
> *beef dripping or bacon fat*
> *2 large onions, thickly sliced*
> *2–3 carrots or 2 parsnips, small to medium, peeled and sliced*
> *1 medium swede or turnip, peeled and cut up*
> *2 stalks celery, sliced*
> bouquet garni, *with 2 extra sprigs of thyme*
> *500 g (1 lb) potatoes, preferably new, or 1 medium-sized old potato per*
> *person, scrubbed*
> *small white cabbage, sliced*
> *salt, pepper, parsley*
> *2–3 slender leeks, sliced*

If you are using shin of beef, brown it and simmer it for 1 hour on its own, before adding the best end of neck which cooks faster.

Brown the meat, then the root vegetables in the fat and transfer to a huge flameproof casserole or pot. Put in the celery, and *bouquet*, then water to come within 5 cm (2 inches) of the rim. Bring slowly to a bare simmer. There should just be an occasional bubble. Remove the scum conscientiously. No need to cover, if you are worried about keeping to a low enough simmer which can be a problem with electric rings: uncovered, you can keep an eye on it more easily, and replace evaporated liquid by the occasional addition of hot water.

Leave to simmer for 4 hours. After 3½ hours, add the potatoes, which should sit on top. After 3¾ hours, put in the cabbage. Season to taste: this late seasoning prevents the meat being tough, and if bacon is being used, gives you a chance to judge the saltiness it has added to the broth. Cut up the meat into convenient pieces. Discard the *bouquet*.

Just before serving, add the leeks and plenty of chopped parsley.

To serve: put the whole thing on the table in a deep wooden bowl, and serve everybody a bit of everything. Have Welsh cheese and wholemeal bread and butter on the table, to make a meal of it.

Or remove meat and vegetables to a serving dish and keep warm, while you serve the soup with bits of leek and parsley.

When Mrs Freeman had a restaurant at Fishguard, she followed the first style, and in summer would float marigolds on top of each bowl. This is an old English habit with all manner of stews: I believe Charles Lamb complained about the dreadful stew and marigolds that were served at Christ's Hospital when he – and Coleridge – were pupils there.

[*British Cookery*]

## COCK-A-LEEKIE

An old and distinguished dish of Scottish cookery, dating back at least to the sixteenth century, made particularly famous on account of its association with the great French statesman, Talleyrand.

'At a formal banquet given by the late Lord Holland, Talleyrand, who was as celebrated for gastronomy as diplomacy, inquired "earnestly" of Lord Jeffrey the nature of "Cocky-leekie" and wished particularly to know if *prunes* (*French plums*) were essential to its scientific concoction. Mr Jeffrey was unable to give the Ex-bishop and Prince any satisfactory information; and the sagacious diplomatist, with his usual tact, settled for himself, that prunes should be boiled in the famous historical soup patronized by "gentle King Jamie", but taken out before the *potage* was sent to table.'

This story appeared in 1826 in Meg Dods's book, *Cook and Housewife's Manual*, with the added comment that prunes are nearly obsolete in Scotland in the soup, but that conservative English cooks still insist that prunes treated in Talleyrand style are what the Scots go for. To me, prunes are what make the soup, the fourth element, the dark accent that pulls the whole thing together both in look and flavour.

Serves 10

*1 kg (2 lb) shin of beef or 2 litres (4 pt) beef stock*
*1 capon or large roasting bird*
*1–1½ kg (2–3 lb) leeks, trimmed and washed*
*18 prunes, soaked*
*salt, pepper*

If you are using beef, put it into a large pot with 2 litres (4 pt) water, bring slowly to the boil, skin and simmer for 2 hours. Put in the bird, plus half the leeks tied in a bundle. Bring back to the boil and simmer for 45 minutes.

If you are using beef stock, start the chicken directly in the heated stock, with the leeks in a bundle.

Add the prunes. Continue simmering until the chicken and beef are tender – about 30 more minutes. Remove the beef and chicken and put in the rest of the leeks, sliced, cooking them 1–2 minutes.

Serve a slice each of beef and chicken with their broth in a soup plate with prunes and some of the barely cooked leeks (discard the bundle), saving the rest of the meat for a cold meal next day. Or strain off the liquor and serve with a little fresh leek as soup, with the hot meats, prunes and leeks remaining as a main course.

A sixteenth-century traveller, Fynes Morison, noted that the top table in a grand Scottish household got 'pullet with some prunes in the broth', and that the lower orders had broth with a little bit of stewed beef – another way of dividing the dish.

[*British Cookery*]

## CREAM OF MUSHROOM SOUP

Here is the basic recipe for mushroom soup. If you can use wild mushrooms, the flavour will be exquisite – field or horse mushrooms, parasols or ceps or fairy-ring mushrooms.

Serves 4–6

*500 g (1 lb) mushrooms*
*juice of a lemon*
*90 g (3 oz) butter*
*1 shallot, chopped, or 1 tablespoon chopped onion*
*1 small clove garlic, chopped*
*salt, pepper*
*60 g (2 oz) flour*
*1¼ litres (2 pt) beef stock*
*125 ml (4 fl oz) double cream*

Chop the mushrooms finely. Sprinkle with lemon juice. Melt one-third of the butter in a pan and cook the shallot or onion and garlic in it until soft and yellow, but not brown. Add the mushrooms and continue cooking until the juices have evaporated, making a *duxelles*. Season.

Meanwhile, melt the remaining butter in a large saucepan, and stir in the flour and moisten with hot beef stock gradually, whisking all the time to avoid lumps. Simmer for 20 minutes. Add the mushroom mixture, and simmer a further 10 minutes. Correct the seasoning and add the cream. Pour into a soup tureen, straining out the bits and pieces if you like; serve very hot.

[*The Mushroom Feast*]


## CURRIED PARSNIP SOUP

This is a wonderful soup, delicately flavoured yet satisfying. One doesn't immediately recognize the parsnip taste, but no other root vegetable can produce such an excellent result.

Serves 6–8

*1 large parsnip*
*125 g (4 oz) chopped onion*
*1 clove garlic crushed*
*90 g (3 oz) butter*
*1 tablespoon flour*
*1 rounded teaspoon curry powder*
*1¼ litres (2 pt) hot beef stock*
*150 ml (¼ pt) cream*
*chives*

Peel and dice the parsnip. Put the parsnip, onion and garlic into a heavy pan with the butter and cook for 10 minutes slowly with the lid on the pan. The vegetables must not brown, but gently absorb the butter. Add flour and curry powder to take up the fat, and gradually incorporate the hot beef stock. Simmer until the parsnip is cooked. Liquidize or push through the *mouli-légumes*. Return to the pan, correct seasoning with salt, pepper and a little more curry powder if liked (but be cautious: keep the flavour mild). Add the cream and a sprinkling of chopped chives. Serve with croûtons of bread fried in butter and oil.

*Note:* liquidized soup may need the further dilution of some stock, or some creamy milk.

[*Good Things*]

## MUTTON AND LEEK BROTH

What I loved about this soup as a child was the pearl barley. It is an odd grain, with a most characteristic mixture of softness and resistance. In soups, I much prefer it to rice. This is a recipe with many variations and it tastes best if you make it well in advance, giving the fat time to rise and solidify on top so that it can be easily removed, before the whole thing is reheated and served.

Serves 6

*125 g (4 oz) pearl barley*
*1 kg (2 lb) scrag end of neck of mutton or lamb, sliced*
*175 g (6 oz) carrot, neatly diced*
*125 g (4 oz) turnip or swede, neatly diced*
*1 small stalk celery, chopped*
*175 g (6 oz) onion, chopped*
*2 medium leeks, thinly sliced, green part discarded*
*½ level teaspoon thyme*
*salt, pepper, sugar*
*chopped parsley*

Wash and soak pearl barley for 4 hours. Drain and put it into a large pot. Cut off any big bits of fat and add the meat to the pot, with 2½ litres (4½ pt) water. Bring to the boil, skim well, and leave to simmer gently for 1 hour. Add carrot, turnip or swede, celery, onion and half the leek, with thyme and a little seasoning. Simmer for a further hour (mutton will take longer than lamb, so be prepared to give it extra time).

When the meat begins to part easily from the bone, remove the slices, discard the bones and, after cutting it into convenient pieces, return the meat to the broth. Skim off surplus fat as best you can – this is particularly important if you are eating the soup straightaway as nothing tastes nastier than mutton or lamb fat in a broth like this.

Taste and adjust the seasoning, adding a little sugar to bring out the flavours. Stir in the last of the leek, bring the soup to a bubbling boil and serve with the parsley scattered on top.

Serve with wholemeal bread and butter, or with cheese and oatmeal biscuits. Follow with fruit or a light pudding, as this soup is a main course in itself.

[*British Cookery*]


## PALESTINE SOUP

Jerusalem artichokes have nothing to do either with Jerusalem or artichokes. When these delicious, warty tubers were introduced into Europe from Canada early in the seventeenth century, their taste was considered to resemble the unrelated globe artichoke's. In Italy, to avoid confusion, the family name was tacked on: the newcomers were distinguished as *girasole* – sunflower – artichokes. We seem to have corrupted *girasol* to Jerusalem, and from Jerusalem artichokes we naturally made Palestine soup.

The French were more deliberately fanciful. Some members of the Brazilian tribe of Tupinamba had been brought to the French court in 1613, and had been a great success, at about the same time as the new vegetable arrived – also from the New World. The name of one bizarre exotic was borrowed for the other – and the French were soon eating *topinambours*, as they still do. Artichokes took so well to Europe that it seemed at one time as if they might provide a basic food for some of the poorer areas. Their flavour, though, was too strong for daily – sometimes thrice-daily – eating; they were soon ousted as a crop by potatoes, and retreated to the kitchen gardens of the middle and upper classes to provide an exquisite winter soup and the occasional purée.

Serves 6

*500 g (1 lb) large Jerusalem artichokes*
*125 g (4 oz) chopped onion*
*1 clove garlic, crushed (optional)*

30 g (1 oz) chopped celery
125 g (4 oz) butter
2 rashers unsmoked bacon, chopped
1½ litres (2½ pt) light chicken stock
2 tablespoons parsley, chopped
60 ml (2 fl oz) double cream
salt, pepper
croûtons

Artichokes can be peeled raw like potatoes, but as they are so knobbly it is less wasteful to scrub and blanch them in boiling salted water. After 5 minutes, or a little longer, the skins can be removed quite easily (but run the artichokes under the cold tap first). Keep the water they were cooked in, unless it tastes very harsh (it does sometimes when the artichokes are becoming old).

Cook onion, garlic and celery in half the butter until soft. Add the bacon and stir about for a few minutes, then the peeled artichokes and 1 litre (2 pt) of the stock. Simmer until the vegetables are cooked. Liquidize or sieve, adding the remaining stock and some of the original cooking water if the soup needs diluting further. Put the remaining butter with the parsley and cream into a warm soup tureen. Reheat the soup to just under boiling point, correct the seasoning, and pour it into the tureen. Stir it well as you do this, to mix in the butter, cream and parsley. Serve with the croûtons.

[*English Food*]

## SMOKED FINNAN HADDOCK SOUP

Serves 4

250 g (½ lb) Finnan haddock
350 g (¾ lb) cod, or other white fish
60 g (2 oz) butter
1 large onion, chopped
1 generous tablespoon flour
600 ml (1 pt) milk
90–120 ml (3–4 fl oz) cream
lemon juice, salt, pepper
chopped parsley

Pour boiling water over the haddock and leave it for 10 minutes. Cut the cod into large cubes. Melt the butter in a large pan, cook the onion in it gently, and when soft add the flour. Cook for a couple of minutes, then moisten with 150 ml (¼ pt) of the haddock water and the milk. Set aside a good tablespoon of haddock flakes, and put the rest – skin, bone and everything – into the pan with the cod. Simmer for 10 minutes. Remove the bones and liquidize the soup – alternatively leave the fish in pieces, so long as you are fairly confident of having removed all the bones. Reheat the soup to just below boiling point, with the cream, and more of the haddock water if it needs diluting; fish soups should not be very thick, particularly when they have a delicate flavour like this one. Season to taste with lemon juice, salt and pepper. Stir in the tablespoon of haddock flakes and the parsley. It is important to buy good haddock for a soup of this kind.

[*English Food*]

## EGGS

'Bless, O Lord, we beseech Thee, this Thy creature of eggs, that it may become a wholesome sustenance to Thy faithful servants, eating in thankfulness to Thee, on account of the Resurrection of Our Lord.' This prayer, appointed by Paul V, pope from 1605 to 1621, for use during mass at Eastertide, opens Venetia Newall's splendid book *An Egg at Easter* (now, unfortunately, out of print). It defines exactly what an egg should be – something good and honest to eat rather than the industrial product it has become.

In the past when I have mentioned *foie gras*, I have sometimes been sent an emotional pamphlet with a nightmarish photograph of a Wicked French Farmer on the cover. I mention eggs all the time and have never yet had a protest about Wicked British Farmers who turn living creatures into egg machines. Yet this is a greater cruelty, and one in which most of us connive.

In the average battery, four to seven birds are crammed into a wire cage the size of a television set. Beaks are cropped so the hens cannot peck each other to death (though they are able to peck each other featherless). Their feet are soon deformed by the wire floor. Their eggs are pallid, so colourants are added to their food to jazz up the yolks. Dieticians tell us that these eggs are just as nutritious as free-range ones.

One solution is to buy other kinds of eggs: you can make up a fine basketful for Easter with quail, duck and goose eggs. Outside London, you might be able to track down someone with Marans or Welsummer hens' eggs for sale: these are a magnificent brown, as if they had been boiled with the deepest onion skins, the yolks are vivid, so too is the flavour. Rarer still are the beautiful blue eggs of the Chilean Araucana hen.

The practical day-to-day solution is to buy free-range eggs. This means the hens have continuous daytime access to open-air runs, which have plenty of vegetation, and that there are no more than 400 hens to each acre of ground. Be wary, all the same. Some free-range producers meet increasing demand by buying in battery eggs. Ask where your free-range eggs come from, and check if you can. Never assume that eggs sold by a butcher, milkman, greengrocer, farm shop or at a thatched cottage down a pretty lane are free-range. Don't be fooled by such phrases as 'farm-fresh eggs', which may quite well mean battery-cage eggs, or 'barn eggs', which can mean eggs from hens packed to a density of twenty-five per square metre (some concentration camp under the nice Cotswold-tiled words). 'Deep litter eggs' are rather better, coming from hens kept seven to the square metre.

## Hen eggs

These are graded into seven sizes by weight. Professional baking manuals give egg quantities by weight, because accuracy is essential, and becomes more essential as quantities increase. I think all books on baking and cake recipes should do this. A recipe for a pound cake, *quatre-quarts* to the French, would then read:

125 g (4 oz) each of self-raising flour, sugar, butter and eggs, plus a level teaspoon of baking powder. Beat together with wooden spoon or in a processor, add a flavouring and a tablespoon of appropriate liquid. Bake for about an hour at gas 4, 180°C (350°F).

As things are, in this imperfect world, take 1 egg to mean an egg weighing 60 g (2 oz, size 3) in modern cookery books and articles. When using older recipes, remember that eggs were smaller – 45 g (1½ oz, size 6) works quite well.

Once an egg is cracked on to a plate, freshness is easily judged. It should have a clear, crisp humpy look: the wider and flatter it spreads, the older it is. FREGG (The Free-Range Egg Association) reports that a group of farmers in Hertfordshire, running a 1,000-bird flock on corn they themselves grow organically, find that their eggs still have crisp whites when they are three to four weeks old. In other words, they keep their liveliness.

Eggs from the refrigerator (and battery eggs) crack if you put them into boiling water. You can prick them, or add a little vinegar or salt to the water. It's easier to start with cold water, starting to time the eggs once the water boils: allow 3 minutes for a size 2 egg (65–70 g (2–2½ oz)).

Another way is to cover the eggs with 2½ cm (1 inch) of cold water, bring the pan to the boil, clap on a lid and remove it from the heat. After 6 or 7 minutes the eggs should be nicely coddled, the whites creamily firm, the yolks runny.

Try Richard Olney's scrambled eggs. Beat 8 eggs and 3 or 4 yolks with a fork until just mixed and sieve. Butter the pan with 45 g (1½ oz) butter. Season eggs and pour them in, plus another 45 g (1½ oz) butter cut into little bits. Stir over another pan of barely simmering water. As the eggs come towards the right creaminess, add a tablespoon or two of double cream, then up to three more.

For a special treat, add at least 90 g (3 oz) sliced truffles to the eggs after beating them, and 3 slices of bread, diced and fried in butter, at the end of the cooking time.

## Duck eggs

Not for soft-boiling, since they are laid in messy places sometimes and there could be a risk of bacterial contamination. They must be boiled for at least 15 minutes. Use duck eggs to make Chinese tea-leaf eggs. First boil them in salted water for 15 minutes. Then cool them under running water and gently tap or roll them on a hard surface so that the whole shell is cracked, but still in place (a few tiny bits may fall off but that doesn't matter). Put them into a clean pan and cover with a strong brew of China tea, plus, if possible, a few strips of dried mandarin orange peel. Simmer for 1 hour. Drain, cool and peel – the whites will be beautifully veined with brown, and the insides will be firm but creamy. This can be done with all eggs. Duck eggs are fine for baking.

## Gull eggs

A delicacy which is becoming rarer all the time though they can still be found in some smart shops. They are not at all fishy, but have a creaminess from the large yolk.

## Quail eggs

The new kitchen toy. Let's hope their price comes down, so that it approaches the more sensible French level. Plainly boiled, they will be firm after 3 minutes. They look beautiful, with their deep blue and brown markings, as an hors d'oeuvre: put them in a basket and serve with mayonnaise, plus brown bread and butter and salt. The proportion of yolk to white is high. Small boiled, peeled quail eggs are a fine embellishment to smoked salmon or sturgeon or halibut. Surround them with sausage-meat for miniature Scotch eggs: eat them warm preferably. Fry a small panful of quail eggs, then cut them into rounds with a petits-fours cutter and put them warm on to identical circles of buttered bread, on top of a sliver of smoked fish or a light spreading of salmon caviare (or the real thing, if you can afford it).

Thai cooks make quail egg and cucumber flowers. Cut 2-cm (¾-inch) ends of 6 very small cucumbers, or substitute courgettes. These will form the cups for the quail eggs; this gives you an idea of the size to aim for. Hollow out the cucumber ends and cut down to make petalled cups. Marinade in 4 tablespoons of white vinegar, 2 tablespoons of sugar, 1 teaspoon of salt and 6 tablespoons of water. Leave for 10 minutes. Shell a dozen hard-boiled quail eggs. Crush together a teaspoon each of salt, ground black pepper, chopped garlic and the chopped roots from a bunch of coriander leaves. Fry the paste in a little oil, then add 4 tablespoons of dark soya sauce and a level tablespoon of sugar. Once it is bubbling and amalgamated, put in the eggs and gently turn them about so that they are evenly coloured. Drain and dry. Put into the cucumber cups and spear in place with a wooden cocktail stick, which makes the stem.

### Goose eggs

A rare treat, especially when fried in a little butter. An occasional extravagance (3/6 d) in days of rationing after the war for undergraduates at Cambridge was goose egg and chips at a small café near Trinity. I still make it for a treat at home with a tomato salad afterwards. As goose gets more popular, which it seems to be doing, there will be more eggs about. They are particularly good for baking.

### Aubergine omelette

For 6 people peel and dice 1¼ kg (2½ lb) aubergines. Heat 150 ml (¼ pt) sunflower oil in a sauté pan and add the aubergine. Cook over a moderate flame, stirring occasionally. After 5 minutes add 2 chopped shallots, plus salt and pepper. Continue cooking until all juiciness has evaporated, leaving a moist mass rather than a stew. Remove half the aubergines to a hot serving dish. Beat 12 eggs, season, pour on to the aubergines in the pan and mix gently. Cook to taste (keep the omelette moist) and turn over on to a dish. Serve with a sauce of fresh, lightly cooked tomato.

[*Observer Magazine*]

## ASPARAGUS AND EGGS

A favourite dish for people who grow their own vegetables, as this simple treatment shows off their fresh flavour well. Purple sprouting broccoli, tiny new peas, artichoke bottoms can all be used instead of asparagus. French recipes often add a flavouring of mustard, chopped herbs such as parsley and chives, and a spoonful of thick cream. A good variation.

Serves 4

*250–350 g ( ½–¾ lb) asparagus tips*
*4 slices bread*
*butter*
*8 eggs*
*salt, pepper*

Cook the asparagus tips in boiling, salted water (keep the thicker ends of the stalks for soup). Drain them well and put in a warm place. Toast the bread, butter it and lay it on a hot dish. Beat the eggs with salt and pepper. Scramble them with a generous tablespoon of butter, keeping them creamy. Arrange three-quarters of the asparagus on the toast, pour the egg on top and decorate with remaining asparagus.

[*English Food*]

## ASPARAGUS SOUFFLÉ WITH MALTESE SAUCE

At the comfortable Mallory Court near Leamington Spa, the chef, Alan Holland, has been described as 'a Trojan with vegetables'. And no wonder since he is so well placed for Evesham. The asparagus season in that part of the world is much celebrated with feasts and asparagus suppers.

Serves 4

*375 g (12 oz) fresh green asparagus, weighed after peeling and trimming*
*75 g (2½ oz) butter*
*1 tablespoon chopped shallot*
*45 g (1½ oz) flour*
*300 ml (½ pt) milk*
*salt, pepper, nutmeg, cayenne*
*4 egg yolks*
*60 g (2 oz) Gruyère or Emmenthal cheese*
*5 egg whites*
*butter and Parmesan cheese for the dishes*

SAUCE
*thinly-cut peel of a blood orange*
*3 egg yolks*
*1 tablespoon lemon juice*
*6 tablespoons blood orange juice*
*175 g (6 oz) melted butter*

Cook asparagus until just tender in boiling salted water. Drain and cut off 12 tips about 4 cm (1½ inches) long and set aside. Finely chop the remaining asparagus. Melt 1 tablespoon of butter in a pan, add the shallot and cook for a moment, before adding the asparagus. Stir while the moisture evaporates, then put aside. Melt the remaining butter, stir in the flour and cook for 1 minute. Meanwhile, bring the milk to the boil. Off the heat, mix the milk into the roux, return to the heat and cook for 1 minute. Stir in the asparagus and season. Beat in the yolks one at a time and half the cheese.

Whisk egg whites with a pinch of salt until firm. Fold a third of the whites into the asparagus mixture. Pour the mixture back on to the remaining egg white and gently fold in. Do not overmix. Preheat the oven to gas 6, 200°C (400°F).

Butter four small soufflé dishes, 10 cm (4 inches) diameter and 6 cm (2½ inches) deep. Line each base with a disc of buttered greaseproof paper. Sprinkle the insides with grated Parmesan.

Divide the asparagus mixture between the dishes. Sprinkle the remaining cheese on top. Place on baking sheet and bake for 15–20 minutes.

Make the sauce while the soufflés are cooking. Shred the orange peel into a thin julienne (thinner than matchstick strips). Cook about 2 minutes in boiling water to make them tender. Drain, run under the cold tap and set aside. Put the yolks into a small saucepan and whisk, adding lemon juice and 2 tablespoons of the orange juice. Place over a gentle heat or a *bain marie* and whisk until the eggs have lightened in colour. Remove from the heat and whisk in the warm melted butter very gradually. Season with salt and the remaining orange juice to taste.

When the soufflés are well risen, remove from oven and run a knife round the soufflés to loosen them. Using a cloth to protect your hand, turn a soufflé on to your hand, peel off the paper, then on to a warm plate. Repeat with the others. Surround soufflés with sauce and decorate with the reserved asparagus tips and julienne of orange peel.

*Note:* Maltese sauce is by definition made with blood oranges (which are about during the asparagus season). Well-flavoured oranges of other kinds can be used instead, though one misses the glowing colour and the bright flavour.

[*British Cookery*]

## MUSHROOM PASTE

A recipe from a small pamphlet entitled *Pottery*. The mixture is excellent with toast, as a first course.

*1 small onion, chopped*
*60 g (2 oz) butter*
*2 slices bacon, chopped*
*125 g (4 oz) skinned, chopped tomatoes*
*500 g (1 lb) mushrooms, sliced*
*2 eggs, beaten*
*1 teaspoon salt*
*a dash of cayenne pepper*

Brown the onion lightly in a little of the butter. Add the rest, and immediately stir in the bacon, tomatoes and mushrooms. When everything is well cooked, put it through a vegetable mill, or liquidize in a blender. Mix with the eggs and stir over a low heat until the mixture thickens (do not let it boil). Season with salt and cayenne. 'This can be put in a jar and will keep some time. It is, however, so good that it can never be kept.'

[*The Mushroom Feast*]

# FISH

I remember as a child listening to my father's tales of going out with the herring boats from South Shields or Tynemouth. He talked about the cold and the fierce sea, the sudden energy required and the cups of strong sweet tea that kept people going. When the nets were pulled in, the silver catch tumbled into the boat for what seemed like hours, the mesh stuck solid with the fish. He came to appreciate Scott's remark in *The Antiquary*, 'It's nae fish ye're buying, it's men's lives.'

Such things had gone on for ever, would go on for ever. The vast shoals would appear as usual at the expected times and places, even if they had not been predicted by the annual arrival of the Scottish fisherwomen. These women knew the seasons and would appear up and down the coasts ready to gut and barrel the herrings, a vast trade for export. They were a tough, loud, cheerful lot, who swore with the best of the men and worked in bitter conditions. Modern methods and refrigeration put an end to this picturesque trade, but the herring still appeared in the sea.

The name herring means army, and even a small shoal in an aquarium is an impressive, unnerving sight, millions of 'soldiers' blindly moving on. Some shoals were the width and breadth and depth of towns, which meant weeks of enormous catches.

It never occurred to most of us that herrings might vanish from our shops. They were eternal, a natural plunder that would never fail. But they did fail. Nets and trawling techniques became so efficiently Hoover-like that even the vaster shoals were sucked up. So depleted were they that for several years herring fishery was forbidden. Only in 1984 was it allowed again.

Herrings are on the slab once more, it is true, but what has happened to them? The ones I see are poor limp things compared to the crisp bright herring of the old days. Is this because they are kept too long in ice between catch and sale? Is it because local fishmongers do not buy the top of the catch, but second and third rate fish? Is it because we fished the heart out of the herring tribes and the few years' peace we allowed them has not been long enough to restore their vigour? It seems to me that they very often have a grey pappiness, that unpleasant softness you sometimes encounter with farmed salmon. Once, a plain grilled herring, well salted and nicely browned, was a treat. All it needed was bread, butter and a squeeze of lemon juice. Now such herrings as I can buy need zippy handling, a tonic of sharp and savoury ingredients to disguise the weariness of what should be one of our finest and most health-giving fish. But perhaps this is just a Wiltshire peculiarity – we are not spoiled in the matter of fish.

Perhaps because herrings were once a cheap and abundant fish, they did not appear much on polite English dinner tables. I wonder, too, if this was because their oily flesh does not stand up well to poaching and papillote treatments? To my mind, they need a high heat, whether in the oven or under the grill, so that the skin becomes brown and crisp in places, even a little burnt at the edges. This leads to strong smells which people worried about far more in the past than they do today – perhaps it is easier to air our houses. The smell of a herring on the grill over hot coals is one of the most captivating I know, it's the smell of holidays in the sun, relaxed parties out of doors.

Since herrings go from 150–350 g (5–11 oz), you will find it easy to adapt sardine or mackerel recipes to them. They all have similarly oily flesh and need contrasts of sharpness (lemons, gooseberries, sharp apples, sorrel) and a hint of sweetness. They stand up well to spicy piquancy (mustard, anchovies, spices, bacon).

The scales of herring fall off easily enough – for this reason they are described as deciduous – under the tap with the minimum of help from a knife. Gutting can be done via the gills, or by slitting the belly with a pair of scissors. Any trace of blood remaining can be removed by dipping a finger in salt and rubbing the mark away.

The head is not usually cut off unless you want to bone the fish or remove the fillets.

Herring roe is much prized, especially the soft kind. It will be of better quality, coming from the fish, than the roe you buy from thawing blocks at the fishmongers. Dip the roes in flour seasoned with salt, pepper and cayenne, fry them in butter and serve on toast with parsley. Alternatively, crush both soft and hard roes together with a little butter, a few crumbs and parsley, and use them to stuff the fish for baking. Roes can also be kept as a filling for omelettes or they can be liquidized with egg and cream or milk as a filling for tarts.

## Devilled Herrings

Serves 6

*6 very fresh herrings with soft roes*
*3 level tablespoons Dijon mustard*
*2 teaspoons sunflower or groundnut oil*
*¼ level teaspoon cayenne pepper*
*salt*
*100 g (3½ oz) fine dried white breadcrumbs*
*100 g (3½ oz) butter, melted*
*sprigs of parsley*

Gut the herrings, extracting the roes carefully. Leave the heads in place. Rinse the fish and dry them, slashing them diagonally two or three times on each side. Rinse and dry the roes.

Mix together the mustard, oil and cayenne pepper with a little salt. Brush the roes with this mixture and put them back into the herring cavities. Brush the herrings with the same mixture. Tip the breadcrumbs on to a baking tray and roll the herrings in them.

Preheat the grill. Line the grill pan with foil. Carefully lay the herrings on top of the rack, sprinkle with melted butter and slide under the grill. Baste the fish from time to time, and turn them

once. Total cooking time, including time for basting, will be about
12 minutes.
Transfer to a dish and garnish with parsley. Serve with buttered,
boiled new potatoes and a sprig or two of rosemary.

[*À La Carte*]


## BRANDADE OF SMOKED MACKEREL

A recipe of George Perry-Smith's that could be served with triangles
of fried bread but, since his Riverside restaurant is in Cornwall, comes
to table as a miniature pasty. The treatment and accompaniments of
the smoked mackerel (a new but well established speciality of the west
of England) show a very English eclecticism – dill cream from
Scandinavia, cucumber *sambal* from India, the *brandade* method from
France.

This responsiveness to the food of other nations can be traced back
for three centuries and more. For better or worse, it marks English
food apart from the cooking of any other country in Europe. When
the combinations and adoptions are made by a master, the results
are splendid but success in such matters is not as easy as we seem to
think it is. For that you need a fine taste, an impeccable taste such
as Elizabeth David's or George Perry-Smith's. In lesser hands it can
turn to pretentiousness or a desperate novelty that makes one long for
a boiled egg and toast.

Serves 6

*about 400 g (14–15 oz) slab of puff pastry*
*250 g (8 oz) smoked mackerel, skinned and boned*
*2 cloves garlic*
*salt*
*60–90 ml (2–3 fl oz) very good olive oil*
*60–90 ml (2–3 fl oz) milk*
*pepper*
*lemon juice*
*egg yolk, beaten, to glaze*

DILL CREAM
*250 ml (8 fl oz) double cream*
*salt, pepper*
*lemon juice*
*1 tablespoon dill seed, pounded*

SAMBAL
*1 cucumber, peeled and diced small*
*1 level tablespoon salt*
*1 small onion, chopped*
*1 stalk celery, chopped, or ½-head fennel, chopped*
*cayenne, black pepper*
*olive oil*
*lemon juice*
*chopped parsley*

Roll out the pastry fairly thinly and cut 7½-cm (3-inch) rounds with a cutter. Chill while you make the *brandade*.

Flake the mackerel, removing the bones attentively. In a mortar, crush the garlic with just enough salt to make it creamy. Add the mackerel, pounding energetically to make a paste smoother than you believed possible (you can use the processor, but pounding does give a better result and does not take long). Remove any whiskery bones that may have escaped you.

Prepare a *bain marie* (in a roasting pan, for instance). When the water is hot but not boiling, stand a pudding basin with the mackerel paste in it, and two jugs, one with the oil, the other with the milk. When everything is warm, not hot, add oil and milk to the mackerel in small quantities, beating them in lightly – the mixture should not be sloppy, but soft and moist. Season to taste with pepper and lemon juice, perhaps a little more salt. Chill the mixture.

When firm with the cold, place a small teaspoon of the mackerel *brandade* on the pastry circles. Fold over the dough into a half moon and twist the edges to seal. Get as much filling in as you can, but be careful to seal well. Chill on a floured tray until just before the meal.

Make the dill cream by whisking the double cream until it is much thickened but not stiff. Add seasonings to taste. For the *sambal*, salt the cucumber for 30 minutes at least, then drain it well and pat dry between two cloths. Mix with chopped vegetables and add seasoning to taste.

Allow six little pasties per person. Brush them with egg yolk and bake in a preheated oven, gas 8, 230°C (450°F) for 12 minutes. Serve very hot with a tablespoon each of dill cream and cucumber *sambal*.

Deep-freeze any left over; they freeze extremely well.

[*British Cookery*]

## CURRIED PRAWNS

Serves 4

*750 g–1 kg (1½–2 lb) cooked prawns in their shells*
*1 large onion chopped*
*60 g (2 oz) butter*
*1 heaped teaspoon curry powder*
*1 rounded tablespoon flour*
*300 ml (½ pt) fish stock*
*150 ml (¼ pt) thick cream*
*salt, pepper*

Shell the prawns first, and use the shells when making the fish stock. Put the prawn meat aside. Melt the onion in the butter until golden and soft, stir in the curry powder and flour, then moisten with the fish stock. Add the cream and reduce to a thick sauce. Season well. Reheat the prawns gently in the sauce for a few seconds and serve in a ring of boiled rice.

Firm white fish can be curried in the same way with great success. The thing is not to overcook the fish in the first place, and not to overheat it in the sauce. Lemon juice can be added for piquancy when cod or haddock are being used.

[*English Food*]

## FISH CAKES

I was never fond of northern ways with fish – fish pies and muddles of that kind, and overcooking generally – but fish cakes are another matter, especially when made with smoked haddock or salmon or crab, or the fresh inshore cod which was taken for granted until lately, but seems such a treat now. I read somewhere a few years ago that Newcastle eats more fish fingers than anywhere else in the country – which seems scandalous for a place that has the makings of excellent fish cakes to hand.

Sometimes fish cakes are smartened up, but I think that food of such basic purity and goodness should be left alone. Anchovy essence is the one permitted flavouring, Lazenby's according to my husband, but unfortunately you cannot get it now: I have the feeling that modern brands are not as good.

Serves 6–8

*250–375 g ( ½–¾ lb) cooked fish, flaked*
*250 g (8 oz) cooked potato, the fresher the better*
*yolk of 1 large egg*
*about 2 tablespoons chopped parsley*
*1 teaspoon anchovy essence*
*60 g (2 oz) butter*
*pepper, salt*
*1 large egg white, beaten slightly*
*fresh white breadcrumbs*

Mix the first five ingredients. Melt the butter in a pan over a very low heat and put in the mixture, beating them together – the warming through makes this easier, but the mixture should not cook properly. Season to taste, then spread out on a plate in a thick layer and cool.

When cold, form into cakes of whatever size is convenient – tiny fish cakes, served with a little crisp bacon make a good first course. Dip in the egg white, then the crumbs and fry in clarified butter or bacon fat according to the fish used: the more delicate the fish, the more delicate the cooking medium. Have the fat 1 cm ( ¼ inch) deep in the pan, so that the cakes brown at the sides.

Drain on kitchen paper, and serve very hot with a béchamel or velouté sauce (use fish stock and cream), flavoured with anchovy and parsley, or just serve them on their own with bread and butter.

[*British Cookery*]


## HERRINGS IN OATMEAL

The best way of eating herrings. If you like, rashers of streaky bacon can be fried first, and their fat used for cooking the herrings. Bacon and fish go well together.

Serves 6

*6 herrings*
*salt, pepper*
*90 g (3 oz) fine or medium oatmeal*
*125 g (4 oz) butter*
*lemon quarters*

Ask the fishmonger to fillet the herrings from the back, so that they look like uncured kippers when they are opened out, with the thin part in the centre. Season them with salt and pepper, then press them, skin side and cut side, into the oatmeal so that they are coated with it. Fry them in the butter until cooked and lightly browned. Serve them with lemon quarters.

*[English Food]*

## KEDGEREE

*Khichri* is a Hindi dish of rice and lentils, which can be varied with fish or meat in all kinds of ways. The English in India worked up their own versions, and soon kedgeree became a popular Victorian breakfast dish. The sad thing is that it became institutionalized as a handy way of using up any left-over fish and rice: it came to table stodgy and tasteless. Left-overs can be used to make a good kedgeree, but the cook's hand should be generous with butter and cream, and the proportion of fish to rice should be more or less two parts to three, cooked weight.

Well-flavoured fish like salmon and first-class kippers and bloaters make a delicious kedgeree. So do shellfish such as mussels: use their liquor to cook the rice.

Serves 4

*500 g (1 lb) piece smoked haddock*
*olive oil*
*1 large onion, chopped*
*175 g (6 oz) long-grain rice*
*1 teaspoon curry paste*
*butter*
*3 hard-boiled eggs, sliced*
*chopped parsley*

Pour boiling water over the haddock and set over a low heat for 10 minutes. It should not boil. Take the haddock from the water, discard the skin and bones, and flake the fish. Meanwhile pour a thin layer of olive oil into a pan and brown the onion in it lightly. Stir in the rice, and as it becomes transparent mix in the curry paste. Pour 600 ml (1 pt) of the haddock water over the rice, and cook steadily until the rice is tender and the liquid absorbed. Watch the pan, and add more water if necessary. Mix in the flaked haddock pieces and a large bit of butter, so that the kedgeree is moist and juicy. Turn into a hot serving dish. Arrange the egg slices on top, sprinkle with parsley, and serve with lemon quarters and mango chutney.

*[English Food]*

## KIPPERS FOR BREAKFAST

Everyone has a favourite way of cooking kippers, but it's worth trying a new method sometimes, even if breakfast does not seem the right meal for experiments. There are only two rules to observe: don't overcook them, and don't add butter until they are served, as good kippers cook in their own juice.

JUGGED KIPPERS are my favourite for breakfast. Put them, head down, into a 1–2 litre (2–3 pt) stoneware jug. Pour boiling water on to them straight from the kettle (as if you were making tea), right up to their tails. Leave in a warm place for 5–10 minutes, drain well and serve. They can be laid in a roasting tin, instead of a jug, but this is dangerous as the boiling water slops about if one makes a careless, half-awake movement.

BAKED KIPPERS: wrap them loosely in kitchen foil. Bake for 10–15 minutes in a moderately hot oven. This saves washing up.

GRILLED KIPPERS: place the kippers *skin side up* on a piece of foil on the grill rack. Grill gently for 5 minutes until the skin is deliciously crisp, not charred. *Or* jug the kippers for 2 minutes, then grill for 2 minutes on each side.

FRIED KIPPERS: grease the frying pan lightly with butter, just enough to prevent the kippers sticking and no more (unnecessary with a non-stick pan). Fry gently for 2–3 minutes on each side.

Whether grilled, fried, baked or jugged, eat the kippers with plenty of bread and butter. Lemon quarters, pats of butter or parsley can be served as well.

[*Good Things*]


## MUSSELS ON SKEWERS

Here is a combination of mussels and bacon that is piquant and savoury. It's a good way of using the large mussels on sale in this country.

For each person

*12 large mussels (450 g, a scant lb)*
*150 ml (¼ pt) water*
*3 rashers fat bacon*

*1 dessertspoon cream*
*1 teaspoon chopped parsley*

Cut the rind off the bacon and divide it into 14 pieces. Open the mussels with 150 ml (¼ pt) of water in a heavy pan in the usual way. Discard the shells. Beginning and ending with bacon, thread mussels and bacon on two skewers. Grill quickly, turning twice, for 5 minutes. As the bacon browns and crisps at the edges, its fat keeps the mussels basted.

Put the skewers on a bed of rice in a warm oven, while making the sauce. Pour the mussel liquor into the juices in the grill pan. Boil hard to reduce the liquid to a good flavour, and scrape in all the little brown bits and pieces. Add the cream to bind, then season to taste, and add the parsley. Serve separately in a sauce boat, with plainly boiled rice.

Alternatively the skewers can be rolled in beaten egg, then in breadcrumbs, and deep-fried. The sauce will then depend solely on the mussel liquor and cream.

This dish is very good when scallops are used instead of mussels. Slice the white part across into two pieces, and grill at a slightly lower temperature to cook the thicker scallops.

*[Good Things]*


## POTTED SHRIMPS

A rare food pleasure I remember from the war years was walking along Morecambe Bay with my sister, each of us with a brown paper bag of shrimps. They were small and brown, the best kind. We chewed without bothering to peel all of them. Something of their vivid sweetness came through in potted shrimps when they went on sale again as food became easier. But then they began to taste dull. Eventually I discovered why – it was not my increasing age, as I had feared, but a complete change in production.

In the old days, the catch was cooked on board and brought in at all hours. Whatever the time of night, wives and daughters and children would set to and peel the shrimps. Then they would pot them in butter, catching the fresh flavour. Nowadays, the shrimps are chilled and then picked (shelled) in ordinary working hours: what is more, they are augmented with frozen shrimp from elsewhere. You have only to think of a crab you have boiled yourself and eaten within an hour or two, and a packet of frozen crab meat to understand the difference.

If you go shrimping, use sea water to cook them in. Bring it to the boil over a very high heat, throw in the shrimps and start tasting them a few seconds after the water returns to the boil. Prawns will take a little longer, perhaps 2 minutes; crabs and lobsters, 7–10 minutes. Most people overcook shellfish, especially when it is boiled in vast quantities.

Pot the shrimps you are not eating immediately. To every 600 ml (1 pt) of picked shrimps – which will serve 6–8 when potted – allow 100–125 g (3½–4 oz) butter. Melt it slowly with a blade of mace, cayenne and a shade of grated nutmeg. Stir in the shrimps and heat them through without boiling. Stir all the time. Remove the mace, and then divide between little pots. Cool quickly in the refrigerator. Cover with clarified butter.

To serve, warm them slightly. Provide brown bread and butter. Prawns, crab and lobster can all be potted in the same way.

[*British Cookery*]

## SALMON BAKED IN PASTRY WITH CURRANTS AND GINGER

This is the most famous of the Perry-Smith recipes. His pupils make it in their restaurants, his customers make it at home. Variations creep in. Here is the true version. At Bath, the best Wye salmon was used. In Cornwall, the best salmon comes from the Tamar. I had gathered that the source of the idea was a medieval recipe, but then I found something almost identical in the *Cook's and Confectioner's Dictionary* by John Nott, published in 1726 and reprinted in 1980, with an introduction and glossary by Elizabeth David. In that more fanciful time, the pastry was shaped and scored to look like a fish: inside were mace, butter and ginger in slices, along with the salmon.

Serves 6

*1¼ kg (2½ lb) piece of fresh wild salmon*
*salt, pepper*
*125 g (4 oz) butter*
*4 well-drained knobs of ginger in syrup, chopped*
*30 g (1 oz) currants*

PASTRY
*500 g (1 lb) flour*
*275 g (9 oz) butter*
*egg yolk, beaten, to glaze*

SAUCE
*600 ml (1 pt) single cream*
*2 egg yolks*
*2 level teaspoons French mustard*
*2 level teaspoons flour*
*125 g (4 oz) softened butter*
*juice of 1 lemon*
*½ small onion, finely chopped*
*a small bunch each of tarragon, parsley and chervil*
*salt, pepper*

Skin and fillet the piece of salmon and season both sides. Mash the butter with the ginger and currants. Spread half on one fillet on the inside. Put the other fillet on top to make a sandwich, reconstituting the salmon, and spread the remaining ginger butter over the top.

Make a rich shortcrust pastry with the flour and butter, mixing it with iced water. Roll out and wrap neatly round the salmon, cutting away lumpiness, to make a neat, refined parcel. Brush with egg yolk. Bake at gas 8, 230°C (450°F) for 30 minutes or until cooked.

To make the sauce, whizz the ingredients in a blender until green. Cook in a double saucepan gently, until thickened. Serve in a warm bowl. Serve a cucumber salad as well.

John Webber of Gidleigh Park in Devon much favours watercress with salmon. He makes a purée of the leaves, blanching them for 30 seconds in boiling water, refreshing them under the cold tap and then blending them to a purée with a sprig or two of fresh tarragon (an affinity of flavours he is pleased to have discovered). This purée is then used to flavour a bearnaise or white wine and cream sauce to go with poached or grilled salmon.

*[British Cookery]*


## STEWED SCALLOPS WITH ORANGE SAUCE

A really delicious eighteenth-century dish. The flavour of orange, particularly of Seville orange, goes beautifully with fish. If you want to make a richer sauce, beat an egg yolk with 3 tablespoons of double cream and stir into the sauce after adding the flour and butter – stir it over a low heat being careful not to boil it. The recipe can easily be adapted to fillets of sole, whiting, etc.

Serves 6

*150 ml ( ¼ pt ) dry white wine*
*150 ml ( ¼ pt ) water*
*1 scant tablespoon white wine vinegar*
*½ teaspoon ground mace*
*2 cloves*
*18 scallops*
*1 tablespoon butter*
*1 tablespoon flour*
*juice of a Seville orange, or the juice of 1 sweet orange plus the juice of*
  *½ a lemon*
*salt, pepper*

Simmer the wine, water, vinegar and spices in a covered shallow pan
for 5–10 minutes. Add salt and pepper to taste, and more spices if this
seems a good idea – their flavour should not be strong but it should
hang unmistakably over the dish. Meanwhile slice the scallops in half
crossways, then slip them into the simmering liquid and poach them
for 5 minutes. They should not be overcooked.

   Transfer the scallops to a serving dish and keep them warm.
Measure the cooking liquor and if there is more than 300 ml ( ½ pt)
boil it down. Mash the butter and flour together and divide into little
knobs. See that the liquid is at simmering point, then whisk in the
butter and flour knobs to thicken the sauce. Keep it at a moderate
heat, without boiling; finally season with the orange juice, or orange
and lemon juice, and more salt and pepper if required. Pour over the
scallops and serve at once.

[English Food]

# MEAT, GAME AND POULTRY

## HEREFORD BEEF OLIVES

The modern white-faced Hereford is a cross between the native red
long-horned cattle and cattle brought in from the Low Countries in
the seventeenth century (from which its size and spectacular white
marking come). T. A. Knight, a great stock-breeder as well as fruit
and vegetable gardener, had a fine herd of Herefords at Downton
Castle and attributed the cross to Lord Scudamore, who brought in a
breed of cattle from Flanders (he died in 1671). Today, Hereford

beef is one of the specialities of Churchills', the Ledbury butchers: they choose, slaughter and hang their meat properly. This is what Mrs Hegarty of Hope End uses for her version of a centuries-old favourite of English cooks; her cider and perry come from the Symonds Cider Co., at Stoke Lacy, south-west of Bromyard.

Serves 6

*1 kg (2 lb) piece of topside*
*250 g (8 oz) thinly-cut green back rashers*
*250 g (8 oz) ripe tomatoes, peeled and quartered*
*olive oil*
*600 ml (1 pt) dry cider*
*stock or water*
*2 level teaspoons cornflour*
*salt, pepper*

STUFFING
*60 g (2 oz) brown breadcrumbs*
*1 medium onion, grated*
*zest and juice of ½ a lemon*
*1 level teaspoon fresh thyme, finely chopped*
*1 level teaspoon fresh marjoram, finely chopped*
*1 egg yolk*
*2 level tablespoons tomato concentrate or paste*
*sea salt, black pepper*

Chill the beef in the coldest part of the refrigerator or freezer until you can cut it into thin slices, measuring roughly 5 × 10 cm (2 × 4 inches), or persuade the butcher to do it for you. The inevitable scraps can be added to the sauce, or kept for another dish.

Blanch the bacon for 2 minutes in boiling water. Gently cook the tomatoes in their own juice and sieve.

Combine the stuffing ingredients to make a crumbly thick paste (brown breadcrumbs are just right for this).

Lay a small strip of bacon on top of each slice of beef. Spread the stuffing on the bacon, roll the beef up and secure with a cocktail stick. This can all be done in advance.

Switch on the oven to gas 2, 150°C (300°F) and brown the 'olives' in olive oil, in batches, transferring them to a casserole. Pour surplus fat from the pan, heat through the sieved tomato with the cider and pour over the beef. Add any meat scraps and stock or water to cover, if necessary. Put on the lid and cook on a moderate heat for 1 hour or until tender.

Remove the olives. Strain liquor into a wide shallow pan and boil down hard to about ½ litre (¾ pt). Meanwhile, remove the cocktail sticks. Thicken sauce with the cornflour and season to taste. Put the olives in a row on each warm plate, or in rows on a warm serving dish, and spoon a sash of sauce across them.

[*British Cookery*]

## SHEPHERD'S PIE

This dish belongs to the whole of Britain, and to France as well, where it is called *hachis Parmentier* in honour of the man who persuaded the French to eat potatoes. Worcester sauce is one of the best seasonings for it, especially if you cannot spare a dash of alcohol to zip up the flavour. No one can deny that this is a family Monday sort of dish, but it can be successful and well worth eating.

Two things, avoid wateriness – I am not quite sure how they managed it, but the shepherd's pie at our school tasted and looked as if it had swum to us across the river Lune – and use rare meat from the joint or a piece of lean meat that you have minced yourself or asked your butcher to mince for you. Bought mince is padded out with fat: if your economy is desperate, take a tip from the French and sandwich the meat between two layers of potato, i.e. use less meat but good meat, and more potato. Another way is to mix some cheap but good offal, like brains, which have been prepared and cooked, into the meat hash before putting it into the dish.

Serves 6

*500 g (1 lb) beef, or lamb, or mixed veal and pork*
*150 g (5 oz) chopped onion*
*3 tablespoons butter, dripping or oil*
*3 cloves garlic, crushed and chopped*
*300 ml (½ pt) meat jelly, clear gravy and stock in whatever proportions*
  *you have them*
*1 level tablespoon flour or cornflour*
*tomato concentrate or paste (optional)*
*1 tablespoon Worcester sauce or 1½ teaspoons wine vinegar*
*thyme, salt, pepper, cayenne*
*1 kg (2 lb) potatoes*
*up to 250 ml (8 fl oz) milk*
*up to 90 g (3 oz) butter*
*1 tablespoon grated dry Leicester cheese*
*1 tablespoon grated Parmesan*

Chop, process or mince the meat. Cook the onion in the fat until soft. Add the meat and garlic, stirring well, then raise the heat so that the meat browns. Turn it over in large sections with a slice, so that it browns all over. Pour off any surplus fat. Add some of the liquid and bubble gently for 5 minutes. Sprinkle on flour or cornflour, stir again and add the remaining liquid. Let it bubble to a rich sauce, adding the various flavourings to taste.

Meanwhile scrub, boil, and peel the potatoes. Set aside a couple and slice them thinly. Mash the rest with the milk and butter, seasoning to taste. Put the meat into a shallow dish. Spread the mashed potato on top and, with the slices, make a ring round the edge. Scatter with the cheese and brown under the grill at a moderate heat, or at the top of a hot oven. Once the dish looks an appetizing golden colour, it can wait for a while in a low oven without coming to any harm.

[*British Cookery*]


## YORKSHIRE PUDDING

This recipe has remained unchanged since the eighteenth century when it first became popular. Here is Hannah Glasse's version for cooking under spit-roasted meat – it can be adapted for a modern spit-roaster:

> 'Take a quart of milk, four eggs, and a little salt, make it up into a thick batter with flour, like a pancake batter. You must have a good piece of meat at the fire, take a stew-pan and put some dripping in, set it on the fire; when it boils, pour on your pudding; let it bake on the fire till you think it is high enough, then turn a plate upside-down in the dripping pan [i.e. the pan under the joint] that the dripping may not be blacked; set your stew-pan on it under your meat, and let the dripping drop on the pudding, and the heat of the fire come to it, to make it of a fine brown. When your meat is done and sent to table, drain all the fat from your pudding, and set it on the fire again to dry a little; then slide it as dry as you can into a dish, melt some butter, and pour it into a cup, and set it in the middle of the pudding. It is an exceeding good pudding; the gravy of the meat eats well with it.'

On roast-beef Sundays, my mother's father, who had reached heights of power and respectability in the Bank of England, forgot what was due to his position and remembered the ways of the Northumbrian farm at Old Bewick which his family had come from. The roast beef went back to the kitchen after the main course, but the Yorkshire pudding remained to be finished up with sweetened condensed milk. I do not know how my grandmother took this – she prided herself on her elegant desserts – but my mother shared his delight in the crisp and sticky pudding. When she had a home of her own, and a family, she passed his taste on to us who only remembered him, in spats and spectacles and pin-striped trousers, from old photographs.

Try it. But the pudding should be roasted *above* the beef, and you will have to forgo the meaty juices, at least as part of the pudding. There is, of course, no reason why you shouldn't just make the Yorkshire pudding on its own, as a straightforward second course.

*125 g (4 oz) flour*
*a pinch of salt*
*1 egg*
*300 ml (½ pt) milk, or 150 ml (¼ pt) each milk and water*

Mix flour and salt, make a well in the centre and break the egg into it. Add a little milk. Beginning at the centre, stir these ingredients into a batter, gradually pouring in the remainder of the milk, or milk and water.

[*English Food*]

## SALTMARSH LAMB IN PASTRY

Michael Waterfield, who made the Wife of Bath restaurant at Wye famous, has now moved to Canterbury. There he has a restaurant – Waterfield's – with a courtyard and a pie shop where he sells smoked haddock pies, pigeon pies, sweet lamb pies, pies of pork and apple, pâtés and terrines, and at Christmas little oblong mince pies, the top crust turned back at one end to look like a manger-cradle.

He has good local sources of supply, a butcher, an old-fashioned grocery, farm shops in the area with Mount's at Littlebourne providing him with blueberries and Kentish cobs. His lamb comes from Romney Marsh, from several breeds since it is the pasture not the breed that gives the flavour. Vegetables served with this dish will of course vary with the season: they may well be cooked to a recipe from the famous classic of Italian cookery, *Leaves from our Tuscan Kitchen* by Janet Ross (1899), since Michael Waterfield is her great-great-nephew and published a tactfully modernized edition of her book in 1973.

Serves 8

*boned whole loin of lamb with its 2 kidneys*
*butter*
*salt, pepper, a pinch or two of thyme*
*flaky pastry made with 500 g (1 lb) flour*
*beaten egg to glaze*

Place the two pieces of loin on the table. Remove the undercuts (fillet) and trim the side flaps, leaving about 2½ cm (1 inch). Use the trimmings for little lamb pies, or some other dish. Cut fat away. Prepare the kidneys by skinning them, cutting them in half and removing the fat, then slicing them finely. Brown the outside of each loin lightly in butter, remove from pan and cool.

Take one piece, turning it cut side up, outer browned side down. Season it with salt, pepper and thyme. Put the slices from the kidneys down the flap, and season again. Lay the second piece of loin on top, boned and cut side down, with the thick part resting on the kidneys, the little flap on top of the thicker part of the piece underneath.

Roll out the pastry into a rectangle. Lay the lamb sandwich carefully on top. Season the top and bring up the pastry, folding the edges over firmly on top to make a neat seam. With the point of a knife, make a few incisions either side of the seam to allow steam to escape. Bake 25 minutes at gas 8, 230°C (450°F). Brush with egg.

Serve with gooseberries cooked with a little sugar and a splash of wine vinegar, or with Madeira sauce, and lightly cooked hop shoots or the thin hop tops, watercress, or appropriate seasonal vegetables.

[*British Cookery*]


## LEEK AND BACON ROLY POLY

A splendid suet pudding for a family lunch. Vary the proportions of filling as you please. This kind of dish is made with whatever is to hand, a bit of cooked gammon left over, or a few rashers, or a mixture. I have never tried it with cheese, but it might work well with the leek and onion. Sometimes the bacon is left out altogether and the roly poly turns up with boiled beef or mutton or pork instead of vegetables. This roly poly will serve 4–6.

Make a suet crust by mixing the following crust ingredients together well with your hands: 300 g (10 oz) self-raising flour, ½ level teaspoon of salt and 150 g (5 oz) chopped fresh suet. Bind to a soft but coherent dough with cold water and chill.

For the filling, chop the white part of 4 medium leeks with 2 large onions. Take the rind off and chop 250 g (8 oz) of cooked bacon or gammon, or 300 g (10 oz) uncooked bacon rashers. Mix together, add seasoning – plenty of pepper – and 1 level teaspoon of dried sage, and spread over the rolled out pastry, leaving a free edge all round. Brush the free edge with water and roll up.

Put on to a generously-buttered piece of foil, large enough to enclose the roll in a baggy parcel (the crust needs room to rise and swell). Seal it well. Enclose in a cloth if you like, for easy handling.

Bring an oblong or oval pan – I use a self-basting roaster – one-third full of water to the boil. Put a trivet in the pan, or a long shallow dish upside down and lay the parcel on top. Cover and steam for 2 hours. Check from time to time and, if necessary, restore the original water-level with more boiling water.

Remove the roly poly and take away the cloth, if used. Unwrap the foil carefully, saving any juices, and turn the roly poly on to a hot serving dish. If convenient, put into a moderately hot oven to crisp the surface slightly.

[*British Cookery*]

## ROASTING GAME

Roasting game is little different from other meats. The thing is to spot the analogies, bearing in mind that since game inclines to be tougher than domesticated meat, it should be cooked rare or pink – the exceptions to this being wild boar and wild rabbit, which are just cooked through, like pork and chicken. Venison is treated like beef. It's really a matter of common sense, the smallest items are cooked very briefly at high temperatures, as you can see from the chart below.

There are all manner of dodges. A chef will often brown a bird all over on top of the stove, then transfer the pan to the oven, to shorten the cooking time. With medium-sized and larger birds, the breast will be cut off to be cooked as a steak, seasoned, even marinaded and set to one side well in advance, while the rest of the carcase is used to make stock for the sauce. Or else the legs and backbone are cut off for stock, and the breast roasted on the bone, just before the meal. There is a lot of fun for the cook, and good eating, in this kind of cookery. You can control things more efficiently and take prompt remedial action.

Two rules for game cookery: try to season in advance and be sure to rest the joint or bird in a low oven for at least 15 minutes, or better still, 30 minutes for larger pieces. And, sub-section to rule two, be sure to have the serving dish, plates, vegetables, etc., very hot.

## Preparation

MARINADING furred game in an appropriate wine, with aromatics and a little olive oil, is not really necessary. I do it with farmed game to reinforce the slightly bland flavour, or if there is to be a delay between acquiring the piece of game and cooking it. With young game for roasting there is no need, if the butcher knows his job. Wild rabbit is often soaked for 12 hours or overnight in water and vinegar, 1 tablespoon vinegar to 1 litre (1½ pt) of water.

BARDING game birds with a jacket of thinly-cut pork-back fat is a classic convention, but few butchers these days can cut the fat to the thinness required. Better to wrap them in caul fat – soften in warm water, stretch out and cut to size – or to tie a nearly transparent rasher of unsmoked streaky bacon round the highest part of the breast.

LARDING is a technique that gives great pleasure to the cook skilful enough to pattern a haunch of venison with regular whiskers of pork fat; similarly the breast of a pheasant, a bird which has a tendency to toughness even when young. The ends of fat catch in the first heat of the oven to make a handsome effect, but it is not necessary if the game is well hung, young enough to roast anyway, and cooked rare or pink. Caul fat is again an alternative to larding.

## Roasting Times

VENISON Brown joint in butter, lard or good oil on top of stove. Oven at gas 8, 230°C (450°F). 20 minutes per kg (2 lb) for rare, 30 for medium rare. (*Note:* a really large piece, a whole haunch of 9 kg (18 lb), only needs 3–4 hours for medium rare.) Use a meat thermometer as for beef.

WILD BOAR    Oven at gas 5, 190°C (375°F), 60 minutes per kg (2 lb).

HARE Saddle only, oven at gas 7, 220°C (425°F), for 20 minutes approx. Whole hare: legs splayed out, oven at gas 5, 190°C (375°F), for 45 minutes approx.

RABBIT Saddle only, oven at gas 7, 220°C (425°F), for 25 minutes approx. Whole rabbit: legs splayed out, oven at gas 5, 190°C (375°F), for 60 minutes approx.

WILD GOOSE   Young ones only, gas 7, 220°C (425°F), for 15 minutes, then 60 minutes at gas 3, 160°C (325°F).

PHEASANT   Oven at gas 5, 190°C (375°F), for 45–60 minutes, according to weight.

MALLARD   Oven at gas 8, 230°C (450°C), for 30 minutes for rare; oven at gas 5, 190°C (375°F), for 60 minutes for pink.

WIDGEON   Oven at gas 8, 230°C (450°F), for 15–25 minutes, according to weight (750–1000 g (1½–2 lb)).

TEAL   Oven at gas 8, 230°C (450°F), for 10–15 minutes, according to weight (325–400 g (11–14 oz)).

PARTRIDGE   Oven at gas 7, 220°C (425°F), for 30 minutes.

PIGEON   Oven at gas 7, 220°C (425°F), for 20 minutes.

WOODCOCK   Oven at gas 8, 230°C (450°F), for 15–20 minutes.

SNIPE   Oven at gas 8, 230°C (450°F), for 10–15 minutes.

These times are based on Game Conservancy recommendations, which are the ones I follow. With larger joints, test with a meat thermometer or push in a metal skewer and leave for 30 seconds, then touch the back of your hand with it. If it is cold, the meat is not ready; if it is warm, the meat is rare; if it is fairly hot, the meat is pink; if it is quite hot – ouch! – the meat is well done.

[*Observer Magazine*]


## JUGGED HARE WITH FORCEMEAT BALLS

The delightful name of this dish describes the old way of cooking it: pieces of hare were fitted into a tall pot or jug – I use a French stoneware *rillettes* pot, like a jug without a lip – and the whole thing went into boiling liquid. Apart from the obvious virtue of gentle cooking for meat which could be tough, it was a neat contrivance for cooks before ovens were a commonplace, since the jug could be suspended in the big iron pot in which things were cooking at the same time.

It reminds us that kitchens were only for the well-off until quite modern times. Cottagers cooked on the open hearth, their pots suspended from a pot hook (the French for house-warming is *pendre la cremaillère*, hanging up the pot hook, which indicates, I suppose, that they made do without kitchens even longer than we did and became urbanized at a much later date). People in town tenements balanced pan or grill or kettle on the grate of small coal fires, and took longer-cooking dishes to the baker's or made use of cook shops.

Jugged hare was a favourite winter dish of ours. Sometimes it was jugged properly, sometimes it was put into a low oven and cooked like the modern stew. No one larded hare then, such refinements would never have occurred to the cook who had grown up in a mining community or to my mother who came from Croydon – which is a bad mark against our domestic cookery. Larding makes a worthwhile difference to other very lean meats, which can be dry as well as tough: I suppose we just prided ourselves on our teeth and chewed on. If you do lard the hare, use stock rather than butter in the cooking.

*1 hare, jointed or 1½–2 kg (3–4 lb) hare joints*
*plus the hare's blood (desirable, but optional)*
*5-cm (2-inch) piece pork back fat or green bacon*
*salt, pepper, mace*
*lard*
bouquet garni
*1 onion, stuck with 3 cloves*
*either 125 g (4 oz) butter or 150 ml (¼ pt) hare, game, beef*
   *or poultry stock*
*150 ml (¼ pt) red or white wine*
*2 anchovy fillets, chopped, or 2 curls of lemon peel*
*a pinch of cayenne pepper*
*1½ tablespoons butter*
*1½ tablespoons flour*
*lemon juice or redcurrant jelly (optional)*

FORCEMEAT BALLS
*125 g (4 oz) fresh white crumbs*
*60 g (2 oz) fresh suet, chopped*
*1 generous tablespoon chopped parsley*
*grated rind of ½ lemon*
*60 g (2 oz) bacon, chopped*
*salt, pepper*
*1 large egg, beaten*
*lard or clarified butter*

Pick out the larger pieces of hare for larding (back legs and saddle), and set the forelegs aside. The poulterer will have added vinegar to the hare's blood to prevent it coagulating, but check this with him. If he has not, add a tablespoon of wine vinegar. Keep covered in the refrigerator.

Chill the fat or bacon, and then cut it into matchstick strips. Use them to lard the hare (any left over can be frozen). Trim the ends so that they stick slightly out of the meat. Sprinkle all the hare pieces with salt, pepper and ground mace. If you have time, leave the hare to absorb the seasoning in a covered dish.

To cook the hare, brown it lightly in a little lard and fit the pieces into a jug or pot as closely as possible, without *bouquet* and onion. If using butter, add it now, cut into chunks. Inspect the pan and if there are nice crusty bits, pour off the surplus fat and deglaze it with wine or stock and wine: if the pan does not look too good, just heat the wine or stock and wine to boiling point and pour over the meat. Add anchovy or lemon and a good pinch of cayenne.

Cover jug or pot closely. Stand on a trivet in a pan of boiling water – it should come at least a third of the way up the side of the pot. Adjust temperature to keep water at a steady simmer. From time to time replenish with more boiling water. Should you be using an aluminium pan, put in a tablespoon of vinegar to prevent it discolouring (do the same for all steaming, where flavour is not involved, e.g. when cooking suet puddings).

Alternatively, put the whole thing into a low oven, which might take about 15 minutes more. Allow 3 hours, but start checking after 1½ hours, and remove the smaller pieces when they are tender. Keep them warm.

When the hare is cooked, strain off the liquid into a pan. Extract and discard the *bouquet*, onion, cloves and lemon peel, if used. Taste and decide on final seasoning and thickening.

BLOOD   Stir some of the hot sauce into the blood, then pour back into the pan and stir over a low heat. Do not overheat or – like egg – the blood will curdle.

KNEADED BUTTER (*BEURRE MANIÉ*)   Mash butter and flour together. Add to the hot sauce in little bits, to thicken it slightly. Keep just below boiling point, and stir constantly. This takes about 5 minutes.

FLOUR   Mix the flour to a paste with a little cold water, then stir in some of the sauce. When smooth, tip back into the pan and simmer until the sauce is thickened and has no taste of flour. This is the best way if you have used butter in the cooking: the last tablespoon of butter is not needed. This was the homely way of doing things, no reduction of the sauce, but plenty of sauce to go with a suet pudding in the absence of forcemeat balls or potatoes.

Last of all, taste the sauce and accentuate its flavour with lemon juice or redcurrant jelly. Bring to just below simmering point and pour over the hare.

Serve with redcurrant jelly in a bowl, and the forcemeat balls which should be ready just before the final thickening of the sauce.

To make the forcemeat balls, mix the ingredients together, using just enough egg to bind (you may not need it all). Form into balls 1½–2 cm (¾ inch) across, and fry them in lard or clarified butter. The mixture can be made up even smaller and used as a garnish for game soups: it makes a good stuffing for veal and poultry as well.

[*British Cookery*]

## PHEASANT WITH SMOKED BACON AND WINE

When George Perry-Smith left Bath for Cornwall in 1972, after twenty years of cooking and teaching at the Hole in the Wall, two of his pupils opened their own restaurant, Cranes, in Salisbury. Sue and Tim Cumming had met and married under his amiable tutelage. They carried on, in their own style, the Perry-Smith theme.

Their generation were the heirs of the Elizabeth David revolution – perhaps the word should be revelation. They had both been brought up in families that loved good food, without puritanism. They could take it more naturally. Which meant that when they bought the Hole in the Wall and opened in 1980, they were not so much intimidated as amused to be back.

Now they have been in the business long enough to be able to look back themselves. They see that people who eat out know more, expect more, will follow their own new excitements more (though they get an occasional client like the man who walked over to the open kitchen area, watched for a moment or two, then said, 'And what do you do for the rest of the day?').

Fish is the big change. Once it was sole or salmon, with a daring red mullet. Now they cook sea bass, John Dory, monkfish, squid, grey mullet, all fresh up from Brixham or Bristol. They buy game easily, and bacon from people who smoke their own. Another advantage, from their Wiltshire days, is Loire and Rhône wines from the Yapps at Mere, who specialize in these two areas. On the last three items, this recipe depends.

Serves 4

*2 pheasants*
*12 rashers smoked steaky bacon, cut on no. 4*
*250 g (½ lb) onions, finely chopped*
*250 g (½ lb) carrots, finely chopped*
bouquet garni
*2 cloves garlic, finely chopped*
*2 cloves, finely ground*
*1 bottle Gigondas, or other red Rhône wine*
*olive oil and butter*
*stock (see recipe)*
*1 heaped tablespoon flour*
*2 tablespoons double cream*
*crème de cassis or redcurrant jelly*
*puff pastry* fleurons

Joint each pheasant into six pieces, cutting the breast off the bone, and wrap each piece in smoked bacon (remove the rind first), pinning with wooden cocktail sticks. Place in a bowl with the onion, carrot, *bouquet garni*, garlic, ground cloves and wine. Leave for at least 6 hours. Make stock from carcases.

Remove, drain and dry the pheasant pieces, then brown them in oil and butter. Put them into a casserole. Drain the vegetables and put them into the frying pan to brown lightly – add a shade more oil and butter if necessary. Sprinkle on the flour, cook for 2 minutes, stirring, then add the wine to make a sauce. Stir and taste for seasoning. Pour over the pheasant, adding a little stock if need be, to cover.

Cook in a low oven, gas 2, 150°C (300°F) until the pheasant is tender – ¾–1½ hours according to the birds.

Cool slightly, then remove the pheasant and extract the cocktail sticks (using pliers if they are firmly wedged in). Put the pheasant on a serving dish and keep warm. Strain the sauce, discarding the vegetables. Stir in the cream and extra seasoning, with a sash of cassis or a small spoonful of redcurrant jelly for sweetness. Pour over the pheasant, decorate with puff pastry *fleurons* and serve.

*Note:* you could serve small triangles of fried bread instead of *fleurons*, though it is sensible to use up the trimmings of puff pastry by making these small devices. They can be stored in the freezer or, if baked, like biscuits in an air-tight tin for a day or two. Heat through to revive them before serving.

[*British Cookery*]

## PRESSURE PIGEONS

On 12 April 1682, John Evelyn joined his friends of the Royal Society at a 'Philosophical Supper'. The meal of various meats and fish had been cooked in the new Digester of Monsieur Denis Papin, in other words the first pressure cooker. In a short time, and with little fuel, it reduced tough mutton and beef to a jelly. The bones became 'as soft as cheese' and crumbly so that they could be eaten on bread (the bones of canned salmon, which is cooked under high pressure, are reduced to the same texture). The great success of the evening was the pigeons, 'which tasted just as if baked in a pie, all these being stewed in their own juice'. The success of the pressure cooker was delayed until this century when aluminium and sealing rings made it light and safe enough to be used at home. There is no need to worry about meat and bones disintegrating: the pressure of a modern cooker is 7½ kg (15 lb) to 2½ cm (1 inch), whereas Papin's was 17½ kg (35 lb) and even 25 kg (50 lb).

Evelyn's pigeons were tender squabs from the dovecote: these you can only find in London at Harrods and a few other butchers' shops. I make the dish with wood pigeons, casserole birds; they require 45 minutes, though I check after 35. Another solution would be to buy two guineafowl, or one chicken.

Serves 6

*6 globe artichokes, boiled*
*butter*
*3 hard-boiled eggs*
*12 tablespoons long-grain rice*
*a lump of pork or bacon fat, chilled*
*6 pigeons*
*lard*
*300 ml (½ pt) beef stock*
*150 ml (¼ pt) dry white wine*
*10-cm (4-inch) celery stalk*
*a generous pinch of thyme*
*¼ teaspoon sugar*
*a level teaspoon of salt*
*nutmeg, lemon juice*

Strip leaves from artichokes, scraping the edible part into a bowl. Remove chokes carefully. Mash artichokes in the bowl with a large knob of butter and two chopped eggs. Slice the third egg and set aside. Fill artichoke mash into the saucer-shaped bases, mounding it up. Set them aside, too, until you boil the rice: then they can be reheated on top of the rice pan in a covered plate.

Cut fat into strips. Lard the birds (no need with chicken), then halve and remove the breast bone. Brown them in lard. Put in the cooker with next six ingredients, and sand them lightly with nutmeg. Bring to a boil, then put on lid and pressure-cook for appropriate time.

Meanwhile, boil and butter the rice and put on a serving dish. Arrange the cooked birds around it, with the artichoke saucers and the sliced egg, and season them. Keep warm. Taste, then degrease the cooking juices. Boil them down to a syrupy liquid, adding extra salt if necessary at the end. Strain over the whole thing and serve.

[*Observer Magazine*]

## VENISON STEW

I suspect it is our image of the Monarch of the Glen that makes us nervous about cooking venison. Admittedly it can be lean and so have a propensity to toughness, but this point is so easily taken care of (by larding and not overcooking) that there is nothing to fear. Basically treat venison like beef.

For those who have some choice in the matter, roe deer is reckoned to be the finest, then fallow and then red deer. Detailed instructions, recipes and seasons are given in Julia Drysdale's *Game Cookery Book* which is one of the most useful books to have in the kitchen.

Most of us will not have much choice in the matter of venison, indeed we can count ourselves lucky to see it at all – although with the increase in deer farming I hope it will become easier to buy. Many people come to prefer it to beef as it is a meat uncontaminated by such things as growth promoters. The advantages of farming are that the herd is fed in the winter when the weather is bad, and culled to keep the herd in good condition. I believe that three-quarters of Scotch venison goes off to Germany, and that there is a good trade in deer pizzles and velvet (from the horns) to China where such items are reckoned to have aphrodisiac properties.

When you buy venison, allow time for marinading, and remember that some item like fat salt pork or fat green bacon is essential either for cooking in with the meat (stew) or for larding (roasting or braising, unless the meat has been well hung).

Serves 8

*1 ½ kg (3 lb) shoulder of venison, trimmed and diced*

MARINADE
*300–375 ml (10–12 fl oz) red wine*
*1 medium onion, sliced*
*3 tablespoons brandy*
*3 tablespoons olive oil*
*salt, lightly-crushed black pepper*

SAUCE
*250 g (8 oz) fat salt pork or green streaky bacon, diced*
*2 level tablespoons butter*
*2 medium to large onions, chopped*
*1 large carrot, diced*
*1 large clove garlic, crushed*
*about ½ litre (¾ pt) beef or venison stock*
bouquet garni
*24 small mushrooms, preferably wild ones*
*extra butter*
*raspberry vinegar or lemon juice or redcurrant jelly*
*salt, pepper, sugar*

Season the venison well and soak in the marinade ingredients for 24–48 hours. Drain the meat well, pat it dry on kitchen paper and turn in seasoned flour.

Meanwhile brown the pork or bacon in the butter, cooking it slowly at first to persuade the fat to run, then raising the heat. Transfer to a casserole. In the fat, brown the venison and then the onion, carrot and garlic: do all this in batches, transferring each one to the casserole. Do not overheat or the fat will burn. Pour off any surplus fat, deglaze the pan with the strained marinade and pour over the venison. Heat up enough stock to cover the items in the casserole and pour it over them. Put in the *bouquet*, bring to a gentle simmer either on top of the stove or in the oven preheated to gas 2, 150°C (300°F), cover closely and leave until the venison is tender.

Test after 1½ hours, but allow for 2½ hours' cooking time. For best results, it is wise to cook this kind of dish one day then reheat the next: this improves the flavour and gives you a chance to make sure the venison is tender.

Towards the end of the cooking time, or when reheating, cook the mushrooms in a little butter and put them with their juices into the pot.

Perhaps this is the moment to say that a venison stew gives an opportunity for Scottish cooks to make up for their past neglect of wild mushrooms. Their woods are thick with chanterelles and ceps, have been for centuries, and yet they never appear in a Scottish recipe: even today they are still ignored to the extent that foreign settlers who came from Europe as a result of the war are able to gather them and send a plane load each week to Paris in the season. A point which always makes me suspect the depth of French influence on Scottish food and cookery.

Finally, taste the venison sauce. It will need seasoning, and very likely sharpening. Raspberry vinegar is not a new fancy idea but a suggestion made well over 100 years ago by Meg Dods. Other appropriate fruit vinegars could be used, or wine vinegar straight, or lemon juice and a little sugar, or redcurrant jelly (be careful not to use too much).

Serve with bread or potatoes.

[*British Cookery*]


## CORNISH CHARTER PIE

When I came across this recipe a year or two ago in Lady Sarah Lindsay's *Choice Recipes*, of 1883, I thought it explained something which had puzzled me for a long time. Now I am not so sure.

The puzzling thing was a couple of references in Parson Woodforde's diary, to the Charter. It occurred in the middle of a list of dishes he had had at a dinner party on 13 July 1775, without any explanation. Obviously it was something to eat, because on another occasion the Parson helped his niece Nancy to make the Charter, this time for a party at his brother's house in Somerset. They put the Charter into the cellar to cool, the dog got into the cellar, and the dog ate the Charter. This suggests something meaty, unless it was an especially greedy dog which guzzled anything it could get hold of. And this is why I was delighted to find the recipe above. It seemed to explain everything.

Or does it? Why should the Parson have helped to make a chicken pie? Although he was always concerned with food – in particular when guests were arriving at short notice – he does not give the impression that he helped in the kitchen, even in an emergency.

Serves 6–8

*375 g (¾ lb) weight rich shortcrust pastry*
*beaten egg to glaze*

FILLING
*2 × 1½-kg (3-lb) chickens, jointed*
*seasoned flour*
*1 large onion, chopped*
*125 g (4 oz) butter*
*90–125 g (3–4 oz) bunch of parsley*
*1 leek, or 6 spring onions*
*150 ml (¼ pt) milk*
*150 ml (¼ pt) single cream*
*300 ml (½ pt) double cream*
*salt, pepper*

Roll the chicken pieces in seasoned flour. Cook the onion gently in half the butter in a frying pan, then remove it to a large shallow pie dish. Add the rest of the butter to the pan and when it is really hot, put in the chicken and brown it slightly – a golden colour is right, not a very crusty brown. Fit the chicken into the pie dish on top of the onions, in a close, single layer. Chop the parsley leaves, and the leek or spring onions, and simmer them for 2 or 3 minutes in the milk and single cream. Pour the whole thing over the chicken, and add about a third of the double cream. Season everything well.

Roll out the pastry and cover the pie in the usual way. Make a central hole large enough to accommodate a small kitchen funnel, and put a pastry rose with a 12-mm (½-inch) stem down through the middle. Surround it with some leaves. Brush over with beaten egg. Bake at gas 7–8, 220–230°C (425–450°F), for about 20 minutes, until the pastry is golden. Lower the heat to gas 4, 180°C (350°F) and leave until the chicken is cooked – about 1 hour. Just before serving ease out the rose from the centre, and pour in the remaining cream, which should be at boiling point. Replace the rose, and serve hot, very hot, or cold (the juices set to a delicious jelly).

[*English Food*]

# VEGETABLES AND FRUIT

## STOVED ARTICHOKES

The very best way of cooking artichokes: it emphasizes their exquisite flavour and the golden-brown crust holds their tenderness in shape so that there is no squash of texture to spoil the dish. Serve them on their own in small dishes, or as a vegetable with veal, lamb, chicken, beef, so long as you can leave the meat to keep warm while you spend time just before the meal attending to their cooking only. The method is a combination of frying and steaming: once you grow used to it, there is no need to concentrate quite so hard. It is a superb way of cooking root vegetables of quality – new potatoes, for instance, and very young turnips – as it concentrates the flavour. For this reason it is no good for older roots; they would taste too strong for pleasure and need blanching before being finished in an open pan in butter.

Serves 6

*about 2 kg (4 lb) Jerusalem artichokes, scrubbed*
*olive oil*
*butter*
*salt, pepper*
*1 large or 2 small cloves garlic*
*small bunch parsley*

Pick out the smoothest, least knobbly artichokes you can find. Cut off any oddities, then peel them into fairly even pieces the size of Queen olives; the larger artichokes can be cut to this kind of shape and then halved. (Keep peelings and cuttings to flavour stock for soups or stews.) Aim to end up with at least 1½ kg (3 lb) of prepared pieces. Put them into acidulated water as you go to prevent discoloration.

As the artichokes need to be cooked in a single layer, you may need to use a couple of pans. Heat them over a moderate flame, putting in enough oil to cover the bases comfortably. Put 1 heaped tablespoon of butter into each pan, or 2 tablespoons if you are using one large pan. Drain and dry the artichokes and put them into the sizzling fat. Cover them for the first 10 minutes, but not too tightly, so that they partly fry and partly steam. Turn them over after 5 minutes, and keep the heat steady so that the fat does not burn although the artichokes begin to turn a nice golden-brown. Remove the covers from the pans, and give the artichokes a further 10 minutes, turning them over from time to time to colour evenly. Remember that they are far more tender than, for instance, new potatoes, and may collapse on you rather suddenly. The idea is to keep the softness inside the skins; you can always remove them gradually from the pans.

Put the artichokes into small individual pots, or round the meat, sprinkling them with salt and pepper. Have ready the garlic and parsley chopped finely together and scatter this evenly over the top. Serve straightaway if possible, though the artichokes can be kept warm for a while, so long as the oven is not too hot, which is helpful if they are being served with the main course.

[*Vegetable Book*]

## CABBAGE

Cabbages have been eaten in this country since the time of the Celts and Romans. These were probably of the loose-headed, green-leaved type. Then round about the 1570s we seem to have had the first Savoys – not from the Savoie but from Holland and as Evelyn pointed out, they were 'not so rank but agreeable to most palates'. The name of Savoy cabbage was introduced into the English language by Henry Lyte in his *Niewe Herball* of 1578. This was not an original work, but a translation of Dodoens' *Cruydeboeck*, and the name was a direct translation of the Dutch *Savoyekool* (*kool* as in coleslaw, etc.). Sir Anthony Ashley, of Wimborn St Giles in Dorset, is recorded as planting in England the first cabbages from Holland, which may have been Savoys or perhaps the white, smooth, hard-packed cabbage that we still call Dutch cabbage today.

Cabbage as a food has problems. It is easy to grow, a useful source of greenery for much of the year. Yet as a vegetable it has original sin, and needs improvement. It can smell foul in the pot, linger through the house with pertinacity, and ruin a meal with its wet flab. Cabbage also has a nasty history of being good for you. Read Pliny, if you do not believe me.

How the Celtic inhabitants of Europe regarded the virtues of the cabbage is not known. Wild cabbage is native to the sea coasts of northern France and Great Britain, and they ate that before the Romans arrived. Wild cabbage is very nasty indeed; the rest of the diet must have been stodgy and dull for the Celts to have tolerated it. In *The Englishman's Flora*, Geoffrey Grigson remarks that wild cabbage used to be sold in Dover market, and that it needed several washings and two boilings before it could be eaten. The garden varieties of cabbage brought in by Roman settlers can only have seemed an improvement, as being somewhat less bitter than the wild sea cabbage and larger-leaved. Whether they regarded it as medicine or food, one cannot know.

As Ireland settled into farming, cabbage asserted itself and became an even more important part of people's diet than elsewhere in Europe. So much so that it came to have a share in celebrations at Hallowe'en, the great festival of the year's end, in the form of colcannon (page 53).

Another favourite Hallowe'en dish was champ, a splendid buttery version of mashed potatoes mixed with greenery including cabbage. On the Isle of Man at Hallowe'en mummers would go round and bang on doors with cabbages and turnips stuck on the end of sticks.

Then they sang and sang until silence was bought by the householder, with a scone or a potato.

### How to choose and prepare cabbage

Cabbage, in a number of varieties, is with us the year round. Usually firm solidity is the thing to look out for, although young cabbages such as 'spring greens' and some early Primo cabbages are much looser. I am a recent convert to the tight round cabbages, and prefer to buy them still in their dark green outer leaves. Dutch white cabbage is always sold trimmed though it seems to taste all right so long as it is not overcooked. Nonetheless if there is any choice in the matter, go straight for the mild and crisp Savoy, with its dark wrinkled outer leaves that look as if they were fresh from some porcelain factory. It is the ideal cabbage for raw salads – always excepting the delicious Chinese leaf – on account of its mild flavour and crunchy texture.

Because of the compact form, cabbage should be sliced before it is rinsed. First cut away the outer leaves and the stalk; discard the withered stringy parts, and slice the rest of this hard part rather thinly. Then slice the inner heart across. Rinse the two lots of cabbage separately and briefly.

If you intend to stuff a cabbage whole, washing it properly is impossible. Rinse the outside as best you can in a bowl of salted water and hope that insects and grubs have found it as difficult as you have to get at the centre. A really firm, unblemished exterior usually denotes a wholesome interior. The problem about stuffing individual cabbage leaves is to get them away from the cabbage without tearing their tight roundness. You can blanch the whole thing, as you do for stuffed cabbage, and then remove the leaves – but this means that you have to use up the inside of the cabbage the same day. It is more convenient to cut away as many leaves as you require, plus a few extra to allow for damage, and blanch them for 3 minutes on their own; they should be pliable enough to roll without breaking, but not completely cooked. In cutting away the leaves, it helps if you first cut the stalk right out and ease the leaves from the base end.

There are a good number of exceptions to the brief cooking rule, but one has to emphasize it in a book for this country as most of us have such appalling memories of overcooked cabbage in childhood. In France and Germany, long-cooked cabbage dishes are much approved. I suppose that *perdrix aux choux* could be described as the best of all cabbage recipes: in it the cabbage is given time to absorb the meaty juices of the partridge.

Many peasant dishes depend on the lengthy cooking of cabbage.

Soup-stews such as *potée* and *garbure* require the slow blending of all the vegetables together for the right flavour; nonetheless you may prefer to keep back half the cabbage and put it into the pot at the end of cooking time, so that the soup may also benefit from its crispness. The Christmas cabbage from Schleswig, and a similar dish from the French Marais, are thick purées of cabbage that must first be thoroughly cooked, then squeezed of all juices: this essence or soul of cabbage is finally enriched with butter or cream and is very good.

[*Vegetable Book*]

## COLCANNON, THE NORTHERN BUBBLE AND SQUEAK

In Ireland, colcannon was a favourite dish for fast-day celebrations, when meat could not be eaten. At Hallowe'en, the eve of All Saints' Day, a wedding ring would be pushed into the crusty mass; whoever found it would be married within the twelvemonth. It is best to make it from freshly cooked vegetables, best of all from cabbage and potatoes straight from the garden.

Serves 4–6

*1 bowlful cooked potatoes*
*1 bowlful lightly cooked cabbage*
*1 large onion*
*dripping, lard or butter*
*salt, pepper*

Push the potatoes through a *mouli-légumes*, sieve or ricer. Chop the cabbage. Mix the two together thoroughly. Cook the onion in the fat in a frying pan – a non-stick one, if possible. When it is soft and lightly browned, press in the potato and cabbage to form an even layer. Sprinkle with salt and pepper. When it is nicely coloured underneath and crusted, cut into pieces – with a wooden spatula if you're using a non-stick pan – and turn them over to form a fresh layer. Repeat until you have a green and white marbled cake, speckled with crisp brown bits. (At this stage the wedding ring was pushed into the colcannon.)

Turn it on to a heated dish to serve, with lightly fried slices of beef if you like. We sometimes have it with sausages. Or have it on its own with a bit of butter.

*Note:* Brussels sprouts and other forms of cabbage can also be used.

[*Vegetable Book*]

## CUCUMBER SAUCE

Slice half a large cucumber thinly. Stew it in a heavy pan with a good tablespoon of butter and about 60 g (2 oz) cooked spinach, or twice that amount of raw spinach. When cooked, drain and purée in the blender. Add to about 300 ml (½ pt) béchamel or velouté sauce, and finish with a spoonful or two of double cream. Reheat gently.

Serve with hot salmon, salmon trout, chicken and veal. It is also good with fat fish such as herring and mackerel, which have been stuffed and baked in a hot oven.

The idea of the spinach is mainly to add colour, but the flavour is pleasant too. It can be omitted, and you could in that case complete the sauce with some chopped cucumber, lightly cooked in the sauce before you add the cream.

[*Vegetable Book*]

## HOW TO CHOOSE AND PREPARE LEEKS

Large leeks can be useful for stuffing and for making soup. On the whole – I risk north-eastern wrath in saying so – medium or small leeks have a much better texture and taste. A thing to watch is leeks at the end of the season in March and April; they may look fine, but the centres can be a hard yellow stalk. Buy them ready lopped if you can, as this exposes the centre core and you can see and feel what you are buying. The rest of the winter, leeks with earth, roots and a bit of reality to them are likely to be fresher than the trimmed, washed, neat cylinders in a plastic pack. Of course this means waste and extra cleaning, but it is worth while. You will notice that most recipes are for prepared leeks, so always buy more than you think you will need.

When you start cleaning, do not slice the top green leaves off recklessly with one stroke. Slit round the outside layer beneath the first green leaf, and you will often find that the white part goes up inside further than you had thought. By judicious cutting away of the layers, you waste less. When the leeks are free of the coarse green part – it can be used in soups and stews – chop off the roots. Then stand the leeks, root end up, in a large jug of water to soak for a while, so that the grit has a chance to float out. If any remains as a dark shadow under the white skin, make small slits so that it can be rinsed away without spoiling the shape of the leek.

If the recipe demands sliced leeks, this soaking can be dispensed with. Just trim and rinse them, then cut them into slices and give them another rinse in a colander. You can soon see any earth remaining, and separate the layers to release it.

Avoid overcooking. Leeks can still be slightly resistant in the middle, but only slightly. Watch them.

[*Vegetable Book*]


## JOHN EVELYN'S BUTTERED PARSNIPS, 1699

Scrub, top and tail the parsnips – 1 medium-sized parsnip per person – and cook them in boiling salted water until just tender. Run them under the cold tap, and strip off the skins. Cut across into slices, about 1 cm (½ inch) thick if you like them soft in the middle, thinner if you like them crisp all through, then roll the slices in seasoned flour and cook them in butter until they are golden-brown. If you can regulate your burners to a steady moderate temperature, you can finish the parsnips in butter straight from the packet; if you feel uncertain, clarify the butter first. You should end up with nice clean fat in the pan and the parsnips a golden-brown. No charring. The flour will form a light delicious coating. Use two pans, so that the cooked parsnips do not have to wait around a long time; this is also convenient if you are making both thick and thin slices. If they do have to be kept warm in the oven, line the dish with kitchen paper to absorb surplus butter.

Have ready two bowls, one with melted butter in it, the other with 1 heaped tablespoon of sugar mixed with 1 heaped teaspoon of cinnamon. Serve these with the parsnips for those who like the extra flavouring.

I find that a watercress salad, or watercress sandwiches, goes well after this dish. Pepper-tasting greenery refreshes your appetite, after the sweet spice and buttery softness. If you intend to serve the parsnips with beef or ham, make a watercress and chicory salad, with a few raw sliced mushrooms, to eat afterwards.

*Note:* you can also sprinkle the sugar and cinnamon over the parsnips towards the end of cooking time.

[*Vegetable Book*]


## A FRUITFUL HARVEST

'*Now it is autumn and the falling fruit*' . . . The opening words of one of D. H. Lawrence's great poems runs through my mind continually as the countryside turns to shades of gold and tawniness. '*The apples falling like great drops of dew*' . . . I reflect that in spite of concrete and six-lane highways, we all feel that we have a particular stake in autumn. Pointless, if you think about it rationally, since our shops and supermarkets are bulging all year round with the harvests of other countries. Evidently our emotions have not yet caught up with our condition of life. Perhaps they never will, since this feeling for harvest which hits us every year just refuses to go away.

In France, and no doubt here, since our ways have been so closely linked, under forest law people had the right to gather, from wild and ungrafted trees, blackberries, quinces, crab apples, plums, walnuts, chestnuts, sorb apples (*Sorbus domestica*) and the tiny fruit of the alisier (*S. torminalis* – distilled in Alsace to make the most delicious almond-flavoured spirit). The family parties out picking blackberries in every untamed lane at this time of year are the last observers of these older and more serious rituals of the autumn – rituals that provided grace notes to a diet that was scanty and stodgy.

Our joy in fruitfulness is muted in part by rain and the vagaries of climate. Not that we do too badly in this country these days. The idea of harvest-home supper invades the soul of even the dullest greengrocer. Suddenly the shelves display a daring pumpkin or two, an extra variety of apples, perhaps from local trees, a tray of filberts from Kent in their frilled jackets, a box of wet walnuts, all giving a feeling of plenty and celebration. Churches smell of an unaccustomed ripeness that mutes the dusty odour of old hassocks; dahlias and bright fruit appear on the sills of lancet windows and apples balance precariously on the font.

Oddly enough, the parish harvest service celebrated in church is a modern institution – 130 years old in 1987, to be precise. Of course, there have been harvest feasts for centuries, since the first crops were brought home in the Middle East thousands of years ago. Experience of today's *vendange* feasts, held when all the grapes are picked and the juice flows from the presses, gives me an idea of what those occasions must have been like before gentrification tamed them into a single parish celebration.

Splendidly licentious and boozy affairs, with dancing, singing, dirty jokes and the occasional fight; such things were tolerated until the nineteenth century laid its civilizing hand on us all. It must have been this spectacle of unbridled revelry that led Archdeacon Denison of East Brent in Somerset, to channel the individual farm feasts into a single parish rejoicing. The idea soon caught on. Hymns were written – *We plough the fields and scatter, The sower went forth sowing, Come, ye thankful people, come* – to tunes that have everyone bellowing cheerily.

If you come to think of it, Somerset was just the right fruitful place for the first harvest festival. There would be figs from a sheltered tree in a south-facing corner; muscat grapes from the vicarage or manor house conservatory; peaches from the kitchen garden wall; black-berries for everyone; and many different apples and pears – the choice then was much wider than it is now.

For a while harvest-home suppers for the farm workers and harvest festival existed side by side, though people could see it might not last. Some did not approve of the church's intervention. They thought it weakened the bond of hospitality that made the labourer think, once a year, that his boss was tolerable after all. In 1864 it was written that 'the modern harvest festival as a parochial thanksgiving for the bounties of Providence is an excellent institution, but it should not be considered as a substitute'.

Over a hundred years on, however, harvest festivals are still celebrated in churches throughout the land, while riotous farmhouse feasts are no more. What has completed Archdeacon Denison's success is the mechanization of farming over the past century. It would be a feeble party these days: most farmers would have difficulty in as-sembling more than twenty-five people, including wives and children.

[*Taste*]


## BLACKBERRY AND DEWBERRY

'This being the commonest wild fruit in England is spoken of proverb-ially as the type of that which is plentiful and little prized.'

That is how the great *Oxford Dictionary* rounds off its definition of blackberry. It is unfair, with a touch of class consciousness, as if in manor houses grapes from the hothouse were to be expected and not blackberries from the back lane. Large and very black and shiny and very juicy, blackberries in a good season are as delicious as any of the related soft fruit we cultivate. After all, a basketful costs nothing except the pleasure of blackberrying; and there they are, ready to be eaten with sugar and cream by themselves, ready to add to breakfast muesli, ready to combine with apples, ready for tarts and pastries, for jam, jelly. And ready for some *jeu d'esprit* like pheasant and bramble or a sauce with duck.

Blackberries are world-wide, but it is in the north that they are most plentiful, where there are not so many juicy sweet wild fruits. So for thousands and thousands of summers, blackberrying must have been going on. And indeed, when a neolithic burial was excavated at the beginning of this century on the Essex coast, there was about a pint of seeds found in the area of the stomach – with blackberry seeds predominating.

What can be done with blackberries can be done with the best of their wild relatives, dewberries, the fruit of *Rubus caesius*, which are blue-grey instead of black. The flavour of dewberries is delicious and individual; it is more delicate than blackberry flavour. But dewberry brambles are not so common, and it is often disappointing that each berry is made up of only a few drupelets.

### How to prepare and use blackberries

This is something most people know all about, from their earliest years. But there are one or two points that are perhaps not so commonly thought of.

When picking blackberries, make a point of picking some red ones as well. They are not ripe, of course, but they fortify the flavour and help the set if you make jelly.

When making blackberry jelly, you will get a better set by adding a proportion of apple; sour windfalls are best, up to equal weight with the fruit. I find a proportion of 2 parts blackberries with 1 part apple gives a good result. Strain off the liquid if you want to make a clear jewel-like jelly in an abundant year. Strain off the liquid and push through as much of the pulp as you feel inclined for a thicker but equally delicious jelly in a meagre year.

Blackberry jelly can be used in apple pies in place of liquid and sugar; it makes a pleasant surprise in February. In one family I know, February is a sort of carnival month: the precious store cupboard, with all its jars that have been carefully guarded, can be raided without thought of tomorrow. This way the shelves are clear for the new season.

[*Fruit Book*]


## GOOSEBERRY FOOL

I used to think – see *Good Things* – that the word fool came from the French *fouler*, to crush. It seemed logical, as to make a good gooseberry fool the berries should be crushed rather than sieved. But I was wrong. It is a word that goes with trifle and whim-wham (trifle without the custard) – names of delightful nonsensical bits of folly, *jeux d'esprit* outside the serious range of cookery repertoire. The kind of thing that women are said to favour, but that men eat more of.

In *Kettner's Book of the Table* (1877), the author, E. S. Dallas, quotes a passage from an old recipe book which connects the pudding with Northamptonshire:

> The good people of Northamptonshire maintain that all our best London cooks, in making gooseberry fool, are themselves little better than fools. There is no way, they insist, equal to their own, which is as follows: After topping and tailing – that is, taking off clean the two ends of the gooseberries – scald them sufficiently with a very little water till all the fruit breaks. Too much water will spoil them. The water must not be thrown away, being so rich with the finest part of the fruit, that if left to stand till cold it will turn to jelly. When the gooseberries are cold, mash them all together. Passing them through a sieve or colander spoils them. The fine natural flavour which resides in the skin no art can replace. The skins must therefore remain unseparated in the general mash. Sweeten with fine powdered sugar, but add no nutmeg or other spice. Mix in at the last moment some rich cream, and it is ready. The young folks of Northamptonshire, after eating as much as they possibly can of this gooseberry fool, are said frequently to roll down a hill and begin eating again.

In spite of E. S. Dallas's strictures, I do sometimes add a little muscat de Frontignan to the gooseberry mash, or cook a couple of elderflower heads with the gooseberries.

[*Fruit Book*]

## HOW TO CHOOSE PEARS

Extremely difficult. Pears should be picked firm and then ripened in the house. A ripe pear gives very slightly round the stem, but should be in no way squashy. All this provides problems for the shopkeeper and supplier. The result is that most people have never eaten a decent pear in their lives. And anyone who read the pear introduction in my *Fruit Book* may well be wondering what on earth the fuss was about when the Doyenné du Comice was first produced.

When commerce was less efficient, I suspect that many more people grew pears. My husband remembers being taken by his mother to the Midlands before the First World War, and visiting house after house where pears were produced from back garden trees, as a special treat. They were sampled and compared as knowledgeably and thoughtfully as wine at a tasting.

Perhaps we shall return to this pleasant occupation of pear growing, now that family trees are on sale. In one bush, three varieties are grafted and the size makes them suitable for the smallest garden. Then at least you may be able to experience perfection. Doyenné du Comice is bound to be one of the three varieties (Williams' Bon Chrétien and Conference the other two). 'The tradition is to pick them on or soon after 1 November and then watch them as they come to perfection (the old legend that towards the end it may be necessary to get up at 3 a.m. to find absolute perfection is not a great exaggeration)' according to R. H. L. Gunyon, who wrote and sent me much information on pears.

Meanwhile, as your family tree grows, you will have to continue with shop supplies. Buy pears firm, and keep them in the kitchen until they are ripe. Eat them as soon as possible, storing them if you must in the bottom of the refrigerator wrapped in newspaper as protection.

One thing I learnt in Italy, in Florence, was that fine pears should be set off by fine cheese. That was thirty years ago. Now the idea has spread. French pear salads are dressed with Roquefort vinaigrette, and at Locket's in Westminster, they serve a pear and Stilton savoury.

I read the other day that the pear in cooking always needs help from another fruit, even if it is only lemon juice to prevent its flesh discolouring as it is peeled and quartered, or lemon peel in the poaching syrup. On reflection, I suppose it is true – think of pears with sauce Melba or simmered in a white wine syrup, finished with orange juice, or mixed with blackcurrants or the red juice of quinces. A pear sorbet requires lemon sharpness, even if the finishing touch is a dosage of Williams' pear *eau de vie*.

[*Fruit Book*]


## PLUM, DAMSON OR GREENGAGE CHUTNEY

A good spicy traditional recipe, which is much improved by using wine vinegar rather than the usual malt. The fruit should be prepared before weighing.

Serves 6

*1 kg (2 lb) stoned plums or damsons or greengages*
*250 g (8 oz) sliced apple*
*250 g (8 oz) sliced onion*
*125 g (4 oz) raisins*
*125 g (4 oz) coarsely shredded carrot*

*250 g (8 oz) demerara sugar*
*1 level tablespoon salt*
*1 level teaspoon ground cloves*
*1 level teaspoon ground ginger*
*1 level teaspoon ground allspice*
*1 small red dried chilli*
*600 ml (1 pt) white wine vinegar*

Mix the fruit, onion, raisins, carrot and sugar together in a basin (use your hands). Put salt and spices into a pan, and pour in the vinegar. Bring slowly to the boil and add the basinful of fruit, etc. Stir up well, and bring again to the boil. Leave to simmer steadily until thick and chutney-like. Remember it will become a little thicker as it cools down. Pot and cover with plastic film or the usual jam pot covers, rather than metal lids which will turn very nasty in contact with the vinegar. Store in a cool dark place for at least a month before using.

[*Fruit Book*]


## RASPBERRY AND LOGANBERRY

The raspberry is that rare thing – a delicious improvement of a wild northern fruit. It is nice to think of Eskimos eating raspberries in Alaska, even if they're the wild, unimproved variety, and of children picking wild raspberries in the woods of Scotland. When we were young, a particular pleasure of ours was being let loose amongst a neighbour's raspberry canes on a sunny afternoon – I understand what Parkinson meant when he said that raspberries were an 'afternoon dish' in summertime. Buzzing and warmth and crushing raspberries with your tongue against the roof of your mouth and everyone pleased that the crop should not be finished by the birds.

It is children, in fact, who come to the aid of the cultivated raspberry crop, commercial raspberries. School holidays are timed to coincide with the six-week harvest. Young heads bob up and down among the raspberry canes of Perth in the Carse of Gowrie and of Angus, all 7,947¼ acres of them, as they pick what amounts to ninety per cent of all the raspberries we eat in Britain. Scottish raspberries are the best in the world, the long summer day in the north, not too hot, suits them exactly. Machines of the sort they have in America to pick raspberries have not been widely used. Our raspberries are juicier and too delicate for mechanical treatment on the whole; though adaptations are being studied, it seems that raspberries are often destined to rot by the ton on the canes of Scotland.

Many gardeners claim that for flavour, the yellow raspberry is superior to the more common red one. This is so, I agree. I have a book written in 1920 about the good things of France, taken month by month, and I read that when the raspberry crop of the outskirts of Paris is exhausted in September, 'the fruit growing between Metz and Thionville is covered with the golden grains of the yellow raspberry, which is mild and sweet'. I wonder if that is still true, sixty years later? It must be a sight, the first of the golden displays of autumn. We had a corner of yellow raspberries once, but the canes were exhausted after a number of years and never replaced. Raspberries of blessed memory.

Buy them, if you see them; if you intend to grow raspberries, ask your nurseryman for a yellow-fruiting variety. You will not be disappointed. In the shops, though, to keep life easy, I imagine that raspberry-coloured raspberries will always be preferred. They are a difficult fruit to sell in any case, red or yellow, turning so easily to dampness and mildew. Some growers have the pleasant habit of picking them into punnets lined with soft green leaves which cradle the berries more gently than the white cardboard punnet on its own.

Raspberries are above all the fruit for eating raw, preferably on their own with Jersey cream and sugar. They are companionable with peaches and melon, if there are just a few of them, or with cream cheese mixtures. These remarks do not of course apply to people who grow so many raspberries that they are desperate to use them up, freezers overflowing, children stuffed and red-mouthed beyond their desires. They will not mind a loss of quality in exchange for variety.

The cooking berry *par excellence* is the loganberry, which can be harsh when raw if not absolutely ripe. It tastes like a cross between raspberry and blackberry but is, like the boysenberry, a cultivar of the Pacific blackberry. Any raspberry and blackberry recipes can be adapted to these two berries, one named after Judge J. H. Logan in whose garden at Santa Cruz it was raised, and the other after Rudolf Boysen who helped to introduce it, in the Twenties.

[*Fruit Book*]

# CAKES AND PUDDINGS

## APRICOT AND ALMOND CRUMBLE

Many other fruits can be used instead of apricots. It is a good recipe for pears, but they should first be stewed in a very little water (just enough to prevent them sticking) with the sugar in the first list of ingredients. Tinned peaches are particularly successful, so long as they are drained well and then rinsed under the cold tap before being arranged on the dish – they will not need the sugar.

*24 fresh ripe apricots*
*60–90 g (2–3 oz) sugar*
*60 g (2 oz) blanched, split almonds*

CRUMBLE
*125 g (4 oz) flour*
*90 g (3 oz) sugar*
*125 g (4 oz) ground almonds*
*175 g (6 oz) butter*

Pour boiling water over the apricots, leave them for a few minutes and peel off the skins. Slice them and, if you have the patience, crack the stones and remove the kernels – this is well worth doing. Arrange the apricots in a shallow baking dish, scatter them with sugar and the kernels. To make the crumble, mix flour, sugar and almonds. Rub in the butter to make a crumbly effect, and spread it over the fruit evenly. Arrange the split almonds on top. Bake at gas 6, 200°C (400°F), for 20 minutes, then lower the heat and leave for another 20 minutes at gas 4, 180°C (350°F). In fact crumble puddings are very good tempered – they can be cooked for a longer time at a lower temperature if this suits you better. The only thing to make sure of is that the top is nicely browned, and not burned. Serve with cream.

[*English Food*]

## AUNTY BELLE'S PARKIN

The best recipe for parkin I've tried: it results in a cake of tender consistency unlike those hard, round parkins which I detested as a child (and still do), though I suspect they are in an earlier style. The texture of parkin is nubbly with oatmeal, the taste dark with treacle.

The origin of the name is unknown. The big *Oxford Dictionary* suggests that it may come from Parkin or Perkin, and the first quotation it gives is from the second edition of the *Craven Glossary* of 1828. I would say it is a much, much older cake than that – perhaps it lurked under the name of gingerbread, for that is what it is, gingerbread made with oatmeal, the grain of the north where wheat was a trickier crop altogether than in the south.

This version from Joan Poulson's *Yorkshire Cookery* shows the modern softening of parkin, oatmeal cut with wheat flour, treacle replaced largely by golden syrup and brown sugar (I use light brown).

> *90 ml (3 fl oz) golden syrup*
> *30 ml (1 fl oz) treacle*
> *125 g (4 oz) soft brown sugar*
> *125 g (4 oz) butter*
> *175 g (6 oz) self-raising flour*
> *175 g (6 oz) medium oatmeal*
> *2 level teaspoons ground ginger*
> *a pinch of salt*
> *1 egg beaten in 125 ml (4 fl oz) milk*
> *½ teaspoon bicarbonate of soda*
> *extra egg to glaze (optional)*

The easiest way to get the right quantity of treacle and syrup is to put a saucepan on the scales and weigh it, then add extra weights as you pour in the golden syrup, then the treacle. If you have scales with a needle, put the pan on the scales, then turn the needle to zero and start from there. To the pan containing the syrup and treacle, add the sugar and butter. Warm gently, stirring, until you have a smooth thick liquid.

Have ready the rest of the dry ingredients in a bowl, and pour on the treacle mixture. Beat the egg and milk and add the bicarbonate, then tip into the bowl and mix to a dough. Pour into a well-buttered tin about 32 × 21 cm (13 × 8½ inches). Brush the top with beaten egg – this can be tricky as the surface is soft, but it gives a good dark glaze; an alternative is to brush it half-way through.

Bake in a preheated oven, at gas 4, 180°C (350°F) for 1 hour, or until firm. Wrap in greaseproof and foil for a few days before eating.

[*British Cookery*]

## BRANDY SNAPS

There are many versions of these biscuits in English cookery, because they were popular as fairings – along with eel pies and gingerbread. Indeed at some fairs, like the Marlborough Mop, you can still buy them in flat, irregular, lacy rounds, much better than candy floss to sustain you on the Big Wheel or at the boxing booth. Old versions use black treacle – golden syrup, a refined product, did not come in until the 1880s.

Makes 20–30

*125 g (4 oz) butter*
*125 ml (4 fl oz) golden syrup*
*125 g (4 oz) granulated sugar*
*a pinch of salt*
*125 g (4 oz) flour*
*2 teaspoons ground ginger*
*1 teaspoon lemon juice*
*2 teaspoons brandy*
*300 ml (½ pt) double cream, whipped*

Melt butter, syrup and sugar over a low heat in a medium-sized pan, stirring until you have a smooth mixture. Do not allow it to become really hot. Remove the pan from the heat, and when the mixture is barely tepid, stir in salt, flour, ginger, lemon juice and brandy.

Spread baking sheets with Bakewell paper and put teaspoons of the mixture on to it, allowing room for them to spread a great deal. About 6 teaspoons a sheet is right – although this will depend on whether the teaspoons were generously measured. Bake at gas 3, 160°C (325°F), for 8–10 minutes.

Press the brandy snaps round the handle of a wooden spoon into cigarette shapes while they are still hot. If they cool and become difficult, replace them in the oven to regain their suppleness. When cold store them in an air-tight tin. Fill them with whipped cream, piping it in at both ends, not long before they are required.

*[English Food]*


## BROWN BREAD ICE CREAM

Serves 6–8

*180 g (6 oz) wholemeal breadcrumbs*
*300 ml (½ pt) double cream*
*250 ml (8 fl oz) single cream*
*125 g (4 oz) icing sugar, or pale brown sugar*
*2 egg yolks*
*1 tablespoon rum (optional)*
*2 egg whites (optional)*

Spread the breadcrumbs out on a baking tray and toast in a moderately hot oven. They should become crisp and slightly browned. Meanwhile beat the creams with the sugar. Mix the yolks and rum, if used, and add to the cream mixture, beating it in well. When the breadcrumbs are cool, fold them in gently and thoroughly, so that they are evenly distributed. Lastly, whip the whites of the eggs stiff and fold into the mixture. Freeze in the usual way, at the lowest temperature. There is no need to stir up this ice cream.

[*English Food*]

## AN EIGHTEENTH-CENTURY QUINCE PUDDING

Make a quince purée, by cooking the fruit whole in water, and then cutting it in quarters and pushing it through a sieve. Sweeten with sugar and add some ginger to taste. Beat 300 ml (½ pt) of cream, double, single or the two mixed, with 2 egg yolks; then add to it a generous 150 ml (¼ pt) of quince purée. Adjust the seasoning of sugar and ginger to taste. Cut 60 g (2 oz) of butter into little pieces and stir into the mixture.

Butter a baking dish, pour in the quince mixture and bake at about gas 5, 190°C (375°F), or less, until set. Eat hot. As this pudding is a kind of fruit custard, it's important not to cook it so fast that the mixture boils – this will curdle the eggs. The proportion of fruit purée to custard may be varied to taste. It's important that the purée should be on the dry side, not in the least sloppy.

[*Good Things*]

## GRASMERE GINGERBREAD

In the early autumn, you may have the luck to find Rydal Mount almost free of visitors. You can wander round the steep garden that Wordsworth designed himself, a garden as beautiful as any I have seen, to be ranked – though entirely different – with Monet's at Giverny. Along the terrace you may reflect that Wordsworth liked to walk on smooth lawn when composing, whereas Coleridge preferred the rough tufty ground. The house sits at the top surveying the small kingdom: in the dining-room which was the living-room of the original house, there is a spice cupboard with a carved door. It was there long before the Wordsworths.

I imagine Dorothy taking out the ginger to make gingerbread, which her brother liked so much. When they lived at Dove Cottage, cramped but again with a delicious garden, William would sometimes have a longing for gingerbread. Once they set out at night in January to walk to the gingerbread seller's house: they were going to make it themselves next day, but William could not wait. There were usually two kinds; the Wordsworths obviously preferred it thick – as in the recipe below – but all the seller had was the thin. This I take to have been similar to the kind sold today, in The Gingerbread Shop in the village, where Mrs Sarah Nelson started her business in 1855, right by the churchyard where William and Dorothy are buried.

Serves 6

*250 g (8 oz) flour*
*125 g (4 oz) pale soft brown sugar*
*2 level teaspoons ground ginger*
*¼ level teaspoon baking powder*
*150 g (5 oz) lightly-salted butter, melted*

Mix dry ingredients to a dough with the melted, tepid butter. Spread out in a layer about 1½ cm (½ inch) thick, in a square pan lined with Bakewell paper. Bake until golden brown at gas 4, 180°C (350°F), 30–35 minutes. Cut into oblong biscuits, but leave to cool in the tin.

Serve as they are, or as a pudding topped with whipped cream flavoured with slivers of preserved ginger and some of the syrup. You can also put a butter cream on top, flavoured in the same way, but make it properly with eggs and unsalted butter, not with salted butter and too much icing sugar in the English teashop style.

*[British Cookery]*

## MAIDS OF HONOUR

The story is that these little puff pastry cheesecakes were first made at court in Henry VIII's reign. Whether or not this is true, they are the most charming and stylish little cakes. The best ones are to be found in Kew, at Newens, 288 Kew Road. The following recipe, based on Theodora Fitzgibbon's in her *Art of British Cooking*, is the closest I can find to the real thing. Well worth making if you are not within reach of London.

*500 g (1 lb) slab of puff pastry*
*300 ml (½ pt) milk*
*4 level tablespoons crumbs from 2-day-old white bread*
*125 (4 oz) butter, cubed*
*2 level tablespoons sugar*
*grated rind of 1 lemon*
*60 g (2 oz) blanched, ground almonds*
*3 standard eggs*

First decide on the tartlet tins – 8 cm (or just over 3 inches) is the ideal, but most domestic tins are either 6¼ cm (2½ inches) or 10 cm (4 inches). I use the smaller size which means about 30 tarts from this recipe.

Roll out the pastry and cut circles to fit the tins. You will have some left over. Chill while you make the filling.

Bring milk and crumbs to the boil, remove from heat and leave for 5 minutes. Beat in the butter, then the sugar, rind and almonds. The mixture should have a texture to it, from the almonds and crumbs. Lastly, beat in the eggs.

Preheat the oven to gas 6, 200°C (400°F).

Half-fill the pastry cases and bake for about 15 minutes, or until the pastry is cooked and light and well contracted from the tins, and the filling is patched appetizingly with golden brown. The secret of success – though the maids of honour will be agreeable anyway – lies, I suspect, in the oven temperature, getting the right colour in as short a time as possible. Everyone's oven varies, and it is worth taking the prudent measure of a trial run and baking a few maids of honour first, to see what adjustment of temperature might need to be made.

[*British Cookery*]


## MRS SLEIGHTHOLME'S SEED CAKE

I had been reading a family manuscript recipe book compiled between 1705 and 1730, in which there were five recipes for seed cake, when I saw this recipe in a copy of *Woman* magazine. The ingredient that set this recipe apart from the many other seed cakes of English cookery, was the ground almonds. And when I made the cake it was indeed the almonds which made it moist and delicious and quite exceptional.

The recipe was given in a series of farmhouse cakes by Mrs Dorothy Sleightholme, who frequently appears on Yorkshire Television. She had had the cake from a Somerset family, but thought that it needed something extra and added the ground almonds – which make all the difference.

*175 g (6 oz) butter*
*175 g (6 oz) caster sugar*
*1 rounded dessertspoon of caraway seeds*
*3 eggs*
*1 level tablespoon ground almonds*
*250 g (8 oz) self-raising flour*
*a little milk*

Cream the butter and sugar, and stir into it the caraway seeds – if you are not sure about the tastes of the people likely to eat the cake, use a level dessertspoonful the first time. Separate the eggs. Whisk the whites until they are stiff, but creamy rather than dry. Beat the yolks together and fold them into the whites carefully, until they are mixed together. Add to the butter and sugar. Lastly stir in the ground almonds and flour, adding a little milk if the mixture doesn't fall off the spoon when you shake it with a firm flick of the wrist.

Line a 1-kg (2-lb) loaf tin with Bakewell paper. Pour in the cake mixture and smooth it down with the back of a spoon. Bake it at gas 4, 180°C (350°F), for 1 hour 5 minutes. It should spring back when pressed lightly with a finger, and if you stick a larding needle into it, it should come out clean. Allow the cake to cool in the tin for 20 minutes, before removing it to a wire rack.

A few blanched, slivered almonds can be put on top of the cake before baking.

*[English Food]*

## NORTHUMBRIAN WHOLEMEAL SCONES

*750 g (1½ lb) stone-ground wholemeal flour*
*1 teaspoon salt*
*60 g (2 oz) lard*
*1 tablespoon golden syrup*
*3 tablespoons very hot water*
*150 ml (¼ pt) milk*
*150 ml (¼ pt) boiling water*
*30 g (1 oz) fresh yeast*

Sieve flour and salt into a basin, and rub in the lard. Make a well in the middle. Melt the syrup in the water. Mix the milk and boiling water, and add a little of this to the syrup so that there is about a teacupful. Into the syrup and milk, fork the yeast. Leave it to work for 10 or 15 minutes. When it is creaming and frothy, tip it into the flour, plus the remaining milk and hot water – go slowly with this, as you need a fairly soft but not sloppy dough. On the other hand, you may need to add extra milk and water – if you add boiling water to the milk in equal quantity, you will end up with the right blood temperature of 37–38°C (98–100°F).

Leave to rise until doubled in volume. This should be done in a draught-free place; temperature doesn't matter – dough will rise in a refrigerator, it merely takes longer. Roll out the risen dough on a floured board, and cut out rounds with a scone cutter. Leave to rise again, to 'prove', for another 30 minutes, then brush with milk and bake in a hot oven, gas 7, 220°C (425°F), for 20 minutes. Eat hot with plenty of butter, honey, or a savoury mixture of chopped hard-boiled eggs and parsley.

[*English Food*]

## POOR KNIGHT'S PUDDING WITH RASPBERRIES

Before the last war, when tea was an occasion for enjoyment and not for guilt, we often used to have home-made raspberry jam sandwiches at my grandmother's house. There were always too many – raspberry jam being her favourite – and next day they would appear as a pudding, having been fried in butter. I always thought, and still do think, that their latter end was more glorious than their debut. This recipe is my adaptation of her economy. It works well, too, with really ripe apricots and peaches. In winter one can use a really good jam, but I find this too sweet.

Serves 6–8

*500 g (1 lb) raspberries*
*125 g (4 oz) icing sugar*
*cinnamon*
*8 slices white bread*
*175 g (6 oz) butter*
*175 ml (6 fl oz) whipping cream, or 90 ml (3 fl oz) each double and*
*single cream*
*1 heaped tablespoon caster sugar*

Sprinkle raspberries with the icing sugar and about a ½ teaspoon of cinnamon. Leave until they produce some liquid and look like a slightly runny whole-fruit jam. Taste and add more cinnamon and sugar if necessary.

Cut the crusts off the bread. Bring the butter to the boil in a small pan, then pour it, through a muslin-lined sieve, into a frying pan; fry the bread in it. This sounds laborious, but it is quickly done, and avoids the risk of the bread browning too much – it should look golden, and be crisp.

Keep the bread warm in the oven, while you whip the creams together and sweeten them to taste with the sugar. Sandwich the bread with raspberries, and top with a generous swirl of whipped cream. You have a delicious contrast between the keen, buttery heat of the bread, and the keen cold of the raspberries, softened by the whipped cream.

[*English Food*]

## QUEEN OF PUDDINGS

A pudding which deserves its name for the perfect combination of flavours and textures, a most subtle and lovely way to end a meal.

Serves 4–6

*150 g (5 oz) fresh brown or white breadcrumbs*
*1 heaped tablespoon vanilla sugar*
*grated rind of 1 large lemon*
*600 ml (1 pt) milk*
*60 g (2 oz) lightly salted butter*
*4 large egg yolks*
*2 tablespoons blackcurrant jelly, or raspberry jelly*
*4 large egg whites*
*125 g (4 oz) caster sugar, plus 1 extra teaspoonful*

Put breadcrumbs, vanilla sugar and lemon rind into a pudding basin. Bring the milk and butter to just below boiling point and stir it into the crumbs. Leave for 10 minutes, then beat in the egg yolks thoroughly. Grease a shallow dish which holds about 1½ litres (2½ pt) with a buttery paper, and pour in the breadcrumb custard. Bake at gas 4, 180°C (350°F), for 30 minutes, or a little less, until just firm – the time will depend on the depth of the dish, and remember that the custard will continue to cook a little in its own heat so that if the centre looks runny underneath the skin do not feel anxious. Warm the jelly (if you use jam, warm it and sieve it) and spread it over the custard without breaking the surface. Whisk the whites until stiff, mix in half the caster sugar, then whisk again until slightly satiny. With a metal spoon, fold in the rest of the 125 g (4 oz) of sugar. Pile on to the pudding, sprinkle with the extra teaspoonful of sugar and return to the oven for 15 minutes until the meringue is slightly browned and crisp. Serve hot with plenty of cream.

[*English Food*]

## ROBERT SOUTHEY'S GOOSEBERRY PIE

Do you follow the country tradition of eating the first gooseberry pie of the season at Whitsunday lunch? If you do, here's a nice proposition of Robert Southey's to stimulate some quiet post-prandial reflection: 'Two gooseberry pies being supposed, their paste made at the same time, and indeed of one mass, the gooseberries gathered from the same bushes and of equal age, the sugar in just proportion, and clotted cream to eat with both, it follows that the largest is preferable. I love gooseberry pie, . . . and I think the case is plain.'

Serves 6–8

*30 g (1 oz) butter*
*250 g (½ lb) shortcrust pastry*
*1 kg (2 lb) gooseberries, young and green*
*175–250 g (6–8 oz) sugar*
*1 egg white*
*extra sugar*

Grease a 1-litre (2-pt) pie dish with the butter. Roll out the pastry; moisten the edges of the pie dish and fasten a strip of pastry round it. Top and tail the gooseberries, put them into the pie dish with sugar between the layers (very sharp gooseberries will need 250 g (8 oz)) and mound them up in the centre above the rim of the dish. Brush the pastry edge with egg white before laying on the pastry lid; knock up the edges, brush the pastry with egg white and sprinkle it with an even layer of caster sugar. Bake at gas 6, 200°C (400°F), for 30–40 minutes. Serve with plenty of cream.

[*Good Things*]


## SUMMER PUDDING

This pudding can be made successfully with frozen blackcurrants – though it seems a shame. One family I know always has it on Christmas Day, after the turkey, as a reminder that summer will come.

Serves 8–10

*1 kg (2 lb) blackcurrants, or raspberries, or a mixture of raspberries,*
*    redcurrants and blackberries*
*175 g (6 oz) caster sugar*
*good quality white bread, 1-day-old*

Put the fruit and sugar into a bowl, and leave overnight. Next day tip the contents of the bowl into a pan, bring to the boil and simmer gently for 2–3 minutes to cook the fruit lightly. It should make a fair amount of juice.

Cut the bread into slices 1 cm (¼ inch) thick. Remove the crusts. Make a circle from 1 slice to fit the base of a 1½-litre (2½-pt) pudding basin or other bowl. Then cut wedges of bread to fit round the sides. There should be no gaps, so if the wedges do not quite fit together, push in small bits of bread. Pour in half the fruit and juice, put in a slice of bread, then add the rest of the fruit and juice. Cover the top with one or two layers of bread, trimming off the wedges to make a nice neat finish. Put a plate on top, with a couple of tins to weight the whole thing down, and leave overnight – or for several days if you like – in the refrigerator. (If the bread is not thoroughly impregnated with the brilliant fruit juices, boil up a few more blackcurrants or raspberries and strain the liquor over the white bits which will occur at the top of the pudding.) Run a thin knife round between the pudding and the basin, put a serving dish upside down on top, and turn the whole thing over quickly. Remove the basin and serve with a great deal of cream; cream is essential for this very strong-flavoured pudding, which because of its flavour goes a long way and should be served in small slices.

[*English Food*]

## YORKSHIRE CURD TART

*250 g ( ½ lb) weight shortcrust pastry, made with lard and sour milk*

FILLING
*125 g (4 oz) butter*
*60 g (2 oz) sugar*
*250 g (8 oz) curd cheese (not cottage or cream cheese)*
*125 g (4 oz) seedless raisins, or currants*
*1 rounded tablespoon wholemeal breadcrumbs*
*a pinch of salt*
*grated nutmeg to taste*
*2 well-beaten eggs*

Line a 20–25-cm (8–10-inch) tart tin with the pastry – use the kind with a removable base. Cream butter and sugar together, mix in the curds, raisins or currants and breadcrumbs. Add the salt and nutmeg and lastly the eggs. Taste and adjust nutmeg, add a little more sugar if you like (I find most recipes too sweet). Pour into the pastry case and bake for 20–30 minutes at gas 7, 220°C (425°F). The pastry should be a nice brown.

[*English Food*]

## TEA AND TARTS

Can there have been life in the north before tea? There was always a brown pot of it, a dreadful brew, on the stove. I would not be surprised to go back home and find the same pot, under a flowered woolly cosy, sitting on the microwave. As early as 1767, the tea-break had been observed in full operation by Arthur Young, but food to go with tea, a special meal with special times known as 'tea', belongs to the mid-nineteenth century. Only then were the Indian tea gardens well established and all set to overtake exports from China. This was the time, especially in the north where temperance movements were strong (and necessary), for chapel teas and church teas, Sunday School teas, missionary teas, charity teas, and the enormous development of home baking.

Looking back, to Sunderland in the Thirties' depression, I find it startling that so wretched a town should have had room for three high-class bakeries, Milburn's, Smythe's and Meng's, with cakes of a quality I never saw again until we reached Vienna three years ago on the European tour. An afternoon tea party or a bridge tea, I now realize, were a highly-developed art form, gastronomically speaking, with rigorous rules of behaviour, dress, and food which was exquisitely small and delicious. A foreign visitor once described our thin bread and butter as being like poppy leaves, a perfect description. Children's party teas often included a cake in the shape of a cottage (complete with a water butt and hollyhocks) or a ship. One May I convinced my mother that asparagus rolled in brown bread was the thing for my sister's birthday: to our ruthless infant delight, nobody else ate it and we lived on asparagus rolls for three days (my mother's reaction after all her work, I do not recall). For the less well-off, teas were more of a triumphant blow-out, a chance to show off with propriety, and at least one was expected to eat (at polite teas, one nibbled). There were teas with tea in a can and gingerbread during haymaking, tea at the beach with apricot and sand sandwiches, egg sandwich and thermos teas on long Northumberland walks. Whatever else one did without, tea could be counted upon, down to bread and scrape, bread and dripping or just bread.

A pleasure of going back to the north again was tea at Betty's in Harrogate, a place of elegant art nouveau twirls, good cakes, unique sizzling rabbits and deep curd tarts: you can have Brontë fruit cake and Wensleydale cheese , too.

[*British Cookery*]

# AT HOME IN FRANCE

A FAMILY HOLIDAY in 1961 took Jane, Geoffrey and their young daughter Sophie to Trôo in the Loir-et-Cher for the first time. They returned in following years and, when the opportunity arose, bought a house there. The word house, though, is a poor description. The cliff that this semi-troglodyte village clings to is honeycombed with medieval quarrying caves. Like so many others, the Grigsons' home was part cave, part house. In the extract from *Notes from an Odd Country* that follows, Geoffrey Grigson describes their first sight of the village, setting it in its geographical and historical context.

Trôo was far more than just a holiday home or a mere escape from the pressures of daily life. It was here that Jane's career as a cookery writer began, as is described in the introduction to the next chapter.

Jane's deep feelings for her French home shine through in the evident pleasure she took in the food, the wines, the customs and the whole life of her adopted part of France. They find expression in many of the recipes in this section and the very personal notes which often accompany them.

We are on the edge of Touraine. Up here on the southern hill at Les Hayes I look back across the river Loir – the Loir and not the Loire – and see Trôo church, a blue circumflex on the parallel hill to the north, towards England.

Past a curly cast-iron wind pump the road goes on quietly southward into Touraine, to the grand Loire, and to the cathedral city of Tours. To the north, beyond Trôo church, dedicated to St Martin, the patron of Tours, are the rather muddy farmlands of the Perche. Not a long way to the west, down the Loir, Anjou begins.

*

I have stopped exactly where we stopped on this minor departmental road fifteen years ago, on our way from Wiltshire to Venice. Now we have it fixed in our minds – why? because I think there can be no genuine evidence – that the ridge to the east and the west was the favourite walk of Pierre de Ronsard, or gave Pierre de Ronsard his favourite view of the Loir valley. Fifteen years ago we didn't know we were looking at the Bas-Vendômois, the downstream country of Vendôme, bordering the Loir and enclosed by these northern and southern hills. We didn't know Ronsard was born a few miles away. We looked down on to the buildings of a farm half tucked into the chalk in a side valley, under the woods, and decided how pleasant a farmstead it would be to own – without an idea that it was called Vaubusson, *val buisson*, Valley of the Thicket; without an idea that we would come to know the soft-eyed eighty-year-old farmer whose property it has been for fifty years.

I am up here now to draw a distant view of Trôo church beyond a telegraph pole which is very evidently French. The fields are open and hedgeless. We have picked a large bunch of cornflowers, of genuine, deep blue, open-eyed, exceedingly French cornflowers, not to be confused with the pallid scabious of cornfields at home. Or is this at home?

I must explain Trôo: it is the hub of the odd country of these notes, which is a country of the mind and a portion of France. First, it is about 354 km (220 miles) south of England, south of Hastings or Eastbourne. It exists partly on, partly inside a hill of hard chalk, which was mined for building houses. On top are remains – enceinte wall and turrets and gateways, and a bare motte – of a castle which belonged once to the Plantagenets. Also that strong, prominent church, associated with the castle. Along the foot of the hill, dividing Trôo from a smaller village, St-Jacques, flows the Loir. Vendôme is 24 km (15 miles) upstream, making this river country the Bas-Vendômois, as I say; the lower country of Vendôme. The river continues through the widest meadows to the Ile Verte, at Couture, on which Ronsard wanted to be buried. Couture is much visited for this island and for Ronsard's first home, La Possonnière, which Ronsard's father covered with Renaissance trickings and such inscriptions as *Voluptati et Gratiis*, to Pleasure and the Graces.

At Trôo vineyards begin, on slopes which wall the river plain. The climate is warm and dry. The Bas-Vendômois contains neolithic dolmens, neolithic polishing-stones, Gaulish camps, Roman camps, Gallo-Roman place-names, Romanesque wall-paintings, abbeys, priories, commanderies, pest-houses, ruins, drinking tables, wine caves, good restaurants, few factories, and riverside holiday huts on high legs.

On that Venetian journey we had spent the night at Trôo, we had seen the cliff in sunshine, had seen that the cliff contained stone mines and houses. We had walked over the Loir to the black-roofed church of St-Jacques-des-Guerets, and looked for a passing five minutes at Christ in twelve-century majesty and at the hand of God in a curve of a window. That was all.

It was years later that we came to stay, in a rented cave house. The pleasant thing this time which happened on the way, when we were already in the Perche, with about 48 km (30 miles) to go, was seeing Deptford Pinks in the rain. The hedge of an ochre lane was starred with them. Runnels of orange water poured down the lane, under an oak tree, past a gateway where we made a picnic pause. The hundreds of sparks of magenta spelt a newness, a new actuality.

The rain stopped. The sun was fierce when we reached Trôo and drove with timidity down one of the cliff lanes. The ground was hard and dry.

[*Notes from an Odd Country*]

# SOUPS AND STARTERS

## ASPARAGUS SOUP *À LA COMTESSE*

Serves 6–8

*375 g (12 oz) trimmed asparagus*
*125 g (4 oz) butter*
*60 g (2 oz) flour*
*600 ml (1 pt) chicken stock*
*salt, pepper*
*2 egg yolks*
*2 tablespoons double cream*
*a pinch of sugar*
*extra knob of butter*

Parboil the asparagus, then cut off the tips – which will be just tender – and set them aside. Cut the stalks into 1-cm (¼-inch) lengths. Stew them in half the butter in a covered pan until they are completely cooked. Meanwhile in another pan, melt the remaining butter, stir in the flour and then the chicken stock. Simmer, then moisten the asparagus in butter with some of the stock and liquidize. Pour through a strainer (to catch the last few stringy parts of the asparagus stalk, should there be any). Reheat gently and season.

Beat the yolks with the cream. Pour in a little of the soup, stirring vigorously, then return to the pan. Stir over a moderate heat, without boiling the soup, for 5 minutes; add a pinch of sugar to bring out the flavour, any extra seasoning required, and finally the asparagus tips, which should be given time to heat through in the hot soup, and the extra knob of butter.

*Note:* thawed frozen asparagus can be used instead of fresh. It will not need parboiling. Add the tips to the soup before thickening it with yolks and cream, so that they have a chance of becoming thoroughly tender.

[*Food with the Famous*]

## PUMPKIN SOUP (Velouté au Potiron)

Pumpkin soups in France are often very simple indeed – a slice of pumpkin cooked and sieved, then diluted with milk and water, plus cream and either salt, pepper and nutmeg or sugar. White wine is drunk with it, and little cubes of golden fried bread set off its creamy orange colour. Here is a general vegetable soup with pumpkin predominating, from the Franche-Comté. If you have no pumpkin, substitute little gem squash, courgettes or Jerusalem artichokes.

Serves 4–6

*150 g (5 oz) peeled, chopped tomato*
*60 g (2 oz) chopped onion*
*250 g (8 oz) peeled, diced potatoes*
*200 g (7 oz) peeled and seeded pumpkin*
*90 g (3 oz) butter*
*1 litre (1½ pt) water*
*60 g (2 oz) tapioca*
*3 egg yolks*
*½ litre (¾ pt) whipping cream*
*1 teaspoon wine vinegar*
*salt and pepper*
*cayenne*
*a pinch of sugar*

Stew the vegetables in the butter in a heavy pan for 5–10 minutes, stirring them occasionally and making sure they do not brown. Pour in the water and simmer until the vegetables are tender. Process or put through a *mouli-légumes* into a clean pan. Reheat, stir in the tapioca and simmer for about 20 minutes.

Meanwhile, beat the egg yolks and cream together. Pour in some of the soup then tip it back into the pan and heat through for 1–2 minutes without boiling. Add the vinegar gradually to sharpen the flavour, and seasonings (the vinegar is to compensate for the blandness of English cream and tomato, but you may not need it, or the sugar).

Serve with toasted bread, covered with thin slices of Comté or Gruyère cheese melted under the grill.

[*European Cookery*]


## SHRIMP AND TOMATO BISQUE (Potage à la Crevette)

Whatever the attractions of travel or Paris were for Dumas, he was always drawn back to the sea (he quotes Byron: 'Oh sea, the only love to whom I have been faithful'). He wrote much of the *Dictionnaire* at Roscoff in Brittany, and some in Normandy at Le Havre, where he met Courbet and Monet. He loved the shrimps and *bouquets roses* (prawns) of that coast, and invented this soup for them. In the end he died near the sea.

The entry on shrimps is delightful, with its picture of Ernestine's establishment near Étretat, at St Jouin (my copy of the *Dictionnaire* says St Jouart, but I think this must be a mistake). Ernestine herself was wise and beautiful. The place was much visited by discriminating people from Le Havre, and 'by the painters and poets of Paris who left drawings and poems celebrating her virtues, in her album'.

Judging by a similar recipe in the soup section, this dish was invented by Dumas himself. It should be made with live shrimps. If you cannot manage this, use boiled shrimps (or prawns, or mussels opened with white wine).

Serves 6–8

*750 g (1½ lb) tomatoes, peeled, chopped*
*500 g (1 lb) onions, sliced*
*150–200 g (5–7 oz) shrimps*
*white wine*
*salt, pepper, cayenne*
*a good beef stock*

Cook tomatoes and onions slowly in a covered pan. When the tomato juices flow, raise the heat and remove the lid. Simmer steadily for about 45 minutes, then sieve.

Meanwhile cover the shrimps generously with white wine, add salt, pepper and cayenne. Bring to the boil, and cook briefly for a moment or two. Try a shrimp to see if it is ready. Strain off the liquid.† Peel the shrimps, setting aside the edible tail part. Put the debris back into the pan with the liquid, and simmer for 15 minutes to extract all flavour from the shells, etc. Strain, pressing as much through as possible. Measure this shrimp liquid, and add an equal quantity both of the tomato purée and beef stock. Bring to the boil, taste for seasoning, and adjust the quantities if you like, adding a little more tomato or stock, or both. A pinch of sugar will help bring out the flavour, if the tomatoes were not particularly good.

Put in the shrimp meats, and heat for a moment, then serve. Do not keep the soup waiting, as this will toughen the shrimp tails.

*Note:* if you use cooked shrimps or prawns, start their preparation at †, covering the debris very generously with white wine.

[*Food with the Famous*]


## ARTICHOKE AND SHRIMP SALAD (Fonds d'Artichauts Ninette)

A fine way to start a special meal – the flavour of shellfish harmonizes beautifully with artichoke. Mayonnaise adds zest and richness.

Serves 4–6

*7 cooked artichoke bottoms*
*cooked purée scraped from the leaves*
*250 ml (8 fl oz) mayonnaise*
*mustard*
*fresh parsley, chervil, tarragon, chives*
*200 g (7 oz) shelled shrimps or prawns*
*6 prawns in their shells (optional)*

Chop then mash one of the artichoke bottoms with the purée from the leaves. Mix with the mayonnaise and add a little mustard, then the chopped herbs. Fold in the shrimps or prawns. Pile this mixture up on the artichoke bottoms remaining and put a prawn in its shell on top of each. Serve chilled on a bed of lettuce.

If the artichoke bottoms are on the small side, and there is too much shrimp salad, pile the remainder in the centre of the serving dish and put the artichoke bottoms round it.

*[Vegetable Book]*

## CEPS BAKED WITH GARLIC AND OLIVE OIL

In recent years, in our part of France, at least, ceps have become so difficult to find, that one can rarely pick enough to give to guests. Around Giverny in Monet's time, in the woods that crest the chalk cliffs of the Seine, they must have been abundant, because ceps baked with garlic and oil was a dish that appeared at his hospitable luncheon table in the late summer and autumn.

Ceps – in French *cèpe* – is the name given to various kinds of edible Boletus. The finest, the *cèpe de Bordeux*, is *Boletus edulis*. Two other kinds are yellowish brown, *Boletus luteus*, and reddish brown, *Boletus granulatus*; they grow under conifers. But whatever the colour, all the ceps are easy to identify from their gills, which are clustered tightly together in tubes, so that they look like a sponge rather than a circle of pleated cloth. These spongy gills need not be removed in small ceps, or in larger ones for that matter unless they happen to be wet and bruised looking. The plump stalks of *Boletus edulis* should always be treasured: peel off the outer layer if it looks tough, and cut away any damaged earthy parts.

Sometimes in France you can buy ceps (at a price), but in this country you have to find them yourself, so it would be foolish of me to specify quantities. You have to share them round as best you can. The recipe can also be made with cultivated mushrooms – allow 500 g (1 lb) for 4 – but the flavour is quite different and far less delicious; you may well have to add a very little stock as bought mushrooms are so much less juicy than the wild kinds from field and forest.

To prepare the ceps for this dish, slice off the stalks level with the caps. Peel and trim them, then chop them with 2–3 cloves of garlic and several sprigs of parsley. The quantity of these two items depend on taste: if the cloves of garlic are small, I would use 4 to 500 g (1 lb) of mushrooms.

Sprinkle the caps with salt on the gill side. Turn them upside down on a rack and leave for upwards of 1 hour to drain. Dry them with kitchen paper.

Choose a deep ovenproof baking dish – an oval pâté terrine is ideal – and pour in a thin layer of olive oil. Fit the ceps, stalk side up, in layers into the dish, sprinkling each layer with the stalk mixture and a little olive oil. Plenty of pepper, too. Add no salt at this stage.

Cover the dish and put into the oven at gas 4–5, 180–190°C (350–375°F). Leave until tender – time will depend on the size and age of the mushrooms. Check after 30 minutes, then every 10 minutes. If the juices become copious, remove the lid and raise the oven temperature; a certain amount of liquid is essential, and delicious, but too much will flood the ceps to insipidity. The quantity of juice that wild mushrooms exude can be surprising, especially if the season has been a wet one. You may even need to pour some off, rather than overcook the ceps. In other seasons, dry seasons, you may get very little. Ceps can be very meaty and substantial.

Towards the end of cooking time, taste the juices and a little bit of cep. Add salt at this stage if necessary, and more pepper.

Serve with plenty of bread, either as a course on its own, or with meat and poultry.

[*Food with the Famous*]


## TWO CHICORY SALADS (Deux Salades d'Endives)

Chicory makes a much better winter salad than floppy lettuce from a plastic bag. It's crisp and juicy, and can quite well be served on its own with just a French dressing, and plenty of freshly ground black pepper. Of all salad vegetables it combines best with other ingredients, in this respect it even tops celery.

> *6 heads prepared chicory*
> *2 large eating apples*
> *60 g (2 oz) raisins, soaked in hot water for 1 hour*
> *90 g (3 oz) shelled walnuts*
> *125 g (¼ lb) mild cheese, diced*
> *French dressing, mayonnaise or cream seasoned with French mustard and lemon juice*

Slice the chicory into 1-cm (½-inch) pieces, and push out the half rings of leaves. Core and dice the apples, but don't peel them. Drain the raisins. Mix everything together, chill and serve.

*4 large heads prepared chicory*
*5 hard-boiled eggs*
*2 tablespoons double cream*
*1 tablespoon chopped parsley*
*2 tablespoons melted butter*
*salt, black pepper*
*12 black olives*

Carefully separate and remove the leaves from the chicory heads, stopping when you come to a core of about 5 cm (2 inches). Shell and mash the eggs with a fork, then mix them with cream, parsley and melted butter. This mass should be lightly coherent, not smooth or pastelike. Season it well. Fill the chicory leaves with the mixture, arranging them on a serving dish. Put a few slices of olive on each one, and the tiny cones of chicory in the centre.

*Note:* 250 g (8 oz) cottage cheese may be substituted for the eggs.

[*Good Things*]

## LAMB'S LETTUCE AND BEETROOT SALAD (Salade de Bourcette)

If you happen to be in Normandy around and after Christmas, you are sure to encounter lamb's lettuce. This soft, tongue-shaped leaf grows in little clumps or bouquets, a number of leaves joined loosely at the base: it is a favourite decoration for meat and poultry but above all it is a favourite salad. The normal French name, often used in this country by nurserymen, is *mâche*: it has local names, too, pet names almost, such as *doucette* which refers to its softness, and *bourcette* from its old-fashioned purse shape. It makes a much better salad than floppy hothouse lettuce, and is usually accompanied by beetroot, one of those classic partnerships. Further south in France, walnuts and walnut oil will be added, or the salad will be served warm with fried cubes of bacon, their fat and the vinegar used to deglaze the pan. Lamb's lettuce is also mixed in with other greens, dandelion leaves for instance, endive and so on, in the green salad that is always served after the main course in France. This kind of salad comes as a first course, on its own.

Serves 4

*250–375 g ( ½–¾ lb) lamb's lettuce*
*1 beetroot, boiled or baked and skinned*
*1 tablespoon wine vinegar*
*4 tablespoons sunflower oil*
*2 tablespoons* crème fraîche *or 1 tablespoon each soured and double cream*
*1 large egg, hard-boiled, shelled*
*salt and pepper*

Rinse and pick over the lamb's lettuce, separating the leaves. Leave them to drain. Cut the beetroot into strips. Mix the vinegar, oil and *crème fraîche* or cream in the salad bowl with seasoning, beating them together. Cross the salad servers on top and put in the lamb's lettuce. Season the beetroot and put it in the centre. Chop the egg to crumbs or mash it with a fork, season it and scatter it over the whole thing. Toss the salad at the table.

[*The Cooking of Normandy*]

## CHILLED MANGE-TOUT SOUFFLÉ

Serves 6–8

*500 g (1 lb) mange-tout peas, prepared*
*1 level dessertspoon finely chopped spring onion or green onion sprouts*
*15 g ( ½ oz) sachet of gelatine*
*a pinch of sugar*
*salt*
*black pepper*
*a squeeze of lemon juice*
*250 ml (8 fl oz) whipping cream*
*2 egg whites, stiffly beaten*
*melba toast*

Set aside 125 g (¼ lb) of the peas. Put the rest into a pan with the onion. Bring 300 ml (½ pt) of water to the boil in another pan, pouring most of it on to the peas and onion, but leaving enough to dissolve the gelatine in when it has cooled down a little.

Cook the peas until just tender, then liquidize or process the peas, onion and cooking liquor. Sieve into a measuring jug. There should be about ½ litre (¾ pt).

Dissolve the gelatine in the reserved warm water and add to the warm purée. Season with a pinch or two of sugar, salt, pepper and just a little lemon juice. Put the purée in the refrigerator.

Whip the cream until very thick but not quite stiff. When the purée is on the point of setting, fold the cream into it, followed by the beaten egg whites.

Chill 16 × 75 ml (2½ fl oz) individual oval moulds lightly. Pour in the mixture and leave to set firmly for several hours or overnight in the refrigerator.

To serve, lightly cook the remaining mange-tout and drain. Turn out 2 moulds on to each serving dish. Surround with a few mange-tout and melba toast.

[*À La Carte*]


## MANGE-TOUT SALAD WITH CHICKEN LIVER AND BACON

Serves 4–6

*375 g (¾ lb) mange-tout peas*
*6 tablespoons groundnut, sunflower or hazelnut oil*
*4 tablespoons white wine vinegar*
*6 chicken livers, cubed, with stringy parts removed*
*salt*
*black pepper*
*6 very thin rashers of streaky bacon, cut into strips*
*bacon fat or extra oil (if necessary)*
*16 small bread dice*

Have 4–6 warm individual serving dishes ready. Top, tail and string the mange-tout. Cook them to the state of tenderness you like best. Drain and put into a warm bowl. Mix the oil and vinegar together and add to the mange-tout. Keep warm.

Season the livers with salt and pepper. Cook the strips of bacon in their own fat, using a little extra fat or oil if necessary. Try to get them crisp and curly. Remove with a slotted spoon, then fry the bread dice until golden. Drain and add to the bacon strips. Finally cook the liver pieces briefly in the remaining fat, adding more fat or oil if need be. The liver should be pink inside. Put the bacon and bread back in the fat for a few seconds to warm through slightly.

To serve, arrange the mange-tout, hot liver, bacon and bread dice in the serving dishes and serve immediately.

[*À La Carte*]

# FISH

## THE WORLD'S YOUR OYSTER

The fashion today is to praise our traditional food and cookery, out of gastronomic patriotism, without much experience of its high spots. Asparagus does not, for instance, appear on every table two or three times a week in May or June as it does in Germany. Oysters are served even less, I would say, judging by our local fishmongers. A pity this, since once they were everyone's delight from the poorest to the Prince of Wales. Today, however, we only seem to eat oysters in restaurants – foolish if you come to think of it, since their preparation is negligible and it would be far cheaper to eat them at home.

In the matter of oysters, there are two main choices. The ardent oyster-lover with a deep pocket goes for *Ostrea edulis*, native indigenous oysters which are round and flattish, their shells ridged. In Britain, the ideal might be Royal Whitstables or Pyefleets from Colchester. In France, Belons or Armoricaines or *gravettes d'Arcachon*. If you are new to oysters, go first for the very best. They are in season over the winter.

The second choice is the cheaper Portuguese or Pacific oyster *Crassostrea angulata* or *C. gigas*. Both are longer than the rounded *Ostrea edulis* and much more frilled and beautiful in their form. They are the oysters you see everywhere in French markets throughout the year: the people's oysters and, although inferior to the fine-flavoured native, by careful cultivation some specimens reach almost as distinguished a glory.

Marennes and the Ile d'Oléron provide nearly two-thirds of France's oysters. There had always been native oysters in those parts, but in 1860 a ship with a cargo of oysters from Portugal had to take refuge in the Gironde from storms in the Bay of Biscay. As time went by and the storms continued, everyone became nervous of the state of the cargo. Eventually it was thrown overboard. The oysters were not in as parlous a state as had been feared. They looked around, liked their new situation, and settled down to make a new home. All went well for a century, but latterly disease weakened the Portuguese oysters, so the Pacific oyster has been introduced with great success. As its scientific name suggests, it is a giant oyster, if left to reach full maturity. In fact it is harvested young, at Portuguese oyster size.

In Britain, where the water is too cold for them to breed, Portuguese and Pacific are started off in laboratories and sold to growers as seed oysters. This means you can have the summer pleasure of grilling scrubbed oysters over hot charcoal, flat side up, so that they steam open by themselves.

Beyond the simple choice that I have described, there is, as you might expect, a world of knowledge and expertise, drama and emotion (as for instance when some disease, such as bonamia, takes out famous oyster beds). My own passion for oysters began when my husband gave me a copy of *The Oysters of Loqmariaquer* by Eleanor Clarke. She describes her own first acquaintance with oysters during a long stay in Brittany, and weaves in much oyster history and many anecdotes. She is poet enough to attempt a description of the oyster's special delight: 'Music or the colour of the sea are easier to describe than the taste of one of these Armoricaines, which has been lifted, turned, rebedded, taught to close its mouth while travelling, culled, sorted, kept a while in a rest home or "basin" between each change of domicile . . . It is briny first of all, and not in the sense of brine in a barrel, for the preservation of something; there is a shock of freshness to it . . . You are eating the sea, only the sensation of a gulp of sea water has been wafted out of it by some sorcery.'

My greatest oyster discovery has been that two people in Scotland – and there may be others elsewhere – are trying to get an experience of oysters to everyone. They are John Noble and his partner Andrew Lane at Ardkinglas on Loch Fyne. They will supply them Datapost and have recently circularized thousands of the more likely fishmongers. They already supply restaurants. Their dream is to see oyster bars on the corners of every sizeable town so that this healthiest of fast food snacks is there for everyone.

## Oysters on the Half-Shell

Allow 6–12 oysters per person. If you do not have special oyster plates, serve on a bed of crushed ice or seaweed. Very fresh oysters will keep quite well if they are kept cool, but as a general rule buy them for eating the same day.

Scrub the oysters under a cold tap. Wrap your left hand in a clean cloth (or your right hand if you are left-handed). Take up an oyster, or steady it on the table, flat side up. Examine the join of the two shells as best you can, and where you see a likely separation, insert the point of a knife and wriggle it so that it cuts the attachment of the oyster to the shell. Lever it open.

If the oysters look messy with bits of shell, tip them into a sieve set over a bowl. Swish the oysters one by one in their own liquor and put them back into their deep shells. Strain the liquor through doubled muslin and spoon it over the oysters.

Add wedges of lemon to each plate, then serve with a mignonette sauce made by mixing 140 ml ( ¼ pt) of white wine with 2 tablespoons of chopped shallots and 2 teaspoons of coarsely ground peppercorns.

Provide good bread, rye, wheatmeal or wholemeal for instance, unsalted butter and a dry white wine. Chablis is the classic but try Quincy, Muscadet or an Alsace wine. Some people prefer Guinness.

[*À La Carte*]

## THREE FISH STEWS (Cotriades)

The fish soup of Brittany; or, if you like, the fish supper, because the liquid is drunk first, as soup, with the fish and potatoes as a main course to follow. The cooking method for the first two recipes is close to that of American chowder. All three come from Simone Morand's *Gastronomie Bretonne*. The point of variation between the three, and between so many other fish soups, lies in the different resources of the places where they're made. For this reason, mackerel is included – an unusual creature in most fish soups.

*Cotriades* are excellent food for large parties of people. One cooking pot to watch (and wash up), the simplest of preparations, which means that everyone can help, and a lavish result after a short cooking time. The only possible mistake is to overcook the fish. Provide a great deal of butter to eat with the fish and potatoes. (Breton butter is often salted, unlike Normandy butter which is too softly creamy for this kind of food.) Failing butter, *vinaigrette* will do instead. Provide plenty of bread, too, and toast some of it lightly for the soup. Another essential item is a bottle of full-bodied red wine.

Simone Morand so feelingly implores her readers not to cut off the heads of the fish, that I'm reminded of a Chinese cookery writer who declared that Westerners missed something through feeling unable to look at a fish with its head on, 'they miss experiencing the delicate taste of fish head'. True.

### From Les Bords de la Rance

Serves 6

*2 onions chopped*
*a spoonful of lard*
*3 cloves garlic, chopped*
*1 kg (2 lb) potatoes, quartered*
*chervil, parsley, chives in quantity*

*salt and pepper*
*1¾ litres (3 pt) water*
*2 medium mackerel, 3 gurnard, piece of conger eel sliced, 2 whiting, 1*
   *bream*

## From Cornouaille

Serves 6

*1 onion chopped*
*a lump of lard or butter*
*a good handful of sorrel*
bouquet garni
*1 kg (2 lb) potatoes, sliced*
*salt and pepper*
*1¾ litres (3 pt) water*
*1 gurnard, 1 red mullet, 1 garfish, cod, etc.*

Cook the onion in the fat until it is lightly browned. Add vegetables, herbs and seasoning, and water. Cover the pan, and simmer until the potatoes are almost cooked, then add the fish, cut into chunks. Add more water if necessary to cover all the ingredients. Bring back to the boil, and simmer for a further 10 minutes until the fish is cooked, but not overcooked.

## From Belle-Île

Serves 6

*1 kg (2 lb) potatoes, sliced*
*4 onions, sliced*
*6 large tomatoes, peeled, pipped (seeded) and chopped*
*1 stalk of celery, chopped*
*the white part of 2 or 3 leeks, chopped*
*parsley, chervil, thyme, bay leaf*
*a tumbler of olive oil or melted butter*
*a pinch of saffron, salt, pepper*
*firm fish (conger, mackerel, pollack, saithe)*
*soft fish (sardines, skate, cod, ballan wrasse, etc.)*
*shellfish (crawfish, lobster, crabs of various kinds, mussels, shrimps)*

The method is slightly different for this feast. First season and cut up the various fish. Put the firm-fleshed ones on a plate with crawfish, lobster and crab. Put the soft-fleshed ones on another plate with mussels and shrimps or prawns. Pour the oil or butter over both piles. Leave while the vegetables cook in plenty of water, with seasoning, herbs and saffron. When the potatoes are nearly done, add the firm-fleshed fish, etc. Boil hard for 5 minutes exactly. Add the soft-fleshed fish, etc., and boil hard for another 5 minutes, not a moment longer. Serve separately in the usual way, after correcting the seasoning of the soup.

[*Fish Cookery*]

## CRAB TART (Tarte au Crabe)

A great pleasure of French eating is the crab, especially spider crabs, many of which come from British waters (the official view is that the British housewife refuses to buy them). You go into some ordinary little port café in Brittany, and these splendid creatures will be brought to your table, often in a heap of shellfish bedded on ice and seaweed, with a bowl of mayonnaise. An ideal way of eating, since it takes a long time to eat quite a small amount.

For this tart you can use either kind of crab, or prepared crab meat so long as it contains no cereal filler to bulk it out (inquire firmly). Other shellfish can be used, too.

Serves 6–8

*1 kg (2 lb) crab, boiled, or 250 g (8 oz) crab meat*
*salt and pepper*
*cayenne pepper*
*3 eggs*
*250 ml (8 fl oz) cream*
*1 tablespoon Parmesan cheese*
*1 tablespoon Gruyère cheese*
*23–25-cm (9–10-inch) shortcrust pastry case, baked blind for 10 minutes*

Set oven at moderately hot, gas 5, 190°C (375°F).

Pick the meat from the boiled crab, discarding the dead man's fingers; the shell can be used as a flavouring for fish stock. Season the crab meat, then beat in 1 whole egg and 2 yolks, then the cream and cheeses.

Whip the 2 egg whites until really stiff, then fold them into the crab mixture and spread in the cooled pastry case.

Bake in the heated oven for about 40 minutes. The mixture will puff up and turn golden brown in light patches: the final test is the centre, which should just have lost its liquid wobbliness under the crust (it will be creamy, however, not solid). Serve straightaway with brown bread and butter.

[*European Cookery*]


## FILLETS OF SOLE WITH MUSHROOMS (Paupiettes de Soles Sophie)

The simple method of baking sole in the oven (or poaching it), can be elaborated into the favourite restaurant dish of *paupiettes de soles*. Fillets, spread with some delicious mixture, are rolled into a neat shape and cooked in white wine, or wine and stock: the cooking liquor is finally used in the making of a creamy sauce. Although such dishes look pretty and often taste agreeable, I do confess to a preference for sole on the bone; it keeps more of its natural flavour when cooked that way. But I make an exception for this recipe from *Les Recettes Secrètes des Meilleurs Restaurants de France*. At first the title and ingredients were irresistible; then I found that the smoked salmon adds a most delicious flavour to the sauce, an unexpected piquancy.

Here you have the basic recipe for all *paupiettes* of fish; it can be adapted to humble herring fillets or varied to make many dishes of sole, lemon sole and turbot. The fish bones can be used to make a little stock to go with the white wine when a larger amount of sauce is required.

Serves 8

*16 fillets of sole*
*250 ml (8 fl oz) dry white wine: Chablis or Sancerre*
*60 g (2 oz) butter*
*salt and pepper*

SALMON BUTTER
*125–180 g (4–6 oz) smoked salmon*
*60 g (2 oz) butter softened*
*lemon juice, pepper, salt*

MUSHROOM DUXELLES
*500 g (1 lb) mushrooms, chopped*
*60 g (2 oz) butter*
*lemon juice, salt, pepper*
*2 generous tablespoons thick cream*

SAUCE
*2 large egg yolks*
*3 generous tablespoons cream*

First make the salmon butter. Reduce the smoked salmon to a purée in a liquidizer or moulinette, with the butter. Season to taste with salt, pepper and lemon juice.

Season the cut side of each sole fillet; spread with salmon butter and roll up – use cocktail sticks to keep the fillets in shape. Butter an oval ovenproof dish and place the rolled fillets in it, packed closely together, side by side. Pour the white wine over them. Bring the liquid to the boil, cover with aluminium foil, and either place in a moderate oven for up to 10 minutes (gas 4, 180°C (350°F)) or leave to simmer gently on top of the stove for 5–7 minutes, turning the *paupiettes* once. Whichever method you use, do not overcook the fish.

Meanwhile cook the mushrooms quickly in the butter. Season with salt, pepper and lemon juice. Remove from the heat, stir in the cream and put on to a warm serving dish.

Pour cooking liquid off the sole into a measuring jug; then into a saucepan, and reduce it by half. Beat the egg yolks and cream together, stir a tablespoon or two of the reduced liquid into this mixture; return to the saucepan and cook slowly without boiling until thick. Place *paupiettes* on the mushrooms, coat them with the sauce and serve. At the Domaine de la Tortinière at Montbazon, where this dish is on the menu, 16 small fish shapes are cut out of a piece of smoked salmon and used to garnish the *paupiettes*.

[*Fish Cookery*]


## FISH STEAKS WITH BACON (Darnes de Poisson au Lard)

Steaks (*darnes*) from several kinds of white fish can be cooked in this way, with slight variations of timing according to their thickness and the texture of the fish. Ling (*julienne* in French) is a favourite in Normandy, but cod, haddock, hake or monkfish are more likely choices here. Try and buy a piece of top-quality smoked streaky bacon, rather than rashers.

Serves 6

*6 fish steaks*
*100 g (3½ oz) unsalted butter*
*250 g (8 oz) chopped onion*
*200 g (7 oz) piece of smoked streaky bacon, skinned and diced*

*seasoned flour plus 1 tablespoon plain flour*
*150 ml (¼ pt) dry white wine*
*150 ml (¼ pt) water*
*150 ml (¼ pt)* crème fraîche
*1 tablespoon wine vinegar*
*chopped parsley*
*salt and pepper*

Season the steaks with salt and pepper and set them aside. In half the butter, soften the onion. When it is tender, raise the heat slightly and add the bacon dice. Fry them until they are lightly coloured. Push them to one side of the pan, or remove them with a slotted spoon to a bowl. Dry the fish steaks, turn them in the seasoned flour and colour them lightly on both sides in the same pan. When they are almost done but still pink at the bone, remove everything from the pan and keep warm.

Add the rest of the butter to the pan, stir in the flour and cook it for 1 minute. Add the wine and water gradually. Let the sauce cook down quickly, bring the *crème fraîche* to the boil and add it with a little of the vinegar. Check the seasoning, adding extra vinegar if you like. Put back the fish, onion and bacon and barely simmer until the fish is cooked, about 5 minutes. Transfer everything to a serving dish, sprinkle a pinch of parsley on each steak and serve.

*Note:* the success of the dish depends on careful cooking in the early stages, never letting the butter burn. This way the flavours accumulate and blend.

[*The Cooking of Normandy*]

## FISH STOCK (Fumet de Poisson)

Fish stock is simple and cheap to make, and essential for Normandy cooking. Any left over can be stored in two ways: either in conveniently sized pots in the freezer or else in the form of a fish glaze that can be kept for weeks in the refrigerator. To make fish glaze, strain the stock into a wide, shallow pan and boil it down to a tenth or even a twentieth of its original volume, depending on how concentrated it was in the first place. When the liquid is thick and syrupy, pour it into a little container and cover it when cold. A teaspoonful will add flavour to many fish sauces without your having to make stock.

Suitable bones and heads for stock are often available at the fish counter. Avoid oily fish debris – such as mackerel, herring and so on –

but sole, monkfish, whiting, cod and haddock are all suitable. If you also include shellfish debris, such as prawn, crab and lobster shells, you have the basis for extra-special soups. Mussel and oyster liquor can also be added.

Makes 2 litres (3½ pt)

*1–1¼ kg (2–3 lb) fish bones and heads*
*1 onion, sliced*
*1 carrot, sliced*
*white part of 1 small leek, sliced*
*a stick of celery, sliced*
bouquet garni
*10 black peppercorns*
*450 ml (¾ pt) dry white wine or good dry cider*
*2 teaspoons white wine vinegar*
*2 litres (3½ pt) water*

Put all the ingredients in a large pan, adding the water last. Bring slowly to the boil, skimming until the liquid is clear. Cover the pan and simmer it – fish stock should never boil – for about 30 minutes. Do not be tempted to cook it longer or the stock will taste gluey. Strain the stock through a double-muslin-lined sieve.

*Note:* salt is not added, since the stock may well need to be reduced if you are making a sauce.

[*The Cooking of Normandy*]


## FRUITS DE MER FILLING

A recipe for seafood bound with a rich velouté sauce is a most useful one to know. It can be rolled into crêpes or piled into a large, pre-cooked, flaky pastry case, or spooned into *vol-au-vent* cases. Most simply of all, it can be served inside a ring of rice or egg noodles.

The quantities given here are enough for six helpings. If you have problems getting one or other of the fish or shellfish suggested, substitute what you can get that is good and fresh: in all you need a minimum of 750 g (1½ lb) total edible weight.

Serves 6

*750 ml (1¼ pt) fumet de poisson (page 97)*
*250–300 g (8–10 oz) boned monkfish, cut in little cubes or strips, or*
   *John Dory, weever or Dover sole fillets, cut in strips*

*6 large scallops*
*175 g (6 oz) prawns, large shrimps or langoustines*
*12 mussels or oysters, shelled, liquid added to* fumet
*meat of a boiled crab or lobster weighing about 500 g (1 lb) or about*
    *175 g (6 oz) shelled crab or lobster meat*
*salt and pepper*

SAUCE
*50 g (2 oz) unsalted butter*
*4 tablespoons plain flour*
*100 g (3½ oz) mushrooms, chopped*
*150 ml (¼ pt)* crème fraîche *or double cream*
*salt, pepper and lemon juice*

Bring the *fumet* to simmering point and poach the white fish until it just becomes opaque. Remove the fish with a slotted spoon, season it and set it aside. Slice the white part of the scallops across, reserving the corals. Cook the discs of white scallop meat in the *fumet*. Remove them, season them and set them aside. Strain the *fumet* and reserve it. Shell the prawns, shrimps or langoustines, reserving any eggs. When the fish has cooled mix it with all the shellfish and season to taste.

Meanwhile, make the sauce by melting the butter, stirring in the flour and cooking it for 2 minutes. Add the strained *fumet* and mushrooms. Cook the sauce down steadily until it is thick but not gluey. Mix enough sauce into the shellfish mixture to bind it nicely, and check the seasoning, adding lemon juice if it seems a good idea. Sieve the *crème fraîche* or cream, scallop corals and shellfish eggs together, and mix in the remaining sauce with salt, pepper and lemon juice as required.

You now have your filling and sauce ready for use and subsequent re-heating. Remember that any shellfish is best eaten the day you buy it.

[*The Cooking of Normandy*]

## MACKEREL IN WHITE WINE (Maquereaux au Vin Blanc)

This is so popular a dish in France that I wonder we do not see cans of it in England and America as well in every supermarket. It is simple to make at home, and good. (Be careful not to get the juice on your clothes as it leaves a searching smell that takes some getting rid of.)

For 6 people – or for 12, if you are serving a mixed hors d'oeuvre or buffet meal – buy 6 fresh, medium-sized mackerel. Ask the fishmonger to cut off the heads and clean them.

Put them into a pan in one or two layers, and pour on water to cover generously. Then tip the water into a measuring jug and note the quantity. You will need half that amount in white wine – Muscadet is the ideal – and half in white wine vinegar. Throw the water away.

Put the wine and vinegar into another pan, with 6 neat slices of carrot, and the rest of a large carrot cut into bits. Add 2–3 cloves, a tiny hot chilli, 1 teaspoon black peppercorns, lightly crushed, and a *bouquet garni* (bay, thyme, parsley, tarragon and a small sprig of rosemary). Simmer for 10 minutes. Meanwhile, tuck a large sliced onion and a sliced lemon between the mackerel. Put them on the heat and when the liquor returns to the boil, give it a bubble or two, then cover and put aside to cool.

Transfer the mackerel to a serving dish, with the neat carrot slices, and 2–3 lemon slices, plus the chilli, the bay leaf from the *bouquet garni*, and a few fragments of onion if they are not too tatty. Add fresh peppercorns. Cover and leave to marinade in the refrigerator for 2–4 days. Serve with bread, butter and Muscadet, or whichever wine you used, to drink.

[*European Cookery*]

## OYSTER LOAVES

Serves 6

*6 brioches or baps*
*150 g (5 oz) unsalted butter, melted*
*24–30 oysters, opened, drained, liquor reserved and strained*
*300 ml (½ pt) whipping cream or* crème fraîche
*cayenne pepper or Tabasco sauce*
*salt*
*freshly ground black pepper*
*lemon juice (optional)*
*samphire*
*julienne strips of carrot*

Cut the lids neatly from the brioches or baps and take out the crumb, leaving a strong wall. Put 3 tablespoons of the butter into a small non-stick frying pan about 20½ cm (8 inches) across. Use the rest to brush out the inside of the brioches or baps; any left over can be brushed over the outside. Put them on a baking sheet into the oven preheated to gas 7, 220°C (425°F) until they are crisp and nicely toasted. This takes about 10 minutes but the lids can catch easily, so be prepared to remove them after 5 minutes. Switch off the oven and leave the door ajar.

Meanwhile, stiffen the oysters briefly in the 3 tablespoons of butter. Scoop them out and cut them into halves, if large. Tip the oyster juice into the pan and boil it down to a strong essence. Stir in the cream or *crème fraîche* and bubble steadily until you have a thick-looking sauce. Taste occasionally. If there is a lot of oyster liquor, you may need extra cream – alternatively you can stir in some extra unsalted butter at the end. The sauce should be strong but not belligerent. Add the cayenne or Tabasco, seasoning as required, and add a few drops of lemon juice if you like.

Place the oysters in the sauce and heat briefly. Divide them between the crisp brioches or baps, replace the lids, garnish with the samphire and carrot, and serve, sprinkled with cayenne.

[*À La Carte*]

## SALMON TERRINE WITH HERBS (Terrine de Saumon aux Herbes)

Most of the salmon on sale in France, whether fresh or smoked, comes from the coasts of Norway these days. Often the quality is so good that it is difficult to distinguish it from wild salmon. The main herbs of Normandy cooking are chives and parsley (I was told that half the parsley sold in French markets and shops comes from one village to the north of Carteret). People grow chervil in their gardens and tarragon in particularly warm and sheltered corners.

Serves 6–8

*a little oil*
*1 kg (2 lb) tailpiece of salmon*
*150 ml (¼ pt) dry white wine*
*about 1¼ kg (3 lb) bones, heads, etc. from salmon and sole or other*
    *white fish*
*1 onion, quartered*
*a generous bunch of parsley, about 30 g (1 oz)*
*1 litre (1¾ pt) water*
*1½–2 teaspoons gelatine (if necessary)*
*a generous bunch of chives*
*a bunch of chervil*
*a small bunch of tarragon*
*salt and pepper*

SAUCE
½ *litre* (¾ *pt*) *mayonnaise or* crème fraîche
*a little tomato purée*
*1 tablespoon small capers*
*salt, pepper and lemon juice*

Preheat the oven to gas 8, 230°C (450°F). Lay a large piece of foil on a baking sheet. Brush it in the centre with oil. Put the salmon on top, pour over the wine and season the fish. Fold up the foil to make a baggy parcel and bake the salmon for 15 minutes; then check and see if it needs more time. This will depend on the thickness of the piece: remember it will cook further as it cools. Leave the whole thing in a cool place until it is tepid; then transfer the fillets to a plate and remove the skin and bones. Strain the juice into a bowl. Put the fillets and juice into the refrigerator.

To make the jelly, put the bones, skin, onion and the stalks of the parsley into a pan. Add the water, bring it to the boil, cover the pan and simmer it for 30 minutes. Strain the stock into a measuring jug and then boil it down to just under 750 ml (1¼ pt). Remove the oil from the salmon juice and add the juice to the fish stock. Put a tablespoonful into the refrigerator to test the set: if it is on the weak side, *and if you wish to turn the terrine out for serving*, dissolve some of the gelatine in a little of the stock and then pour it back into the main part. If you do not wish to turn the terrine out the jelly need not be too stiff (which also means it will taste nicer). Season the stock.

Rinse the herbs, keeping then separate. Set half of each bunch of herbs aside. Plunge the rest into a pan of boiling water. After 1 minute, tip them into a sieve and run them under the cold tap. Dry them on kitchen paper, liquidize or process them to a purée and keep them for the sauce.

Chop the remaining herbs and put them in a basin. Flake the salmon and mix it in, with seasoning to taste.

If you intend to turn out the terrine, pour a layer of the stock into the terrine or soufflé dish, making it a good 5 mm (¼ inch) thick. Leave to set in the refrigerator. Then mix the remaining stock with the salmon and herbs; spoon this into the dish and chill until set. If you don't intend to turn it out, pour most of the liquid into the salmon and herbs, but reserve enough to make a smooth final layer about 5 mm (¼ inch) thick. Leave to set firmly in the refrigerator.

Now complete the dish, by adding the salmon and herbs and remaining liquid, and by pouring the last of the liquid over the top to make a smooth final layer if you are not turning it out. Chill until it is set and you are ready to serve it.

For the sauce, add the herb purée to the mayonnaise or the *crème fraîche*, along with the remaining items. Serve with a light brown bread.

*Note:* the precise quantity of herbs will depend on what you like, and what you have. The dish should be well speckled with green.

[*The Cooking of Normandy*]

# MEAT, GAME AND POULTRY

## BEEF BURGUNDY STYLE (Boeuf à la Bourguignonne)

Here is the basic recipe for many kinds of French stew. Alter the beef to chicken, and you have a version of coq au vin; use hare and you have a civet; oxtail and you have a hochepot. Use veal with white wine, and finish with cream and egg yolks, and you have a blanquette, or a coq au Riesling if you choose a young cockerel and the appropriate wine.

Serves 8–12

*1½ kg (3 lb) braising or stewing beef, cubed*

MARINADE
*½–1 litre (¾–1½ pt) red wine*
*5 tablespoons brandy*
*1 large onion, quartered*
bouquet garni
*a sprig of rosemary, optional*
*12 peppercorns, lightly crushed*
*1 level teaspoon salt*

SAUCE
*60 g (2 oz) beef dripping, bacon fat or butter*
*200–250 g (7–8 oz) piece of green bacon, diced*
*2 large onions, chopped*
*2 large carrots, chopped*
*3 cloves of garlic, crushed*
*beef, veal or poultry stock*
*salt, pepper, sugar*

TO FINISH
*500 g (1 lb) small or pickling onions, peeled*
*2 level tablespoons sugar*
*1 tablespoon butter*
*salt and pepper*
*250–375 g ( ½–¾ lb) small, closed mushrooms, fried*
*3 slices of bread, cut in triangles, fried*
*chopped parsley*

Leave the meat in the marinade ingredients overnight. The next day, remove and dry the meat. Keep the marinade.

In the fat, brown the bacon, then the vegetables and put into a casserole. Then brown the beef and add to the vegetables with the garlic. Pour off fat. Deglaze with the marinade minus the onion and pour on to the meat. Add stock to cover. Put on the lid and simmer until the meat is tender – about 2–3 hours. If the sauce is on the copious side, strain it into a wide pan and boil it down hard. Add salt and pepper and a very little sugar. Pour back over the meat, leave to cook for 10 minutes.

While the meat is cooking, caramelize the onions. Put them into a pan in a single layer. Cover with cold water, add the sugar and butter. Boil, without a lid, until the water has evaporated, and the sugar has caramelized to a glossy brown juice. Turn the onions in this, and season.

Arrange the onions and mushrooms on top of the stew, tuck the bread round the side and scatter with parsley.

[*European Cookery*]

## WALNUT-STUFFED BEEF WITH ARTICHOKE MOUSSE

Serves 4–6

*700 g (1½ lb) fillet of beef*

MOUSSE
*3 artichokes, cooked and dismantled*
*1 plump clove of garlic, crushed*
*1 tablespoon lemon juice*
*salt, freshly ground black pepper*
*125 g (4 oz) cream cheese*
*150 ml (¼ pt) double cream*
*mayonnaise*
*60 g (2 oz) packet of powdered gelatine*
*4 tablespoons chicken stock*

STUFFING
*1 small onion, chopped*
*2 tablespoons salad oil*
*125 g (4 oz) walnut halves, roughly chopped*
*1 tablespoon freshly chopped parsley*
*1 egg, beaten*

SAUCE
*4 tomatoes, peeled, seeded and chopped*
*250 g (8 oz)* fromage frais
*a pinch of sugar*
*150 ml (¼ pt) single cream*

GARNISH
*700 g (1½ lb) tomatoes, peeled and seeded*

For the mousse: scrape the artichoke leaf pulp into a bowl. Trim, quarter and add the bottoms to the leaf pulp. Mash or blend this with the garlic, lemon juice and seasoning. Add the cream cheese, cream and enough mayonnaise to make the purée up to 370 ml (13 fl oz). Dissolve the gelatine in the stock and fold into the purée. Leave until it begins to thicken then spread into a fluted 18-cm (7-inch) shallow mould. Chill until set.

Trim the beef of any fat and insert a barding needle or pointed knife through the length of the meat. Open the slit into a deep pocket by pushing a thick skewer or wooden spoon handle into it.

For the stuffing: gently fry the onion in 1 tablespoon of the oil until soft. Take off the heat and add the walnuts and parsley. Season and stir in the beaten egg. Press the walnut stuffing well down into the pocket in the beef. Smear the outside of the meat with the remaining oil and brown it all over in a really hot, heavy-based, lightly oiled frying pan. Lift into a baking tin and roast in a preheated oven at gas 7, 220°C (425°F) for 25–35 minutes or until cooked to your liking. Cool. Slice carefully.

For the sauce: blend the tomatoes with the *fromage frais*, seasoning and a pinch of sugar. Sieve, stir in the cream.

To serve: cut the tomatoes into small dice. Turn the artichoke mousse out on to a serving platter and top with a mound of diced tomato. Arrange the slices of beef overlapping each other on top of the tomato and garnish with a few more tomato dice. Spoon round the sauce.

[*À La Carte*]

## LEG OF LAMB IN PEASANT STYLE (Gigot Paysanne)

Beans of all kinds are a favourite accompaniment to lamb in France. In early summer, there will be a dish of the beautiful stringless *haricots verts*. They will be followed by shelled green flageolet beans, first fresh, then half-dried as summer passes. In winter the lamb will be served on a bed of white haricot beans. Sometimes they will be cooked together.

Serves 8

*1½–2 kg (3–4 lb) leg of lamb, boned*
*2 cloves garlic*
*500 g (1 lb) haricot beans, soaked*
*1 onion stuck with 3 cloves*
*1 large carrot, sliced*
bouquet garni
*60 g (2 oz) butter*
*250 g (8 oz) piece smoked streaky bacon*
*2 large onions, sliced*
*500 g (1 lb) potatoes, peeled and cubed*
*1 litre (1½ pt) light stock, preferably prepared from lamb bones*
*salt, pepper*

Cut the garlic into slivers, and insert them into the lamb (make little cuts with a sharp pointed knife first). Season well and tie firmly into a roll. Put beans, onion stuck with cloves, carrot and herbs into a saucepan; cover with water and simmer for 1 hour. Meanwhile, brown the lamb in butter, in a large oval, enamelled iron pot. Cut the rind from the bacon, then cut it downwards into strips, about 2½ cm (1 inch) long, by 6 mm (¼ inch) wide and thick. Add bacon to the lamb when it has browned, and transfer the pot to a moderate oven to roast (calculate cooking time according to whether you like lamb well- or slightly under-done). Half an hour before the lamb is cooked, remove the pot from the oven. Put in the sliced onions first, slipping them underneath the meat, then the beans cooked and drained, the potatoes and the stock, which should be at boiling point. Cover the pot and return to the oven for about 30 minutes, or until beans and potatoes are done. Serve in the cooking pot.

*Note:* in Brittany, salt marsh lamb is often served with haricot beans, but the two are cooked separately. No potatoes or bacon are included. I think the peasant style is more succulent, particularly for our often inferior lamb.

[*Good Things*]

## SWEETBREADS À LA CASTILLANE

The French way of cooking sweetbreads produces a richer result, with more sauce. The usual accompaniment is mushrooms, but in this recipe (which I've adapted from one given to me in Tours) the sweetbreads sit on a purée of apple and banana. Out of the ordinary and very good.

Serves 6

*750 g–1 kg (1½–2 lb) prepared sweetbreads*
*4 medium eating apples*
*125 g (4 oz) butter*
*4 small, very ripe bananas*
*a liqueur glass of cognac*
*120 ml (4 fl oz) double cream*
*lemon juice, salt, pepper, sugar*

Slice the sweetbreads into pieces about 12 mm (½ inch) thick. Cut up the apples and stew them in 60 g (2 oz) of butter in a covered pan; sieve them and throw away remains of peel and core. Mash the bananas thoroughly and mix them with the apple purée. Sweeten if necessary, and add a little lemon juice – very good apples and scented bananas will need hardly any additions. Keep this purée warm. Brown the sweetbreads in the rest of the butter; pour in about 150–300 ml (¼–½ pt) of their cooking liquor little by little, so that it reduces to a rich glaze on the sweetbreads. Arrange the sweetbreads on the fruit purée, swill the pan juices round with cognac and scrape all the nice brown bits into the sauce as it bubbles. Stir in the cream and cook gently for a few moments. Season this smooth rich mixture with salt, pepper and lemon juice to taste, pour over the sweetbreads and serve immediately. Boiled rice is a good accompaniment.

*[Good Things]*

## EASTER PIE FROM BERRY (Gâteau Berrichonne)

I remember once in Paris buying a wedge from a steaming wheel of pie, labelled *Gâteau Berrichonne*. It was obviously just sausage-meat in pastry, but it was cheap and we were hard up. Wandering into the Palais Royal nearby to see where Colette had lived, we started chewing unenthusiastically. We took time to appreciate how delicious that pie was. Ever since, I've had much respect for food from Berry, a province unharmed by too many visitors in spite of the reputation of Georges Sand, Alain Fournier and Bourges Cathedral – and of the flinty wines of Sancerre. The 'Easter' part of the title it not obligatory – just part of the Easter egg tradition.

Serves 6

*shortcrust pastry, made with 500 g (1 lb) flour*
*750 g (1½ lb) pork from throat, about ⅔ lean to ⅓ fat*
*3 rashers unsmoked bacon*
*1 large clove garlic*
*a handful of parsley*
*1 tablespoon chopped chives*
*1 teaspoon salt*
*plenty of black pepper*
*¼ teaspoon each nutmeg, cinnamon, ginger and cloves (or more, according to taste)*
*125 g (4 oz) chopped mushrooms*
*6 hard-boiled eggs*
*1 beaten raw egg*

Roll out the pastry into a rectangle a little longer than a baking sheet, but about the same width. Line a baking sheet with foil and grease it well. Cut the pastry to fit inside it, keeping the trimmings (to be used for the lid).

Now make the filling: mince pork and bacon coarsely, then mince half of it again finely. Season well with garlic, herbs and spices.

Lay half this sausage-meat on the pastry in a rectangle, leaving a clear 5–7½-cm (2–3-inch) margin all the way round. Spread the mushrooms evenly over the meat. Cut the eggs in half and place the halves, cut-side down, on top of the mushrooms to make a double row of little white domes. Tuck the remaining sausage-meat in between the eggs and over the top, so that they are completely enclosed.

Nick triangles from the corners of the pastry margin to the filling, and moisten the cut edges so that you can bring them up together to make a box which encloses the sausage-meat, etc. Press them firmly. Roll out all the pastry trimmings and cut an oblong lid to cover the pasty. Moisten the edges of the lid and invert it over the pie. Press the lid edges together with the box edges, making scallops with your fingers. Cut some pastry leaves and arrange in two parallel rows the length of the lid, and make some decorative slashes in the middle to let the steam escape. Brush the whole thing over with beaten egg (or top of the milk), and bake for 1¼ hours at gas 4, 180°C (350°F).

Eat cold or just warm, with a green salad.

[*Good Things*]

## NORMANDY PHEASANT (Faisan à la Normande)

One of the classic dishes not just of Norman but of French cooking. Remember that the taste in France is for much milder-flavoured game, which tends also to mean tougher game: hence the success with this braising method. It may be heretical to say so, but I think that this recipe tastes even better when cooked with a brace of well-hung British pheasants; the gaminess is balanced by the apple and softened by the cream. Hare, partridge and pigeon, guinea-fowl, rabbit and chicken can all be cooked in the same style with success; adjust the time accordingly and, in the case of chicken, be prepared to skim fat from the juices.

Serves 4–6

*2 pheasants*
*750 g (1½ lb) Reinettes, Cox's Orange or other aromatic eating apple*
*125 g (4 oz) unsalted butter*
*¼ teaspoon cinnamon*
*6 tablespoons Calvados or 10 tablespoons Pommeau*
*150 ml (¼ pt) dry cider or game or chicken stock*
*200 ml (7 fl oz) crème fraîche*
*salt and pepper*

Preheat the oven to gas 6, 200°C (400°F). Season the pheasants inside and out with salt and pepper. Peel and core the apples and cut them into 8 or 12 wedges according to size. Set aside about half of the neatest pieces for the final garnish, keeping them in a bowl of acidulated water to prevent them from discolouring. Cook the rest in 25 g (1 oz) of the butter, gently, with the cinnamon, turning the pieces until they are lightly browned and half-cooked. Put them into the base of a deep casserole that will hold the two birds snugly, with any juices.

Rinse out the pan and brown the pheasants in a minimum of the remaining butter. Flame them with the Calvados or Pommeau. Put them breast-side down on top of the apples in the casserole. Deglaze the pan with the cider or stock, and pour it while bubbling-hot over the pheasants. Cover the casserole and put it into the oven. After 20 minutes, turn the pheasants over and put them back to complete the cooking for another 25–30 minutes.

Meanwhile, cook the remaining apple pieces in a little of the remaining butter. Do not be in too much of a hurry; aim for a golden, lightly browned effect. Arrange them round a warm serving dish.

Remove the casserole from the oven. Put the birds to one side, in the warm, for the moment. Sieve the apple and juices into a wide shallow pan. Boil them down vigorously, skimming off any murky bits, to concentrate the flavour and consistency: apples vary in their wateriness and you want to end up with a light apple sauce consistency that will not be made too liquid by the addition of the *crème fraîche*. In a separate pan, bring the *crème fraîche* to the boil and stir it into the apple. Taste for seasoning, and whisk in the last of the butter.

As the sauce boils down, take the opportunity to joint or carve the pheasant and arrange it on the serving dish. Spoon a little of the finished sauce over it and pour the rest of the sauce into a warm jug. In France the dish will often be garnished with sprigs of watercress, or – around and just after Christmas – with lamb's lettuce.

[*The Cooking of Normandy*]

## YOUNG RABBIT WITH CHIVES (Lapereau au Ciboulette)

Although this French recipe is intended for domestic rabbit, it can be used most successfully with young wild rabbit, but be sure it's young. Older rabbits need slow stewing.

Serves 4

*1 rabbit, jointed, or 1½ kg (3 lb) rabbit joints*
*seasoned flour*
*60 g (2 oz) butter*
*a liqueur glass of Calvados or brandy*
*16 small onions*
*150 ml (¼ pt) chicken or veal stock*
*175 ml (6 fl oz) cream*
*salt, black pepper, cayenne pepper*
*a thick bunch of chives*

Cut the hind legs of the rabbit into two joints. Turn all the rabbit pieces in seasoned flour, and fry to golden brown in butter. Use a large, heavy frying pan, cast-iron is best. Warm the Calvados or brandy, set a light to it and pour over the rabbit, turning the pieces about in the flames.

Add the onions, giving them a few moments to colour slightly in the pan juices. Stir in the stock, cover the pan (silver foil will do, if it has no lid) and simmer for 40 minutes or until the rabbit is cooked. Remove meat and onions to a warm serving dish. Reduce the liquid in the pan by boiling it down, then stir in the cream. After a few moments' bubbling, the sauce will have thickened nicely. Add salt and pepper if required; then a pinch of cayenne pepper and the chives snipped into tiny pieces. Pour the boiling sauce over the rabbit and onions and serve.

*Note:* chicken can be substituted for rabbit, and tarragon for the chives. Add a teaspoon of tarragon to the pan with the stock.

[*Good Things*]

## BOURBONNAIS CHICKEN AND SALSIFY PIE (Tourtière de Poulet de Grains)

The *tourtière*, the utensil that has given its name to this pie, is an old style of copper pie dish. It belongs to the days before ovens were common, when much cooking was done *au foyer*, on the hearth. With the pot cranes and hooks, grill racks and huge iron pot, cooking *au foyer* was quite a difficult technique. It is still in use on some small farms where the old people are hanging on. Occasionally you will meet an elderly Parisian with country roots, who can still produce a splendid meal all from the fireplace, just as her mother and grand-mother had done every day. This kind of thing is still much closer to the French than it is to us: their equivalent phrase to our 'house-warming' is '*pendre la crémaillère*', to hang up the pot-hook. The *tourtière* was used at the side of the fire, where it would stand on a bed of hot cinders raised up on its three legs. More hot cinders would be pulled on to the rimmed lid. This is what is meant in old French cookery books, when they stipulate 'heat below and above', an instruction that also applies to the stew pot known as a *daubière*, which has no legs, and a far more deeply concave lid.

This recipe comes from Roger Lallemand's *La Vraie Cuisine de Bourbonnais*. The ingredients were listed without quantities, so I have worked out the ones that seem best, but there is a certain amount of give and take. The recipe following is very slightly adapted from *La Bonne Cuisine du Périgord*, by La Mazille, which was first published in 1929.

Serves 4–6

*shortcrust pastry made with 500 g (1 lb) flour*
*2–2½ kg (4–5 lb) farm chicken, jointed*
*butter*
*500 g (1 lb) salsify, cooked*
*250 g (½ lb) mushrooms, sliced*
*18 small onions, blanched 5 minutes*
*18 black olives, stoned*
*salt, pepper, ground nutmeg, ground cloves*
*chopped parsley, tarragon*
*beaten egg to glaze*

Line a metal pie dish with two-thirds of the pastry, keeping the rest back for the lid. Brown the chicken in butter. Put into the dish in a good jumble with the remaining ingredients. Cover with the pastry lid, and decorate with a few pastry leaves. Brush over with egg glaze. Bake at gas 6, 200°C (400°F) for 20 minutes, then at gas 4, 180°C (350°F) for 30 minutes. Push a larding needle or skewer carefully through the central hole in the lid and see if the chicken is tender: it should be by this time. If not, put the pie back in the oven for a further 10 minutes, and protect the lid with paper if necessary.

You will notice that no liquid is added to this pie. The juices of bird, mushrooms and onions provide enough moisture. The mixture of flavours is delicious, even if you have to resort to canned salsify.

[*Vegetable Book*]

## CHICKEN FRICASSÉE IN THE BERRY STYLE (Poulet à la Berrichonne)

The Berry lying between Touraine and Burgundy, and partly enclosed by a great sweep of the Loire, is not so famous for food as its two illustrious neighbours, which is unfair. The wide farmlands centred on Bourges produce fine unpretentious dishes like this one.

Serves 4

*1½–2 kg (3–4 lb) chicken, jointed*

STOCK
*chicken giblets*
*1 medium carrot*
*1 leek*

*1 medium onion*
bouquet garni
*600 ml (1 pt) water*

SAUCE
*60 g (2 oz) butter*
*1 kg (2 lb) carrots, cut into 4-cm (1½-inch) strips*
*2 shallots, or 1 mild onion, chopped*
*1 clove garlic, crushed*
*1 heaped tablespoon flour*
*150 ml (¼ pt) double cream*
*1 tablespoon wine vinegar*
*2 egg yolks*

Make the stock by simmering the ingredients together for 1 hour. Then blanch the carrots in boiling salted water for 5 minutes, pour them into a sieve and rinse under the cold tap. Drain them well.

Melt the butter in a large heavy pan, cook the carrots in it until they are lightly browned. Remove them, and put in the chicken, shallots or onion and garlic. When they are golden brown, stir in the flour, and then the strained stock. Bring to the boil, then add the carrots. Leave the chicken to simmer, uncovered, for about 45 minutes, or until it's cooked, removing the breast joints, when they are done, to a warm dish. Mix cream, vinegar and yolks together. Put the cooked chicken and carrots on to the serving dish with the breast joints. Pour a little boiling liquid into the cream and egg mixture, return to the pan and cook without boiling until thick. Pour over chicken, etc., and serve very hot.

[*Good Things*]

## CHICKEN WITH CALVADOS (Poulet Vallée d'Auge)

The Normandy style means cooking poultry, game or pork with Calvados (apple brandy) and cream, sometimes with apples as well. Occasionally the dish will be labelled pays d'Auge or vallée d'Auge, since that part of Normandy is strong in those three ingredients. It's an attractive land of timbered manor houses, dovecots, farms and orchards, and includes the village of Camembert.

For the simplest *poulet vallée d'Auge*, gently fry a plump young chicken in 150 g (5 oz) butter, turning it over from time to time, until it is tender. Flame with 100 ml (3½ fl oz) Calvados (whisky is the best substitute), deglaze with a very little stock, then stir in 500 ml (¾ pt) cream. Give the chicken a moment or two longer, then cut it up, put on a hot dish and pour over the sauce. Serve with rice, and mushrooms or apple slices (use Cox's Orange Pippins or a similar eating apple), fried in butter.

Serves 4

*750 g (1½ lb) Cox's Orange Pippins apples, peeled, cored and sliced*
    *(reserve 3 for the garnish)*
*butter*
*1 level teaspoon powdered cinnamon*
*sugar*
*a brace of pheasant or guineafowl, or large chicken, or*
    *1 kg (2 lb) boned, rolled loin of pork*
*100 ml (3½ fl oz) Calvados or whisky*
*250 ml (8 fl oz) appropriate stock*
*150 ml (¼ pt) each whipping and double cream*
*salt and pepper*
*lemon juice*

You need enough apple slices to make a layer in the bottom of an ovenproof pot which will hold the game, poultry or pork closely.

Set oven at moderate, gas 4, 180°C (350°F).

Fry apple slices in butter, then as they soften, sprinkle with cinnamon and 1 tablespoon of sugar, turning them over in the juices. Put into the pot. In the frying pan, brown the birds or meat and flame with Calvados or whisky. Put the birds, breast down, or the meat on top of the apples. Deglaze the pan with stock, pour into the pot and add the whipping cream. Cover and cook in the heated oven, turning once, for about 45 minutes for the game birds, 1¾ hours for the chicken or pork.

Meanwhile, peel, core and slice the remaining apples, and fry them in butter, caramelizing them with sugar towards the end.

When birds or meat are done, carve and put on to a hot dish, with the caramelized apple slices. Skim fat from the sauce and sieve, taste for seasoning and heat through. Stir in the double cream and a squeeze of lemon juice. Pour some of the sauce over the meat, and serve the rest separately.

A rice pilaff is the usual accompaniment, with perhaps a few sprigs of watercress tucked round the dish with apple.

[*European Cookery*]

## SIMPLE SAUCE NORMANDE

This simpler, domestic version of Sauce Normande is primarily intended for vegetables, poultry and meat. It can also, of course, be served with fish, though I think it would be considered a little too simple for the fine soles and turbot which are the glory of the Norman table, at least by chefs. As one writer sternly remarks, the success of the sauce depends on using the finest unsalted butter and the finest cream, which for us is Jersey cream.

Makes ½ litre (¾ pt)

*1 large onion, chopped finely*
*125 g (4 oz) unsalted butter, quartered*
*2 tablespoons plain flour*
*300 ml ( ½ pt) good dry cider or white wine*
*300 ml ( ½ pt) light stock*
*nutmeg or ground cinnamon*
*about 150 ml ( ¼ pt) Jersey cream*
*lemon juice*
*salt and pepper*

Soften the onion in one piece of butter, without browning it, in a heavy pan. It should be mellow in flavour. Add another piece of butter and when it has melted, stir in the flour. Bubble gently for a minute, stirring continuously. Add the cider or wine and the stock. Season with salt, pepper, and a light grating of nutmeg or a pinch of ground cinnamon. Leave to cook down slowly, giving an occasional stir. Sauce Normande should be rich and fairly thick, but not stodgy.

To finish the sauce, have it at simmering point. Stir in the remaining butter and then cream to your taste. Check the seasoning and sharpen it slightly with lemon juice.

### Variations
To the finished sauce, add 20–24 oysters and 12 small mushrooms cooked lightly with a little butter and lemon juice. The oysters will firm up in the heat of the sauce. The oyster liquor and mushroom juices can be used in place of some of the stock. If this sauce is served with very good potatoes, or salsify, or chicory, you have an excellent first course.

For a prawn or shrimp sauce, shell 375 g ( ¾ lb) cooked prawns or shrimps, using their debris to flavour the stock, which can be a fish stock or a light chicken stock. Make the sauce, and add the prawns or shrimps to heat through at the end.

[ *The Cooking of Normandy*]

# VEGETABLES AND FRUIT

## ARTICHOKE

The artichoke is an edible thistle. To John Evelyn it was the 'noble thistle'; to a nineteenth-century writer on food, E. S. Dallas, it was an amusing moral lesson, 'It is good for a man to eat thistles, and to remember that he is an ass'. John Evelyn – as one might expect – is nearer the mark, for the artichoke was the aristocrat of the Renaissance kitchen garden, as the asparagus was of the Roman. It is sobering to realize that they are still the two finest vegetables we can grow. Nothing we have developed since comes near them for delicious flavour or for elegant form.

The artichoke above all is the vegetable expression of civilized living, of the long view, of increasing delight by anticipation and crescendo. No wonder it was once regarded as an aphrodisiac. It had no place in the troll's world of instant gratification. It makes no appeal to the meat-and-two-veg. mentality. One cannot attack an artichoke with knife and fork and scoff it in three mouthfuls. It is first for admiration, then each leaf has to be pulled away for eating and dipped in sauce. When the leaves have gone, there is still the fibrous and tickly choke to be removed before the grey-green disc – the *bonne bouche* – can be enjoyed.

Although the artichoke is easily grown – someone observed that it flourishes, or can flourish as far north as the Orkneys – it has remained the pleasure of people who mind about good food. At first it was the passion of rulers, of the Medici in Florence, of François I and his court in Tourane, of our Henry VIII. François's daughter-in-law, Catherine de Medici, ate so many at a wedding feast in 1575 that she nearly burst (she was given to over-eating: on another occasion she suffered from a surfeit of melon). Henrietta Maria, queen of Charles I and daughter of Henry IV and Marie de Medici, kept a garden devoted to artichokes at her manor in Wimbledon. It was large – forty-four perches – and its spiky vigour was enhanced by the contrast of five dark bays of splendid growth. When a contemporary painter in France, Abraham Bossé, painted a series of *The Five Senses* round about 1635, he chose an artichoke to embody Taste. He depicted a dining room, with a young couple at table. The maid brings in a fine melon, but the painting centres on a huge artichoke in a raised dish, as the lady stretches out her hand to remove the first leaf. It could have been Henrietta Maria and Charles I enjoying an especially fine artichoke from that Wimbledon garden, though it is really a scene from French court life under Henrietta Maria's brother, Louis XIII.

Although the name, from *al-kharsuf*, indicates an Arab origin, perhaps in gardens on the Barbary coast, the Italians must take the credit for developing the fine varieties of artichoke that captured the courts of Renaissance Europe. Italians would still take the prize for the largest repertoire of artichoke dishes; they make much of the young artichoke before stalk, fibre and leaf have hardened, so that it can be eaten whole. My first acquaintance with artichokes, in the mid-Fifties before they were commonly on sale in our greengroceries, was in Venice where they have been growing for five centuries. We were visiting Torcello in the lagoon, walking along from the landing stage to the church by a canal, when a man swept into view punting a great boatload of artichokes. Presumably they were for the Rialto market. The blue sky swept by the strong wind, the orange and red bignonia trumpets pouring over every fence, the man's slow confident movements as he stood ankle-deep in the green and purple artichokes, made a first encounter of Medicean colour. We could understand how Rabelais – the first person in France to mention *artichaut* in print, in 1534, though it seems to have been grown in Brittany around Tréguier, since about 1508 – put them as a final delight of the offerings to the Gastrolaters' god of good living. After the salads, which included asparagus, and the fish, came the dessert, ending with prunes, dates, walnuts, hazelnuts, parsnips – and artichokes.

The other great writer of the time, the poet Ronsard, loved artichokes too. Asparagus, artichokes, melons, he declared, are much better than the finest of meats: they should be served in great mounds. When he got fed up with studying, he sent out a friend to buy a picnic. 'Don't forget the wine. Remember that I hate meat in summer –

> *Achète des abricots,*
> *Des pompons, des artichauts,*
> *Des fraises, et de la crème:*
> *C'est en Été ce que j'aime,*
> *Quand sur le bord d'un ruisseau*
> *Je la mange au bruit de l'eau,*
> *Étendu sur le rivage,*
> *Ou dans un antre sauvage.'*

Apricots, melons, artichokes, strawberries and cream, the sound of water, a cool cave – could there be a better picnic for a hot day? This poem of 1554, twenty years after Rabelais was publishing his adventures of Pantagruel, shows that the artichoke was well settled into French life.

It took a little longer to establish the artichoke in England, though by 1629 when the great apothecary and herbalist John Parkinson wrote his *Paradisus in Sole* and dedicated it to Queen Henrietta Maria, he was able to say that even the youngest housewife knew how to cook artichokes and serve them with melted butter seasoned with vinegar and pepper.

A last curious thing about artichokes. Sheila Hutchins mentions it in *English Recipes*. She describes how popular they were until the end of the last century, then they seemed to vanish, so that now – she was writing in the Sixties – they are appearing in the shops 'like some exotic foreign import'. She had heard 'English people on returning from holiday in Brittany where the vegetable is grown in quantity, protest after eating it in an hotel, that they had been fed on boiled water lilies'. I remember my mother, who had always been an adventurous eater, going out one day soon after I saw that boatload of artichokes at Torcello and returning with a couple for supper. We boiled them, then neither of us had the least idea what to do. We worked it out slowly. When it came to the choke, we worked it out the hard way. A quarter of a century later some greengrocers still feel the need to put a paper collar round artichokes explaining how to cook and eat them. This is why it seems important to go into some detail in the section following.

### How to tackle artichokes

There are a few general points that apply to nearly every method of preparing artichokes. Unless they are tightly closed, soak them upside down in a bowl of salted water for an hour, to dislodge earth or insects that might be concealed between the leaves. Provide yourself meanwhile with a piece of lemon to rub over any cut surfaces before they blacken. No lemon? Have a small bowl of wine vinegar to dip the cut parts into. When preparing artichokes in quantity, keep them in a big bowl or bucket of acidulated water (malt vinegar will do at that kind of dilution) until you have finished the last one; even if you have rubbed them with a lemon, they can still discolour slightly with a long wait.

Snipping the sharp points from the leaves with scissors or knife is an accepted thing to do. Why? There is no point in deforming such a beautiful object. I have never done this, and no one has pricked their finger and fallen asleep for a hundred years at our table.

BASIC METHOD: when the artichokes are ready to come out of the salt water, put on a huge pan half full of acidulated salted water. Use 2 tablespoons vinegar to 1 litre (1½ pt) of water. Cut the stalks from the artichokes, close to the leaves, and put them into the boiling water, cut end down. If the artichokes seem fresh and lively, put in the stalks as well; the inner part can often be scraped out and eaten. Once the water returns to the boil, allow 30 minutes. Remove a leaf from the base of the largest artichoke; if the nugget of flavour at the base is tender when you nibble it, the artichokes are done. If not, give them more time, testing every 10 minutes. Drain the cooked artichokes in a colander, upside down.

If you want to eat them hot or warm, serve them with melted butter and lemon juice, or with hollandaise sauce. When cold, they taste most delicious when eaten with vinaigrette, mayonnaise or sauce tartare. Another good sauce is clotted cream, sharpened with lemon and seasoned with salt, pepper and a pinch of sugar.

Set the table with a large dish in the centre for discarded leaves. Provide everyone with a cloth napkin. Small bowls of water are also a good idea, for people to rinse their fingers. Unless you have space in the china cupboard, there is little point in buying special artichoke plates, though there is no denying that they do look pretty. If you make a runny sauce such as vinaigrette or melted butter, it is perfectly satisfactory to tilt the plates by sliding a knife underneath one end. The sauce gathers into a neat pool, so that mess is avoided. With firmer sauces such as mayonnaise or hollandaise you do not need to worry.

To eat an artichoke, pull away the leaves beginning at the bottom. Dip the tender base of each one into the sauce before chewing it from the leaf, which can then be discarded. The last inner rows of leaves will come away in one piece like a pointed egg cosy; nibble around the edge. This leaves you with a thick grey-green saucer of artichoke – the final reward. Alas, it is topped with a tight circular pad of whitish fibres. This is the 'choke'. If you are not careful, you will find out how apt the name is. The French call it the *foin*, or hay; I think our name is a better warning. The choke is quite easy to remove if the artichoke is properly cooked. You can do it by sliding a knife between the fibres and the artichoke bottom, but you risk losing quite a lot of the edible part. It is better to take wedge-shaped sections of the fibres between your thumb and a knife blade and pull them away with a flick of the wrist. You will be left with the artichoke bottom, the whole point of the enterprise. Eat it with a knife and fork, with plenty of sauce.

HOW TO MAKE ARTICHOKE CUPS: if you want to serve artichokes stuffed, you need to form them into cups.

Cut off the artichoke stalk and the two lower rows of leaves. Trim the exposed base part if it needs tidying up. Then slice across the top, about a third of the way down. Boil and drain the artichokes as above. When they are cool enough to handle, pull out the centre leaves to expose the choke, leaving several outer layers of leaves to form the cup. Using a pointed teaspoon, scrape away the choke. Pour a little well seasoned vinaigrette into the base, and leave the artichokes to cool down. The mayonnaise or salad can be piled into the centre – the flavours should be vivid not stuffy, which is why shellfish is so successful in this kind of artichoke recipe.

Artichokes cooked in this way have to be eaten with a knife and fork.

For serving stuffed artichokes hot, you have to cut the raw artichoke into shape. This is easier than it looks if your knives are sharp. Slice off the stalk and the two outer rows of leaves as described above. Then slice off the top third, or what you judge to be the right amount to make a nice shape; artichokes can vary in height or squatness – you have to go by eye rather than rule. Open out the inner middle leaves with your fingers, then tug and cut them away. You will now find that the uncooked bottom is hard enough to stand the vigorous scraping required to dislodge the choke – a strong teaspoon is the best utensil. Now you are ready either to boil the cups so that they can be served with separately cooked mixtures inside them, or to stuff and braise them with a breadcrumb mixture.

HOW TO PREPARE ARTICHOKE BOTTOMS: If you need cooked artichoke bottoms, this is simply a matter of boiling the whole artichoke, then dismantling it in the kitchen. The leaves should be scraped free of the edible part which can often be incorporated into the dish in some way.

If you need uncooked artichoke bottoms, cut away the stalk, then the rows of large leaves. The centre leaves can be pulled away and the choke discarded, as above.

In Venice, where artichokes are cheap, you will see people sitting on the quays preparing artichoke bottoms for sale. Leaves and stalks go into the canal at flashing speed and the neatly turned bottoms drop into a bucket of acidulated water to await a sale.

HOW TO PREPARE YOUNG ARTICHOKES: This is a paragraph for gardeners only (unless you happen to be housekeeping in southern Europe where such things can be bought). When the artichoke plants have to be pruned of their lateral buds so that the large ones can develop, don't throw them out. Sometimes the whole of their stalk can be eaten, they are so tender. Sometimes you may need to scrape away the tough outer layer.

HOW TO CHOOSE CANNED ARTICHOKES: Don't. And don't be caught by cans labelled 'artichoke bottoms'. Look at the picture. They quite often turn out to be tiny whole artichokes, which are even more tasteless preserved in this way than the proper artichoke bottoms.

[*Vegetable Book*]


## ARTICHOKES AND EGGS ROC EN TUF (Oeufs Brouillés Aux Fonds d'Artichauts)

I have a friend in France whom I admire greatly. She is the complete eighteenth-century manor house wife. Her vegetable garden bulges with unusual things such as huge tufts of perpetual lettuce as well as the standard items. Her poultry yard quacks continually with ducks, geese, hens, guinea fowl, turkeys, pigeons. In the meadow beyond the garden a few sheep browse by the stream that supplies her trout. When we go to dinner we sit on chairs she has upholstered and embroidered. We drink cordials, apéritifs and wine that she and her husband have made. The things we eat have been grown, fed and cooked by her. One of the best meals we have eaten there started with this seventeenth-century dish that La Varenne describes in *Le Cuisinier François*. She was surprised when I commented on its antiquity. I think she had it from her mother-in-law, but she had added her own special seasonings. The recipe works well, too, with asparagus tips, young peas and many other vegetables of quality.

Serves 6

*6 large artichoke bottoms, cooked*
*12 eggs, beaten*
*4 large sprigs parsley, chopped*
*a small bunch of chives, chopped*
*100 g (3–4 oz) butter*
*1 tablespoonful Dijon mustard*
*2 tablespoons double cream*
*salt, pepper*

Cut the artichoke bottoms into 1-cm (½-inch) pieces, and reheat them if necessary. Mix the eggs with the herbs and scramble them lightly in the butter. Add mustard to taste gradually, then the cream and finally add seasoning to taste. Put the artichoke pieces over the base of a warmed serving dish and pour on the scrambled eggs. Set triangles of toast round the dish, or serve with baked bread, or French bread.

*Note:* be careful not to overcook the eggs in the first instance. They will continue to cook in their own heat, and in the heat of the serving dish.

[*Vegetable Book*]

## HOW TO MAKE THE MOST OF ASPARAGUS

Serves 4–6

*1 kg (2 lb) bunch of asparagus*
*750 g (1½ lb) new potatoes*
*4–6 hard-boiled or mollet eggs*

Scrape the new potatoes and leave them in water until required. Peel the hard part from the asparagus stems, then trim 5–7½ cm (2–3 inches) from the bottom – this is the part usually left on the side of the plate. Tie the asparagus into bunches.

Take a large saucepan. Put 5 cm (2 inches) of water into it with a teaspoon of salt, and bring to the boil. Stand the bunches of asparagus upright in the pan, put the stem trimmings round them, and the new potatoes on top. Put the lid on the pan, or arrange a domed cover of silver foil on it if the asparagus heads come above the rim. They will cook in the steam and be tender by the time the lower part of the stalks is done. Allow 20 minutes.

Special pans with an internal strainer can be bought, in France, for cooking asparagus. One or two shops in London may be able to supply them, but usually one has to improvise with pan and foil. Unless you grow asparagus, the cost of a special pan is hardly justified.

Remove the asparagus, when cooked, to a colander to drain, or arrange it on an old-fashioned meat dish with a removable strainer. Put the potatoes, which will be delicately flavoured with asparagus, round the edge of the dish, with the eggs, cut in half. Serve hot, warm or cold, with a sauce.

This dish makes an excellent main course for a summer lunch, but if you want to make it a little more substantial, wrap thin slices of Bayonne, Westphalian or Parma ham round bundles of asparagus. In Switzerland, air-dried beef from the Grisons is eaten with asparagus in this way.

You are left with the asparagus water and stalk trimmings, enough to transform the evening's soup into something unusually good:

*250 g (8 oz) peeled and cubed potato*
*125 g (4 oz) chopped onion*
*1–2 cloves garlic, chopped*
*60 g (2 oz) butter*
*1 dessertspoon flour (see recipe)*
*asparagus water and trimmings*
*milk or chicken stock*
*cream to finish, or butter*
*chopped parsley and chervil, or a head or two of asparagus*
    *saved from lunch*

Stew potato, onion and garlic gently in the butter, without browning them. If you intend to put the soup through a sieve or *mouli-légumes*, stir in the flour: if you're going to liquidize it, the flour is unnecessary. Pour in the asparagus water and simmer until the potatoes are just cooked. Add the asparagus trimmings, and when they are heated through sieve or liquidize the soup.

Return it to a clean pan, and bring it to the right consistency by adding milk or stock. Reheat to just below boiling point, and finish the soup with a spoonful of cream per person, or a knob of butter. Sprinkle with the chopped herbs, or with the asparagus cut into pieces the size of peas.

*[Good Things]*


## STUFFED CABBAGE IN THE TRÔO STYLE (Chou Farci)

I went into our neighbour's house in France one Saturday, and remarked on the wonderful smell. Madame Glon was making a *chou farci* as her grand-daughters were coming to supper. She lifted the lid of the red enamelled pot to show me. I expected to see a round cabbage, swollen out with the filling, but all I could see was a flat layer of cabbage, bubbling and heaving gently. She soon convinced me that her quick method was just as good as the classic one; certainly it is now one of our favourite dishes. I have tried it with various spicy and aromatic additions, tomatoes, bits of bacon, herbs and so on, but reject them all in favour of the Trôo simplicity of cabbage, good sausage-meat and butter. It has a pure directness that is just right, and cannot be improved. One can use either a Savoy or Dutch cabbage; or a Chinese cabbage for greater delicacy. Adjust the blanching and cooking times accordingly.

Serves 6

*1½–2 kg (3–4½ lb) cabbage*
*750 g (1½ lb) good sausages or sausage-meat*
*salt, pepper, butter*

Cut the cabbage across into slices, and blanch it for 5 minutes in hard-boiling, salted water. Drain it and run it under the tap to prevent further cooking at this stage. Butter an ovenproof or flameproof pot (according to whether you intend to cook the dish on top of the stove or in the oven). Put in a third of the cabbage. Remove the skin from the sausages if necessary, and put half over the cabbage. Then repeat, and cover with a final layer of cabbage. Season each layer as you go. Dot over with butter and cover tightly. Bake at gas 2, 150°C (300°F) for 2½ hours, or simmer on top of stove very gently. With a Chinese cabbage, you would need 2–2½ hours.

[*Vegetable Book*]

## PURÉE OF CELERIAC

This purée goes well with game or with turkey or chicken. It's a recipe that can be adjusted to taste, but the result should never be watery.

*1 large celeriac*
*⅓ its weight in potatoes*
*125–175 g (4–6 oz) butter*
*parsley, chervil, salt, pepper*

Quarter, peel and cut the celeriac into 2½-cm (1-inch) cubes. Cook in boiling salted water for 10 minutes. Drain well, then stew in 90 g (3 oz) butter (cover the pan) for 20 minutes, or until celeriac is cooked. Put through a sieve or *mouli-légumes* – don't liquidize the celeriac or it will be too soft and smooth.

Meanwhile scrub, boil and peel the potatoes. Sieve in the same way and add to the celeriac. Add chopped herbs, salt, pepper and more butter to taste. Reheat and serve.

*Note:* if you have some thick béchamel or cream sauce, this may be substituted for the potatoes.

[*Good Things*]

## GARLIC

'I find, as I suspected, that garlic is power; not in its despotic shape but exercised with the greatest discretion.' That was the Reverend Sydney Smith, in 1826, after his first visit to Paris. I would add that learning the whole range of garlic is, for a northerner, one of the more rewarding aspects of cookery.

When I was young, people shuddered at garlic. Dashingly you rubbed the salad bowl with it and kept quiet. There was a story about a cook 'whose salads bore the faintest, the merest suggestion of garlic. All questions failed to elicit the guarded secret of its fame. Nothing ... could account for the extreme delicacy of the result. Diners asked each other: "Do I detect garlic, or do I not?" It was only on his deathbed that the master bequeathed the secret to his son. The cook chewed a fragment of garlic, and puffed a few faint breaths over his salad.'

Nowadays we puff more than a few faint breaths. Indeed, I am told the English eat more garlic than the northern French. Surprising, too, that America grows well over 150 million pounds of it a year and that Gilroy, California, claims to be the garlic capital of the world. Its annual festival is in August, an occasion for which Alice Waters invented the superb Garlic Soufflé when she ran a garlic dinner at Chez Panisse. My own favourite festival – of basil as well as garlic – takes place in Tours on 26 July, St Anne's day. There we buy the year's supply, mainly from a grower in Bourgeuil, the wine commune, great trusses of tight white heads for long keeping (in good years, right round to July again) and lavender and green striped bulgy garlic for immediate eating. This young garlic makes a vegetable crown (*La Couronne d'Ail*) for lamb and poultry, and when puréed has a savoury sweetness that is unidentifiable to anyone not in the know. We also buy small bundles of garlic from the Charentes and from the Gers, garlic capital of France. Some claim that the further south you go, the sweeter and milder the note. Since garlic could not be more gentle than ours from the sandy fields of the Loire valley, I suspect that variety and cultivation may have more to do with it.

If you use garlic raw, for instance in salads chopped fine with parsley and scattered on beetroot, remember its power. People who stink of garlic, very few bearing in mind the quantities consumed, are, I am sure, eating a good deal of it raw. Perhaps it is a matter of digestion. Sprigs of parsley are supposed to prevent the smell lingering.

Avoid the garlic press: it releases an unpleasant bitterness. Just take a clove, in its skin, put it on a chopping board and press down slowly but firmly with the blade of a palette knife. This will crack and loosen the skin which can be picked off easily. A heavier pressure will crush the garlic to a state at which creaming with salt or chopping finely with a knife becomes an easy chore. If you are blanching garlic in boiling water, remove the skin afterwards when it will slip off with no resistance.

There are many marriages, happy ones, for garlic – with parsley and fine lemon peel (to scatter on *osso bucco*), with basil (*pesto*), with thyme and goat cheese, with olive oil on bread or in a pan bagna (try cooking 3 whole cloves gently in a little olive oil, then chopping them when tepid and adding them with the oil to 500 g (1 lb) of bread dough). Make a sauce by blending 12 large cloves of garlic, blanched and skinned, with 10 anchovy fillets, 1 heaped teaspoon of capers, a splash of wine vinegar, and then pouring in slowly about 12 tablespoons of olive oil: splendid with eggs, or cold chicken. When you make a tomato salad, add onion slices, chopped fresh basil and a pinch of dried oregano, and dress it with 2 or 3 crushed and creamed cloves of garlic mixed with 4 tablespoons of olive oil (no lemon, no vinegar, the acidity of good summer tomatoes is enough).

## Crown of Garlic

The garlic crown is a traditional French dish which varies slightly from region to region. Here is the Périgord version.

Brown a 2 kg (4 lb) leg of lamb or a good chicken in a little poultry fat or clarified butter. Put it into a deep heavy pot and add 50 or 60 peeled cloves of garlic.

Warm 3 tablespoons of brandy in a ladle, set it alight and pour over the lamb. Then add 150 ml (¼ pt) of medium-dry or sweet white wine and 150 ml (¼ pt) of chicken or veal stock. Cover with a tight-fitting lid and cook as slowly as possible on top of the stove or for 3 hours at gas 2, 150°C (300°F). Turn the meat occasionally.

Dish up the meat and surround it with the garlic. Strain the juices, removing as much fat as possible and reduce to concentrate the flavours. Add seasoning and pour over the garlic. This will serve 6–8.

## White Gazpacho

Put 60 g (2 oz) of blanched almonds or pine kernels, 4 fat garlic cloves, peeled and halved, and 90 g (3 oz) of unbleached white bread (weighed without crusts) into a food processor or blender. Whizz to a paste with a little water. Gradually add 4 tablespoons of olive oil, then 1 tablespoon of white wine vinegar and 1 teaspoon of salt. When blended, slowly pour in about 600 ml (1 pt) of water to obtain a smooth soup. Add more salt, vinegar and water, according to the seasoning and consistency you prefer.

Chill thoroughly in a large, covered bowl. Serve in individual bowls, adding an ice cube and 3 skinned, halved and pipped grapes (preferably Muscat) to each bowl. This is sufficient for 6 people.

## Potatoes with Garlic and Walnut Oil

Peel enough potatoes to fill a large sauté pan and cut them into fairly thick slices. Gently heat enough walnut oil to cover the base of the sauté pan by just under 3 mm (⅛ inch) and put in the potatoes. Cook them very gently – walnut oil loses its flavour if overheated – and season with salt, pepper and grated nutmeg. Cook for about 40 minutes, turning the potatoes occasionally.

Meanwhile, peel and chop 4 cloves of garlic with a good bunch of parsley and chives. About 5 minutes before the potatoes are ready, stir in the herbs and garlic. Do not let them cook for too long. Serve very hot. Enough for 4–6.

## Garlic Soufflé

First make a béchamel: melt 90 g (3 oz) of butter in a saucepan, stir in 5 tablespoons of flour and cook slowly for 2 minutes. Heat 375 ml (12 fl oz) of half cream with 250 ml (8 fl oz) of whipping cream and pour into the roux, stirring. Add salt, 1 medium onion, peeled and quartered, 2 or 3 peeled cloves of garlic, ½ teaspoon of dried thyme, 1 bay leaf, 4 sprigs of parsley and 10 black peppercorns. Set the pan over another pan of simmering water (*bain-marie*) and leave to cook gently for about 1 hour, stirring occasionally. Then strain out the aromatics. This can be done in advance.

To prepare the soufflé, have ready 1 generous tablespoon of garlic purée (see below). Butter a shallow metal or earthenware dish about 30 cm (12 inches) long and preheat the oven to gas 8, 230°C (450°F). Separate 5 eggs, then beat the yolks into the tepid béchamel sauce. Add the garlic purée and 90 g (3 oz) of grated Gouda or Gruyère cheese. Measure out 150 g (5 oz) of grated Parmesan cheese and sprinkle 1 tablespoon of it into the soufflé dish. Mix half of the remaining Parmesan into the soufflé mixture with salt, cayenne and black pepper to taste.

Whisk the egg whites until stiff, beat 1 tablespoon into the soufflé mixture to slacken the texture, then fold in the rest. Turn into the dish and sprinkle on the remaining Parmesan and 1 teaspoon of dried thyme. Bake at the top of the oven for 10–20 minutes or until golden brown but still creamy inside. This will serve 6 or 7 people.

## Garlic Purée

Break up 4 large heads of garlic into cloves and put them, unpeeled, into a large pan in a single layer. Cover with 500 g (1 lb) duck or goose fat, light olive oil or clarified butter. Add 3 sprigs of fresh thyme (or 1 teaspoon dried), 2 sprigs of fresh marjoram (or 1 teaspoon dried) and 2 bay leaves. Simmer slowly for 30 minutes, remove the garlic and peel when cooled, or sieve unpeeled if you need a purée.

Either way, the garlic can be used to flavour *ragoûts*, sautés, soufflés, braised dishes and purées.

For a garlic paste, cook and peel the garlic cloves as above, add 60 g (2 oz) of chopped shallots to the strained garlic and continue to cook for 5 minutes. Process or blend the mixture and reheat to just under boiling point, then pour into small, hot sterilized jam jars. Cool and cover with 6 mm (¼ inch) groundnut or sunflower oil. Seal the jars and store in the refrigerator. They will keep for several weeks, but once a jar is open use it up quickly.

## The Poor Man's Cure-all

Allow 1 head of fresh garlic per person. Remove the papery outer skin, keeping the clusters of cloves intact. Put the heads close together in an ovenproof dish so that they fit neatly. Pour over a little olive oil, then cover with buttered paper and foil.

Preheat the oven to gas 1–2, 140–150°C (275–300°F). Bake the garlic for 30 minutes. Carefully remove the foil and baste the heads, then cover again. Cook for about another hour, basting them occasionally. The garlic should be creamy inside the skin.

Give each person a head of garlic with a little of the cooking juices plus slices of wheatmeal or unbleached white bread and butter (ideally the fine unsalted butter from the Charentes) or goats' cheese, mixed to a sauce with a little cream.

## Garlic Butter

This will fill at least 48 large snails or mussels. Put 500 g (1 lb) of unsalted butter, cut into cubes and softened, into a food processor or blender. Add the leaves of a large bunch of parsley, 60 g (2 oz) of peeled shallot or mild onion and 4 or 5 large, skinned and halved garlic cloves. Blend until smooth. Add salt to taste and about 1 teaspoon of freshly ground black pepper.

To serve with snails or mussels, put the snails back into their shells, and leave the mussels on the half shell. Cover them with the butter, sprinkle with fine breadcrumbs and bake at the top of a very hot oven, or under the grill, until the butter is bubbling and the crumbs are lightly browned.

To keep the butter, form it into a roll and wrap well with greaseproof paper. Store in the refrigerator for a couple of days, or in the freezer for up to a week.

[*À La Carte*]

## PURSLANE IN FRANCE

A neighbour of ours at Trôo sent me along some purslane one day. We were instructed to make it into a salad with beetroot, like the lamb's lettuce salad on page 87.

A book on Périgord cookery describes purslane as having fleshy leaves with a fine flavour of hazelnuts. In those parts they leave them 24 hours with a sprinkling of salt. Drain them well and mix in a salad bowl with olive oil, wine vinegar, fresh milled black pepper and some slices of sweet red pepper (remove the skins first by grilling them). Hard-boil 2 eggs, shell them, and chop the yolks and whites separately: scatter the two decoratively over the salad.

[*Vegetable Book*]

## SALSIFY AND SCORZONERA

Salsify and scorzonera have much in common. They both provide us with long carrot-shaped roots of a succulence unusual in root vegetables. They have the same delicious flavour, though people in a position to know say that scorzonera has a slight edge over salsify. They are both natives of southern Europe, and belong to the same family. The difference between them is that salsify's skin has a whitish, parsnip look, while scorzonera's is a brownish black.

Italian gardeners developed the wild scorzonera root into its present state of tender firmness, although it early became popular in Spain and so acquired its botanical name of *Scorzonera hispanica*.

Salsify came in to this country about 1700, rather later than scorzonera, probably via France, though it was originally developed in Italy too. Often it was called vegetable oyster, a name one still finds in seedsmen's catalogues, or oyster plant. One authority says that this must have been because it had a slightly oysterish flavour, and could be used in meat pies instead of oysters which were often added for piquancy in the days when they were cheap (see the recipe for *tourtière*, on page 111). If the flavour was once there, modern varieties have it no longer. Salsify tastes of nothing but itself – and scorzonera, of course. Other people have compared it to the parsnip, but this won't do either. Parsnip has a softer texture than the clean waxy bite of salsify, and is much sweeter.

The odd thing is that neither vegetable has ever really caught on, at least with the general public. Intelligent gardeners, from John Evelyn onwards, have always grown either salsify or scorzonera. People who write books on gardening have been pushing them from the seventeenth to the twentieth century, but outside a few specialized and resourceful greengrocer's shops one can rarely buy them.

### How to choose and prepare salsify

Choose roots that are as smooth as possible, and firm: avoid flabby ones. Top and tail the roots, then run them under the cold tap and scrub away any soil with a small scrubbing brush.

At this point the French scrape away the dark brown skin, putting the pieces into acidulated water as they go to keep them white. Then they cut them up into pieces 5–8 cm (2–3 inches) long, and cook them for at least an hour in a *blanc à légumes* (page 131).

I find it just as satisfactory, and a good deal quicker, to cook the roots in their skins in salted water. Leave them whole if possible, only cutting them in half if absolutely necessary to fit them into the pan. All the salsify I have cooked has been tender in 30 minutes: to have left it longer would have reduced it to a stringy mush. Perhaps French salsify is thicker and tougher; the kind I have bought has usually been about 2 cm (¾ inch) thick, or a little less. After cooking, run the roots under the cold tap until you can peel away the skin. Then cut the creamy roots into whatever lengths the final preparation may require. By this method you cannot use the cooking liquor in a sauce, as it turns dark brown. It follows that for soup it is better to follow the French method of scraping, as you want the liquor to draw out the flavour.

[*Vegetable Book*]


## SALSIFY WITH FINES HERBES

If the salsify is to go with grilled and fried meat, chops, escallops and so on, this is the way to finish it.

Fry the blanched and cut up salsify in butter until golden-brown, scattering over it at the start the leaves of a good sprig of thyme, or a small branch of rosemary. When it is ready, put it into a hot dish and scatter generously with chopped parsley, tarragon and chives.

Instead of this typically French mixture, you can use the Italian *gremolata*, which is easier from the point of view of ingredients, as autumn turns to winter. Mix 2 good tablespoons of chopped parsley with the grated rind of half a large lemon and 1 small clove of garlic, finely chopped.

[*Vegetable Book*]

## STEAMING AND BLANCHING VEGETABLES

### Steaming

Steaming is not used enough in vegetable cookery, which is a shame as it has several advantages. First the flavour is preserved, as vegetable juices are not lost into the water. Secondly, steaming takes longer than boiling, which in the case of delicate vegetables can be a good thing when you are preparing a meal: it gives you more chance to catch the vegetables when they are perfectly cooked, before they can overcook. And thirdly, if you have a multi-storeyed steamer, two or more vegetables can be cooked on a single burner.

Put plenty of water in the lower pan. Bring it to the boil. Arrange the vegetables in the steamer and season them well. Put the steamer in place – it should be well above boiling water-level – and cover.

The time required varies from 5 minutes for delicate asparagus peas, to 10 or 15 minutes for green beans and cauliflower florets, to 20–25 minutes for young carrots, sliced leeks, seakale, and 30–45 minutes for peeled, cut up root vegetables. Obviously this can only be a rough guide. Everything depends on the size and thickness of the vegetable.

A compromise is a method in which green and stalk vegetables are partly steamed, partly boiled. Put 1½ cm (½ inch) of water into a pan with salt, bring it to the boil, and put in the vegetables. Cover so tightly that no steam can escape, and lower the heat so that the water boils steadily but not hard. Shake the pan occasionally. Test after 5 minutes for young or tender vegetables.

### Blanc à légumes and blanching

Certain pale vegetables are sometimes cooked in a *blanc à légumes* to preserve their light colour and prevent them darkening: celeriac for instance, white asparagus (not the greener English kind), cardoons, seakale, chicory, salsify, hop shoots, the stalks of Swiss chard, the heart or *fond* of globe artichokes, Jerusalem artichokes. When there is a real risk of blackening, say with celeriac, the vegetables are put straight into a bowl of acidulated water, as they are cleaned, to keep the cut surfaces from the damaging air. When the *blanc à légumes* is ready, they are quickly drained and put into it. To acidulate water, add 1 tablespoon of vinegar to 1 litre (2 pt) water.

A *blanc* is simple to make. Put 2 level tablespoons of flour into a bowl and gradually mix in 1 litre (2 pt) water until the mixture is smooth. Tip it into a pan with the juice of a lemon, salt, pepper and 1 heaped tablespoon of butter or chopped suet or 2 tablespoons of oil (an extra precaution to ensure that vegetables do not come into contact with the air as they rise to the surface). Bring the *blanc* to the boil, leave for 2 minutes, then add the drained, prepared vegetables.

Blanching means that a vegetable is parboiled in salted water, cooked until it is almost tender. Then it is tipped out into a sieve and 'refreshed' under the cold tap (this helps to preserve colour, in green beans for instance). This practice is essential if you are cooking potatoes in their skins, or salsify or scorzonera, because the skins have to be removed before the finishing process. If the blanching, refreshing and finishing are carried out in rapid succession, you get the most delicious result. Have the liquid at a rolling boil, plunge in the vegetables and time the cooking from the moment the liquid returns to the boil.

[*Vegetable Book*]

## JANE GRIGSON ON FRUIT

I grew up in a town devoid of fruit. There were of course apples, oranges and bananas in the shops, and one or two friends had kitchen gardens, but fruit trees were not part of our lives. There was nothing to raid when summer came along. The few blackberries were dry and sooty.

This, I imagine, is why certain experiences of fruit in my childhood remain bright, an orchard in Gloucester where old trees bent into tunnels and tresses of plums, a huge basket of strawberries that an uncle produced one day when we were visiting him in Worcestershire, raspberry canes blobbed with red and yellow fruit that met over our heads in a Westmorland cottage garden, unending peaches and water-melons of a student summer in Florence.

This special feeling towards fruit, its glory and abundance is, I would say, universal. We have to bear the burden of it being good for us – though I would not think many people in man's history agreed with one sixteenth-century doctor who said that fruit should not be eaten for pleasure, but because it did us good. An apple a day, an orange a day have not spoilt our feelings. We respond to strawberry fields or cherry orchards with a delight that a cabbage patch or even an elegant vegetable garden cannot provoke.

As with vegetables, what moved me about fruit was the centuries of patient work that have built up the repertoire of apple, pear and strawberry varieties, that have developed cherries, peaches, plums and citrus fruit for different tastes and places. Before farming began, people cleared space round certain trees so that their fruit could grow in better light with less competition. Later soldiers, travellers and explorers brought new fruit, or better versions of familiar fruit home with them. The excitement of the Renaissance extended to gardening too, which is something that historians leave out of their accounts. Northern gardeners took from Italy the idea of planting apricots, peaches and so on against walls so that they might benefit from the stored warmth of the bricks and stones, and the espalier method of growing fruit trees was developed particularly in France. Such methods extended the range of fruit-growing. 'No longer do we have to travel down to Touraine for a Bon Chrétien pear,' wrote one enthusiastic Parisian – pears from Burgundy and Anjou as well were being grown on the outskirts of Paris, and sold in abundance in the markets.

It was in Paris that I discovered what had moved the skilful gardeners of that period. Not just the pleasure of the fruit or the triumph of intelligence, but a grand design. I was in the Bibliothèque Nationale reading room at the end of a long day. Knowing it would be several months before we'd be back in France, I had crashed through a pile of French books without moving from the chair. Twenty minutes was left for one English book, John Evelyn's *Compleat Gard'ner*, of 1693, his translation of a book by Jean de la Quintinie, one of Europe's great gardeners, expert on melon cultivation and the conduct of orangeries. He had made the gardens at Versailles from mounds of rubble, and was in charge of all Louis XIV's other gardens. No sinecure, as Louis had a passion for fruit and vegetables and inspected their progress regularly.

I opened the book in a tired blur, started at the beginning with resignation – and suddenly woke up. Here were these two voices speaking about what had moved them to their labours, de la Quintinie producing fruit with the least faults for 'the man who has most merits' – i.e. the Sun King – and Evelyn trying to turn Britain into an Elysian parkland, dotted with fine gardens. To explain what they were about, they chose fruit – 'Fruit, as it was our primitive, and most excellent as well as most innocent food, whilst it grew in Paradise; a climate so benign, and a soil so richly impregnated with all that the influence of Heaven could communicate to it; so it has still preserved, and retained no small tincture of its original and celestial virtue.' Even in its fallen state, fruit is still the most 'agreeable closure' to a meal, however grand and princely. And so it is the gardener's labour 'to repair what the choicest and most delicious fruit has been despoiled of, since it grew in Paradise'. To aim, in other words, at recovering the original flavour of Eden, even if such transcendent perfection can never quite be achieved.

I suppose we no longer believe that God Almighty first planted a garden. Heavy cropping seems to be the aim of fruit breeders today, rather than fine quality of flavour. For this reason I am grateful to have been able to live and work part of my life in France during the last twenty years, in one of the great fruit-growing areas. In that genial climate, in private gardens at least, it is possible to sense what Evelyn and de la Quintinie and their tribe were after. People in Kent and Herefordshire, in Gloucestershire, Evesham and the Carse of Gowrie, may sometimes have a chance to sense it, too – so will people who stop by the occasional box of perfect fruit, nectarines perhaps or muscat grapes, on a market stall or in a supermarket, if they are not in too much of a hurry.

[*Fruit Book*]


## PEACH AND NECTARINE

'Renoir used to say to young artists longing to paint – like him – the pinkish-brown tones of an opulent breast: "First paint apples and peaches in a fruit bowl." My greengrocer sold me worthy models for painting. Their curves were perfect and graceful. Their grooves were in exactly the right place. Their gradations of colour were an art school exercise, and as for the velvety down of their skin . . . "It's the left cheek of my girl", as a Japanese poet has written.'

So began an article by James de Coquet at the height of the peach season some years ago. Peaches for painting, peaches for writing poems about – but peaches for eating? His beauties were hard. When cooked, they were tasteless and still not tender. Horticulture has come into perilous times. Everything is selected, trained, peaches are now the children of arranged marriages. Perhaps they would have more taste and succulence if they were love-children? People understand the problems in France, where in every heart there sleeps a peasant. They are on the grower's side. They know he has to decide which currency he is growing for, the mark, the pound or the Swiss franc. They know he has worked hard to produce strains that will be roadworthy and can earn a living in the markets of Europe. They appreciate that he has produced the peaches of Renoir, with exultant curves, pretty enough to eat. But should they not also be eatable?

We can appreciate James de Coquet's sentiments, and feel an added crossness that our beautiful, unsatisfactory peaches cost nearly twice as much as his, although coming from the same growers.

Somewhere, surely, there must be the perfect peach? I thought I would try and find it, and started off with the famous Montreuil peach, because on every classic French menu Montreuil means peaches, just as Montmorency means cherries and Argenteuil means asparagus.

According to legend – perhaps it is true? – the peach began its career at Montreuil to the east of Paris in the seventeenth century. A retired soldier living there grew his peaches on the espalier system, which was a new idea, and took off most of the tiny fruit from the trees, leaving only a few to ripen on each one. This man, Monsieur Girardot, was a friend of de la Quintinie, Louis XIV's gardener, and one day confided in him that he would like to ask the king a favour. Knowing the king's fondness for fruit, de la Quintinie suggested that he present a basket of his wonderful peaches at Versailles, anonymously. This he did. The king was entranced by the quality of the fruit and by their mysterious arrival. Next time he was hunting over in the direction of Montreuil, de la Quintinie told him that the peaches had been grown by a friend of his not far away. Of course the king had to go and see for himself, the man asked his favour and it was granted. After that, year by year until the Revolution, the family and other growers of Montreuil who were helping to supply the increasing demand for the fruit, sent a basket of them to the royal family.

Louis was not the only king who was captured by these peaches. Edward VII was dining incognito with a young woman in Paris. When the bill came, he was astounded at the price of the Montreuil peaches, and called the waiter over.

'Peaches must be very rare this year,' he said.

'Ah yes, sir, but not as rare as kings,' came the reply.

I rang up the Hôtel de Ville at Montreuil. No one knew, but passed me on to a local college of agriculture. 'No, we do not grow Montreuil peaches here,' I was told. 'Never heard of them.' When I went to see the district, I found that the old back gardens – once divided by espalier lines of peach trees – have quite disappeared into tower blocks and concrete. The big road to Charles de Gaulle airport goes through it.

Stumped, I went and told a friend about my search. 'Why didn't you ask me before?' he said. 'I remember eating Montreuil peaches after the war at the Escargot restaurant in Paris, in the rue Montorgeuil. They were sensational. And each one was presented in a special box as if it had been an expensive brooch, a black or navy box, I think, with the name of the restaurant printed on it in gold. You paid, but they were worth it.'

Off again, to the rue Montorgeuil with a friend, and the Escargot. There under the sign of the golden snail, in all that cherished decor of the past, surely I would find the answer? But no. Even the oldest cleaner was 'new', from the last eighteen years and less. I remembered that it was over thirty years since the war ended. We had an excellent meal – ending with strawberry fritters, which reminded me of my failure since strawberries were another speciality of Montreuil in the past. Does anyone anywhere tend a last surviving Montreuil espalier? It seems not. The French are more careless of their past than we are. Those magnificent peaches have gone for ever.

My journey was nothing, though, to the undertaking of Professor Edward Schafer, of Berkeley University. His quest for the finest possible peaches has produced one of the best and most thorough books about food that I know, *The Golden Peaches of Samarkand*, a study of T'ang exotics. Now peaches are native to China. They have the kind of place in Chinese myth and poetry that apples have in ours.

When golden peaches, the size of goose eggs, were sent from Samarkand, T'ang courtiers must have thought they were seeing the mythical peaches of immortality that fruit every six thousand years, so that the gods can eat them and continue to live for ever.

The peaches were sent twice in the seventh century from Samarkand. Trees came with them. They must have been cherished, as T'ang emperors had the same kind of passion for fruit and vegetables as Louis XIV, ten centuries later. No one recorded what they tasted like.

For me, the exotic peach is the *pêche de vigne*, covered with a fine grey down, and deep-coloured through to the stone. In the past, every vineyard had its peaches, and the small ones still do. The fruit is ripe at vintage time, and the trees renew themselves, growing true from the fallen stones. A friend gave us a small peach tree from his vineyard and we planted it in Wiltshire. For years and years it did nothing, then suddenly it had thirty-nine peaches. The year was not warm enough to ripen them properly, but cooked they had a superb flavour. Even better were the purple vineyard peaches we found by accident, in Vendôme two years ago. They were purple right through, even and perfect in size. Someone was growing them commercially, for the following week I saw some in Paris and bought them. After the first lot, they were disappointing – the hand of commerce, presumably.

We went back to Vendôme, but the peaches were finished, and last autumn there were none at all.

If anybody cares to grow fruiting trees and writes to the Ministry of Agriculture for a permit to bring in plants, they might on a journey through the wine districts of France be able to pick up a young *pêchier de vigne*. For the non-gardeners, look out in the markets for these peaches at the end of the summer, late August and September. They may also be marked 'sanguines', blood peaches, like blood oranges, on account of their rich coloured flesh.

Nectarines are smooth plum-skinned varieties of peach. They come white and orangey-yellow, just as peaches do and, as with peaches, the white ones taste better. The difference is quite marked, nectarines being both sharp and richer at the same time. In Italy, the peach is *pesca* – the nectarine *pesca noce* – because the Romans thought it came from Persia (hence, too, our peach and French *pêche*). In France, the *nectarine* may also be labelled *brugnon*, because the fruit was a great speciality around Brignole in the Var. And should you ever come across the word *pavie*, it means a clingstone peach, grown originally at Pavie near Auch, a part of France where vast orchards now stretch kilometre after kilometre.

### How to choose and prepare peaches and nectarines

If you are housekeeping in Italy or France with a family to feed, buy peaches and nectarines in trays and boxes, rather than by the kilo. They will be a little cheaper and a continuing source of contentment in hot weather. In August, peaches, melons and late strawberries dominate the markets of both countries with their colour and smell.

An infinitesimal number of readers may live near an English peach orchard or big house where wall peaches and nectarines are still grown. All I can say is that if they can buy them, they are to be envied. My parents once said that the finest they had ever eaten anywhere had been grown in Mr Perrin's – or was it Mr Lea's? – garden in Worcestershire. But that was a long time ago, longer ago than the last Montreuil peaches.

Being on the whole so remote from the orchards, and being so used to the Golden Delicious apple which never changes, we can be taken by surprise that peaches from the same suppliers vary from year to year. Even from tree to tree it would seem, judging by the way 1 kg (2 lb) of peaches will vary from superb to tasteless. This means that you are gambling rather than choosing. All you can do is make sure your horse is not lame or blind, by refusing peaches that are bruised or soft. Softness indicates woolliness and cannot be redeemed, as hardness sometimes can, by cooking.

To skin peaches and nectarines, pour boiling water over them. If they are very ripe, they will be peelable after about 15 seconds. Extra time will be needed for the rest. If you are poaching the fruit, leave the skins on – they improve the colour of the syrup and can easily be strained out or peeled off at the end of the cooking time.

The easiest way to cut up a peach is to run a small sharp knife down from top to bottom, going through to the stone. Turn the peach slightly in your hand and make another cut, so that the wedge falls out, on to a plate, or better still into a glass of wine. Continue like this all round the peach. If you are doing a bowl of peaches in wine, do not prepare them more than an hour before the meal. The grandest form of what is basically a rustic affair is peaches in champagne, with a few wild or wood strawberries added. Myself, I prefer the simple version; at least you can add some sugar to the wine if the peach is not as sweet as it should be, without feeling that you are desecrating a noble example of the wine-maker's art. We open a bottle of a reasonable local white or red wine, whatever we have, just as our neighbours do.

If the peaches you buy are not quite as ripe as they should be, pour some boiling light syrup over the slices. It cooks them as it cools down. If they are slightly harder than that, slip them into some boiling syrup and bring the liquid back to a thorough boil before taking the pan from the stove. This kind of technique is ideal for cooking many foods that are tasteless and which spoil if they are overcooked.

[*Fruit Book*]


## GRILLED PEACHES

Cut the peaches in half and remove the stones. Brush the cut sides with butter and sprinkle with sugar generously. Grill cut-side up, gently at first to heat the peaches through, then more fiercely to brown the sugar. Serve hot with vanilla ice cream, or with whipped cream.

[*Fruit Book*]


## QUINCE JELLY (Gelée de Coings)

A French recipe that is practical for people who grow quinces, and end up with the usual mixed bag of fruit, some perfect, some blemished, some a bit twisted, some very small. If it is a bad year, add windfall apples or cooking apples up to half the weight of quinces.

Set aside 3 or 4 fine quinces, after washing them all and rubbing away the grey fluff. Cut up the rest roughly into chunks and put them into a preserving pan, half full of water.

Peel your best quinces, then slice and core them neatly. Throw peel and core into the pan. Lay the slices on top. If the water does not cover the fruit, add some more. Bring to the boil and simmer until the fruit on top is completely tender – remove the slices with a slotted spoon. Boil the panful hard to get the most out of the debris. Crush it down occasionally with a potato masher. When the fruit is completely pulpy, strain off the juice through a jelly bag.

Measure the quantity: to each 600 ml (1 pt) of water allow 500 g (1 lb) of sugar. Put the reserved slices into the juice, bring to the boil, stirring, then boil hard until setting point is reached. Concentrate the slices in two or three sterilized jam jars. Top them up with jelly, then pour the rest into more jars. Cover and store in a cool dark place.

The quince slices come in handy, when stored like this, for adding to apple pies throughout the winter.

Spices can be added to quince jelly if you like, cinnamon stick and a few cloves for instance; put them in with the sugar.

[*Fruit Book*]

# CAKES AND PUDDINGS

## DUCLAIR CHERRY TART (Tarte Aux Cerises de Duclair)

Ducks are a speciality, so is this unusual cherry tart. The tricky bit is cooking the cherries so that they caramelize without becoming overcooked: you need a high heat once the butter, sugar and Calvados are blended, but take care the cherry juices do not burn – this kind of thing is much easier to do on a gas burner than an electric ring.

You need a puff pastry case, baked blind in a 23–25-cm (9–10-inch) tart tin. This can be done in advance, and the case reheated to freshen it if necessary. The cream and cheese can also be mixed earlier in the day. But the cooking of the cherries and the final assembly should take place not too long before the meal.

*500 g (1 lb) firm red cherries, stoned weight*
*60 g (2 oz) butter*
*100 g (3½ oz) granulated sugar*
*3 tablespoons Calvados or malt whisky*
*250 g (8 oz) fromage frais*
*caster sugar*
*150 ml (¼ pt) double cream*

Drain the cherries in a sieve. Melt the butter, stir in the granulated sugar and Calvados, or whisky. When they are blended, raise the heat and put in the cherries. They should caramelize lightly, so keep them moving and do not take your eye off them. Drain and cool.

Beat the *fromage frais* with caster sugar to taste. Whip the cream and fold it in, check again for sweetness and taste a cherry to make sure that you do not over-sweeten the mixture.

To assemble, spread the cream cheese and cream on to the pastry. Put the cherries on top.

[*Fruit Book*]

## EPIPHANY CAKE (Galette des Rois)

As we drove into Giverny one winter day, past the church and churchyard where Monet and his family are buried, we saw a baker's van ahead. Bright blue. We were hungry and suddenly had a desire for the childish treat of a *pain au chocolat* – a bar of chocolate baked inside a roll. So we chased the van. Down the village street, sharp right, down a lane, sharp right again to a sudden stop by a farmyard gate. Yes, the baker did have *pains au chocolat*. He also had two round puff pastry discs, nicely browned and puffed. What can that be? '*Galettes des rois, Madame*,' and I remembered that it was after all only 12 January, within the octave – just – of the feast of the Epiphany.

We continued our day's programme, visiting Monet's garden and so on, and ended up at the house of a young Monet scholar who showed us photographs of Giverny, when the garden was in its lush prime, photographs of many paintings never or rarely reproduced, and books on Monet.

Turning over the pages of one book, we came suddenly to a painting in the Durand-Ruel collection – and there were our two *galettes* of the morning. Painted by Monet, as they cooled on those round open wicker trays that everyone in the countryside in France has for drying small cheeses. We have a couple ourselves. So now I put our *galettes* on the trays when I make them, with a sharp knife alongside, black-handled like Monet's. It reminds me of our visit to Giverny, and recalls the day in 1882 when Monet kept his large family waiting for their treat while he made his sketches: his own little boys were fifteen and nearly four, then there were the children of Madame Hoschedé who shared his life after the death of Camille and eventually became the second Madame Monet. It was the year before they found Giverny, while they were still living at Vétheuil.

Monet's cakes had a swirling design and roundly curled edges. Sometimes the design is more like the star that led the Three Wise

Men, with five points. Sometimes it is in criss-cross diamonds like a half-extended trellis, and the edges are cleanly cut so that they bake up into layers like the edge of a book. Some *galettes* are no more than pastry, but the better ones are filled with a sort of almond frangipane cream. Whatever the decoration and filling, all galettes have one thing in common – a *fève* or 'bean' in the middle. Long ago the 'bean' was a bean, a dried haricot. Nowadays it is a tiny faience fancy representing a motorcycle or a duck or some other bit of nonsense. The person whose teeth find the 'bean' becomes king or queen of the feast, and has luck for the year.

If you have a large party, make two or more *galettes*, rather than one big one. They can be made early in the day, and heated through when required. For one *galette*:

> *about 500 g (1 lb) total weight, or 1 large packet frozen puff pastry*
> *egg yolk or cream to glaze*

> FILLING
> *100 g (3–4 oz) blanched almonds, ground not too finely*
> *100 g (3–4 oz) vanilla sugar*
> *1 slightly rounded tablespoon cornflour*
> *3 large egg yolks*
> *a pinch of salt*
> *75 g (2½ oz) butter, melted*
> *1–2 tablespoons kirsch or rum (or whisky, if you like)*
> *1 dried haricot bean*

Roll out the pastry and cut two circles 22–25 cm (9–10 inches) across. Place one on a baking sheet and brush its rim with beaten egg or cream – the rim should be about 2½ cm (1 inch).

Mix the filling ingredients in the order given, and spread the mixture inside the rim of the pastry. Place the second circle of pastry on top, pressing down round the rim, and making a centre hole.

Now you can either trim off the edge with a pastry cutter, and knock up the edges, cutting parallel with the baking sheet. Or roll up the edges of the lower sheet of pastry – the top sheet should be just inside it, being raised up over the mound of filling – to make a plump, curving roll.

With the point of a sharp knife, decorate the top swirling lines out from the centre, or scoring a star or narrowed trellis. Bake at gas 7, 220°C (425°F) for 20–30 minutes, then lower the heat to gas 4, 180°C (350°F) for 10–20 minutes.

*[Food with the Famous]*

## LAVARDIN CAKES

A year or two ago a new pastrycook arrived in Montoire, a small market town in the department of Loir et Cher. Everyone watched his window – Montoire is careful of its gastronomic reputation – to see what sort of show he would put on (and how he would compare with his two rivals). Very soon, among the evanescent stars of the usual repertoire, the éclairs, the *barquettes aux fraises*, the *amandines*, the *présidents*, rows of plain, white-iced discs appeared. They were labelled *Lavardins, notre spécialité*. Now Lavardin castle, or its remains, on one side of Montoire, together with Trôo church on the other, dominates our valley landscape of the Bas-Vendômois. Could these cakes be a local speciality we had all missed? We bought some – feeling a little piqued – and they were so delectable that I asked for the recipe.

I learnt, in the simple, beautiful kitchen behind the shop, that lavardin cakes had nothing to do with Lavardin at all, that they came from the south-west of France, via an old pastrycook in Normandy who had specialized, against the dominant French tradition, in cakes which keep. And these do. They are also very much to the English taste. In fact of all the recipes in this article, I think that lavardins show off best the flavour and texture of walnuts.

SWEET PASTRY
*500 g (1 lb) flour*
*250 g (8 oz) butter*
*250 g (8 oz) caster sugar*
*3 standard eggs*

FILLING
*300 g (10 oz) sugar*
*60 ml (2 fl oz) water*
*180 ml (6 fl oz) tin evaporated milk*
*scant 60 g (2 oz) unsalted butter*
*generous 60 ml (2 fl oz) double cream*
*a pinch of bicarbonate of soda*
*300 g (10 oz) walnuts, roughly chopped*

ICING
*2 egg whites*
*125 g (4 oz) icing sugar*

First make the filling: bring sugar and water to the hard crack stage over a brisk heat, stirring with a wooden spoon from time to time.

Remove from heat and quickly stir in the evaporated milk, butter, cream and bicarbonate of soda. Stir until the mixture reaches firm soft ball stage, add the walnuts and pour out on to a marble slab or a sheet of greased paper. It will cool to a soft nut toffee.

While the filling cools, make the pastry in the usual way. Roll it out thinly and line 7½–10-cm (3–4-inch) flan rings laid on a greased baking sheet (or smooth-sided tart tins) leaving a little frill of pastry overlapping the edge. Fill slightly over half-full with the walnut mixture. Brush the pastry edges with water and fit in lids of pastry, which have been pricked half a dozen times with a fork. Take off the surplus pastry by running a rolling pin across the tins. Bake at gas 3, 180°C (350°F), or a little less, until the pastry is cooked but not brown – about 15 minutes. As with mince pies, the point is to bake these little cakes so that the pastry cooks without the filling bursting through. Remove the lavardins from their rings or tins, and cool upside down on a wire rack.

Set a pudding basin over a pan of boiling water, put in the egg whites and icing sugar, and whisk until they blow up to a fairly stiff meringue, which feels hot but not uncomfortably so. Spread thinly over the top and sides of the cooled and inverted cakes with a palette knife, leaving the pricked surface exposed. Dry overnight in a cool place, or in the refrigerator, and store in an air-tight tin.

If time is short, there is no reason why you shouldn't make 2 or 3 large lavardins, instead of the 20–30 small ones. Use a French flan ring, a tart tin with a removable base, or a straight-sided tart tin.

[*Good Things*]

## MADELEINES AND LIME TEA

Madeleines, said to have first been made in Lorraine at Commercy, are plump little cakes that look 'as though they had been moulded in the fluted scallop of a pilgrim's shell'. Special tins are needed, which not only shape the base of the cakes in the characteristic way, but cause the mixture to rise into a central dome. If you use ordinary bun tins, madeleines will look as gently curved as any other small plain cake. It also follows that you can bake a variety of mixtures in the tin and achieve the same effect: I sometimes feel that the many brands of madeleines on sale in France in plastic bags – some of quite good quality – have been made from an easier pound-cake mixture (125 g (4 oz) each of butter, sugar, self-raising flour, eggs – i.e. 2 eggs). Indeed, if you flavour this with orange-flower water, you can get a good result, although the following is closer to the real thing:

scant 100 g (3 oz) butter
125 g (4 oz) caster sugar
3 large eggs
120 g (scant 4 oz) self-raising flour
1 tablespoon orange-flower water (or milk)

Cream butter, add sugar, and cream again. Beat in eggs one at a time, alternating with the flour. Stir in the orange-flower water. Fill buttered and floured tins to their rim, then bake until golden brown at gas 7, 220°C (425°F), about 10–15 minutes.

Lime tea is made from dried lime blossoms. Every year people pick the flowers on a warm day at the height of their scent, and spread them out on newspapers in a dry place until they are brittle. Store in plastic bags if you are confident that all the moisture is gone, or in brown paper bags; close them well. When you want to make the *tisane*, or lime tea, remove enough dried flowers to fill a large stoneware jug; don't ram them in, just put in enough to fill the jug lightly. Pour on boiling water almost to the top, and leave to infuse for about 5 minutes. Strain this *tisane* into a warmed jug, and serve with madeleines. A soothing end to a Proustian evening, or a pleasant tea in winter time. Health food shops and delicatessens often sell packages of lime tea from France. They will be labelled *tisane*, with *tilleul* underneath, meaning lime, as opposed, say, to mint or vervain.

[*Food with the Famous*]

## NECTARINE BAVAROISE

Not a correct classic bavaroise, but a lighter mixture that allows the flavour of nectarine to come through particularly well. My original version, and the most successful, contained *orgeat*, an almond and orange-flower syrup tasting very much of the past that you can buy in high-class groceries and foodshops in France. Worth looking out for when you're on holiday. Kirsch can be used instead, or an orange-based liqueur.

6 nectarines, approximately 750 g (1½ lb)
125 (4 oz) sugar
1 × 15 g (½ oz) packet gelatine
juice of 1 orange
2 tablespoons orgeat or appropriate alcohol
100 g (3½ oz) fromage frais or yoghurt, drained weight
100 ml (3½ fl oz) double cream, whipped
lemon juice (see recipe)

Into a wide shallow pan, section nectarines into 8 wedges each. Sprinkle with the sugar and 2 tablespoons of water. Cook on a low heat until the juices run, then raise the heat and finish the cooking. The red skins of the fruit will dye the syrup a glowing pink. Remove, drain and skin 12 sections. Put them in a whirligig star shape in the base of an oiled and sugared charlotte mould or other plain dish (use almond or a tasteless oil).

Put the rest of the fruit, skins and all, with the syrup into liquidizer or blender. Sprinkle on the gelatine, orange juice, and *orgeat* or alcohol. Whizz or process until very smooth. Strain into a basin, mix in the *fromage frais* or yoghurt, then fold in the cream. Taste and see if any lemon juice is needed to bring out the flavour. Add extra sugar if you like – icing sugar will mix in best at this stage, caster next best.

Carefully spoon some of the bavaroise over the nectarine sections in the dish, so as not to disturb them. Put in the coldest part of the refrigerator, or into the freezer, until almost set. Then spoon in the remaining mixture, starting round the edge so that it runs gently into the middle. Put back to set and chill.

To turn out, run a knife blade round the edge. Put a dish on top, then turn the whole thing over, and give a shake or two. If it is reluctant to turn out, put a cloth wrung out in very hot water over the metal mould, and shake again.

[*Fruit Book*]

## ORANGE TARTLETS (Mirlitons de Rouen)

Mirliton is a nonsense word from the refrain of old songs; it suggests a cheerful twirling of skirts and light feet and suits these little tarts well.

Makes about 12

*250 g (8 oz) puff pastry*
*4 egg yolks*
*50 g (2 oz) caster sugar*
*1 vanilla pod*
*125 g (4 oz) butter, plus extra for greasing*
*1–2 teaspoons orange-flower water or orange liqueur*

Preheat the oven to gas 7, 220°C (425°F). Roll out the pastry and line 12 greased tartlet tins. Put them into the refrigerator to chill for 30 minutes at least.

Beat together the yolks and nearly all the sugar, keeping 1 tablespoon back, until the mixture is pale and thick. Slit the vanilla pod and scrape the soft black seedy pulp into the egg and sugar. Mix well.

Cut up the butter, melt it in a small pan and cook it to a golden-brown colour; it should have an appetizing smell of nuts. Mix it vigorously into the egg yolks and flavour it to taste with orange-flower water, adding this ½ teaspoon at a time (it is much stronger than you might think). An orange liqueur does not taste at all the same, but it gives a slight zip to the mixture.

Fill the tartlet cases two-thirds full. Sprinkle them with the remaining sugar. Bake them in the oven for 10–15 minutes; they may sink a little.

[*The Cooking of Normandy*]

## PEARS IN BATTER (Tarte de Cambrai)

On arriving in France, we usually go straight to the *droguerie* to buy paraffin for the stoves. We are always greeted enthusiastically – being the first of the returning cuckoos of summer – but one year was exceptional. No preliminaries of health, weather and absent friends, straight to business. 'I've been waiting for you,' said Madame Guilbaud. 'I've a recipe for your readers. Easy. Quick. Delicious. Take it down.' I obeyed, and have been grateful ever since.

*4–5 large ripe pears*
*1 tablespoon lemon juice*
*60 g (2 oz) butter*
*extra sugar*

BATTER
*10 level tablespoons self-raising flour*
*6 level tablespoons vanilla sugar*
*4 tablespoons oil*
*8 tablespoons milk*
*2 whole eggs*
*a pinch of salt*

Peel, core and slice the pears. Sprinkle with the lemon juice, turning the slices over.

Mix the batter ingredients in the order given. Grease a 25-cm (10-inch) flan or shallow cake tin with a butter paper and pour in the batter. Arrange the pear slices on top. Dot with butter, and sprinkle evenly with extra sugar. Bake for about 50 minutes at gas 6–7, 200–220°C

(400–425°F), or until golden brown and risen, with bits of pear showing through. Eat warm, and serve with cream, if it's being eaten as a pudding.

*Note: Tarte de Cambrai* can also be made with apples, and with peaches (they should be lightly cooked first, to draw off most of the juice). Bananas work well, too. To make the top extra good, scatter 30 g (1 oz) blanched slivered almonds over it before putting in the oven.

[*Fruit Book*]

## RICE PUDDING (Riz à l'Impératrice)

As a child, Proust was already a lover of the theatre, 'a Platonic lover, of necessity, since my parents had not yet allowed me to enter one'. When they were living in a street near the Madeleine, he would study the playbills stuck on to the nearest Moriss column, imagining fantastic performances. At last his parents told him to choose between two plays. 'I had shewn myself such vivid, such compelling pictures of, on the one hand, a play of dazzling arrogance, and on the other a gentle, velvety play, that I was as little capable of deciding which play I should prefer to see as if, at the dinner-table, they had obliged me to choose between rice *à l'impératrice* and the famous cream of chocolate.' Anyone who feels an aversion to rice puddings, may be encouraged to try this one and think again.

> *125 g (4 oz) long grain rice*
> *600 ml (1 pt) milk*
> *½ a vanilla pod*
> *4 egg yolks*
> *125 g (4 oz) sugar*
> *2 heaped teaspoons gelatine*
> *300 ml (½ pt) double cream*

Boil the rice in water for 3 minutes, then drain and rinse it under the cold tap. Return to the pan with half the milk, cover and simmer until very tender. Bring the rest of the milk to the boil with the vanilla pod, then whisk into the yolks and the sugar. Pour back into the pan and stir over a lowish heat until the custard thickens (use a double boiler if you are not accustomed to making egg custards). Melt the gelatine in 2 tablespoons of hot water and add to the hot custard. Strain into a bowl, and add the cooked rice which will have absorbed all the milk. Cool. Whip cream and fold in. Turn into a lightly oiled mould. Chill, and serve with soft fruit or stewed pears that have been lightly poached in syrup.

[*Food with the Famous*]

## STUFFED PRUNES, TOURS STYLE (Pruneaux Fourrés de Tours)

Walking along the main street of Tours, one's eye is caught again and again by the cake and confectionery shops. And of all these shops, the finest is the Maison Sabat. There in the ravishing window display, among the other specialities of the Sabat family, are charming little baskets, miniature hampers, filled with rows of stuffed prunes. These *pruneaux fourrés* are one of the great specialities of Tours. Each house makes its own (no sweet factory to vulgarize the old recipes). What I like about them is that they are not too sweet, that their flavour is rich but subtle, with just a hint of kirsch or rum. Discerning natives of Tours prefer the original *pruneaux noirs* which go back I think to the eighteenth century – they are stuffed with a prune and rum purée. I find it difficult to choose between them and the ones filled with pale green almond paste or an orange apricot purée, flavoured in both cases with a little kirsch.

Mlle Madeleine Sabat finds it more and more difficult to get traditional baskets for the prunes. They are only made now by the old ladies of Vilaine, a village in Balzac country near Chinon which once relied on supplying baskets to local prune-packers at Huismes. (With the decline of the prune trade, the young people of Vilaine concentrate on fashionable and profitable wicker furniture.) Soon the *pruneaux fourrés* will all be packed in paper boxes. Soon, too, the prunes may come from California – at the moment they come from Agen.

*1 kg (2 lb) giant prunes, soaked, stoned and dried*
*250 g (8 oz) sugar*
*75 ml (½ gill) water*
*125 g (4 oz) ground almonds*
*kirsch*
*a few drops of green colouring*
*125 g (4 oz) prunes or apricots, soaked*
*about 125 g (4 oz) sugar*
*rum or kirsch*
*250 g (8 oz) sugar*
*75 ml (½ gill) water*

Leave the soaked and stoned prunes to dry on a rack in a warm kitchen.

To make the almond paste, bring sugar and water to the soft ball stage. Pour in the almonds, remove from heat and beat until cold (use an electric beater), adding kirsch to taste, and just enough green colouring to produce a delicate tone. Knead the paste on icing sugar spread over a formica or marble surface, until the marzipan is coherent and firm.

To make the fruit purées, stew apricots or prunes with a very little water until they begin to be soft. Drain and weigh (discard prune stones first). Add about half the weight of fruit in sugar and sieve, or blend in a liquidizer using a little of the cooking liquor if the fruit sticks. Put the purée into a heavy pan and cook slowly over a steady heat until it dries to a thick mass. Extra sugar may be added but these purées should not be over-sweet. Remove from heat, flavour with kirsch (apricots) or rum (prunes) and leave to cool.

To fill the prunes, roll the paste or purées into fat nuggets and slip them into the prunes. The filling should show an almond-shaped bulge through the split in the prune. Make two or three light indentations across the filling at a slant, for decoration.

At the Maison Sabat, the fruit purées are piped into the prunes with a forcing bag before they have set. I think it's easier to shape the mixtures with a teaspoon, rolling them in caster sugar if they are a little sticky.

Bring sugar and water to the hard ball stage to make the coating syrup, and have ready an oiled rack. Quickly dip the prunes into the syrup (use a larding needle or knitting needle), and transfer them to the draining rack. This makes them shiny. It also makes them sticky, so put them into tiny paper cases before handing them round, or packing them into a small basket.

[*Good Things*]

# CHARCUTERIE

CHARCUTERIE AND FRENCH PORK COOKERY
was the first of Jane's long series of books on food and cooking.
Living in France, she became fascinated and delighted by the
skill of local *charcutiers*. A scheme was hatched with a friend to
write a book on the local subject, Jane as researcher, the friend
Adey as writer. In the end the task of writing it fell to Jane as
well, and *Charcuterie and French Pork Cookery* was published in
1967. It remains the best and only dedicated book written in
English on this vast and intricate subject, and deserves a chapter
all to itself.

Anyone visiting France soon becomes aware of the importance
of charcuterie shops in French daily life. The choice of pork
products is almost bewildering, many of them unfamiliar to
foreigners, all of them tempting. For Jane, at the beginning of
the French part of her and Geoffrey's life, the whole subject was
a treasure trove into which she plunged with characteristic
energy and lively curiosity.

The pleasure with which her chosen publisher must have
read Jane's manuscript can only be imagined. The pleasure the
published book has given, and will go on giving, may be judged
from the extracts which make up this third chapter of *The
Enjoyment of Food*.

It could be said that European civilization – and Chinese civilization too – has been founded on the pig. Easily domesticated,
omnivorous household and village scavenger, clearer of scrub and
undergrowth, devourer of forest acorns, yet content with a sty – and
delightful when cooked or cured, from his snout to his tail. There has
been prejudice against him, but those peoples – certainly *not* including
the French – who have disliked the pig and insist that he is unclean

eating, are rationalizing their own descent and past history: they were once nomads, and the one thing you can't do with a pig is to drive him in herds over vast distances.

The pig as we know him is of mixed descent. An art of *charcuterie* – the *chair cuit*, cooked meat, of the pig – could hardly have been developed very far, however much people relied on pig meat, fresh or cured, as the staff of life, with the medieval pig carved on misericords, or painted in the Labours of the Months (pig-killing in November, or pig-fattening with the acorn harvest). He was a lean, ridgy and rangy beast, with bristles down his back. Two thousand years ago the Gauls in France were excellent at curing pork, and Gallic hams were sent to Rome. But what made the pig of the European sty – rather than the pig of the autumn oak forests – really succulent, was a crossing of the European and Chinese pigs in England round about 1760, by the great Leicestershire stock-breeder, Robert Bakewell.

The Chinese porker was small, plump and short-legged. The European pig was skinny and long-legged like a wild boar. The cross between the two resulted in the huge pink beast of prints by James Ward of 160 years ago. Cobbett wrote that the cottager's pig should be too fat to walk more than 100 yards. Spreading through Europe, this was the creature on which French cooks got to work when the Revolution turned them out of their princely, aristocratic kitchens along the Loire and in the Île de France.

The trade of *charcutier* goes back at least as far as the time of classical Rome, where a variety of sausages could be bought, as well as the famous hams from Gaul. In such a large town slaughterhouses, butchers' and cooked meat shops were necessarily well organized to safeguard public health. This system was still being followed – after a fashion – in medieval Paris, although in the later Middle Ages a great increase in cooked meat purveyors put an intolerable strain on such control as there was. From this insalubrious chaos the *charcutiers* emerged and banded together, by edict of the king in 1476, for the sale of cooked pork only, and raw pork fat. But they did not have the right to slaughter the pigs they needed, which put them at the mercy of the general butchers until the next century. At the beginning of the seventeenth century *charcutiers* gained the right to sell all cuts of uncooked pork, not just the fat. Now the trade could develop in a logical manner. Incidentally in Lent, when meat sales declined, the *charcutier* was allowed to sell salted herrings and fish from the sea.

In the larger cities of the eighteenth century the *charcutier* developed a closer connexion with two other cooked meat sellers – the *tripier* who bought the insides of all animals from both butcher and *charcutier* and sold cooked tripe, and the *traiteur* who bought raw meat of all kinds and sold it cooked in sauces as *ragoûts*, either to be eaten at home or on his ever-increasing premises. Remember that for many people at all income levels the private kitchen was a poor affair, often non-existent; everyone sent out to the cooked food shops for ready-made dishes. It was a big trade, jealously guarded, so that the *traiteurs* considered that their functions as *ragoût*-makers had been usurped when a soup-maker, Boulanger, who described his dishes as '*restaurant*' or restorative, began to sell sheep's feet in sauce, to be consumed on his premises. He was taken to court in 1765 by the *traiteurs*, but he won, thereby gaining enormous publicity and a fashionable trade. More important still, he had broken through the closed shop organization by which the cooked food purveyors worked.

By the end of the century the guillotine had put many great cooks out of work. They soon saw the opportunities offered by the growing restaurant trade and the old cooked food trades *vis-à-vis* the more widely distributed prosperity of a new social order. The *traiteur* began to specialize in grand set pieces which he supplied on a catering basis to nineteenth-century bourgeois homes. The *charcutier* increased the range and quality of his pork products, and began to sell cooked tripe to his middle-class clients as well. Only the *tripier* seems to have lost in prestige, supplying poor families and shabby hotels with what Henry James described as 'a horrible mixture known as *gras-double*, a light grey, glutinous nauseating mess'.

In the twentieth century all these categories have become blurred at the edges and interdependent. They have also benefited from most stringent food laws. French small-town hoteliers and restaurateurs now delight their clients with delicious preliminaries to the main course, supplied usually from the *charcuterie* near-by rather than their own kitchens. This is where English hotels outside London are at such a disadvantage. There are no high-class cooked meat and bakery trades in this country. The chef with a small staff cannot send out for *saucisses en brioche*, *quiches lorraines*, or a good pâté, leaving him free, as in France, to concentrate on his meat, fish and sauces.

Towards the end of the nineteenth century, France, like every other European country, benefited from the development of refrigeration. Nobody needed the huge pig anymore. With cold storage, mild round-the-year ham and bacon curing became possible, which meant that less fat was needed to mitigate harsh-tasting lean meat. At the same time there was a big increase in machine and sedentary occupations, which lessened people's need for a high fat diet. So the pig grew smaller. Now his weight is watched as carefully as any film star's.

Probably the English pig is now being taken too far towards leanness, at any rate for the finer points of *charcuterie*. He has become too much a factory animal: we neglect his ears, his tail, his trotters, his insides, his beautiful fat and his flavour (pig's ears by the hundred thousand are fed to mink, from one of the Wiltshire bacon factories, which is a bit like feeding caviare to canaries). But with a little care and persistence the housewife can bully out of her butcher what is known as 'over-weight pig', and for very little money she can obtain the fat parts, as well as the extremities and the offal – the basis of many of the most delicate and delightful dishes it is possible to make. The skilful and economical housewife can buy a pig's head for very little; this is what she can make from it – pig's ears with a piquant sauce, brains in puff pastry, Bath chap, 750 g (1½ lb) of sausage-meat for making pâté, or *crépinettes*, and some excellent *rillons* which are more usually made from belly of pork. There is on average 2¼ kg (4½ lb) of boneless meat on a pig's head. And an excellent clear soup or aspic jelly is to be made from the bones.

So I hope that *Charcuterie and French Pork Cookery*, in some degree, will contribute to reinstating the pig in its variety in English kitchens, as well as help the holiday maker travelling in the country where the pig is most valued.

# TERRINES AND PÂTÉS

## WHAT IS A TERRINE, WHAT IS A PÂTÉ?

A meat loaf is a terrine, a pork pie is a pâté. But only from an academic point of view. Nowadays the words pâté and terrine are used interchangeably by French and English alike.

*Terrine*, with the same origin as our English *tureen*, means something made of earth, of *terra*; we use the word to describe a deep, straight-sided oval or oblong dish, and stretch it to include the contents.

*Pâté* shares a common Romance origin with English words such as patty, pastry, and paste, and with Italian and Spanish words like *pasta*. Even though derived from the Greek verb, Πασσω, to sprinkle, it early acquired cereal connotations. Sometimes pâtés are hot, sometimes cold. Pastry is kept mainly for hot pâtés (what we call pies), and for the finest cold pork-based pâtés, or game terrines. Flat strips of pork fat are used to preserve moisture and flavour in more humble mixtures.

Many modern English cookery books give excellent recipes for making pâtés. *Pâté maison* is on the menu in many English restaurants. It is the first thing travellers in France think of buying for a lunchtime picnic. In the midday shade of a walnut tree, or poplars bordering a canal, two or three pâtés are laid out on the cloth, with new crusted bread, good butter, fruit, cheese and wine – not always very good wine perhaps, but very good pâté, and each day's choice differing in flavour from the one before.

I am not thinking of exotics – the Pithivier lark pâté, for instance, the truffled *foie gras* pâtés of Perigord, or the superb range of Battendier's game pâtés in Paris – but of the simple pâtés produced in unique variety in every village in France, above the size of a hamlet.

Our small market town, Montoire, with its 2,708 inhabitants, has four *charcuteries*. There are three pâtés on sale daily (the number increases dramatically at the great Feasts and on Sundays) in each shop, *pâté de foie*, *pâté de campagne* and *pâté de lapin*. But none of them are quite the same, although the four *charcutiers* are using roughly similar recipes. So there is an immediate choice of twelve. Our own village of 549 inhabitants produces two pâtés – not counting *rillettes*, and *fromage de tête* and *hure* which further extend the picnicker's choice.

When you go into a strange *charcuterie*, be brave. Take your time and buy small amounts of all the pâtés. There will not be sulks and sighs *à l'anglaise* – nor murmurings from the other customers behind. An enterprising greed is the quickest way to any French person's generosity and kindness. Often persistence is rewarded by kindly hand-outs of *saucisson* and black olives to small daughters and sons.

All pâtés have a basis in the pig (though with the mouse-like ones it is a tenuous connexion, rather than a solid basis). Hare and game pâtés, for instance, often consist of small pieces or strips of the said creature layered with a pork forcemeat. As they cook slowly, pâtés have a permanent basting from the bards of pork fat which line the dish.

Variety, as I have said, is infinite. By the addition of different alcohols, different combinations of spices and herbs, orange juice and rind, an egg, a little flour, some truffle parings, one recipe can be stretched interestingly over months. You can chop the meat larger or smaller, or mince it. You can layer large pieces with a virtual mousse. You can pour off the fat after cooking and substitute a jelly made from game-bones, or flavoured with Madeira, or port, or lemon-juice. You can alter the flavour by keeping the pâté for a couple of days (indeed you should do this), or for weeks (run a good layer of lard or butter over the top) not in the deep freeze but just in the cool.

## PORK TERRINES

### Pâté de Campagne

*750 g (1½ lb) lean, boned shoulder of pork* (épaule)
*90 g (3 oz) veal, ham, or lean beef*
*250 g (½ lb) flair (leaf, flead, body) fat* (panne)
*250 g (½ lb) back fat* (gras dur), *cut into strips, or streaky bacon*
*250 g (½ lb) belly of pork* (lard de poitrine)
*seasonings – salt, pepper,* quatre-épices, *nutmeg, mace, crushed juniper*
　　*berries, thyme, parsley, garlic, etc.*
*150 ml (¼ pt) dry white wine*
*60–90 ml (2–3 fl oz) brandy, Calvados,* marc *or eau-de-vie*
*250 g (½ lb) onions, chopped*
*90 g (3 oz) butter or lard*
*1 level tablespoon flour*
*1 large egg, beaten*

If the butcher won't cut the back fat into thin slices, and you can't do it without slicing yourself, cut it as thin as you can safely manage, then beat it out with a wooden mallet. Salt and pepper lightly, leave in the cool. Caul fat, softened in tepid water, is a good substitute.

Chop all the other meat finely. Put it through the mincer if you must, but the Moulinette 68 is better. Mix in the seasonings you have chosen, and the alcohol, and leave to marinade overnight.

Next day cook the onions gently in the butter or lard until they are a golden hash. Do not brown them.

Beat the flour and egg together to a smooth paste, and add with the onions to the meat mixture.

Grease a terrine with lard. Any ovenproof dish will in fact do – there is no need to buy one of those dramatic dishes with dead hare lids, and simulated pastry sides. Provided it holds 1 litre (2 pt), it doesn't matter what shape it is. If you like, you can divide the mixture between several smaller dishes.

Some people line the terrine next with shortcrust pastry, and cover the meat with a decorated pastry lid. But unless you want that kind of a showpiece (which adds considerably to your labour), a lining of pork fat strips is quite enough.

The seasoning of pâtés is a personal affair, but allow for the fact that foods to be eaten cold need more seasoning than foods to be eaten hot. It's prudent to try out a small *rissole* (fried or baked), before irrevocably committing the pâté to the oven. Should you have overdone the seasoning, add more chopped meat, or – in desperate situations – some breadcrumbs.

Fill the terrine absolutely full, and mound over the top – it will shrink in the cooking. Lay a lattice of fat pork strips on top and cover with foil.

Stand the terrine in a larger pan of hot water, which should come about half-way up the side, and bake in a slow oven for 1½–3 hours, according to the depth of the dish: small but deep dishes of pâté take longer than wide, shallow ones. Oven temperature should be about gas 3–4, 170°C (340°F). The pâté is done when it appears to swim in fat, quite free of the sides of the terrine; you can also test it with a metal knitting or larding needle – if it comes out clean the pâté is cooked.

You can also cook pâtés like steamed puddings, on top of the stove. If you want an addition to the store cupboard, try bottling the pâté in preserving jars like fruit. It needs 2 hours' cooking. This is widely done in France.

Pâté can be served straight from the cooking dish. If you do this, remove the foil 20 minutes before the end of cooking time so that the top can brown appetizingly. Cool for 1 hour, then weight it gently.

Remember that it will taste better the next day.

For very elegant meals, the pâté is finished with meat jelly. If there is much fat, pour it off, add the jelly in a liquid state, and don't weight the pâté until the jelly is beginning to set. Be careful to eat the pâté within three days if you have a refrigerator, within two days at most if you haven't for jelly sours quickly. Flavour finally with Madeira or port.

If the pâté is to be the main dish of a meal, serve a green salad with it, and some small pickled gherkins. In France crusty bread is always served too, but English factory bread is flabby and needs toasting, or, better still, baking in thin slices to a golden brown crispness.

Although bottling is the best way of keeping pâté, it also keeps well under a 1-cm (½-inch) layer of lard, in a cool dry larder. A month is a safe length of time. To do this, allow the pâté to cool for an hour, then weight it not too heavily (a dish with a couple of tins on top, or a foil-covered board). Next day melt plenty of good quality lard and pour it over the pâté, so that it is completely covered to the depth of 1 cm (½ inch). When the lard has set cover it with silver foil, smoothing it on right close to the fat. Then put another piece of foil over the top, as if you were finally covering a jam pot. Store in the fridge if possible.

## Pig's Liver Pâté (Pâté de Foie de Porc)

> 750 g (1½ lb) pig's liver, weighed when hard bits are removed
> 750 g (1½ lb) belly of pork, salted in mild brine for 12 hours or
>   500 g (1 lb) fresh belly, 250 g (½ lb) green streaky bacon
> 250 g (½ lb) flair fat
> strips of hard back fat to line terrine and cover or a large piece
>   of caul fat
> 1 large egg
> 2 tablespoons flour blended with 150 ml (¼ pt) dry white wine
> seasonings to taste

Follow the recipe above.

## Veal and Pork Pâté (Pâté de Foie Fine)

> 500 g (1 lb) pig's liver
> 250 g (½ lb) lean veal (fillet) weighed without bone
>   (rouelle de veau)
> 250 g (½ lb) cooked ham fat, or very fatty ham
> 175 g (6 oz) fresh white breadcrumbs soaked in a little milk
> 2 large eggs
> 75 ml (½ gill) brandy, or other hard liquor
> 2 heaped tablespoons of parsley
> salt and spices according to taste, including a bay leaf
> 4 heaped tablespoons onion melted in some lard (do not brown it)
> plenty of fat bardes to line the terrine and cover

Mince the meat finely – mix everything together, except bards and bay leaf.

## Pâté in Pastry (Pâté de Viande de Chartres)

> FORCEMEAT
> 500 g (1 lb) lean shoulder of pork
> 500 g (1 lb) lean fillet of veal
> 250 g (½ lb) chicken livers
> 750 g (1½ lb) hard back fat
> 45 g (1½ oz) spices
> 30 ml (1 small liqueur glass) cognac or other brandy
> 60 ml (2 small liqueur glasses) port
> 5 egg yolks
> 250 ml (8 fl oz) cream

FILLING

250 g ( ½ lb) tongue
250 g ( ½ lb) ham
125 g ( ¼ lb) fillet veal
125 g ( ¼ lb) hard back fat
} *all cut in strips and marinaded for 2 hours in some brandy*

750 g (1 ½ lb) puff pastry

Line the terrine with pastry, keeping back enough for the lid. Layer forcemeat, filling, forcemeat, filling, and finally forcemeat. Put on the pastry lid and decorate. Do not stand in a pan of water, but bake in a slow oven for 2–2½ hours, protecting the top when necessary with greaseproof paper.

When the pâté is quite cold, pour in meat jelly flavoured with port. Do this through a funnel by way of vents in the pastry lid. Or remove the lid carefully with a sharp, pointed knife, so that it can be replaced tidily when the jelly has been poured over the filling.

## SWEETBREAD PÂTÉ (Pâté Chaud de Ris de Veau, or d'Agneau)

Here is a hot pâté of delicate flavour, whose ingredients are within the range of nearly every supermarket-goer. The result, though, does not betray its origins.

500 g (1 lb) sweetbreads (calves' or lambs')
chicken stock and a little lemon juice
375 g (¾ lb) lean pork, weighed without bone, or veal and pork
375 g (¾ lb) hard back pork fat
2 large eggs
1 tablespoon of flour, heaped
125 ml (4 fl oz) double cream
seasoning, salt, pepper and thyme
125 g (¼ lb) mushrooms
60 g (2 oz) butter
enough pastry to line and cover, made of:
250 g (8 oz) flour
150 g (5 oz) butter and lard, or butter
1 level tablespoon icing sugar, pinch salt, cold water

Stand the sweetbreads in cold, salted water for 1 hour. Then simmer them for 20 minutes in chicken stock, sharpened with a little lemon juice. Drain and take off the gristly hard bits and divide them into smallish pieces.

The forcemeat can be made whilst the sweetbreads are cooking. Mince the pork and fat as finely as you can. Add beaten eggs, flour, and cream. If you have an electric blender whirl the mixture in this. Season with salt and pepper, and thyme.

Slice the mushrooms (more than 125 g (¼ lb) does not hurt, and if you can use field mushrooms, or even better *Trompettes des Morts* (*Craterellus Cornucopioides*) the flavour will be greatly improved). Fry them lightly in butter. If you have plenty, mix half into the forcemeat after it has been whirled in the blender.

Now assemble the pie. Line a pie dish with pastry, then line the pastry with a thick layer of forcemeat, keeping aside enough to cover. Next put in the sweetbreads and mushrooms, and cover with the last of the forcemeat. Put on a pastry lid, decorate, knock up the edges and brush with egg yolk-and-water glaze. Bake in a moderate oven for 1 hour, protecting the pastry lid with greaseproof paper if necessary.

## CHICKEN LIVER PÂTÉ

Elizabeth David's version, quoted from *A Book of Mediterranean Food*, is the most popular with our visitors. I do it in the blender, however, putting the liquid from the pan in first then tipping the lightly cooked livers on to the fast whirling blades. Half quantities and a little more butter do very well – however the quantity can be divided amongst several small pots, covered with 1 cm (½ inch) of melted butter, and a foil lid, for eating on different occasions.

'Take about 500 g (1 lb) of chicken livers or mixed chicken, duck, pigeon or any game liver. Clean well and sauté in butter for 3 or 4 minutes. Remove the livers and to the butter in the pan add 30 ml (a small glass) of sherry and 30 ml (a small glass) of brandy. Mash the livers to a fine paste (they should be pink inside) with plenty of salt, black pepper, a clove of garlic, 60 g (2 oz) of butter, a pinch of mixed spice and a pinch of powdered herbs – thyme, basil and marjoram. Add the liquid from the pan, put the mixture into a small earthenware terrine and place on the ice.

'Serve with hot toast.'

## HARE PÂTÉ

Here is an old recipe for a hare pâté. Try it if you are having a large party, but it is prudent to bake the mixture in several terrines rather than in the one large stewpan recommended, then you can run a layer of lard over any you do not use at the time, and keep them for several weeks.

'Chop all the meat of a hare, and of a rabbit, half a leg of mutton, [1 kg] two pounds of fillet of veal or fresh pork, and [1 kg] two pounds of beef suet; season these with pepper and salt, fine spices pounded, chopped parsley, shallots, [125 g] a quarter of a pound of pistachio nuts peeled, about [500 g] a pound of raw ham [use uncooked gammon] cut into dice, [250 g] half a pound of truffles or mushrooms also cut into dice, six yolks of eggs, and [60 ml] one glass of good brandy; garnish a stew-pan all round with slices of lard, put all your preparation close into it, and cover it over with slices of lard [i.e. hard back fat, not the modern lard but the French *lard*] also, rather thick; stop the pan all round with a coarse paste, and bake it about four hours; let it cool in the same pan, then turn it over gently; scrape the lard quite off, or leave a little of it, and garnish it with any sorts of colours; or to make it more even, and to give it a better form, cover it over with hog's lard or butter, in order to garnish it with different colours according as your taste shall direct.'

## RABBIT PÂTÉ (Terrine de Lapin)

I find that this is the most successful hot rabbit recipe, as well as one of the simplest. It is, in effect, a hot pâté or pie – which I have put here as it does not require pastry, as most hot pâtés do.

> *1 rabbit*
> *plenty of strips of hard back fat*
> *plenty of chopped onions – about 250–375 g ( ½–¾ lb)*
> *2 medium carrots, chopped*
> *plenty of thyme*
> *garlic, spices, salt and pepper, according to taste*

Joint the rabbit, then cut the joints into suitable serving pieces. Do not bone.

Line the terrine with strips of fat, as if you were going to make an ordinary pâté.

Put in a layer of rabbit, then a good layer of chopped vegetables, thyme, spices and so on, then a few strips of fat – no need to cover the layer completely. Then another layer of rabbit, the rest of the vegetables and spices, then a complete cover of strips of fat. Pour in enough dry white wine or *rosé* to come about half-way up the meat, and 2 liqueur glasses (60 ml or 2 fl oz) brandy or *eau-de-vie de marc*.

Fix the lid on with flour-and-water paste, or use a double-layer of foil as a lid, stand the terrine in a shallow pan of hot water and cook in a slow oven for 2 hours.

Serve with boiled potatoes, and a plain green salad to follow.

This recipe sounds disgustingly fatty – but it isn't. The best flavour is obtained by using a wild rabbit (*lapin de la garenne*).

## PORK AND GAME PÂTÉ (Terrine de Porc et de Gibier)

Here is one of Elizabeth David's recipes for a pâté that is on a somewhat larger scale, suitable for a party or for a buffet supper. It will be sufficient for 20–25 people, and is all the better for being made 3 or 4 days in advance.

Quantities are 1 kg (2 lb) each of belly of pork and leg of veal (the pieces sold by some butchers as pie veal will do, as these are usually oddments of good quality trimmed from escalopes and so on), 250 g (½ lb) of back pork fat, and 1 wild duck or pheasant. For the seasoning you need 250 ml (2 teacups or 8 fl oz) of dry white wine, 1 tablespoon of salt, 8–10 juniper berries, 1 large clove of garlic, 10 peppercorns, 2 tablespoons of stock made from the duck carcase with a little extra white wine or Madeira.

Mince the pork and the veal together, or to save time get the butcher to do this for you. Partly roast the duck or pheasant, take all the flesh from the bones, chop fairly small, and mix with the pork and veal. Add 150 g (5 oz) of the fat cut into little pieces, the garlic, juniper berries, and peppercorns all chopped together, and the salt. Pour in the white wine, amalgamate thoroughly, and leave in a cold place while you cook the duck carcase and the trimmings in a little water and wine with seasonings to make the stock. Strain it, reduce to 2 good tablespoons, and add to the mixture (if it is necessary to expedite matters, this part of the preparation can be dispensed with altogether; it is to add a little extra gamey flavour to the pâté).

Turn into a 2-litre (3-pt) terrine; cover the top with a criss-cross pattern of the rest of the pork fat cut into little strips. Cover with foil. Stand in a baking tin containing water, and cook in a low oven, gas 3, 160°C (330°F), for 2 hours. During the last 15 minutes remove the paper, and the top of the pâté will cook to a beautiful golden brown.

One wild duck or pheasant to 2 kg (4 lb) of meat sounds a very small proportion for a game pâté, but will give sufficiently strong flavour for most tastes. Also the seasonings of garlic, pepper, and juniper berries are kept in very moderate proportions when the pâté is for people who may not be accustomed to these rather strong flavours, and with whose tastes one may not be familiar.

## GALANTINES

The derivation of the word galantine is obscure. Snowdrops, rushes with aromatic roots, Chinese galangale (a mild spice of the ginger family), gelatine and the popular fish galantines of the Middle Ages, have all assisted, incongruously, in the speculations. But from a *charcuterie* point of view, the word takes on interest in the mid-eighteenth century, meaning then 'a particular way of dressing a pig'. By the turn of the century galantine was used in France in its modern sense to describe a cold dish of chicken, turkey, etc., and veal, boned, stuffed, simmered in a cloth and pressed, making an elegant appearance swathed in and surrounded by its own jelly. Although talking of fish, Chaucer nicely described the emotions a galantine in its jelly might arouse:

> *Was never pyk walwed in galauntyne*
> *As I in love am walwed and y-wounde.*

Such enthusiasm is particularly delightful to the cook, because a galantine is not at all a difficult dish; its preparation is lengthy, but the result is never in question. Like pâtés, it should be prepared at least a day in advance for all the ingredients to settle down together and mature.

In the *charcuterie*, the galantines look like pale-coloured pâtés, with a geometric patterning of fat, truffles, pistachio nuts, tongue, *foie gras*, and jelly. From a commercial point of view it is necessary to prepare them in long metal loaf-tins, rather than with boned birds, so that every customer's slice has its exact share of all the good things. I find these galantines disappointing, very often. Their almost classical intarsia prepares one for a supreme experience, and of course one is let down. Galantine of rabbit or pig's head is inevitably prepared in this way, but for attractiveness and flavour, poultry, veal and game galantines should be tackled like this:

*chicken, weighing about 2 kg (4 lb) when dressed*

FORCEMEAT
*625 g (1¼ lb) lean meat (pork, pork and veal, or veal and ham)*
*500 g (1 lb) hard back pork fat*
*125 g (¼ lb) streaky bacon*
*2 eggs*
*herbs, spices, salt and pepper*

OPTIONAL SALPICON
*pistachio nuts, blanched*
*125 g (¼ lb) cold pickled tongue*
*125 g (¼ lb) ham fat or pork fat*
*truffles*
foie gras
*liver from the chicken*
*brandy, Madeira, sherry or* eau-de-vie

STOCK
*calf's foot, or pig's trotters*
*veal, ham or pork bones*
*1 onion stuck with 4 cloves*
*1 carrot*
bouquet garni
*375 ml (½ bottle) dry white wine*
*stock made from chicken bouillon cubes*

Choose a mature bird. Battery chicken is useless, as flavour is needed.

Cut the flesh from neck to tail down the back, and by using a very sharp knife to scrape the flesh off the bone, you will not find it difficult to achieve a flat, if locally lumpy, oblong of bird. Do not pierce the skin, though this can be remedied by removing a piece of flesh from, say, the leg and lying it over the small tear. The worst part is the legs. Take your time, and gradually pull the muscles and skin off inside out, as your knife loosens them from the bone. Lay the final result, skin side down, on a clean cloth and distribute extra bits of flesh over the thinly covered parts. But don't get fussy and niggly with it. Sprinkle on some salt and pepper; leave in the cool.

Put the carcase on to boil in a large pan, together with a calf's foot or pig's trotters, a ham bone if you have one, 1 onion stuck with 4 cloves, 1 carrot, *bouquet garni*, and a mixture of wine and stock. Any other scraps of pork skin, or pork, veal or poultry bones, would not come amiss. You need as good a stock as you can make.

Assemble any attractive bits and pieces that you can manage – the liver of the bird, *foie gras*, truffles, pistachio nuts, cold tongue, cold ham, ham fat or pork fat – and decide whether you are going to make a formal arrangement, or whether you are going to dice these and mix them right in with a fine forcemeat. This collection of larger pieces is known as a *salpicon*. Leave them to marinade in some brandy or Madeira or sherry.

Make the forcemeat – as fine as you can – of *equal parts of lean and fat meats*: pork entirely, with a little bacon, if you like; or lean veal and lean ham and fat pork; or the lean flesh from an extra bird and veal or pork or both, and an equal quantity of fat pork. You need about 1 kg (2 lb) for a 2 kg (4 lb) chicken, correspondingly more for a turkey, less for a partridge or pheasant. Bind with 2 eggs; season with salt, pepper, herbs, spices, according to your preference and the creature concerned.

I don't advise the use of shop-bought sausage-meat, ever. It's too stodgy. If you can't face the tough mincing required, ask the butcher to do it for you.

If you want to include the *salpicon*,
*either* add it to the forcemeat, stirring it in well, so that you have an evenly marbled mass to lay on the boned chicken,
*or* put two layers of it, attractively arranged, between three layers of forcemeat, on the boned chicken.

If you are omitting the *salpicon*, lay the forcemeat by itself on the chicken.

The next step is to wrap the back edges up and over the forcemeat, etc., and sew it into a rough chicken-shape. Wrap this tightly in cheesecloth and tie the ends securely.

Meanwhile the stock ingredients have been bubbling away. Let them have 2 hours before adding the bird, which also requires 2 hours once the liquid has returned to the boil. Keep it simmering gently, not galloping.

Take the pan off the heat, but don't remove the chicken for another hour. You have to squeeze a good deal of liquid out of it, so you don't want it too hot. On the other hand, don't squeeze it dry either, and don't put too heavy a board and weight on it – you want a succulent galantine. Forget about it overnight.

For the jelly, you use the simmering liquid. Strain it and taste. Reduce if necessary, or zip it up with extra seasonings, lemon juice, Madeira, port, sherry. Leave it in a bowl to cool – it will be much easier to remove fat from jelly than from liquid.

If the liquid doesn't gel, or doesn't gel firmly enough, add gelatine crystals (15 ml to 600 ml (½ oz to 1 pt)).

If the jelly is murky, clarify it.

Next day unwrap the chicken, very carefully, remove the button thread, and put it on a wire rack over a dish. Melt a little of the jelly until it just runs and brush it over the bird. You can then put some decorations on, once the jelly has reset. Brush on another layer to hold the decorations. When that has set, transfer the chicken to the final serving dish. Arrange round it chopped jelly, holding back some to whip into mayonnaise.

Everyone has their own ideas on decoration. But I would recommend the abstract and simple – tomato flowers and cucumber leaves raise suspicions that the cook has got something to hide. Picot-edged oranges and daisied eggs are for spoiling the fun at nursery teaparties, where chocolate biscuits and sardine sandwiches would be much more welcome, and at wedding receptions, where one begins truly to understand how England acquired her unenviable gastronomic reputation.

# SAUSAGES

## SAUSAGES AND SAUSAGE-MEAT

Sausage, *saucisse*, *saucisson*, derive ultimately from the Latin *salsus*, salted, probably by way of a Late Latin word *salsicia*, something prepared by salting. The Romans are, in fact, the first recorded sausage-makers, their intention being – as the derivation suggests – to preserve the smaller parts and scraps of the pig for winter eating. Though unwise to say so in a Frenchman's hearing, the Italians are still the supreme producers of dried and smoked sausages. They use beef, as well as pork, but not usually donkey as some Frenchmen firmly believe.

For the fresh sausage, France is the country. It is still an honourable form of nourishment and pleasure there, protected by law from the addition of cereals and preservatives, produced in ebullient variety – both regional and individual – by thousands of *charcutiers*. In other words, the French sausage is freshly made, well-flavoured, and, apart from seasonings, 100 per cent meat. Inevitably you pay more than in England, but the money is better spent. For picnickers the sausage is an ideal alternative to pâtés; cook it in foil in hot wood ashes, or unwrapped on a metal grill. At the weekends, look out for the light puff-pastry sausage rolls, *friandises*, and on Sundays for the luxurious *saucisse en brioche*, which can be bought by the piece – though if you want to be sure of it, order on Thursdays, no later.

Although the meat is basically pork, from neck and shoulders and fat belly, a resourceful use of seasonings (spices, onions, sweet peppers, chestnuts, pistachio nuts, spinach, quite large amounts of sage or parsley, champagne, truffles) produces a variety of sausages that an English traveller, going through France for the first time, may find bewildering.

Making a good sausage is a simple affair, though you mightn't think so from the nasty pink packages sold in grocers' and butchers' shops in this country. Even if you haven't an electric mixer with a sausage-making attachment, you have two alternatives: prepare the mixture and take it in a bowl to your butcher for him to put into skins; or else buy a good sized piece of caul fat as well as the pork and make *crépinettes* – little parcels of sausage-meat wrapped in beautiful veined white fat and either fried or grilled – or *gayettes*, or faggots which closely resemble *gayettes*. Some cookery books suggest frying the meat in a *rissole* shape, with perhaps an egg and breadcrumb coating, but *crépinettes* are a more succulent solution.

First of all, though, sausage-meat. It is so simple to buy the necessary lean and fat pork and put it through the mincer that I cannot see why butchers find it worth their while to sell sausage-meat, with its high proportion of cereal and its poor seasoning.

### Sausage-Meat (Chair à Saucisse)

> *500 g (1 lb) lean pork from neck or shoulder*
> *250 g (½ lb) hard back fat*
> *1 level tablespoon salt*
> *½ teaspoon* quatre-épices, *or spices to taste*
> *freshly ground black pepper*
> *plenty of parsley, or sage, or thyme*

Put the lean and fat pork through the mincer once, or twice, according to the texture desired. Season.

> *Or*
> *500 g (1 lb) lean pork from neck or shoulder*
> *500 g (1 lb) hard back fat*
> *1 rounded tablespoon salt*
> *1 teaspoon spices or* quatre-épices *or cinnamon alone*
> *freshly ground black pepper*
> *plenty of parsley, or sage, or thyme*

Prepare as above.

> *Or*
> *250 g (½ lb) lean pork from neck or shoulder*
> *250 g (½ lb) veal*
> *250 g (½ lb) hard back fat, or green bacon fat*
> *seasonings to taste*

*Or*
*250 g ( ½ lb) poultry, game*
*125 g ( ¼ lb) pork, lean*
*125 g ( ¼ lb) veal*
*250 g ( ½ lb) hard back fat*
*seasonings to taste*

*Note:* if you want to bind these sausage-meats or forcemeats ( *farces*), say for stuffing a bird, or making a pâté, remember these proportions:
To 500 g (1 lb) of meat (lean and fat)

*1 whole egg*
*1 level tablespoon salt*
*1 level teaspoon spices*

Optional extras:
*60 ml (2 fl oz) brandy*
*30–60 g (1–2 oz) breadcrumbs*

## FAGGOTS (Gayettes de Provence)

*Gayettes*, a French equivalent to our West Country faggots, are often to be found in *charcuteries* and homely restaurants in Provence and the Ardèche, where they make a speciality of *gayettes aux épinards* (page 171). They look like faggots, very appetizing in their brown hummocky rows. Strictly for hungry picnickers on chilly days, when they taste delicious if you wrap them in a double layer of silver foil and reheat in wood ashes on the edge of the fire. The non-spinach *gayettes* are often eaten cold, in slices, as an hors d'œuvre. I recommend black olives with them, and plenty of bread and unsalted butter.

*500 g (1 lb) pig's liver*
*125 g ( ¼ lb) hard back fat*
*125 g ( ¼ lb) lean pork (neck or shoulder)*
*pieces of caul fat*
*2 cloves of garlic, crushed*
*salt, pepper and spices to taste*
*plenty of parsley, or other herb, chopped*

Mince the meat, season and wrap in pieces of caul fat – as for *crépinettes*, but *gayettes* are more the shape of small round dumplings. Lay them close together in a lard-greased baking dish. The oval, yellow and brown French gratin dishes are ideal.

Melt a little lard and pour over. Bake for 40 minutes in a medium oven. The top will brown nicely, and you can turn them over after 20 minutes, though this is not the conventional thing to do. Like faggots, *gayettes* are good tempered – you can stretch the cooking time with a slower oven and raise the heat to brown them at the end. Eat cold, sliced, as an hors d'œuvre.

## Poor Man's Faggots (Gayettes)

From the *charcutier's* point of view, *gayettes* are a way of using up the pig's lungs and spleen. If you want to be really economical, you can do the same and ask the butcher for a mixture of liver, lights and spleen, with more liver than anything else. Cut off all the gristly bits when you get home, weigh the result, and add one-third of the weight in sausage-meat (half fat, half lean pork).

Then follow the above recipe.

## Spinach Faggots (Gayettes aux Épinards)

> 250 g (½ lb) sausage-meat (half lean pork, half back fat)
> 250 g (½ lb) Swiss chard leaves, or spinach or perpetual beet (poirée)
> 250 g (½ lb) spinach (épinard)
> a few leaves of garden sorrel (oseille)
> 60 g (2 oz) plain flour
> a dash of hard liquor
> caul fat
> salt and pepper and spices

Wash the beet greens and spinach, shake off as much water as possible, and put in a pan over a low heat with a knob of butter or lard. No extra water should be needed, if you keep the pan covered and shake well from time to time to prevent sticking. Drain well, and chop with the *uncooked* sorrel. Stir in the flour, then the sausage-meat and seasonings. Finish like *gayettes de provence*, but eat them hot.

*Note:* Frozen spinach does quite well, follow instructions on the packet and dry thoroughly. Allow for different quantity.

If you can't get beet leaves, use all spinach and a stalk of celery chopped finely but not to a mush.

If you can't get sorrel, use a squeeze or two of lemon juice. Though I should say, go out and buy of a packet of sorrel seed immediately. Once sown, it's there for ever, welcoming the spring with its clear sharp taste and lasting until the first severe frosts. Invaluable for soups, spinach purées and sauces for veal or fish.

## LARGE SAUSAGES (Saucissons)

On a row of hooks in the *charcuterie*, above the small, fresh sausages, the *boudins blancs*, and the *boudins noirs*, hang the medium-sized saveloy-type *saucissons*, for boiling and eating hot or cold. Beside them are ranged the very large keeping sausages (*saucissons secs*), which the *charcutier* sometimes makes himself, but which are usually supplied from a factory, as they are to delicatessen shops in this country. They are easy to recognize, meshed in string, wrapped in gold, silver and coloured foils, and cheerfully labelled. Like the fresh sausage, they must be all meat, predominantly pork – if horse-meat, for instance, is used, the label must say so. The more unfamiliar, black-skinned *andouilles*, or large tripe sausages (page 189), hang with them, slicing to a greyish-brown, beautifully marbled surface.

You can buy these sausages whole, for storing from hooks in your own larder, and in miniature for modern, small-family convenience, but mostly they are sold in slices, by weight. Eat them as they are, with hunks of bread and butter; olives go well too and can be bought at most *charcuteries*. A good picnic idea is to heat through some garlic sausage (*saucisson à l'ail*) and a piece of *petit salé* (cooked, pickled pork) with a large tin of pork and beans French-style (*cassoulet*, page 173).

In town *charcuteries* you will often find a variety of regional, national and international *saucissons*. Forget about the ones you know. Buy 50 g (just under 2 oz) of as many as you can afford – if they are well wrapped, then re-wrapped after the picnic, they will survive days of heat and car-travel in good condition. Often there will be local names, so point and don't lose heart. French patience is endless in matters of food, even in busy shops. Explain that you would like to make an hors d'œuvre of as many kinds of *saucisson* as possible, particularly *les spécialités de la région*. One name that we always remember is *gendarme*, given to flat, strappy, yellow and brown speckled sausages in the Jura.

Buying *saucissons* in small quantities, whilst coping simultaneously with decimal weights and currency, one is only dimly aware of the high cost per pound. With an all-meat sausage you expect to pay more, but in the case of *saucissons secs* there is inevitably a good deal of shrinkage in the processes of drying and maturing, which pushes the price up higher still.

To make these sausages at home, you need skins made from the large intestine. If you have a farmhouse kitchen, with a solid fuel stove and plenty of old hooks attached to the beams, you are well away because the *saucissons* need to be dried at a temperature of 15°C (60°F), and a steady temperature at that. You can store them in a cooler larder when the drying is completed, but once again they should hang so that air circulates all round them. Avoid a steamy humid atmosphere.

As well as the right physical conditions, you need patience too because this type of sausage needs at least a month in which to mature, whether or not it is smoked; some kinds need six months. They will be covered with white powdery flowers from about the sixth day: '*cette fleur est constituée par des micro-organismes de la famille des levures, qui préparent le climat idéal pour le développement d'autres microbes qui feront subir à la viande la transformation voulue d'onctuosité et de goût.*' In other words, leave the white organism alone to do its work of maturing the sausage. Don't worry if the sausage shrinks, it will lose up to 40 per cent of its weight.

## CASSOULET

The tastiest form of baked beans is *cassoulet*, a rich slowly-cooked dish of dried white haricot beans, goose, salt pork, sausages large and small including the Toulouse sausage, small squares of pork skin to make the sauce smooth and bland, and breadcrumbs to form the crusty golden top. Languedoc is the native home of *cassoulet*, more specifically the small town of Castelnaudary on the Canal du Midi, whose classic version was described by Anatole France as having 'a taste, which one finds in the paintings of old Venetian masters, in the amber flesh tints of their women'. At Toulouse and Carcassonne cooks add mutton and partridge.

This dish needs careful planning and preparation. It is not cheap. The ideal time to choose for it is when you are able to have a goose: keep the legs to one side, turn them over daily in a mixture of 60 g (2 oz) unadulterated salt and a small pinch of saltpetre. Invite your guests and assemble the other ingredients.

Good beans are worth an effort. Most grocers sell dried white haricot beans vaguely described as Foreign. Better quality and a creamier texture are to be found in Soho, where grocers import beans from France, varieties known as Soissons and Arpajon from the market-gardening centres near Paris where they were first developed. Like geese, dried beans are at their best in the autumn; with time they become drier and harder and harder and drier, so beware the grocer with a slow turnover.

The other main requirement is a deep wide earthenware pot in which all the ingredients are finally amalgamated. Correctly a *cassole* or *toupin*, any earthenware or stoneware casserole will do, provided it is deep and wide.

Serves 6–8

BEANS
*500 g (1 lb) haricot beans*
*a good-sized piece of pork or bacon skin, cut into squares*
*a knuckle of pork*
*500 g (1 lb) salt belly of pork*
*1 large onion stuck with 4 cloves*
*1 carrot*
*4 cloves garlic*
bouquet garni

PORK AND GOOSE, OR MUTTON RAGOÛT
*500 g (1 lb) boned shoulder of pork*
*750 g–1 kg (1½–2 lb) preserved goose (*confits d'oie*), or duck, or*
*either made up to weight with boned loin or shoulder of mutton*
*3 large onions, chopped*
*4 large skinned tomatoes, 3 tablespoons tomato extract*
*6 cloves of garlic, or according to taste*
bouquet garni, *salt and ground black pepper*
*beef stock*
*goose or duck fat, or lard*

SAUSAGES
*500 g (1 lb) Toulouse sausages, or* saucisses de Campagne, *or a*
*large 500 g (1 lb) boiling sausage of the all-meat* cervelas *type, or*
*the pork boiling rings sold in delicatessen shops*
*500 g (1 lb) saucisson à l'ail*

*plenty of white breadcrumbs to form a top crust*

Soak the haricot beans overnight. Drain and put them in an earthenware pot with the other ingredients; cover with water. Bring to the boil, and cook in a gentle oven for 1½ hours, or until the beans are tender but not splitting.

Meanwhile prepare the pork and goose *ragoût*. Put the chopped onions on to melt to a golden hash in a large frying pan (preferably cast iron). Cut the various meats into eating-sized pieces, or joints, and add them to the onions. Turn up the heat a little so that they can brown, without burning. Pour off any surplus fat, then add the tomatoes skinned and chopped into large chunks, and a little stock, about 150 ml (¼ pt), to make enough sauce for the meat to continue cooking in. Flavour with concentrated tomato extract and seasonings, push the *bouquet garni* into the middle. Cover the pan, and keep the contents at a gentle bubble until the beans are ready – about 30 minutes.

Add the large *saucisson à l'ail* and the *cervelas* to the beans, so that they have 30 minutes' simmering. If you are using sausages, stiffen them in a little goose fat or lard for 10 minutes.

When the beans are cooked, drain off and keep the liquid; remove the onion, carrot, *bouquet garni*, and knuckle bone, and slice the salt pork and knuckle meat. Use the bacon skins, or pork skins, to line the deep earthenware pot you intend to use for the final cooking. Put in half the beans, then the pork and goose *ragoût*, the sliced meats from the bean cooking pot, the small and large sausages, and the rest of the beans. Pour over 150 ml (¼ pt) of the bean liquid, and finish with a 1-cm (½-inch) layer of breadcrumbs dotted with pieces of goose fat or lard.

Cook very slowly, about gas 2, 150°C (300°F), for 1½ hours. The crust will turn a beautiful golden colour, and traditionally you should push it down with a spoon 3–7 times, so that it can re-form with the aid of another sprinkling of breadcrumbs.

The point of this last cooking is to blend all the delicious flavours together gently, without the meat becoming tasteless and stringy. Everything has, after all, already been cooked. If you find that the *cassoulet* is becoming too dry, add a little more of the bean liquid, but don't overdo this.

The quantities can be varied; the essentials are beans, sausages, pork and goose (or goose and mutton, or a small roasting duck). Pork and beans alone are very good (see below, and recipes for Boston baked beans, etc.), but it is the goose or duck that makes the difference.

This is an ideal dish for a winter's Sunday lunch-party – it pleases everybody from children to grandparents. The cook should be pleased too, because her guests should not be allowed to eat too much beforehand, and can't eat much afterwards, so her labours are cut to a minimum.

**Cassoulet with Gascogne Butter** (Cassoulet au Beurre de Gascogne)

Here is a simple family version of *cassoulet*. An excellent filler on a cold day, which can be prepared after breakfast – if you omit the sausage, or use small ones – and left to look after itself until 30 minutes before lunch.

Serves 4

*500 g (1 lb) haricot beans*
*pieces of fresh pork skin*
*500 g (1 lb) piece of* petit salé, *uncooked, or brine-pickled pork belly*
*1 large French sausage of the boiling type, or small smoked sausages*

BEURRE DE GASCOGNE
*8 cloves of garlic*
*90 g (3 oz) lard, goose, duck or chicken fat*
*2 tablespoons chopped parsley*

Soak the beans overnight.

Next day line the casserole with the fresh pork skin, outside down, and put the piece of pork on top. If you use *petit salé*, make sure that the salt is washed off first. Pack in the beans around and on top. Just cover with water, and put on a close-fitting lid. Give it 3 hours in a slow oven, gas 2, 150°C (300°F). Add no salt at this stage.

If you use a large sausage, add it 1 hour before the end of cooking time. If you use small sausages, add them 30 minutes before. Taste the *cassoulet* whilst you do this and add salt, pepper, etc. Make the *beurre de Gascogne* by blanching the cloves of garlic in salted boiling water for 5–10 minutes. Pound them to a paste adding the 90 g (3 oz) of fat and finally the parsley.

Just before serving, strain off the liquid from the beans and pork, taste again and adjust the seasoning. Mix in the *beurre de Gascogne* at the last moment before serving.

*Note:* if you have no pure fat or dripping, use olive oil or butter.


## CABBAGE HOT POT (Potée)

*Potée* is basically a cabbage soup, in the way that *cassoulet* is basically beans and pork. But the addition of other vegetables as well as sausages and pickled meat makes it a complete meal in one pot, again like *cassoulet*. In the south-west of France, this thick soup is called *garbure* and contains, inevitably, *confits d'oie*. Country housewives use what they have to hand in their own kitchens and attic store, so the ingredients vary; but here is a suggested list and basic method:

Serves 4–6

*1 good crisp Savoy cabbage*
*500 g (1 lb) salt belly of pork, or green streaky bacon in a piece*

*a large piece of pork skin*
*3 leeks, sliced*
*6 medium-sized potatoes*
*12 new carrots, or 4 old ones cut in pieces*
*4 small onions*
*a piece of garlic sausage, or boiling sausage* (saucisson à l'ail)
*green beans and peas, if in season*
*Toulouse or Country sausages, or dried or smoked sausages*

Cut the cabbage into quarters, plunge it into boiling water to blanch for 10 minutes. Leave it to drain.

Put the pork or bacon and pork skin in a pot and cover with water. Don't add salt. Simmer for 30 minutes.

Add the leeks, potatoes, carrots and onions, and any other root vegetables you want to use. Simmer for 30 minutes. Add the garlic sausage, peas and beans – and the smoked or dried sausages if you are using them. Simmer for 30 minutes.

Meanwhile slice up the blanched cabbage, stiffen the fresh sausages for 10 minutes in lard or butter, and add them to the *potée* 5 minutes before serving. Remove the piece of salt pork, so that it can be sliced too, then returned to the pot. Taste, and correct seasoning.

One French custom is to add thick slices of wholemeal bread just before serving the soup, but it is usually best to leave people to do this for themselves in case they are watching their weight. A more popular tradition is the addition of a glass of red or white wine to the last few spoonfuls of soup in one's plate – this is known as a *goudale* in the Béarn, where much *garbure* is consumed.

# HAMS AND SALT PORK

## COOKING AND CARVING

With home-cured ham particularly, make absolutely sure that it is still good before you cook it. It should smell unsuspicious and appetizing. Push a larding or metal knitting needle right into the middle of the ham, it should come out clean and sweet.

### Soaking
The point of soaking is to remove excess salt, and to restore moisture to the dried-out tissues.

It follows therefore that salt pork and very lightly cured hams (*Jambons de Paris*) need no soaking.

On the other hand, home-cured hams, which have been subjected to a prolonged curing followed by smoking, need to be left in water overnight.

With commercial hams, follow the instructions provided with them. Otherwise make enquiries from the supplier. For mild cures 4–6 hours soaking may well be enough.

Very large hams need longer than small hams cured in the same way.

But don't worry. You will have a further chance to rectify saltiness in the cooking process.

### Cooking utensils

Borrow or buy a ham kettle.

If this is impossible, try to find a pot large enough to hold the ham with *plenty of water*. In the case of a large ham, a washing copper is a good solution. This also enables you to suspend the ham, by a strong, clean cord, so that the more quickly cooked knuckle end is out of the water.

### Cooking

Weigh the salt pork, or soaked ham. Calculate the cooking time. *Salt pork and smaller hams, up to 2 kg (4 lb)*, reckon 30 minutes per 500 g (1 lb), plus an extra 30 minutes. But watch the joint – the last 30 minutes may be unnecessary: if so, take the pot to the side of the stove and leave the joint in the liquid to keep hot. Or glaze it in the oven.

*Hams of 2½ kg (5 lb) and over, up to 5 kg (10 lb)*, 20 minutes per pound, plus 20 minutes.

*Hams of 5 kg (10 lb) and over*, the period of time gets progressively less. The diagram on page 179, from Bulletin 127, Ministry of Agriculture and Fisheries, *Home Curing of Bacon and Hams*, gives you the answer.

Draw a vertical line from the kg/lb to the diagonal, and a horizontal line from the point where they intersect to the hours' scale. In other words, a ham just over 8 kg (16 lb) needs 4 hours' cooking.

Put the joint or ham into the pot, cover with plenty of cold water and bring slowly to the boil. Count your cooking time from now, and keep the water at a simmer. After 10–15 minutes, taste the water. If it is unpleasantly salty, throw it away and start again, reckoning the cooking time from the second boiling point, *less 10–15 minutes*.

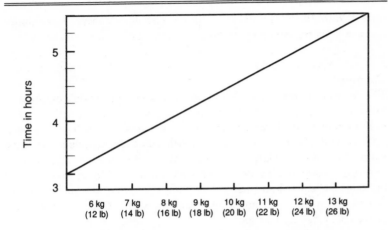

## Finishing – cold ham

When the ham is cooked, leave it to cool for 1–2 hours in the liquid. Then remove it, and take off the skin. Toast plenty of white breadcrumbs and press them into the fat of the ham whilst both are still warm.

(If the ham was cooked boneless, let it cool for 1 hour in the liquid, remove the skin, and press the ham, either with a board and weight, or with a weight into an appropriately-shaped mould. Remove string afterwards, and cloth, if it was cooked in a cloth.)

Leave the ham to set in a cool place for 12 hours. This makes it much easier to carve.

## Finishing – hot ham

The simplest and most attractive way to finish a hot ham is to glaze it.

Remove the ham from the cooking liquid 30 minutes before the end of cooking time. Peel off the skin, and smear the ham with, for instance, a mixture of brown sugar and French mustard, or brown sugar and mustard powder, moistened with a little of the cooking liquor.

Put it in a moderate oven for the rest of the cooking time.

There are endless variations and complications on this theme. You can invent more for yourself, remembering that the most successful glazes combine sweetness and spiciness. One attractive finish is achieved by scoring the fat of the ham in a lattice pattern, studding the intersections with cloves, and then smearing the glaze on gently. Be careful not to score right through the fat to the lean. The juices from the glazing can be turned into the sauce, with a little extra liquid from the boiling operation, or cream, or a wine like Madeira, Marsala, port, sherry, etc.

## Carving

The essential requirement is a very sharp knife, preferably one with a long, thin blade.

Remember that there are right and left hams, if your ham has been cooked on the bone. If the ham is boneless and pressed, you will carve it straight down, so right and left are of no consequence. The knuckle must lie towards the carver – to his left for a right-hand ham, and to his right for a left-hand ham. Cut each slice from alternate sides, as thinly as possible with an even smooth movement of the knife – this prevents a ridgy appearance.

## HAM IN MADEIRA SAUCE (Jambon au Madère)

Cook the ham in a bouillon for three-quarters of its cooking time – reckon 20 minutes per 500 g (1 lb) plus 20 minutes, from the time it reaches simmering point. See page 178.

Skin the ham and transfer it to a closer-fitting pot. Pour ½ litre (¾ pt) of Madeira, put on the lid and cook in a moderate oven for 50 minutes or the rest of the cooking time – whichever is the longer.

Transfer the ham again to a shallow dish, sprinkle it with icing sugar, or a brown sugar, spices and French mustard glaze, and put it to melt in a hot oven. See that it doesn't burn but turns to a succulent golden sheen.

Meanwhile deal with the sauce. Taste the braising liquid – add some stock or Madeira, reduce it or leave it alone, according to your judgement. Thicken it by adding a little knob of *beurre manié* (1 tablespoon of flour kneaded into ½ tablespoon of butter).

## Variations and accompaniments

Use another fortified wine – Marsala, port, sherry, or any heavy wine, instead of Madeira.

Serve with a cream sauce made by reducing the braising liquid and adding 300 ml (½ pt) of double cream. Surround the glazed ham with little piles of vegetables cooked in butter (new carrots, tiny onions, mushrooms, young peas (young green beans). This is *jambon à la crème*.

Serve *jambon à la crème* with a purée of spinach, or spinach and sorrel, instead of the little piles of vegetables. Get the spinach as dry as possible and flavour the purée with a little sugar, salt, pepper, cheese, cream as you think fit – spinach varies so much that you have to use your discretion. If you do grow sorrel, add a few leaves for their sharp, spring flavour.

Belgian chicory (*witloof* or *endive de Bruxelles*), blanched for 15 minutes in boiling water, then braised in butter in the oven, makes a good accompaniment to *jambon au Madère*.

Most popular of all, *jambon au Madère*, or *à la crème*, served with young green peas and new potatoes in the early summer.


## BURGUNDIAN HAM (Jambon Persillé de Bourgogne)

This is the famous and beautiful Eastertide dish of Burgundy. The major requirements are plenty of white wine, the ham, plenty of parsley, and one of those old-fashioned bedroom wash-bowls. I use a leg of pork cured in the York or American style, or a 1½ kg (3 lb) piece of gammon. It goes into a ham kettle with plenty of cold water, which is slowly brought to the boil to draw out excess salt. Pour off the water if it is very salty and start again. When the water is once more at the boil, simmer the ham very gently for 45 minutes.

Remove from the water and cut the meat off the bone in sizeable chunks. Put them into a pan with a large knuckle of veal, chopped into pieces; 2 calf's feet, boned, and tied together; a few sprigs of chervil and tarragon tied together with a bay leaf, 2 sprigs of thyme and 2 sprigs of parsley; 8 peppercorns tied into a little bag. Skim off fat as it rises, and leave the ham to cook very thoroughly, as it will need to be mashed and flaked with a fork.

However, before you do this, attend to the jelly. Pour off the cooking liquid through a strainer lined with a piece of clean cotton sheeting. Taste it to make sure it is not too salty. Add 1 tablespoon of white wine vinegar, and leave it to set a little.

Meanwhile crush the ham into a bowl.

Before the jelly sets altogether, stir in plenty of chopped parsley – at least 4 tablespoons, and pour over the ham. Leave to set overnight in a cold place. Turn out the *jambon persillé*, and serve. When it is cut, it will display a beautifully marbled, green and pink appearance. If you like you can keep back some of the parsley jelly, remelt it gently next day and pour over the ham in an even green layer.

## SOUFFLÉ AU JAMBON

Serves 4

*250 g ( ½ lb) lean cooked ham*
*30 g (1 oz) butter*
*30 g (1 oz) flour*
*a generous 125 ml ( ¼ pt) milk, or single cream*
*3 egg yolks*
*3 egg whites*
*salt, pepper*

Mince the ham twice and pound to a smooth mass in a mortar. Make a very thick white sauce with butter, flour and milk or cream, cooking until it comes away from the side of the pan. Use a wooden spoon for stirring. Add the ham and season well.

If you have an electric blender, mince the ham once or chop it roughly. Put it in the blender goblet with the thick white sauce and whirl at top speed. Reheat in the pan, but not to boiling point. The egg yolks should now be added, one by one.

Beat the egg whites until they are stiff, fold lightly into the pan mixture with a metal spoon, and pour into a soufflé dish with an oiled greaseproof collar.

Bake in a moderate oven for 25 minutes. Serve immediately – remember to remove the paper collar – to seated guests.

This soufflé can be cooked in small individual soufflé dishes. They will only take about 10 minutes to cook and the oven should be hotter than for a large soufflé.

## CROQUE-MONSIEUR

This delightfully named hot sandwich, can be served as an hors d'œuvre.

Choose good bread, milk loaf, *pain de mie* or *pain brioché*. Cut thin slices, butter them, and make them into sandwiches with a layer of Gruyère cheese and a layer of lean ham on top. Cut into elegant triangles, and fry in half butter, half oil, until they are golden brown, on both sides.

### Variation

Fry slices of bread on one side only, butter the unfried side, lay thick slices of ham on top and cover with a paste made of grated Gruyère cheese, French mustard and thick cream – enough to make the mixture spread. Grill gently until gold and bubbly – serve on very hot plates.

# FRESH PORK

The most obvious, visible difference in the French cooking of fresh pork – apart, of course, from the elegant butchery – is the lack of crackling. In the *charcuterie*, the *porc rôti* will be a neat boneless cylinder, pale pink from its night in brine, studded with an occasional clove of garlic, and sold by the succulent slice.

The outer layer of fat and skin will have been used in pâtés, sausages and *crépinettes*. If the *charcutier* is the butcher as well, you will see nicely-cut oblongs of white fat barding the lean roasts of beef. If you want to buy a fillet of beef for roasting, you can also buy fat to cut into larding strips. The skin, *la couenne*, is available too, for additional flavour and texture in beef casseroles. Crackling is not unknown in France, but it is served quite separately from roast pork.

The finest roasting joint of all is the loin, usually divided into two on account of its length. The leg end is known as the *filet* or *longe*, and the smaller end as the *carré*. When the *filet* is cut into chops it becomes escalopes, or the small round *noisettes*. When the *carré* is cut into chops, it becomes *côtes* and the smaller *côtelettes*.

The leg, together with the loin, are the *parties nobles* of the pig, but the leg is most usually turned into ham. The French for both is *jambon* (though *gigot* is often used for a fresh roasting leg), and the adjective *frais* to designate an uncured leg is often omitted. Be careful of this when using a French cookery book, or an English one derived from French sources. Read the recipe very carefully before visiting the butcher, and decide which is most likely – fresh leg of pork, gammon or cooked ham.

The cheaper joints of pork benefit even more than leg and loin from being salted in brine before they are cooked. Boned shoulder of pork (*épaule desossée*), for instance, spare ribs (*échine*) and blade bone (*palette*), and the often despised belly of pork (*poitrine*), gain in flavour and tenderness for three days in *saumure anglaise*. They can then be stewed or braised to advantage, or simmered in water and finally glazed. Try combining belly of pork, salted or not, with shin of beef in the casserole; the pork supplies a bland smoothness which greatly improves the flavour and texture of the sauce.

The extremities of the pig can also be eaten fresh (page 187).

### Roasting
Unlike beef or lamb, there is nothing to be gained by undercooking pork. Indeed it is neither desirable nor safe to do so. Pork should be well and gently cooked, whatever the cut and whatever the method of cooking used.

Prepare a joint of pork for roasting by boning, salting, marinading or seasoning. Then weigh it, and reckon 30 minutes' cooking time for joints up to and including 2 kg (4 lb). Add 20 minutes per 500 g (1 lb) for each 500 g (1 lb) over. Put the joint on a rack in the roasting pan, and set it in a low oven, gas 3, 160°C (325°F). There is no need to add fat or water. Test the joint near the end of the cooking time with a larding or knitting needle. The liquid which oozes out should be colourless. If it is pink the joint is not ready.

Make a sauce from the pan juices after pouring off excess fat, according to taste and recipe.

**Roast Pork with Carrots and Onions** (Porc Rôti à la Bourgeoise)

An hour before the pork is cooked, add small new carrots and tiny onions to the roasting pan. Turn them over from time to time so that they glaze. Serve the vegetables round the meat, garnish with parsley.

If small new potatoes are cooked in the pan as well, you have pork *à la bonne femme*.

**Roast Pork with Chestnuts** (Porc Rôti à la Berrichonne)

Shell and simmer 500 g (1 lb) chestnuts for 20 minutes, blanch 500 g (1 lb) of small onions, and add them with a few rolls of bacon to the pork 45 minutes before the end of cooking time.

An attractive way of serving chestnuts with pork or ham is to cook them to a purée, flavour with pan juices from the pork or crumbs of crisply fried bacon, and serve it in small *barquettes* or *tartelettes* of short pastry, baked blind.

**Roast Pork with Herbs** (Porc Rôti aux Herbes)

Sage is not often associated with pork in France, but if you grow it, here is a way of combining it with pork in the French style (don't use dried sage):

Make incisions in the joint of pork and insert small sprigs or leaves of sage. Mix 1 tablespoon of salt, 1 tablespoon of thyme, and half a bay leaf crushed, and rub this over the fat and boned sides of the joint. Leave overnight. Rub the seasoned salt in again next morning, before tying up the joint for roasting.

In Provence, plenty of crushed garlic, breadcrumbs and some olive oil are mixed together into a paste, and this is spread over the joint 45 minutes before the end of cooking time. It forms an appetizing golden crust.

## BRAISING, POT-ROASTING AND STEWING

The first two methods amount to much the same thing in the case of pork, as the meat is moist enough to require very little additional liquid. What moisture there is, is conserved by covering the pot with a tight-fitting lid, which means that it is a good method for cheaper joints of pork. If you tell the butcher that you wish to braise a joint *en casserole*, he will probably give you a piece of *échine* (spare ribs and blade bone joint), or the fillet end of the leg.

Here is a typical way of pot-roasting very popular in small French villages, where not everybody has an oven:

Choose a heavy cast-iron pan, melt some lard in it, or butter and oil, and brown the neatly-tied joint of pork all over, including the two ends. Warm some *eau-de-vie de marc*, brandy (or vodka) in a small pan, set alight to it and pour over the browned pork.

Add a *mirepoix* of carrots and onions, some crushed garlic and a large glass of *rosé* wine – about 150 ml (¼ pt). Grind salt and pepper over, put on the lid and turn the heat down low enough to keep the liquid gently bubbling. Allow 30 minutes per 500 g (1 lb).

Turn the meat over from time to time. Add new potatoes for the last 30 minutes.

Taste the sauce and adjust the flavour and seasoning as you like. Skim off the fat. The French like their *jus* or gravy to be concentrated and well-flavoured – this means that there can't be a vast quantity of it, just a spoonful or two for each person.

Some farmers say that if the pork is accompanied by a hash of onions, sautéed in butter and flamed in brandy, it will keep you sober through a day's hard drinking. Recommended for market-day breakfast.

Use a cast-iron pot which has been enamelled if you can – otherwise the sauce turns a disconcerting blackish colour, due to the wine. It tastes all right, but the appearance may put people off.

### Pork with Prunes, Tours Style (Noisettes de Porc aux Pruneaux de Tours)

This bland combination of pork, prunes, cream and the white wine of Vouvray embodies what Henry James described as 'the good-humoured and succulent Touraine'. The wine is made – as the best white wines are – from grapes which are almost rotting on the vines. As local *vignerons* say: 'They piss in your hand'. The first time I made this dish I couldn't afford the Vouvray, so I improved on the very ordinary white wine in the larder by using Christmas prunes, which had been steeping in a mixture of half *marc*, a crude *eau-de-vie*, and half syrup. Delicious, if unorthodox.

> *375 ml ( ½ bottle) white Vouvray (drink the other half with the dish)*
> *500 g (1 lb) large Californian prunes (unless you can find prunes from Agen)*
> *salt, pepper, a little flour*
> *2 noisettes or 1 chop per person*
> *1 tablespoon redcurrant jelly*
> *300 ml ( ½ pt) thick cream*
> *a dash of lemon juice*

Put the prunes to soak overnight in the Vouvray. Next day pour off about 60 ml (2 fl oz) of the liquid, and put the rest of it with the prunes into a slow oven to cook. Three-quarters of an hour is enough, but in fact you can leave them there for up to 1½ hours provided they simmer slowly enough. Cover them so that the juice does not evaporate.

Season and flour the *noisettes*. Cook them gently in the butter on each side, making sure that the butter doesn't go brown. Add the 60 ml (2 fl oz) of steeping juice and leave the pork to cook for 40 minutes with a lid on the pan.

Pour on the juice from cooking the prunes. Cook for 3 minutes then remove the pork to a large flat serving dish, and arrange the prunes around the *noisettes* whilst the sauce in the frying pan boils down to a thinnish syrup. Add the redcurrant jelly, then the cream bit by bit, stirring it in well so that after each addition it is properly amalgamated. Because English cream doesn't have that slightly sour tang of French cream, I add a dash of lemon at the end before pouring the sauce over the *noisettes* and prunes. Leave in the oven for 5 minutes. Serve this dish on its own.

## FRYING AND GRILLING

These methods involve the small cuts of pork, and are virtually interchangeable according to your circumstances. If you have really good pork chops, grill them. If you are in the least bit dubious, fry or braise them. Either method should be applied gently – unlike fillet steak, pork chops will take about 20 minutes under the grill, or in the sauté pan.

**Pork Chops in White Wine** (Côtes de Porc au Vin Blanc)

After a long day's work, or excursion, grilled pork chops are everybody's solution to the evening meal. With a little forethought, you can improve on everybody else's solution and enjoy a much better meal.

Season the chops. Put previously cooked potatoes into a pan with milk, to heat through for mashing.

Grill the chops fast for 1 minute, then lower the heat and give them 9 minutes. Turn over, and repeat with 1 minute fast, and 9 minutes slow.

Deal with the potatoes, adding plenty of butter and nutmeg or mace; arrange the chops round them and put the dish into the oven whilst you make the sauce.

Take the rack out of the grill pan, pour in some white (or *rosé*) wine, bubble it all together on top of the stove. Taste and season.

Be sure to scrape in all the little brown bits. Pour over the chops and serve. Have French mustard on the table.

(Watercress always makes a good appearance with pork chops.)

**Pork Chops with Cheese** (Côtes de Porc Avesnoise)

A delicious way of serving pork chops from Avesnes-sur-Helpe in the very north of France. The method can be adapted for use with other glazing mixtures; but this French rarebit style is the best of all.

Grate a quantity of Gruyère or Emmenthal cheese (60 g (2 oz) is enough for 3 chops), mix it to a thick paste with half-and-half French mustard and cream. It should spread but not run.

Grill the chops on both sides as in the recipe for *côtes de porc au vin blanc*. When they are done, spread one side of each chop with the Gruyère paste and set under the grill. The mixture will melt, bubble and turn gold.

One of the most appetizing ways of serving pork, the smell is irresistible and draws the whole family into the kitchen.

# EXTREMITIES

## THE HEAD

Pig's head, like the other extremities, is sold cheaply in this country. It makes an excellent brawn (*fromage de tête, hure*) or galantine, if suitable attention is paid to its preparation. Anyone can grill a steak or chop; the cheaper cuts require careful and sophisticated cooking.

This does not mean that the methods are difficult or tortuous, but they do require judgement and care over detail. Lack of proper care, above the statutory requirements of hygiene, and insensitivity to flavour make many manufactured meat dishes in England uneatable. This commercial debasement of brawn, black puddings, meat pies and sausages has misled people into feeling that only the expensive parts of a pig are worth eating.

There is little difference between *fromage de tête* and *hure* and *galantine de porc*. *Fromage* is a mixture of the meat set in jelly, *hure* is a mixture of the meat enveloped in the skin of the head, galantine is a mixture of the meat with hardly any internal jelly, but a coating of jelly round the outside.


## PIG'S TROTTERS (Pieds de Porc)

I once commented on the limited variety of prepared and cooked pork on sale in this country to an executive in a large pork factory. He recalled that in the early days of this century the Managing Director always had pig's trotters to start his important dinner parties, but that nowadays the housewife was ashamed to be seen coming out of the butcher's shop with a packet of trotters and tail. In France there is a usually a tray of them in most *charcuteries*, breadcrumbed (*pieds panés*), waiting to be taken home and grilled for an hors d'œuvre. As one is lucky enough to buy them so cheaply in England, I usually serve them in various ways for a main luncheon dish, accompanied by mashed potato. They have often spent 48 hours in brine, but this is not essential, though it certainly improves their flavour.


### Pig's Trotters in Breadcrumbs (Pieds de Porc à la Sainte-Ménéhould)

The most famous of all the French ways of cooking pig's ears and pig's trotters, the Sainte-Ménéhould method, gives a crisp texture to gelatinous meat, which has been boiled, by rolling it in breadcrumbs, then grilling or frying. But in Sainte-Ménéhould itself, in the Argonne where pigs once ran in the huge woods of the plateau (scene of much of the Verdun fighting in the First World War), pig's trotters with a difference can be bought for reheating. Spiced with *quatre-épices* and rolled, like *pieds panés* in breadcrumbs, they have been cooked for so long – 48 hours – that they can be eaten bones and all. This gives three textures – crisp, gelatinous and the hard-soft biscuit of the edible bones. An extremely delicious combination. They are served in local hotels quite dry, without sauce, and you eat them with French mustard.

One *charcutière* told me that it's the addition of a certain vegetable or herb that causes the bones to soften, as well as the prolonged slow cooking. Local sceptics tartly hint at '*produits chimiques*'.

# INSIDES

## TRIPE OR CHITTERLING SAUSAGES (Andouilles, Andouillettes)

*Andouilles* are large, invariably salted and smoked, sold in slices by weight, like salami, and eaten cold. *Andouillettes* are smaller, the size of a large sausage or a little bigger, occasionally smoked or salted, and eaten hot after a gentle grilling.*

If the *charcutier* orders his *andouilles* from Vire in Normandy, the capital of the *andouille*, they will be hanging up among the other *saucissons secs*. They are easily distinguishable on account of their black skins and their mottled greyish-brown section, with the pieces of tripe looking like the fossilized coral in Frosterley marble, or else graded by size and drawn into each other, so that the slices look like regular growth rings across a tree-stump. If the *charcutier* makes his own, they may well be a lot smaller, about the size of a man's clenched fist and about as knobbly. Their skins are probably more succulent and wrinkled black, and when you go near to choose one your mouth waters with their sharp smell of a white wine marinade.

*Andouillettes* are about the same size as *boudins blancs*, but craggier with the pieces of tripe. Some *charcutiers*, however, mould them into squared prisms cut off into exactly similar lengths, and pile them up quite architecturally into a pyramid. Or they may be wrapped up, each one, in a roll of greaseproof paper. It may be pure coincidence, but the nicest *andouillettes* we've ever eaten belonged to the more rugged, tied-at-each-end school and we bought them in the Dordogne at Montignac, after an unusually solitary hour in the Lascaux caves.

---

* *Andouille*, which sounds unusual, is in fact most appropriately derived from a Late Latin adjective, *inductibilis*, 'that may be drawn over something'. When you come to the method of filling the skins, you will understand how nice the derivation is. In Palsgrave's *Lesclaircissement de la langue francoise*, 1530, he gives 'Chyterlyng, Endoile', a good half-way name between *inductibilis* and *andouille*.

They were fried too quickly over a picnic stove from Woolworth's, but no other *andouillettes* have ever tasted so good.

*Andouilles* and *andouillettes* are quite easy to make at home, the most difficult part is acquiring the large intestine and belly of the pig. Chain butchers are no help in this, you need to find a butcher who chooses his own meat at the local slaughter house. Pig factories are sometimes obliging. If you have to clean the tripes yourself, the bath is the best place because, as well as having plenty of room, you can fix the ends of the intestines over the cold tap and run plenty of water through. When it comes to the manufacture, a relay of unsqueamish helpers with neat fingers is an advantage.

The basic mixture is the same for both *andouilles* and *andouillettes*, apart from local variations. It's the size that distinguishes them as far as the home cook is concerned.

> *large intestine and belly of the pig (or part)*
> *fat bacon (⅓ of above weight)*
> *spices*
>
> BOUILLON
> *half-and-half milk and water to cover, 2 or 3 onions stuck with 4 cloves
>     each, 3 medium carrots, salt, pepper,* bouquet garni, *spices*

(If the intestines, etc., have not been cleaned, soak in cold water for 24 hours in a cool place. Overnight only in warm, humid weather. Then clean and scrape them. Simmer for 1 hour in water.)

Set aside enough intestine for the casings – thinner pieces for *andouillettes*, fatter for *andouilles* – and cut them into suitable lengths. Sprinkle with salt and store in the refrigerator, or the coolest part of the larder.

Slice up, with scissors or a sharp knife, the rest of the intestine and the belly, into strips 8–12 mm (⅓–½ inch) wide and little shorter than your lengths of casing. Put them in a bowl and sprinkle with plenty of salt, freshly ground black pepper and a mixture of spices such as *quatre-épices*. Remember that *andouillettes* and *andouilles* need a strong spice contrast to the slightly rubbery smoothness of the tripe filling. Let the strips macerate in the seasonings for 24 hours, in a cool dry place.

Next day, cut the bacon fat into pieces about the width and length of the tripe pieces. If you refrigerate the fat first, this job becomes quite easy. Divide the tripe and bacon strips into bundles and tie each one, at one end, with a length of button thread.

Wash the salt off the casings, and draw the bundles in, by means of the button thread (this is where the neat-fingered are at a premium). Cut away the thread and tie the *andouilles* or *andouillettes* at each end.

(If this process appals you, you can, more simply, chop the tripe and bacon fat rather than slice it into regular lengths. If you have a sausage-making attachment to an electric mixer, you can treat the mixture like sausage-meat and fill the skins that way – but use the very large-holed plate as the final result should not be too smooth or solid in texture.)

If the knobbliness of your *andouilles* and *andouillettes* seems excessively exaggerated, roll them backwards and forwards with the palm of your hand on a smooth surface (Formica, marble slab).

### Cooking andouillettes

Prick them with a darning needle and arrange evenly in a large saucepan. Cover with milk and water in equal quantities, add the other bouillon ingredients and bring to the boil. Simmer gently for 3 hours. Leave them to cool down in the liquid until tepid, then lay them side by side closely in a shallow dish and put a lightly weighted board on top. This gives a handsome squared-off appearance, which is not strictly necessary but gratifying. In France they are often glazed with a mixture of lard and veal fat in equal quantities, or – when the weather gets warmer – with one-fifth mutton fat and four-fifths veal fat.

Now they can be fried, or else slashed across in three or four places and grilled. Serve them on their own, as a starting course, with French mustard; or with mashed potato as a main luncheon dish. Well-spiced *andouillettes* are a great treat, and worth the trouble of making them.

### Cooking andouilles

The *andouillettes* cooking programme can be followed entirely – or when the *andouilles* have quite cooled under a light weight, they can be sliced and served as part of an hors d'œuvre.

It is better to salt, or salt and smoke, them first. Four days in brine is a great improver, two days in brine and three days smoking is better still. Smoking produces a wrinkly, brownish-black exterior, which is most appetizing.

Substitute white wine for milk in the bouillon recipe.

Although, as I have said above, *andouilles* can be eaten hot like *andouillettes*, they are at their best salted, smoked and smelling of white wine, and served cold in thin slices.

Although *andouilles* are served like *saucissons secs*, they are not when domestically produced a keeping sausage. When salted and smoked they keep good longer than *andouillettes*, which should be eaten within two days of manufacture, but it is wise to eat them within the week.

## THE KIDNEYS

Along with all the other parts of the pig, you can buy kidneys at the *charcuterie*. They are usually sold raw – and very fresh, which is how they should be. If you can, order them in advance, with some surrounding flare fat. To my mind, the most delicious way to cook kidneys is to pop them into a moderately hot oven, encased in flare fat, and roast them for 1 hour. This applies to lambs' and calves' kidneys as well. And you will have a basin of beautiful fat, superb for pastry-making. The next most simple way is to grill them.

### Skewered Kidneys (Rognons–Brochette Grillés)

Skin the kidneys; then slit them in two so that they are not completely separated into two halves, but can be laid out flat. Remove the small hard white part. If you have some very fine skewers, you could skewer them crosswise in the French style, otherwise use two skewers for each kidney side by side across the two halves.

Brush the cut side with melted butter, and season with salt, freshly ground black pepper, and perhaps some ground sage – be discreet about this. Set the kidneys, cut side up, of course, under the grill for several minutes at a moderate heat. Then turn them over, brush with melted butter, and grill the outside.

The usual garnish is butter, pounded with chopped parsley and some lemon juice. In other words, *à la maître d'hôtel*.

#### Variations and accompaniments

When you have brushed the kidneys with melted butter, sprinkle them with breadcrumbs.

With *Beurre Colbert*, butter, pounded with tarragon, and salt and pepper.

With *Beurre de Ciboulette*, butter, pounded with chopped chives, salt and pepper.

With *Beurre de Moutarde*, butter, blended with mustard (French).

With *Beurre d'Échalote*: shallots, chopped, then blanched for 3 minutes in boiling water, and pounded to a mash. Add butter.

With a nice arrangement of bacon, boiled or mashed potatoes, and watercress (*à l'anglaise*), with the addition of one of the butters suggested above, served in little pats, one on each half of each kidney.

On a bed of *risotto*.

Encircled by crisp fried potatoes, whether as straws, or crisps, or
fluted crisps. Add pats of butter, and a sprinkling of chopped parsley
or tarragon or sage, as appropriate.

Here is another simple but delicious way of cooking kidneys:

### Kidney Kebabs (Rognons en Brochette)

Skin the kidneys, cut them into suitable sized pieces of a uniform
thickness. Alternate them on the skewers with squares of streaky
bacon and small mushroom caps. Brush with melted butter, roll them
in breadcrumbs, and grill. Turn them every few minutes, so that they
are cooked all round.

Serve them on a bed of mashed potato, laid side by side, with the
juices from the grill pan poured over them. Sprinkle them with
chopped chives, or parsley, or sage.

This recipe can be varied in all kinds of ways. The main thing is to
alternate lean, dry ingredients with fat or juicy ones. I learnt this at
open-air lunch-parties, organized, *en brochette*, by an Anglo-French
friend years before the barbecue became fashionable. The day before,
he would go down to the butcher's shop, and return with a load of
kidneys, liver, belly of pork, heart and smoked bacon, conveniently
cut up into rough cubes. Then he prepared a fearsome marinade in
his cave-house kitchen – oil, red wine, herbs, garlic, spices, and raw
onion – and soaked the meat in it overnight.

### Sautéed Kidneys (Rognons de Porc Sautés)

Skin the kidneys, remove the hard white core, and slice thinly. Melt
some butter to a froth in a heavy frying pan, add the kidney slices and
sprinkle with salt and freshly-ground black pepper. Cook quickly on
both sides. Serve with lemon quarters.

### Sautéed Kidneys with Rice (Rognons de Porc Sautés en Pilaff)

Soften a medium, chopped onion in 90 g (3 oz) of butter until it is
golden. Add 250 g (½ lb) of rice and stir in the melted butter until it
is transparent. Pour in 600 ml (1 pt) of hot water and boil until the
rice is cooked. Meanwhile blanch and fry 60 g (2 oz) of almonds.
Cook 4 pig's kidneys as in the above recipe. Drain the rice, arrange
on a serving dish in a ring, put the kidneys in the centre and garnish
with the fried almonds. Make a little sauce by swilling 150 ml (¼ pt)
of good stock round the kidney pan, and quickly reducing it – pour
over the kidneys and serve.

## THE LIVER

Pig's liver can be bought at the *charcuterie*, but makes its usual appearance in *pâté de foie*, page 160. It must be confessed that pig's liver is neither so delicate in flavour nor so tender as the fine calf's liver to be bought at a high price in France (English calf's liver cannot be compared with it – I imagine this is due to methods of rearing, or a more lax definition of the word 'calf'). Nonetheless, pig's liver is nutritious and inexpensive, and can be turned into dishes that are well worth eating, apart from the delicious pâtés.

### Liver and Bacon (Foie de Porc à l'Anglaise)

Slice the liver thinly, turn it over in seasoned flour.

Prepare the bacon, as many rashers as slices of liver, and fry it in butter, arranging it nicely on an oven dish. Have some scrubbed, unpeeled potatoes boiling at the same time, so that they will be cooked when the liver is finished. Pour off and keep the bacon fat.

Keep the bacon hot in a low oven, and fry the liver very quickly in a fresh lot of butter. Two minutes a side should be ample, unless your slices are rather thick. Time this carefully – the liver should only just be cooked to a point of juicy succulence. Nothing is worse than leathery liver. Remove to the serving dish which already contains the bacon.

Add the bacon fat to the liver fat and juices, add some lemon juice, and pour over the dish. Sprinkle with chopped parsley.

Drain the potatoes, cut them to a convenient size, take off the skins, and finish them with butter and parsley.

A simple dish, but very much better for taking care with its preparation.

### Porc Liver and Truffles (Foie de Porc Rôti aux Truffes)

This is a magnificent recipe, accompanied by a magnificent sauce, *sauce Périgueux*; Périgueux is the capital of the Dordogne, the most important truffle area, and any dish described as *Périgueux* means that it's been prepared with truffles.

> *1 large piece of pig's liver 1–1½ kg (2–3 lb)*
> *125 g (¼ lb) very fat pork*
> *125–150 g (4–5 oz) truffles*
> *1 large piece of caul, enough to wrap easily round the liver*
> *250 ml (2 wineglasses) olive oil*

*125 ml (1 wineglass) Madeira*
*salt, pepper, spices*
*a little good brown jelly from roast meat or poultry to glaze at the end*

First prepare the liver. Lard it with small strips of the fat pork, make small incisions with the point of a sharp knife and push in tiny pieces of truffle so that they are well distributed. Leave the liver for 24 hours in a marinade of the oil, wine and seasonings.

When you are ready to cook, assemble two sheets of greaseproof, plenty of silver foil and a shallow oven dish, or baking sheet with raised edges, in case the juices from the meat leak out.

Oil the greaseproof paper on one side only, and put one piece, un-oiled side down, on top of the other piece, oiled side up. Wrap the liver in the caul (run under a warm tap for a moment to make it pliable), and lay it, with the juices from the marinade, on the greaseproof paper. Wrap the liver up, lay it on a sheet of silver foil and crinkle the edges together to make a loose, but firmly sealed parcel. Lay this in the oven dish, or baking sheet, and put in a medium oven for 1½ hours.

Just before taking the meat out of the oven, melt down a little jelly from a roast. This you will pour over the caul-wrapped liver, when the greaseproof and foil have been removed, and return it to the oven for a moment or two to glaze, whilst you finish off the *sauce Périgueux*.

*Sauce Périgueux* might just as well be made from a *good sauce espagnole*, since the truffles cost so much, rather than the remains of the gravy from a roast or stew. Do the hard work the previous day, and add the Madeira and truffles just before the liver is ready to serve. *Remember that the sauce must not boil* after the truffles and Madeira have been added.

# PICNIC GUIDE TO THE CHARCUTIER'S SHOP

Every small town in France, at any rate in the more prosperous districts such as Touraine, Burgundy or the Île de France, is likely to have more than one *charcuterie*. Probably one, and one only, will be worth going to. It will be on the *place* or in the main street, its windows crowded with a variety of good things, its marble slabs and its tiled floors clean and inviting, with a brisk white-coated wife in attendance (the *charcutier* himself leads a pale, mainly nocturnal existence, at the back, transforming pork into his delicacies).

The other *charcuteries* will be mediocre, even a little grey, with fewer lines, tucked away in a side street. Only the master in each town can afford the good position, and match up to the standard which many of the townspeople demand. He is likely to have as neighbours, more or less, the one good *pâtisserie* (pastry-cook) and the best *boulangerie* (baker), with its many varieties of bread.

The *charcutier* will sell olives, anchovies, condiments, and a few proprietary goods (e.g. *saucissons secs*, salami of one kind and another). He will sell various salads of his own making, and a few confections of rabbit (e.g. *pâté de lapin*), chicken or beef. But transmutations of the pig are his mainstay.

Occasionally the butcher (*boucher*) is *charcutier* as well, particularly in smaller places, and, as you would expect, his range of *charcuterie* is fairly restricted – sausages, black puddings, a simple pâté or two, and some *rillettes*.

Many of the *charcutier's* products can be eaten cold, with salads (which are sold in cartons by weight), or bread. Below are listed his standard items, for quick use in the day's picnic shopping. It must be understood that items vary according to season and province.

### Ready to eat

*Rillettes.* Potted belly of pork, sometimes with the addition of goose or rabbit. A major delicacy of Touraine and Anjou; but not infrequently made in factories (tins of very good *rillettes* may be bought in some grocer's shops), as well as by the *charcutier* himself.

*Rillons.* Small pieces of browned belly of pork. These sometimes have an unappetizing look, altogether belied by their taste. They are among the finest products of *charcuterie*.

*Petit Salé.* Belly of pork and spare ribs salted and boiled, sold in larger pieces than *rillons*, delicately pink and white.

*Galantine de Porc.* Nearer to brawn than to galantine, made of the head-meat and scraps of the pig.

*Fromage de Tête.* Brawn, often breadcrumbed on the outside.

*Hure.* Brawn, once again, but often presented with a 1-cm (½-inch) layer of jelly on the outside.

*Pâté de Campagne.* Pâté made from the lean and fat meat of the pig, veal, ham, etc. Ingredients vary locally and according to season and taste.

*Pâté de Foie de Porc.* Pâté made from the lean and fat meat of the pig, with the addition of pig's liver.

*Pâté de Lapin.* Pâté made from rabbit and pork.

*Pâté de Gibier.* Pâté made from pork and game, which may be specified, e.g. *pâté de lièvre*, hare pâté.

*Jambon* (ham), including mild cures such as *jambon de Paris, jambon de York* (i.e. ham cured in the mild York style, but often a tinned and insipid travesty), and the delicious smoked hams, many of which are eaten raw, in very thin slices, like the famous *jambon de Bayonne.* Many regions make their own not so famous *jambons crus*; always enquire.

*Jambonneau.* Picnic ham, mildly cured, from the hock. Charmingly presented as small breadcrumbed cones, with a neat piece of bone sticking out of the top, like a stem. Sold by the half, or quarter, if you do not want a whole one. Much cheaper than *jambon de Paris* or *jambon cru.*

*Porc Rôti.* Roast pork, most usually the loin, boned and rolled, and very lightly salted.

*Saucissons Secs.* Salami of various kinds, regional, national and international, and other dried or smoked sausages including *saucisson à l'ail* (garlic sausage), *andouille* (large, black-skinned, tripe sausage), the slightly smaller *chorizos* or *saucisses d'Espagne* (red-pepper sausage). The *charcuterie* will usually stock frankfurters, and the very similar *saucisses de Strasbourg*, of good quality.

*Museau de Bœuf en Salade.* Boiled ox-muzzle, sliced thinly and dressed with plenty of parsley and chives, and vinaigrette.

### Charcuterie which requires warming or cooking
*Quiche Lorraine.* Bacon, egg and cream flan – many variations, and sizes, according to region.

*Oreilles de Porc.* Pig's ears, cooked, in jelly. Tasty, though seldom eaten in England. In France the crisp cartilage is eaten as well as the meat, and they are usually served grilled, with a coating of egg and breadcrumbs, though you need do no more than warm them through.

*Pieds de Porc.* Pig's trotters, often split in half and breadcrumbed. Sold by the piece. Fry in butter, or brush with melted butter and grill.

*Queues de Porc.* Pig's tails, cooked, and finished with a coating of breadcrumbs. Fry in butter, or brush with melted butter and grill.

SAUCISSES (page 168). Sausages for cooking divide into:

*Saucisses de Porc.* Small pork sausages, sold, as in England, in chipolata and larger sizes. By French law they are 100 per cent meat, and do *not* contain preservatives.

*Andouillettes.* Small tripe sausages, of bland and mild flavour, making an excellent picnic lunch. They may be contained in very knobbly lengths of gut, for which they are none the less delicious. Usually grilled when served on their own. Sometimes wrapped in stiff white paper, sometimes pressed into four-sided shapes and neatly glazed with a mixture of pork and veal lard. As they are expensive, buy one or two according to the size of the family, break them up in the pan when they are cooked, and add beaten eggs, 1–2 per person, to make an omelette.

*Boudins Blancs.* White puddings, though more sausage-like and less puddingy than their counterparts in England. Of delicate flavour, containing (from the best *charcuteries*) a proportion of chicken with the pork. The most expensive of all the sausages.

*Boudins Noirs.* Black puddings. Spicier and tastier and with more character than the factory-made black puddings of England. Whether presented sausage-style, or in an immense coil, the cheapest of all the sausages. Delicious with fried apples.

*Saucisson-Cervelas.* Saveloy, or larger sausage for poaching in nearly-boiling water. Eat with potato salad, improved with some chopped raw onion, and mustard.

*Saucisses de Francfort.* Usually a proprietary brand, sold in plastic wrappings. Five minutes in nearly-boiling water. Eat with potato salad, etc., like the *cervelas* sausage above.

*Saucisses de Strasbourg.* See above entry.

*Crépinettes.* Small flattish cakes of sausage-meat, encased in veiny, white caul fat (*crépine*). Fry or grill.

*Chair à Saucisse.* All-pork sausage-meat, on a tray, in a mound. Sold, as in England, by weight, and used for stuffings and home-made pâtés.

*Saucisse en Brioche.* A large pork sausage, up to a pound in weight, encased in *brioche*, and sold by the slice. It has been described as an extra fine toad-in-the-hole; an extra fine sausage-roll would be a better description. Eat warm.

*Friandises.* Small sausages enveloped in puff-pastry, in other words, sausage-rolls. Best eaten warm.

*Pâtés Chauds*. Mixtures of meat cooked in shortcrust pastry, pasty or turnover style. Best eaten warm. Occasionally hot pies are baked on a large shallow plate, and sold by the slice, which will be weighed to determine the price; see *Gâteau à la Berrichonne* (page 107).

*Tripes*. Tripe is sold in various forms apart from tripe sausages (*andouillettes* and *andouilles*, above). Often it is sold in hunks from a jellied slab, starred with carrot rungs; sometimes in pots and cartons. Needs warming through, and is intended to be improved, according to taste, by the addition of wine, hard liquor, tomatoes and parsley.

*Lard* is, confusingly, the French for bacon (*tranche de lard* is a rasher of bacon). *Saindoux* is the name given to what we call lard. Bacon is not much sold in France, though it is always available; housewives there use fresh pork fat cut in strips or belly of pork in cooking, where we might use fat bacon.

### Cuts of fresh pork and offal
The *charcutier* also sells uncooked fresh pork and offal, including:
*échine* spare ribs, bladebone
*gorge* neck, and part of hand  ⎫
*épaule* shoulder  ⎬ hand of pork, shoulder
*poitrine* belly of pork
*lard de poitrine* fat belly of pork
*côtes* fore loin
*carré* fore loin in a piece
*côte* single chop
*longe* or *filet* hind loin and part of fillet
*noisettes* small round cuts from the fillet
*jambon* leg of pork
*jambonneau* hock, and hand
*tête de porc* pig's head
*pieds de porc* pig's trotter
*queues de porc* pigs' tails
*abats de porc* pig's offal
*cervelle de porc* pig's brain
*rognons de porc* pig's kidneys
*foie de porc* pig's liver.

# THE MEDITERRANEAN

FROM THE BRITISH ISLES we look outwards at a sea that is, more often than not, in grey and angry mood. In sharp contrast, those countries which border the Mediterranean gaze over a sea that has its dangers, but is for the most part blue, warm and tranquil. No wonder then that for centuries the British have been drawn to its shores, as pilgrims, explorers, travellers, scholars and, latterly, as tourists in their unseeing millions, and it is unsurprising that so many English writers and artists have found a source of inspiration there. Since the end of the Second World War, food writers have joined them, invigorated by the vitality and richness of Mediterranean cookery. Elizabeth David was the first and remains the greatest, beginning the mass transformation of our eating and drinking habits. Jane shared Elizabeth David's love for the food of the region and was much inspired by the earlier writer's work and so too wrote affectionately and knowledgeably about the Mediterranean.

The subject is so wide and diverse, the amount of source material so great and the strands that link food with history and culture so myriad that almost every book that Jane wrote will have somewhere in it a recipe or reference deriving from the Mediterranean, and this is reflected in this chapter.

Sitting outside a small taverna on Rhodes, hard by the water's edge, sipping retsina and nibbling olives, pistachio nuts, little cubes of cheese and bits of octopus, I realized that 2,000 years ago and more, Greeks were drinking the same resinated wine and eating the same food. Only the very rich would have enjoyed extra dishes of consummate skill.

Greek chefs then had the same reputation as French chefs have today – 'Cook and poet are alike: the art of each lies in his brain,' said one Greek writer. And he reported a chef's remarks to a young commis: 'I'm a gourmet – that's the key to our skill. If you aren't to spoil the ingredients entrusted to you, you must love them passionately ... Cook and taste often. Not enough salt? Add some. Something lacking? Keep tasting and adding until the flavour is right. Tighten it, as you would a harp, until it's in tune. Then when everything is in harmony, bring on your chorus of dishes, singing in unison.'

Such statements have been made again and again since then, each chef in turn heralding a revolution (nouvelle cuisine?) whereas he is really restating the principles of fine cookery that, for Europe, were first enunciated in Greece. Our Greek chef saw good food, food in its season, as an integral part of the harmony and pleasure of life.

Meat and game were plentiful. Our chef dealt with lamb, veal, pork, ham, sausages, and hare. Flour came, perhaps, from one of the new watermills. For dessert, he was able to produce almonds, walnuts, pine kernels, pistachio nuts with their green and purple tones, and dried raisins. If his cheesecakes were not quite up to Athenian standards, he would serve them with Hymettus honey, a much prized delicacy from the nearby Mount Hymettus.

He might have agreed with the chefs of Kos that cooked lettuce stalks were the best of vegetables, in spite of their reputation for cooling sexy desires. His salads contained bitter rocket and green coriander, with sorrel added for sharpness. And, of course, he had olives and olive oil. He was sharp, too, in the market, poking down into the punnets of figs to see what was beneath the fine ones on top, and bargaining with fish-sellers.

Then, as now, fish was the favourite food of chefs and other discriminating eaters. They knew the best parts of the tunny fish, that octopus needs bashing to tenderness on the rocks, how squid should be stuffed, and the special deliciousness of red mullet. They loved shellfish like oysters, mussels, crabs, lobsters, and prawns, as well as the apricot-orange creaminess of sea urchins, enclosed in purple-brown spikes. The best foods of Greece have not changed.

I wonder what our chef would have thought of new foods that came later with Arab merchants and Turkish invaders, or after the discovery of America? If he considered the tomato to be over-used today, he would surely enjoy spinach in flaky pies ... the elegance of okra. Or the transforming lemon and the clarity its flavour brings to food. He might also envy modern pastry-cooks the neutral sweetness of sugar (the assertive sweetness of honey, the only sweetener he had, limits variety in dishes), but what would he make of the thick black coffee needed to balance the tooth-piercing syrups? And the accompanying glass of water?

Except in top restaurants or hotels, the way of ordering a meal in Greece demands nerve. You will be handed the universal printed menu, listing every Greek dish you can think of – there are no great regional differences. Here and there, inky smudges on the plastic indicate the day's dishes. Or yesterday's. You must at this point, earlier for preference, make for the kitchen to see what bubbles on the stove. On account of Greek willingness to feed you at any time of the day, meat dishes can be overcooked. Best to stick to the little *meze* dishes – the appetizers, such as stuffed vine leaves and vegetables, little pastries and so on. Then grilled fish, which came out of the sea that morning, with a Greek salad. Then figs, oranges or grapes and the superb coffee: if you value your teeth, order *metrios* (lightly sugared coffee), or *sketos* (without sugar).

Buying picnic food is another great pleasure. You find the baker's shop simply by looking out for people carrying pans of meat and potatoes under white cloths, or a tray of buns on their head. They are going to and from the baker's ovens, where these foods are baked for them as they have always been. Butchers' shops are stark and you may prefer to look for sausage and cooked meats at the grocery, along with honey and cheese, fruit, wine and olives.

On leaving a village one day in November to look for a sheltered picnicking place, I stopped at a spot where people were knocking down olives from their tree. I joined in, and later was rewarded by dipping bread into the green-gold stream of oil that came from the presses. Everything in the pressing shed had a soft sheen of oil – sacks, mats, walls, floor, the dog – even the farmers, who had brought in their crop and were watching it pass through the unchanging process, the centuries-old system hurried along by machinery.

[*European Cookery*]

# SOUPS AND STARTERS

## AVGOLEMONO SOUP

The name means egg and lemon, which are the two important finishing ingredients of this soup. In Greek restaurants here, it's usually made with a basis of chicken stock – but try using fish stock as they often do in Greece. Most fishmongers are delighted to hand over free plaice bones, or cheap fish pieces, left over from filleting, which gives you a luxurious soup at a low price. Avgolemono has a light foamy texture, which tastes particularly agreeable on warm days.

Serves 6

STOCK
*750 g–1 kg (1½–2 lb) fish bones and pieces*
*1¾ litres (3 pt) water*
*150 ml (¼ pt) wine vinegar*
*1 medium onion, stuck with 4 cloves*
*1 medium carrot, sliced*
*8 peppercorns*
*½ bay leaf, sprig of thyme and parsley*

Simmer together for 1 hour. Strain and reduce to about 1½ litres (2½ pt). Correct the seasoning.

*60–90 g (2–3 oz) rice*
*3 eggs*
*1–2 lemons*

Simmer the rice in the stock until cooked. Have ready in a bowl the eggs beaten up with the juice of 1 lemon. Add a ladleful of hot soup, whisking all the time. Return to the pan, and *without boiling*, cook until slightly thickened. Keep whisking. Add more lemon juice to taste. Serve at once.

[*Good Things*]

## FISH SOUP IN THE MEDITERRANEAN STYLE

Mediterranean recipes for fish soups often include tomatoes and saffron and a good mixture of fish, including shellfish. Our varieties in the north of Europe and in the United States, too, are different, so we can never hope to produce a bouillabaisse. But we can make a good soup on the same lines, and enjoy it for its own qualities. I have not specified exactly which fish should be used. First because it doesn't matter precisely, and secondly because fishmongers vary widely in their stock in different parts of the country, and on different days of the week. Generally speaking, you need a cheap fish for background flavour: conger eel is good, but redfish, often sold as bream, will do instead (in the United States anything from ocean perch to porgy would be fine); then a better type of fish to add fineness and an agreeable texture, red mullet, John Dory, brill or turbot (in the States, perhaps red snapper or sea bass would be best); and lastly shellfish for sweetness and piquancy.

When you have made your choice, take the fish home and prepare them appropriately. Mussels will need to be scrubbed and opened and their liquor should be carefully strained and added to the soup in place of some of the water. Then all the fish should be cut into nice chunks and divided into three piles – 10 minutes of cooking (conger), 5 minutes of cooking (most white fish), and 2 minutes of cooking (shellfish). If these times seem short to you, remember that the fish continues to cook in the broth as it is served and brought to the table, and that nothing is worse than soup with a flannel-like mush of overcooked fish.

Serves 6–8

*1 kg (2 lb) fish (see above)*
*500 g (1 lb) mussels or other shellfish*
*60 ml (2 fl oz) olive oil*
*1 large onion, sliced*
*3 cloves garlic, chopped*
*250 g (½ lb) tomatoes, peeled, chopped*
*250 g (½ lb) mushrooms, chopped*
*1 heaped tablespoon rice*
*1¾ litres (3 pt) water*
*bouquet garni*
*a pinch of saffron*
*salt, freshly ground black pepper, sugar*
*tomato concentrate (optional)*
*6 thick slices French bread*
*extra olive oil*
*grated Parmesan cheese*
*chopped basil or parsley*

Clean and separate the seafood as described above. Heat olive oil and fry onion and garlic until lightly browned. Add tomatoes, mushrooms and rice, and stir over the heat for a few moments. Pour in water, and add *bouquet* and saffron. Season with salt, pepper and a little sugar (many commercial tomatoes are tasteless by comparison with French ones – some extra tomato concentrate may also be a good idea). Simmer for about 15 minutes, then add the fish at the intervals described above. Correct the seasoning.

Meanwhile brush the slices of bread with oil and place under grill until lightly browned. Sprinkle one side of each slice with cheese, and return to the grill until it is melted and bubbling. Either place these in the soup tureen or put on a separate plate.

Pour the soup into the tureen, scatter the basil or parsley over the top, and serve boiling hot.

[*The Mushroom Feast*]

## TUSCANY BEAN SOUP

The people of Tuscany are the great bean-eaters, the *mangiafagioli*, of Europe. They have so many bean dishes that I'm surprised they've never invented any bean cakes, or buns, in the Japanese style. But they have invented a special pot for cooking beans in, a *fagiolara*. Apart from being a beautiful object, the *fagiolara* is practical: it can be used over low, direct heat, or in the oven, and, on account of its chianti-flask shape, the top is easily sealed against loss of heat and flavour. In these pots, beans simmer in water seasoned with olive oil, garlic, sage, tomato, and perhaps some pickled pork, to make Tuscan – not Boston – baked beans. But for a small party of tired urban stomachs this is the Tuscan recipe I would choose:

Serves 6

*250 g ( ½ lb) dried haricot, or butter beans*
*1¼ litres (2 pt) water*
*5 or 6 large tablespoons olive oil*
*2 large cloves garlic, chopped not crushed*
*a bunch of parsley, chopped*
*salt, black pepper*

Soak, then simmer the beans in the water *without salt* until cooked. When they are soft, remove a quarter to half of the beans, and liquidize or *mouli* the rest. Season well, diluting the soup with more water if necessary. Reheat, with the whole beans. In a separate pan cook the garlic slowly in 2 tablespoons of the olive oil, until it turns golden. Add to the soup, with the parsley and the rest of the oil. Serve immediately.

*Note:* if you can't buy good olive oil, don't make do with corn oil, which is tasteless. Use butter instead. The result will be quite different, more like a French soup, but still very good.

[*Good Things*]


## BAGNA CAUDA

A *bagna cauda* – 'hot bath' – of anchovy sauce, with vegetables to dip into it, is a favourite dish in Piedmont. The vivid collection of vegetables is arranged on a platter or in a basket, or on plates with individual pots of the sauce, if the party is a small one. Cardoon (only available here if you grow it yourself), celery and Florentine fennel are popular, and there must be red pepper, too, for its juicy sweetness. Green and yellow peppers, chicory, radishes, broccoli, carrots cut into long sticks – choose whatever is fresh in the shops that day. For special occasions, the Piedmontese grate thin slivers of white truffle into the sauce.

Serves 6

*18 plump cloves of garlic, skinned and sliced*
*milk*
*18 large salted anchovies, soaked and filleted, or 3 × 50 g (1¾ oz) tins*
  *of anchovy fillets in oil*
*60 g (2 oz) butter*
*240–270 ml (8–9 fl oz) olive oil*
*6 eggs (optional)*

Simmer the garlic until tender in enough milk to cover. Use a small pan with no lid, so that the milk can reduce (but take care it does not burn). Add the anchovies, cut in pieces, with their oil if they are tinned. Crush them down with a wooden spoon or masher, keeping the heat low. As they dissolve, put in the butter, and then the oil gradually. You should end up with a fairly smooth brown sauce under a layer of oil. This can all be done in advance.

When ready to eat, bring the sauce to boiling point and put in a pot over a table burner, or in individual pots with nightlights underneath. (It is normal for the oil to separate and come to the top.) To eat, dip in vegetable pieces, stirring up the sauce. Provide long stubby bread 'soldiers' and bread-sticks (*grissini*), too.

If you include the eggs, put them on the table in a small basket. When the sauce reduces to a sediment, break in the eggs and scramble them with a fork. Scoop them up quickly before they overcook, with vegetables, bread or a fork.

[*Dishes of the Mediterranean*]


## CHICK-PEA AND SESAME SALAD (Hummus bi Tahina)

This recipe lifts chick-peas far above their basic role of standard nourishment. A blender or food processor is essential. Soaking time can vary: best quality chick-peas may only require 12 hours, but it is prudent to allow 48. The general rule for dried pulses is that when they have more or less doubled their weight, they have soaked for long enough. There is no magic about soaking – the point is to reduce cooking time, as the less you soak the more you cook, which wastes fuel.

Serves 4

*125 g (4 oz) dried chick-peas (not canned ones)*
*juice of 2 lemons*
*2 cloves of garlic, sliced*
*100 g (3½ oz) tahina paste*
*approx. 2 tablespoons olive oil*
*salt and pepper*
*cayenne pepper or finely chopped parsley, to garnish*

Soak the chick-peas, as described above. At the end of the soaking period simmer them for 1–1¼ hours. Then drain them, saving the liquor. Put 4 tablespoons of this liquor in a blender or food processor with the lemon juice and garlic. Start the blades whizzing and gradually tip in the chick-peas and tahina alternately. If the machine clogs, add a little more liquor, and some olive oil. You should end up with a thick, cohesive purée of a grainy creaminess. Be prepared to add extra olive oil, or tahina, to taste. Season with salt and pepper.

Put in a bowl. Smooth the top and cover with a barely perceptible layer of oil. Sprinkle with cayenne or parsley.

Hummus can be served on its own or as part of a mixed *meze* course. Scoop it up with bits of pitta bread. Or use it with okra and tomatoes (page 248), *cerkes tavugu* (Circassian chicken, page 237), felafel, peperonata and so on, to fill the pitta bread.

[*Dishes of the Mediterranean*]

## EGGS FLORENTINE

The Italians love spinach, and make more use of it than we do. All those green pasta, the *pasta verde*, are not coloured and flavoured by drops from a bottle, but by the addition of spinach and spinach juice. Sometimes ravioli and tortellini are filled with a mixture of spinach and cream cheese and Parmesan. When eggs, fish and ham are cooked and served with spinach and cheese sauce, we describe them as 'Florentine', in the style of Florence.

Serves 6

*1½–2 kg (3–4 lb) spinach, cooked*
*30 g (1 oz) butter*
*30 g (1 oz) flour*
*300 ml (½ pt) hot milk*

*150 ml (¼ pt) single cream*
*1 heaped tablespoon Parmesan cheese, or Cheddar to taste*
*salt, pepper, nutmeg*
*6 medium eggs*
*2 crumbled rusks or biscottes*

As the spinach cooks, make the sauce. Melt the butter in a heavy pan, stir in the flour with a wooden spoon. Cook gently for 2 minutes, then incorporate the hot milk gradually, to avoid lumps, and the single cream. Season with half the cheese or a little more to taste, with salt, pepper and nutmeg, and leave to simmer over a low heat for at least 15 minutes.

Meanwhile, having drained the spinach, put it into a buttered ovenproof dish, and prepare the eggs. They can be poached, but, if, like me, you're not an admirer of poached eggs, try cooking them this way – put them into a pan of fast-boiling water *for exactly 5 minutes*. Then plunge them into a pan of cold water, set under a gently running cold tap. The moment they're cool enough to handle, tap them all over carefully and peel them (remember that the yolks will not be hard-boiled, so do this gently).

Make 6 depressions in the spinach with the back of a tablespoon, and set the eggs well down. Strain the hot sauce over the dish. Mix the rest of the cheese with the rusk crumbs, and sprinkle over the top. Bake in a hot oven for about 10 minutes, until the sauce bubbles and the top turns golden brown.

## *Variations*

FOR SOLE OR PLACE FILLETS FLORENTINE: roll up the fillets and secure them with a toothpick. Put them on the spinach instead of the eggs. Finish the dish as above, but bake for 30 minutes in a moderate oven to cook the sole or plaice. The top can be browned under the grill, if necessary.

FOR HAM FLORENTINE: roll up slices of cooked ham, spear with a toothpick, and lay on the spinach. Pour over the sauce and finish as for eggs Florentine. If uncooked gammon is used, pour boiling water over the slices and leave for 5 minutes to remove excess saltiness. Lay them, overlapping each other, on top of the spinach, and finish as for eggs Florentine.

FOR INDIVIDUAL EGGS FLORENTINE: put a spoonful of spinach (4-day spinach is ideal for this dish) into a buttered ramekin. Break an egg and slide it on top of the spinach. Bake in an oven (or in a pan of simmering water) until the white just starts to look opaque. Pour in 1 tablespoon of double cream; sprinkle with cheese, salt, pepper, and rusk crumbs; brown quickly under the grill. Don't overcook. Serve with toast fingers.

[*Good Things*]


## GREEK SPINACH PIE (Spanakopitta)

Thin fila pastry dries rapidly and breaks, so have a damp cloth handy to put over it the moment it is unwrapped. Extract a sheet at a time, and wrap up immediately any you are not going to use.

Serves 8

> *60 g (2 oz) chopped spring onion or onion*
> *300 g (10 oz) butter*
> *750 g (1½ lb) cooked spinach, chopped*
> *225 g (8 oz) grated feta cheese, or mixed Parmesan cheese and dry grated Cheddar cheese*
> *4 large eggs (size 1–2)*
> *2 tablespoons dried dillweed*
> *2 tablespoons chopped parsley*
> *12 sheets (½ packet) fila pastry*
> *salt and pepper*

Preheat the oven to gas 4, 180°C (350°F). Cook the onion slowly in 90 g (3 oz) of the butter until soft but not brown. Mix in the spinach. Remove from the heat and stir in the cheese, eggs, herbs and seasoning (remember that the cheese and butter also contain salt).

Melt the remaining butter. Take a shallow tin into which a sheet of fila will fit, come up the sides and overhang the top – approximately 28 × 20 cm (11 × 8 inches) in area. Brush a sheet of fila with some of the melted butter and lay it in the tin. Repeat with 5 more fila sheets, putting each on top of the last. Put in the filling, sprinkle with a few spoonfuls of melted butter and flip over the fila at the edges.

Cut the remaining sheets to fit the top of the pie with a slight tuck-in. Brush them with butter and lay them on the pie. Score the top lightly into diamonds or squares, and sprinkle or spray with water: this prevents the pastry curling. Bake for about 45 minutes, until the top is golden brown.

### *Variation*
Creamed chicken, made piquant with feta and Parmesan, is another

popular filling. Lamb or beef mixtures, well spiced, sometimes with raisins and pine kernels added, also work well.

*[Dishes of the Mediterranean]*

## GREEK SUMMER SALAD (Salata)

This is the dish that makes me most homesick for Greece. Not because it was the best thing I ate there, but because it appeared in every small taverna on every beach, at every market or monument or site that I visited.

Serves 6

*1 lettuce, separated into its leaves*
*6 fine large tomatoes, peeled and quartered or sliced*
*½ cucumber, scored with a fork or zester, sliced*
*salt and pepper*
*12 spring onions, or 1 sweet onion*
*12 sprigs of fresh mint, chopped*
*1 heaped teaspoon* rigani
*4 tablespoons olive oil*
*2 tablespoons lemon juice*
*about 175 g (6 oz) feta cheese, crumbled, or sliced or cubed*
*18 black olives*

Roll up the lettuce leaves and slice the rolls across thinly with a stainless-steel knife. Scatter all over a serving dish. Arrange the tomatoes and a cucumber on top of the lettuce, leaving a good lettuce rim, in receding layers, seasoning as you go. Scatter with onion and herbs. Beat the oil with lemon juice and pour over the whole salad. Put the cheese and olives on top (sometimes rings of sweet pepper are added, too).

Serve straightaway – if this salad stands around for long the shreds of lettuce will wilt and the cucumber will weep.

*[European Cookery]*

## ITALIAN STUFFED MUSHROOMS (Funghi Ripieni)

Ceps are the ideal mushroom for this dish, but large field or cultivated mushrooms can be used instead.

Serves 4–6

*13 large mushrooms*
*1 medium onion, chopped*
*1 small clove garlic, crushed*
*olive oil*
*4 anchovy fillets, chopped*
*1 heaped tablespoon chopped parsley*
*salt, pepper*
*1-cm ( ½ -inch) slice of bread, crusts removed*
*1 egg*
*breadcrumbs*

Remove mushroom stalks and chop them up with one of the mushrooms. Stew onion and garlic in a couple of tablespoons of olive oil until they begin to soften. Add chopped mushrooms, raise heat, and cook for 5 minutes. Stir in anchovies and parsley, and cook for another 5 minutes. Remove from heat and correct seasoning. Meanwhile squeeze bread to a thick paste with a little water. Mix with fried mushroom mixture and bind with the egg. Fill the caps. Pour a little oil into a shallow ovenproof dish, and arrange the stuffed mushrooms in it close together. Sprinkle with breadcrumbs and olive oil. Bake in a fairly hot oven, gas 6, 200°C (400°F), for about 20 minutes – field and cultivated mushrooms will not need quite so long, so keep an eye on them after 10 minutes.

[*The Mushroom Feast*]

## MARINADED MUSHROOMS (Champignons à la Grecque)

This popular French dish is best served as part of a mixed hors d'oeuvre. When serving mushrooms like this on their own, the recipes which include tomato or tomato and orange are to be preferred on account of their extra piquant flavour. Be careful not to overcook the mushrooms: they should still be crisp in the centre.

Serves 4–8

*125 ml (4 fl oz) olive oil*
*300 ml ( ½ pt) water*
*juice of ½ lemon*
*¼ teaspoon peppercorns, crushed*
*¼ teaspoon coriander seeds, crushed*

*salt to taste*
*bouquet of ½ small bay leaf, sprig each of parsley, thyme, and fennel,*
*    plus 1 celery leaf*
*500 g (1 lb) small mushrooms*

Boil all the ingredients except the mushrooms together for 10 to 15 minutes to make a marinade. Add mushrooms, and boil for about 3 minutes, then leave to cool. Serve with a little of the marinade, well chilled.

## Marinaded Mushrooms with Tomatoes (Champignons à la Grecque)

Serves 4–8

Prepare the marinade and boil the mushrooms in it as directed in preceding recipe. Remove mushrooms, and reduce sauce until it is thick. Skin and chop 3 large tomatoes, add to sauce, and boil for a few minutes. Pour boiling sauce over mushrooms. Serve chilled, sprinkled with a little chopped parsley.

[*The Mushroom Feast*]

## MUSHROOM RISOTTO (Risotto ai Funghi)

When the French have a few ceps, they stretch them with potatoes. The northern Italians choose rice; the plump melting grains produced in the Po valley go well with mushrooms. The recipe is simple, the standard *risotto* with one extra ingredient.

Serves 4–6

*125 g (4 oz) butter*
*1 medium onion, chopped*
*250–375 g (8–12 oz) ceps, caps sliced, stalks chopped*
*500 g (1 lb) Italian rice*
*250 ml (8 fl oz) dry white wine*
*up to 1½ litres (2½ pt) meat stock*
*salt, pepper*
*Parmesan cheese, grated*

Melt half the butter, and sweat the onion in it. When it is soft, stir in the ceps and cook for another 5 minutes. Add the rice, and when it becomes translucent, pour in the wine. This will soon be absorbed, so add a quarter of the stock, then another quarter as that disappears. And so on, until the rice is cooked – about 20 minutes. Different kinds of rice, even different brands, need different amounts of liquid, so this is a dish to be watched.

Correct the seasoning and stir in the remaining butter and several tablespoons of cheese. Serve at once, with more grated cheese in a separate bowl.

[ *The Mushroom Feast* ]


## OLIVE AND ANCHOVY FLAN (Pissaladière)

If you're a cook living in the Mediterranean area, the sun does half the work for you. Tomatoes and onions have acquired a concentration of sweet richness; olive oil, olives and anchovies flavour them to perfection. This combination is well known to us all in the form of the *pizza*, which has sadly become a cliché, now, of snack bars and cookery demonstrations, and as tasteless as you'd expect. For this reason I'm concentrating on *pissaladière*, which is less known. I happen to prefer the filling when set off by pastry rather than by bread dough as in the *pizza*; and it's easier for most housewives to make; unless they bake their own bread, in which case *pizza* can be one of the delicious side-products.

*Pissaladière* comes from the area of Nice, where they use a conserve of anchovies flavoured with cloves called *pissala*, rather than anchovy fillets. *Pissala* is the modern descendant of those vigorous Roman confections known as *garum* or *liquamen*; they were made of anchovies, or anchovies and various other fish, pickled and fermented in brine, and were used in many dishes, as a kind of antique monosodium glutamate. *Pizza*, which sounds rather the same, means pie, so any connection between the two words is probably coincidental. Both, after all, are made in areas where tomatoes, olive oil, olives and anchovies are to be had in abundance. You don't need to be a diffusionist to arrive at similar dishes.

Serves 6

*shortcrust pastry, made with 250 g (8 oz) flour, and seasoned with*
   *1 tablespoon of cinnamon*

FILLING
*6 tablespoons olive oil*
*1 kg (2 lb) onions, sliced*
*3 cloves garlic, crushed*
*400 g (14 oz) can tomatoes*
*2 lumps of sugar*
bouquet garni
*1 tablespoon tomato concentrate*
*2 tins of anchovy fillets, 60 g (2 oz) each*
*125 g (4 oz) black olives*

Line a 26-cm (10¼-inch) to 28-cm (11-inch) flan tin (with a removable base), and bake blind, until the pastry is firm and set, but not brown.

Cook the onions and garlic slowly in the olive oil for 1 hour, until they're reduced to a soft mass. They must not brown at all (it helps to cover them for the first 30 minutes). In another pan, boil down the tomatoes, sugar, and *bouquet garni*, until the mixture is reduced to about 6 tablespoons of purée. Stir in the concentrate, and remove the *bouquet*. Mix with the onions. Season well, having regard to the saltiness of the anchovies, and spread out evenly over the baked pastry case. Split the anchovy fillets in half lengthwise. Arrange them in a lattice over the filling, then put an olive into each diamond-shaped compartment. Brush over lightly with olive oil. Bake in a fairly hot oven (gas 6, 200°C (400°F)) for 20 minutes or so, until the pastry is properly cooked, the filling thoroughly heated, and the olives beginning to wrinkle. Eat hot, cold or warm, with a glass or two of red wine.

It makes marvellous picnic food, particularly if you can manage to bake it just before leaving home. Wrap it loosely in foil, and it should still be warm by early lunch-time. You may find it more convenient to bake small *pissaladières*, as they often do in northern France in the grander *charcuteries*; use patty pans, the ones with almost perpendicular straight sides, and a diameter of 11 cm (4½ inches). Naturally, more shortcrust pastry will be required; about double the amount.

[*Fish Cookery*]

## PIPERADE (Piperrada)

A Basque dish of cheerful colour and flavour, and an ideal summer
lunch especially if you grow your own tomatoes. The tomato and
pepper sauce (*sofrito*) can be prepared in advance, but the eggs and
ham must be dealt with at the very last moment.

Serves 6

*750 g (1½ lb) red or green peppers, or both mixed*
*375 g (12 oz) chopped onion*
*150 ml (¼ pt) olive oil*
*3 cloves of garlic, crushed and chopped*
*750 g (1½ lb) tomatoes, peeled and chopped*
*a good pinch of thyme*
*salt and pepper*
*sugar, to taste*
*6 slices of Bayonne or Parma ham, or thin gammon*
*6 eggs, beaten*

Grill, or bake the peppers in a hot oven gas 8, 230°C (450°F), or turn
them over a gas flame, until the skin turns black and blistered. Rub it
away under the cold tap; seed and slice the peppers.

Make a *sofrito* in a shallow earthenware pot (use a heat-diffuser for
gas) by cooking the onion slowly in about two-thirds of the olive oil,
then adding the garlic as the onion begins to look transparent. When
the onion is soft and yellow, add the tomatoes. Stir them about and
when they are cooking away, put in the pepper strips, thyme and
seasoning, adding sugar if the tomatoes are not as well-flavoured as
they should be. Keep the mixture bubbling so that all wateriness
disappears.

In the rest of the oil, heat the slices of ham briefly. Stir the eggs into
the vegetable mixture. Take the pot off the heat straightaway as egg
cooks rapidly and it should not be allowed to harden. Tuck the ham
round the edge or place it on top. Serve immediately.

[*European Cookery*]

## RICE AND PEAS (Risi e Bisi)

Driving along between the arcaded de Chirico towns of Cuneo and
Turin, one may round a corner to find that life has shifted suddenly
to the Far East. Rows of girls, with skirts kilted up and low conical

straw hats on the back of their necks, paddle along pushing rice plants into flooded fields. The extra large grains that these paddy fields produce give the rice dishes of Northern Italy a special succulence. For this dish of *risi e piselli*, or *risi e bisi* to Venetians, who make it a great deal, try to buy some of this delicious rice from an Italian delicatessen.

Serves 4

*90–125 g (3–4 oz) chopped onion*
*3 tablespoons olive oil*
*250 g (8 oz) Italian rice*
*½ litre (¾ pt) water*
*500 g (1 lb) shelled peas*
*sugar, salt, black pepper*
*grated Parmesan cheese*

Brown the onion lightly in the oil. Add the rice and stir it over the heat until transparent – about 5 minutes. Add ½ litre (¾ pt) water, and leave to simmer with the lid on the pan, until the rice is tender and the water absorbed. You may need to add more water, so watch the rice as it cooks. Meanwhile cook the peas in boiling water, seasoned with salt, pepper and a little sugar. Drain and mix with the cooked rice. Stir in 2 tablespoons of Parmesan cheese, and serve extra grated cheese in a separate bowl.

By adding hot chicken stock at the end, this dish can be turned into a hearty soup.

[*Good Things*]

# FISH

### FISH STEW (Bourride)

Any firm white fish can be used; one alone, or a mixture. The ideal fish is monkfish, turbot or John Dory, but squid make an excellent *bourride* as well. Saffron is occasionally used to scent and colour the soup, but the most usual flavouring is orange peel, 1–2 good strips of it, preferably from a Seville orange. The *ailloli* is used to thicken the soup. Croûtons rubbed with garlic are served with it, as with *bouillabaisse*. Potatoes can be cooked and presented separately, or included in the soup.

Serves 6

*1½–2 kg (3–4 lb) firm white fish, or squid*
*2 large onions, chopped*
*1 leek, chopped*
*4 cloves garlic*
*2 tomatoes (optional)*
*500 g (1 lb) potatoes sliced (see above)*
*bouquet of herbs: thyme, fennel, parsley, bay*
*strips of orange peel*
*salt, pepper*
ailloli *(see below)*
*12 slices French bread, toasted lightly in the oven, fried in olive oil, and*
   *rubbed with garlic*

Clean the fish and cut into good-sized slices. Put onions, leek, garlic, tomatoes, and potatoes (if included), into a large pot. Lay the fish on top, with the herbs, orange peel, and seasoning. Add 1¼ litres (2 pt) of water, or enough to cover the fish; stock made from head and bones of fish can be used instead for a finer result; in some places sea water is used. Cook *gently* for 10 minutes at simmering point. Remove fish, and potatoes, to a warm serving plate. Boil the liquor hard to less than 600 ml (1 pt). Correct the seasoning. Then strain slowly on to the *ailloli*, in a large bowl, mixing the two together carefully. Return to a clean pan and stir over a low heat until the mixture thickens slightly. Pour over the fish, sprinkle with extra parsley, and serve with bread as above, and with potatoes if not included in the soup-making.

[*Fish Cookery*]

## GARLIC MAYONNAISES (Ailloli and Aillade)

*Ailloli*, the garlic mayonnaise from Provence, gives its name to the great spread of cold food for which that part of France is so famous. Salt cod and other fish provide the centrepiece (page 221). The sauce can quite well accompany the salt fish in simpler combinations or even alone; though I think a modifying salad of some kind is a good idea.

   *up to 8 cloves garlic*
   *salt*
   *2 egg yolks*
   *300 ml (½ pt) Provençal olive oil*
   *pepper*
   *lemon juice*

Crush the garlic with a little salt in a mortar. (The first time you make the recipe start with 4 cloves of garlic; when everyone's got used to the idea, work up gradually to 8.) Add the egg yolks and finish the mayonnaise with the rest of the ingredients.

The unexpected ingredients of *aillade*, another garlic mayonnaise, are hazelnuts and walnuts. To me, this is the ideal sauce for a simpler arrangement of cold fish:

*8 large shelled hazelnuts*
*8 shelled walnuts*
*3–6 cloves garlic*
*salt*
*2 egg yolks*
*300 ml ( ½ pt) Provençal olive oil*
*pepper*
*lemon juice*

Grill the hazelnuts lightly, until the skins can easily be rubbed off; pour boiling water over the walnuts, and remove their skins. Crush the nuts with the garlic and a little salt in a mortar, and continue with the mayonnaise in the usual way.

[*Fish Cookery*]


## AILLOLI GARNI WITH SALT COD

The most spectacular dish of summer holidays in Provence is *ailloli garni*. At its most flamboyant, it is a Matisse-coloured salad of salt cod and other fish, vegetables fresh and dried, raw and cooked, hard-boiled eggs, snails occasionally, and lemon quarters. With it comes a huge bowl of mayonnaise, a special garlic mayonnaise. The flavour has nothing to do with rubbing a clove of garlic discreetly round a salad bowl. It comes from clove after clove after clove. So important is this sauce that the dish carries its name of *ailloli* – *ail* being French for garlic – with all the rest reduced to the status of a garnish, lordly abundance being just an excuse as it were for eating the sauce. Although mayonnaise has a way of dominating nomenclature – *mayonnaise de saumon, mayonnaise de homard* – I think no other name touches the grandeur of *ailloli garni*.

The sauce (see preceding page) is the last thing to be made. First you must assemble the other ingredients. A nice piece of salt cod is the first requirement. Soak it for at least 24 hours, changing the water, then drain it and put it into a large pan. Cover with cold water, and add *bouquet garni* and a little salt. Bring slowly to the boil and simmer for about 20 minutes (or less) until the fish flakes away from skin and bone. Don't overcook. Put on a perforated dish to cool. Remove the skin, and put on a large serving dish. Surround it with as great a variety of vegetables as you can assemble. Crispness is required (raw Florentine fennel, cauliflower, radishes, peppers and celery); so, with that sauce, is mild solidity (potatoes, haricot beans). Decorate finally with lemon quarters, egg quarters, and unshelled prawns.

[*Fish Cookery*]


## MARINADED SEAFOOD (Seviche)

Serves 6

It is magical to watch citrus juice 'cooking' fish. If you put it into a glass bowl, and look into the refrigerator from time to time, you will see the scallops or bass or sole losing transparency and beginning to look exactly as if you had steamed or poached it. The blend of sharpness and fresh fish is most refreshing.

As well as the fish mentioned above, you can use John Dory, brill or weaver, sea bream or mackerel. Go for freshness.

Skin and cut 500–750 g (1–1½ lb) of fish fillets into strips or cubes about 2½ cm (1 inch) long. Large scallops can be sliced across into 2 discs. Put them into a dish and cover them with lime juice or lemon juice. Seed a hot pepper, a Jamaican Scotch bonnet pepper for instance, and slice it, adding it to the fish. Cover and leave for up to 3 hours in the refrigerator. Taste occasionally to see whether the hot pepper is making too powerful an effect, and remove it if necessary.

Drain and dress with Seville orange juice. Serve on salad leaves, with thin slices of purple onion, avocado, tomato and a little sweetcorn. Sometimes slices of cooked white sweet potato are added.

[*À La Carte*]


## PAELLA

Like couscous (page 230), paella is one of those magnificent dishes that need a party to share them. A picnic by the sea in this case, I think, with the shallow pan bubbling gently over a driftwood fire. Again like couscous, there is no one 'right' recipe. The only essential ingredients are rice and saffron (do not be tempted to substitute turmeric – make your economies elsewhere if necessary!). Flavourings can be meat and poultry alone, or fish and shellfish alone, or vegetables alone. Or – as in this recipe – a mixture of all three. I have come to regard squid as essential for its piquant sweetness; mussels help to flavour the broth, and huge *gambas* (Mediterranean prawns) give an air of luxury, though the usual pink prawns do well enough.

Serves 8–10

*1½ kg (3½ lb) roasting chicken, with giblets*
*2 litres (3½ pt) light stock or water*
*1 small lobster, uncooked or ready-boiled, cut up by the fishmonger*
*1 medium-size squid, approx. 250 g (½ lb) in weight*
*500 g (1 lb) prawns, preferably of varying sizes*
*500 g (1 lb) mussels*
*250 g (½ lb) monkfish*
*olive oil*
*1 large onion, chopped finely*
*250 g (½ lb) tomatoes, peeled and chopped*
*1 heaped teaspoon paprika*
*3 large cloves of garlic, chopped finely*
*tomato paste or sugar, if needed (see recipe)*
*500 ml (¾ pt) Spanish or Italian rice (approx. 400 g (14 oz))*
*a generous pinch of saffron*
*175 g (6 oz) shelled young peas*
*1 large red pepper, grilled, skinned, de-seeded and sliced*
*4 large artichoke hearts, cooked (optional)*
*3 lemons, quartered*
*salt and pepper*

Use a wide, shallow pan or *paellera* of at least 35 cm (14 inches) diameter. Alternatively, use two pans once the rice is half-cooked, transferring some of the rice to a second pan before putting in the chicken. Paella is not a dish for the small family. Remember that if you alter the quantity of rice, you need to alter that of the liquid.

First, prepare the chicken and fish. If you intend to make the paella out of doors, on a picnic, this should all be done in advance, leaving the final cooking of the rice and so on to be done on the spot.

Set aside the chicken wings and drumsticks. Cut away the chicken breast and keep for another meal, if you are only feeding 8 people. Cut the thigh meat off the bone, dividing each piece into three, and remove the oysters. If you are using the chicken breasts, bone them and cut into two pieces each. Leave the carcase to simmer in the stock or water. Cut up the lobster so that there will be a chunk for each person.

Clean the squid and cut the bag into rings and the tentacles into short lengths: keep the trimmings and left-overs. Peel most of the prawns, leaving a few whole for garnishing: put the debris with the squid's. Open the scrubbed mussels in a heavy covered pan over a high heat: shell most of the mussels, keeping some for the garnishing, and strain the juice into the chicken stock pan. Add the fish trimmings after the stock has been simmering for at least 30 minutes. Cut the monkfish into chunks: add the bone and skin, and the small claws of the lobster, to the stock pot. Give it another 30 minutes and then strain off the stock – you will need just over 1 litre (approx. 2 pt) or a little more, so add water if you are short, or boil it down if there is much too much. Season the chicken and fish.

Now you are ready for the cooking. Bring the stock to simmering point and keep it there. In a large pan or *paellera* heat enough olive oil to cover the base. Put in the onion and cook it slowly until soft and yellow. Add the tomatoes, paprika, garlic, seasoning and a little tomato paste or sugar unless your tomatoes are very well ripened. When the mixture is a thick purée, push it to the side of the pan and brown the chicken pieces. Remove them to a plate. Stir in the rice and move it about until it looks transparent. Pour about half the hot stock on to the rice. Pour a little more stock into a cup and dissolve the saffron in it. Leave the rice to bubble gently.

When the rice is half-cooked, put in the chicken, pushing it down so that only the drumstick and wing bones stick up. Pour in the saffron stock and most of the remaining stock.

After 10 minutes put in the squid. In another 5 minutes, add the vegetables and uncooked lobster pieces. Check the chicken breast pieces and remove them if they are done: they should not get too dry and can be put back at the end to heat through with the prawns and mussels. Another 8–10 minutes and everything should be cooked. Add any remaining stock or water, if necessary to prevent sticking. Shake the pan from time to time, but avoid stirring it up.

Just before serving, put in the shelled mussels and cut-up, cooked lobster meat, if you had to buy a ready-boiled lobster. Then add the shelled prawns. Last of all, arrange the reserved whole prawns and mussels in their shells on top, after checking the seasoning. Tuck in the lemon wedges and serve.

*Note:* in Spanish restaurants, the *paellera* is sometimes placed in a slightly larger basket tray, with a ring of flowers and fruit in the gap – red and white carnations, yellow lemons, echoing the colours of the food. Festive but confusing.

[*Dishes of the Mediterranean*]

## SEAFOOD PUDDING (Strata)

One of the best bread-and-butter puddings, but made with crab or prawns. For economy, a proportion of lightly cooked and flaked white fish can be used with the crab or prawns, but never more than half.

Serves 6

*butter*
*12 slices from a small sandwich loaf*
*meat from a large crab, or 250 g (½ lb) shelled crab or shelled prawns*
*1 tender celery stalk, chopped finely*
*1 tablespoon chopped onion*
*150 ml (¼ pt) mayonnaise*
*3 tablespoons mixed herbs – chopped parsley, tarragon, chervil and chives*
*3 tablespoons grated Parmesan cheese*
*approx. 175 g (6 oz) Gruyère, fontina or Gouda cheese, grated*
*4 eggs*
*250 ml (8 fl oz) milk*
*250 ml (8 fl oz) single cream*
*salt, pepper and cayenne pepper*

Butter the bread and cut off the crusts. Season the crab or prawns. Mix the celery and onion with the mayonnaise, herbs and Parmesan and then fold into the shellfish. Make six sandwiches with the mixture.

Butter a dish that will take the sandwiches in a single layer. Cut them in half and place in the dish. Dot with the grated Gruyère, fontina or Gouda. Beat the eggs with the milk and cream and pour into the dish. Leave in the fridge 2 hours or longer (overnight will not hurt).

Bake in the oven, preheated to gas 4, 180°C (350°F) for 30–40 minutes, lowering the heat as the top browns.

[*Dishes of the Mediterranean*]

## SEAFOOD VOL-AU-VENTS (Croûte aux Fruits de Mer)

The success of this dish depends on the quality of the seafood, its freshness and sweetness, and on your skill in seasoning. It's a matter of attractive assembly and taste, rather than of any cooking skill. If lobsters are impossibly expensive locally, use chopped mussels or lightly simmered scallops instead. Or even some fine, cooked white fish such as sole, John Dory, turbot, or anglerfish. The thing to avoid is canned lobster and crab, they are too tasteless for this French recipe – and for any other, I think.

Serves 6

*1* vol-au-vent *case, about 20 cm (8 inches) across*

CRAB SALAD
*1 large crab, boiled*
*4 finely chopped shallots*
*a small bunch of parsley, chopped*
*a small bunch of chives, chopped*
*5 tablespoons oil*
*1 tablespoon wine vinegar*
*juice of 1 lemon*
*1 avocado pear*
*salt, pepper, cayenne pepper*

LOBSTER SALAD
*1 boiled lobster, 1 kg (2 lb) in weight*
*avocado mayonnaise (page 227)*

*1 avocado pear, peeled, stoned and sliced*
*tail meat from lobster above*
*175–250 g (6–8 oz) unpeeled prawns*

If you make the *vol-au-vent* case at home, you will need 500 g (1 lb) total weight puff pastry. Bake in a very hot oven (gas 8, 230°C (450°F)) until risen and brown. Leave to cool.

Remove the meat from the crab and mix it with the other crab salad ingredients, and the avocado pear, peeled, stoned and diced.

For the lobster salad, remove the claw meat and meat from the head, and mix it with avocado mayonnaise. Slice the tail meat neatly across and set it aside for the garnish.

Put a layer of lobster salad in the pastry case, then all the crab salad, then another layer of lobster salad. Arrange a circle of avocado slices on top as garnish, with tail meat in the centre. Stand prawns, head up, around the outside of the pastry case. *Serve immediately.*

[*Fish Cookery*]

## Avocado Mayonnaise

Excellent with shellfish, on account of its beautiful colour, as well as its flavour. I do not find it very harmonious with other fish; it seems to need the sweetness of shellfish for complete success. Here are two recipes, the first quick and simple, the second a little more work but much better in flavour and so worth the trouble.

*1 avocado pear, peeled and stoned (pitted)*
*1 egg*
*4 tablespoons salad oil*
*juice of ½ lemon*
*½ teaspoon salt*
*½ teaspoon mustard*

Cut avocado into rough cubes. Mix in blender with other ingredients, at top speed, for 10 seconds, until creamy. Adjust seasoning to taste. A hint of sugar may be needed.

*basic mayonnaise made with salad oil*
*1 tablespoon tomato ketchup*
*1 teaspoon Tabasco sauce*
*a pinch of cayenne pepper*
*1 avocado pear, peeled and stoned (pitted)*
*1 measure vodka (optional)*

Season the basic mayonnaise with the next three ingredients. Mash or sieve avocado to a fine purée. Fold it into the mayonnaise and add vodka if used. Adjust seasoning to taste.

[*Fish Cookery*]

## SHELLFISH RISOTTO

One of the pleasures of eating is good rice. By this I mean Italian rice, or French rice from the Camargue, huge oblong grains which cook to a juicy *risotto* without losing their individual form. I cannot conceal my preference for this European rice; or my affection for the man-made landscape of the Po, where oriental paddy fields separate one Renaissance or Mannerist city from the next. To the rice add shellfish, as they do in Venice – clams, mussels, oysters, lobster or crawfish, cockles, prawns and shrimps of all kinds – and you have one of those perfect unions which stimulate high respect for the civilization where it came about.

Serves 4–6

*60 g (2 oz) butter*
*1 medium onion, chopped*
*500 g (1 lb) rice*
*250 ml (8 fl oz) dry white wine*
*1¼ litres (2 pt) water*
*300 ml (½ pt) concentrated fish stock or mussel liquor*
*salt, pepper*
*1 small lobster, shelled and cut up*
*or 1 crawfish, shelled and cut up*
*or 3½ litres (6 pt) mussels*
*or 3½ litres (6 pt) clams*
*or 3½ litres (6 pt) cockles*
*or 375 g (¾ lb) shelled prawns or shrimps*
*or 30 scampi*
*90 g (3 oz) butter*
*1 clove garlic*
*parsley*
*60 g (2 oz) butter*
*60 g (2 oz) grated Parmesan cheese*

Use suitable shells from the fish for making a fish stock, plus the usual trimmings; or keep the liquor from opening mussels etc., and use as well as, or instead of, fish stock.

To make the *risotto* cook the onion in the butter until soft and golden (don't brown it). Stir in the rice and when it looks transparent, pour in the wine. This will soon be absorbed, so add 300 ml (½ pt) of the hot water, and as it disappears, another 300 ml (½ pt). Use the fish stock next, and the rest of the water if required. The rice will take 20–30 minutes to cook. It should be tender but not mushy to the tongue, and juicy – juicier, for instance than curry or pilaff rice – but not wet.

When the rice is done, quickly reheat the cooked or opened shellfish in their butter, with the finely chopped clove of garlic. A matter of seconds only, or the fish will toughen. Stir into the *risotto* with the parsley and the final 60 g (2 oz) of butter. Turn on to a serving dish and sprinkle with the Parmesan.

*Note:* 500 g (1 lb) of tender young squid, cut in rings and fried in olive oil until cooked, can also be added to a *risotto*. So can pieces of eel fried in olive oil. Chopped anchovies are sometimes used, with a little more garlic, and plenty of parsley. The only rule is that the fish must be piquant in flavour, and firm.

[*Fish Cookery*]

## SPAGHETTI WITH CLAMS (Spaghetti alle Vongole)

Small clams in a tomato sauce are often served with spaghetti in central and southern Italy. In the north, in Venice, they would be added to a *risotto* (page 227), with a lump of butter rather than tomato sauce.

Serves 6

*500 g (1 lb) spaghetti*
*3 kg (6 lb) clams, washed*
*3 tablespoons olive oil*
*1 large onion, chopped*
*3 cloves garlic, chopped*
*400 g (14 oz) can tomatoes*
*60 g (2 oz) chopped parsley (large bunch)*

Cook the spaghetti in plenty of boiling salted water in the usual way, until it is cooked but not slimily soft. Drain and keep warm until the sauce is finished.

Start the sauce as soon as the spaghetti goes into the pan. Open the clams in a large pan over a moderate heat, discard the shells and strain off the liquid from the fish. Brown the onion and garlic lightly in the oil. Add the tomatoes and some of the clam liquor. Boil down to a rich sauce. Add clams, which will be adequately cooked, just to re-heat them. Remove sauce from the stove, stir in the parsley and pour over the spaghetti, mixing it well.

*Note:* mussels can be used instead of clams.

[*Fish Cookery*]


## TUNNY KEBABS (Crostini di Tonno Fresco)

A recipe for fresh, good quality tunny fish. Be sure to place the sage leaves next to it on the skewers for the full benefit of the flavour.

Serves 6

*600 g (1¼ lb) tunny*
*bread*
*small sage leaves*
*olive oil*
*salt, pepper*
*lemon juice*

Cut the tunny into regular slices about the thickness of a finger, and divide the slices into squares. Cut an equal number of squares of bread, without crusts, of a similar size. Wash plenty of sage leaves.

Thread the tunny and bread on to six skewers, with sage leaves on either side of each piece of tunny. Half-leaves of bay can be substituted for some of the sage leaves.

Brush the skewers with olive oil, and season them. Grill at a very moderate temperature for about 30 minutes, brushing tunny and bread with oil whenever they begin to look in the least dry.

Squeeze lemon juice over them and serve.

[*Fish Cookery*]

# MEAT, GAME AND POULTRY

## NORTH AFRICAN STEW (Couscous)

Couscous is a magnificently hospitable dish for a number of people. Meat and vegetables can be varied with the season. If one or two extra people turn up, just add extra couscous. The explanation may sound laborious, but once you understand the stages, couscous is very little trouble – especially if you make it at the weekend when there is help around. Then the preparation is nearly as much fun for everyone as the eating.

The traditional *couscoussier* is a huge double pot. In the large base part, meat and vegetables are cooked; in the perforated upper part, the couscous itself is steamed. A large stew or stock pot and a colander or steamer can quite well be substituted.

Serves 8–10

*375–750 g (¾–1½ lb) shin of beef*
*4 sections of marrow bone shank, 13–18 cm (5–7 inches) long*
*4–8 slices of scrag end of mutton or lamb*
*½–1 chicken (boiling or roasting fowl)*
*oil*
*1 large onion, sliced, plus the skin*
*a generous pinch of saffron*
*8-cm (3-inch) stick of cinnamon*
*4 tomatoes, peeled and chopped*
*4–6 medium-size carrots, peeled*
*175 g (6 oz) chick-peas, soaked for 36 hours*
*1 red, hot chilli, de-seeded*

500 g (1–1¼ lb) couscous
a heart of 1 cabbage, sliced
3–4 small white turnips, peeled (optional)
250 g (8 oz) shelled broad beans (optional)
250 g (8 oz) pumpkin, cubed (optional)
8 tiny courgettes
60–100 g (2–4 oz) raisins
2 tablespoons coriander
harissa or cayenne pepper and paprika
butter
salt and pepper
extra coriander and chopped parsley, to garnish

Trim surplus fat from the beef and cube the meat. Block the ends of the marrow bones with tied-on foil, to stop the marrow falling out. Trim fat from the lamb. Season the chicken inside and out and set aside in the refrigerator. (If you use a boiling fowl rather than a roaster, cook it from the start with the beef and so on.)

In a frying pan, brown the beef and lamb lightly in a little oil. Put it in a stew pot or the base of a *couscoussier*. Brown the onion in the pan and then put it with its skin on top of the meat. Add the marrow bones. Pour in water to cover generously. Bring to the boil and skim conscientiously, adding cold water to replace what the skimming has removed and to encourage the foam to rise. When clear, add the saffron, cinnamon, tomatoes and carrots, and the drained chick-peas tied in a muslin bag. Simmer at about 90°C (190°F) for 1½ hours, covered. This gives the fat a chance to solidify on the surface, so that it can be removed.

Two hours before the meal, reheat the beef. Put in the chicken and the chilli. Add extra water if necessary, but the chicken does not need to be covered if it is a roaster. Bring to simmering point, skim and remove a mugful of liquid.

Line the top of the *couscoussier* or a colander with stockinette or muslin. Stir the couscous round with some water in a basin, and then drain it and put it in the cloth. Raise the heat under the meat pot so that the liquid boils steadily. Put the top section in place. Tie a tea towel round the join to prevent steam escaping and leave for 30 minutes. Occasionally, dip your hands in some oil and run them through the conscous to air it. When you remove the couscous after 30 minutes, taste the liquid and remove the chilli if it is hot enough for your tastes.

Tip the couscous into a bowl, sprinkle it carefully with cold water and stir through to separate any lumps. Use more water or a little oil so that it runs freely. Add salt and then put the top part back on the boiling meat and stock, after slipping in the remaining vegetables, raisins and coriander. Give it a further 30 minutes. By this time the couscous should be tender and much swollen. Try it, and be prepared to give it longer, though this is rarely necessary with the packaged couscous.

To make the fiery sauce to go with couscous, simply stir 1 tablespoon of *harissa* into the mugful of stock previously removed and reheat it, stirring. Alternatively, mix in paprika and cayenne. This sauce is used in dabs, like mustard.

To serve, heap the couscous on an earthenware dish. (In North Africa a shallow earthenware dish with a tall conical lid is used. This is called a *tajine*; the base of it is a *kesra*.) Melt a good lump of butter and pour it over. Gently make a crater in the top for the meat. Keep it warm. Remove the meat you wish to serve from its bones. Season the pieces and place them with the best bits of vegetable on top of the couscous, or in a separate dish. Carefully remove the foil from the marrow bones, so that the marrow can slip out and lie on top, like the delicacy it is. Scatter with coriander and parsley. Strain off the broth into a pan, season and boil it down if need be. Remove the chick-peas from their bag and add to the broth. Drink it first, or put bowls on the table for people to drink it with the couscous itself. Finally, serve the couscous, and give everyone a tiny pot of the hot sauce.

*Note:* if you bring back *ras-el-hanout* or the French *quatre-épices* from a holiday in North Africa, use it in the seasoning of couscous.

[*Dishes of the Mediterranean*]

## PILAFF

Another recipe with many variations. Different nuts can be used – pine kernels are a favourite choice. Sultanas make a substitute for raisins, and saffron will give a better colour and flavour than turmeric. For a plain pilaff, omit spice, almonds and raisins. Bulghur can be substituted for rice. Serve as an accompaniment to grilled or stewed meat.

Serves 6–8

*1 large onion, chopped*
*olive oil*
*500 g (1–1¼ lb) long grain rice*
*approx. 1½ litres (2½ pt) stock appropriate to the accompanying meat,*
*    or water*

*1 rounded teaspoon turmeric or a large pinch of saffron*
*4 heaped tablespoons slivered almonds or pine kernels*
*4 heaped tablespoons raisins or sultanas*
*chopped parsley*
*salt and pepper*

Brown the onion lightly in just enough oil to cover the base of the pan. Stir in the rice, and when it goes transparent, pour in about 500 ml (¾ pt) of the stock or water, with the turmeric or saffron. Simmer gently, covered, adding extra stock or water as required. The rice should never be swamped and by the time it is cooked (20–25 minutes) there should be no more liquid visible: the top of the rice will have little holes in its flatness. Stir in the nuts and fruit, with enough seasoning and chopped parsley to give a lightly speckled effect.

Turn the rice on to a hot dish and place the cooked meat in the centre. Scatter with a very little more parsley and serve.

[*Dishes of the Mediterranean*]

## LIVER AND ONIONS (Fegato alla Veneziana)

Quite the best version of a favourite European combination, but you should use calf's liver. The tricky thing is to cook it so briefly that it remains slightly pink inside.

Serves 4

*375 g (¾ lb) piece of calf's liver*
*750 g (1½ lb) onions, sliced*
*3 tablespoons olive oil*
*salt and pepper*
*chopped parsley, to garnish*

Half-freeze the liver, so that it is solid enough to cut into thin, tissue-paper slivers. Put them on kitchen paper to thaw and drain and then pat them dry.

Cook the onions slowly in just enough oil to cover the base of a large, heavy frying pan. Put a lid or some foil on top at first. As the juices run, remove the lid or foil so that they can evaporate, to leave you eventually with a soft golden mass of onion, not browned but very tender. Season with salt and pepper. This can be done in advance.

Just before serving the dish, and after the first course if you are eating one, set the pan over a high heat. When it is sizzling, stir in the leaves of liver and keep stirring for about 30 seconds, or until the liver is brown in part, but still a little pink – you are in effect stir-frying. Remove the pan and season again. Tip everything into a warm serving dish, or divide immediately between four warm dinner plates. Sprinkle with a little parsley and serve.

[*Dishes of the Mediterranean*]

## CYPRIOT SAUTÉED PORK (Afelia)

Pork in Cyprus is excellent. I suspect that farmers there are not yet breeding the skinny modern pig, since the chops are of a size and tenderness difficult to find in this country. When making this dish, which should be succulent, be careful not to overcook it.

Serves 6

*6 thick pork chops*
*salt, pepper and sugar*
*olive oil*
*250 ml (8 fl oz) red wine*
*1 heaped tablespoon coriander seeds, lightly crushed*

Cube the meat from the chops, discarding bones, skin and obvious gristle, but including the fat. Rub in salt and pepper, sprinkle with a pinch of sugar, cover and leave overnight in the refrigerator.

To cook, heat a thin layer of oil in a heavy sauté pan (large enough to take all the meat in one layer) and sizzle the cubes rapidly, until they are brown all over. Pour off any surplus fat. Add the wine and let it bubble fast for a minute. Half-cover the pan, lower the heat and leave the pork to finish cooking. Turn it over regularly. It will need upwards of 2 minutes. The sauce should boil down to a little rich gravy. Stir the coriander seeds into the pan, leave for a few moments and then serve with new potatoes, bulghur or rice pilaff (page 232), and a salad.

[*Dishes of the Mediterranean*]

## VEAL OR TURKEY ESCALOPES (Saltimbocca)

A quick appetizing dish – the name means 'leap into the mouth' – which should not be kept hanging about. With veal the price it is,

Italians are beginning to use sliced turkey breast for dishes of this kind. But be careful, turkey is a much drier meat than veal and should be cooked more briefly. Chill it thoroughly in the ice-making compartment of the refrigerator, so that you can cut paper-thin slices on the slant.

For 4–5 people you will need 500 g (1 lb) turkey slices, or 4–5 escalopes of veal, which need to be beaten out between greaseproof paper or clear film. You also need 125 g (¼ lb) *prosciutto crudo* and enough small fresh sage leaves to give you one for each *saltimbocca* – 18 to be on the safe side.

Spread out the turkey slices, or cut the flattened escalopes into 2–3 pieces each, and spread them out. On each put a piece of *prosciutto* cut to fit, and a sage leaf. Roll up the little pieces and secure them with a wooden cocktail stick or toothpick. (In some versions, the sage leaves are put between veal and ham, and the pieces are not rolled up: this shortens the cooking time to 4 minutes.)

Brown the little rolls on both sides in butter. Pour in 90 ml (3 fl oz) Marsala, cover and simmer for a further 3–5 minutes, turning the rolls once. Serve immediately with the pan sauce.

*Note:* if you replace the sage with batons of Gruyère cheese, the dish is known as *bocconcini* (little mouthfuls).

[*European Cookery*]


## VEAL WITH TOMATO SAUCE (Ossi Bucho)

Find an intelligent butcher who will cut 4 cm (1½ inch) thick veal slices for you, across the shin of the animal. These are *ossi bucho*, hollow (marrow) bones, a favourite Milanese food. Season and brown these bones carefully, so that the marrow doesn't fall out, in olive oil. Pour over a large glass of dry white wine. Boil hard to reduce, for about 5 minutes. Transfer the bones to a casserole, where they can lie flat in a single layer. Add a good 600 ml (1 pt) of tomato sauce to the pan juices, bring to the boil and pour over the veal. Simmer gently in a low oven until tender. This can be done in advance, and the dish reheated just before the meal.

Serve sprinkled with 2 tablespoons chopped parsley, mixed with the grated rind of half a large lemon, and 1 chopped clove of garlic. Boiled rice is the usual accompaniment to this excellent dish.

[*Good Things*]

## SWEET-SOUR RABBIT (OR HARE) ITALIAN STYLE, WITH CHOCOLATE

It may need an act of faith to include the chocolate, but please don't leave it out. And make sure it's the bitter kind. Pine kernels can be bought at delicatessen or health food shops.

Serves 4

*1 rabbit, jointed (or 1 young hare)*
*seasoned flour*

MARINADE
*½ litre (¾ pt) red wine*
*2 heaped tablespoons each onion and carrot*
*1 tablespoon each parsley and thyme*
*1 bay leaf*
*3 cloves*
*plenty of black pepper*
*½ teaspoon salt*

SAUCE
*60 g (2 oz) lard*
*60 g (2 oz) fat bacon, diced*
*90 g (3 oz) chopped onion*
*beef stock*
*1 heaped tablespoon sugar*
*90 ml (3 fl oz) wine vinegar*
*60 g (2 oz) sultanas*
*60 g (2 oz) pine kernels*
*60 g (2 oz) candied peel, cut in strips*
*30 g (1 oz) grated bitter chocolate*
*salt, pepper, lemon juice*

Soak the rabbit or hare in the marinade ingredients for at least 4 hours. Drain and dry the meat, roll in seasoned flour and brown in the lard, together with bacon and onion. Put into a casserole. Strain the marinade liquid over the rabbit and add enough beef stock to cover it. Season well and simmer for 1½ hours, or until the meat is cooked. Melt sugar in a thick saucepan until it turns pale brown, add vinegar, stirring vigorously – the mixture will become a brown syrup. Pour into the casserole, and add the sultanas, pine kernels, peel and half the chocolate. Simmer 5 minutes. Correct the seasoning with salt, pepper, lemon juice and remaining chocolate to taste. No accompanying vegetables are needed.                                    [*Good Things*]

## CHICKEN LIVER SAUCE FOR VEAL (Salsa di Fegatini)

One of the family sent me this recipe from La Lanterna restaurant in Perugia. I thought it most original – until I came across an almost identical sauce the following week, in the *Forme of Cury*, that roll of medieval recipes compiled about 1390 by the cooks of Richard II. *Sawce noyre* was served with capon in those days: at La Lanterna it's spread on hot, thin slices of veal (lightly fried escalopes or roast veal), and served with pieces of toast in between also spread with the sauce. You can order it too as a first course on its own, when it's eaten with toast like a pâté.

*30 g (1 oz) dried* porcini *or ceps, or 60 g (2 oz) mushrooms, chopped*
*500 g (1 lb) chicken livers, chopped*
*1 slice raw Parma ham or unsmoked gammon, chopped*
*1 small onion, chopped*
*1 clove garlic, finely chopped*
*25 g (¾ oz) chopped sage*
*a sprig of rosemary*
*1 slice lemon, chopped*
*olive oil*
*½ litre (¾ pt) dry white wine*
*juice of ½ lemon*
*salt, pepper*

Pour hot water over the dried mushrooms, and leave to soak for 15 minutes or according to the instructions; drain and chop. Cook the first eight ingredients in a little olive oil, until the livers are half-cooked. Mince finely, or use a food mill. Add wine and a little lemon juice. Simmer for 30 minutes, uncovered. Correct seasoning and add the rest of the lemon juice if necessary. The liquid evaporates to leave a strongly flavoured, spreadable paste rather than a sauce. It can be stored for up to 10 days in a screw-top jar in the refrigerator: it can also be made in half-quantities quite successfully.

[*The Mushroom Feast*]

## CIRCASSIAN CHICKEN (Cerkes Tavugu)

Usually served cold, as part of the *meze* course, though it can quite well be eaten as a main dish, hot or cold. The important thing is to find a well-flavoured chicken. In practice this means the larger the better: I have sometimes used half a huge capon or small turkey. The ideal is a plump boiling fowl.

Serves 6 as a main course or 12 as part of a first course

*1 large chicken, approx. 2 kg (4 lb) in weight, with giblets
    (minus the liver)*
*375 g (¾ lb) onions, complete with skins*
*125 g (¼ lb) outer celery stalks*
*125 g (¼ lb) carrot, quartered*
bouquet garni
*250 g (8 oz) walnut halves, almonds or skinned hazelnuts*
*2–3 tablespoons nut oil (walnut, almond or hazelnut as appropriate) or
    groundnut oil, if required (see recipe)*
*1 tablespoon paprika*
*60 g (2 oz) bread, crusts removed*
*salt and pepper*

Put the chicken and its giblets in a large pot or pan, together with the onions, celery, carrot and *bouquet garni*. Add enough water to cover the legs if it is a roasting bird, or to cover it completely if a boiling fowl. Bring to simmering point and skim. Adjust the heat to maintain a low simmer, 90°C (190°F), and cover. A roasting chicken will need 1 hour or so, a boiler anything over 2 hours. Do not overcook the chicken. (The drumstick should move easily when pulled and the flesh between it and the body should not be pink.)

Remove the cooked bird. To serve hot, cut it into serving pieces, season and keep warm. To serve cold, allow to cool and then cut into pieces and remove the bones.

For the sauce, blend or process the nuts (no need to blanch almonds, unless you like a very white sauce). Turn them into a piece of stockinette and squeeze as much oil out of them as you can. There is no need to do this if you are using nut oil or a good groundnut oil. Stir the paprika into the oil and set aside.

Boil the cooking stock to reduce to a good, concentrated flavour, aiming to end up with 300 ml (½ pt), or slightly more. Return the nuts to the blender or processor, if necessary. Add the bread and then whizz to as smooth a sauce as possible, using the reduced stock to moisten it slightly. You may well not need it all. Aim for a consistency that will coat the chicken nicely, and keep tasting to make sure that the sauce does not become too strong – it should be delicate but not insipid.

To finish the hot version, put the pieces on a dish surrounded with well buttered, plainly cooked rice. Heat the sauce through (add a little more stock if it is unmanageably thick) and pour over the chicken. Dribble the red oil over the top and serve immediately.

To finish the cold version, consider the sauce. It should have almost a mayonnaise consistency, as thick but not quite as light, since nuts and bread are heavier than oil. Add more stock if it is too thick. Layer the chicken pieces into a glass bowl with the sauce, leaving enough sauce to cover the top completely. Sprinkle with the red oil. Serve very cold, or slightly chilled.

[*Dishes of the Mediterranean*]

## LEMON CHICKEN (Kotopoulo Lemonato)

One of the best and simplest chicken recipes, clear and vigorous yet delicate.

Serves 6

*large roasting chicken*
*125 g (4 oz) butter*
*grated zest and juice of 2 lemons*
*1 level tablespoon* rigani
*125 ml (4 fl oz) giblet stock or water*
*2 level teaspoons salt*
*plenty of freshly ground black pepper*
*3 eggs*
*extra lemon juice*

Set oven at moderate, gas 4, 180°C (350°F).

Stuff the bird with half the butter mashed with lemon zest and some of the *rigani*. Brown it in the rest of the butter and put into a deep casserole. Pour over the juice of the 2 lemons, plus the stock or water, salt, pepper and the rest of the *rigani*. Cover and bake in the heated oven, basting every 15–20 minutes until the chicken is cooked (about 1 hour). Transfer the chicken to a heated dish and keep warm.

Beat the eggs vigorously and strain in the chicken juices to make an *avgolemono* sauce (see below) using extra lemon juice to heighten the flavour. Serve the chicken with boiled rice.

### Avgolemono Sauce

As its name implies, the popular sauce of Greece is made from eggs and lemon. It tastes rich and clear, more lemonish than our northern hollandaise egg sauce, and lighter since the bulk consists of stock rather than butter. It is served with vegetables, poultry, meat or fish, either separately or poured over.

The basic mixture is 4 egg yolks or 3 eggs beaten with the juice of a large lemon (to extract the maximum juice, pour boiling water over the lemon and leave a few minutes before squeezing it). First beat the yolks of eggs in a large bowl or in the top of a double boiler, using an electric beater if you have one, then beat in the lemon juice. Now you are ready to complete it.

Pour 250 ml (8 fl oz) hot liquid slowly into the egg and lemon mixture, beating all the time. The liquid should be appropriate to the dish or from it. Place the bowl or pan over simmering water and stir or beat until the sauce is thick, light and smooth. As with any egg mixture, do not overheat or the egg will curdle. When the consistency seems right, dip the base of the bowl or pan into very cold water to prevent overheating.

*[European Cookery]*


## MOROCCAN MEAT STEWS WITH QUINCE

One of the interesting things about Middle Eastern and Arab cooking from an Englishman's point of view, is its similarity to our own medieval food. The abundant use of sweet substances with meat, the strong seasoning of ginger and various peppers, remind us that once dishes and courses were not so separately conceived as they are now (the well defined three- or four-course dinner, soup, fish, meat, dessert and so on, is really a nineteenth-century institution). To jump from reading a modern Middle Eastern cookery book to a fifteenth-century English one is much less of a change than going from the fifteenth-century one to Mrs Beeton. It may seem obvious to say 'Crusaders!', but I'm reluctant to believe such romantic notions, remembering that Marco Polo didn't bring back from Cathay half the things he's credited with. Let's be cautious, and say that such dishes, whatever their origin, came to us via France and our medieval French court.

Serves 4–6

*1 large chicken, jointed, plus 2 tablespoons butter (or 1¼ kg (2½ lb)*
  *cubed mutton or lamb)*
*2 large finely chopped onions*
*a bunch of parsley, chopped*

*about ½ teaspoon ground ginger*
*salt, black cayenne and paprika pepper*
*90 g (3 oz) butter*
*500 g (1 lb) quinces (or more to taste)*

Put meat (and, in the case of the chicken, its butter) into a large pan with onions and parsley. Just cover with cold water and season with ginger, salt and peppers. Bring to the boil and simmer for about 1 hour, until cooked. Slice and core the quinces (leave peel on), brown them very lightly in butter, and add to the stew 30 minutes before the end of cooking time.

*Note:* the meat is not browned before cooking, and lamb has enough fat of its own to do without the butter.

[*Good Things*]

## SWEETBREADS IN THE ITALIAN STYLE

The Italians have a good way of cooking delicate pieces of lean meat such as turkey or chicken breasts, or poultry livers, or sweetbreads. The system is to brown them lightly in butter, then to stew them for a little with Marsala until they are glazed and succulent. The result is delectable, sharply stimulating to the appetite, but not in the least heavy.

Serves 4

*500 g (1 lb) prepared sweetbreads*
*4 thin slices lean smoked bacon, or, more correctly, Italian* proscuitto
*6 fresh sage leaves (1 teaspoon dried sage)*
*90 g (3 oz) butter*
*scant 150 ml (¼ pt) Marsala (or Madeira, port, brown sherry)*
*4 large croûtons of bread, fried in butter*

Divide the sweetbreads into nuggets. Cut the bacon into matchstick strips, discarding the rind. Snip the sage into tiny pieces with scissors. Fry the sweetbreads in butter quickly until they begin to brown (be careful not to burn the butter) with the sage. Add the bacon and cook for another 2 or 3 minutes. Pour in some of the Marsala, and, as it boils down, add some more, and so on until it's used up. This takes about 10 minutes, and the heat should be turned up to evaporate the wine. Turn the sweetbreads over and over all the time, to acquire a brown, syrupy glaze. Serve them on the croûtons of bread, with the small amount of sauce left in the pan poured over them.

[*Good Things*]


## TURKEY BREASTS WITH MARSALA (Filetti di Tacchino al Marsala)

Like the preceding recipe, this is another Italian way of cooking delicate cuts of meat. As well as being suitable for veal and pork, it can be adapted to sweetbreads, which should first be soaked, blanched and trimmed.

Serves 4

*500 g (1 lb) turkey fillets (or blanched sweetbreads)*
*salt, pepper*
*flour*
*butter*
*225 ml (1½ gills) Marsala, or 125 ml (4 fl oz) each Marsala and stock*
*250 g (8 oz) mushrooms, sliced (or thinly sliced white truffle)*

Flatten, season and flour the fillets (if using sweetbreads, do not flatten but divide into convenient pieces, or cut into slices). Cook gently until lightly browned in 90 g (3 oz) of butter – about 5 minutes a side. Pour on the Marsala, or Marsala and stock, and bubble for a few moments before removing meat to a warm serving dish. Boil pan liquids down to a slightly syrupy sauce, stirring all the time. Beat in 30 g (1 oz) of butter and pour over the meat.

Meanwhile cook the mushrooms in 60 g (2 oz) of butter, unless you are using white truffles, which need no cooking but can be heated for a moment in some butter. Place mushrooms around the fillets.

[*The Mushroom Feast*]


# VEGETABLES AND FRUIT

## AUBERGINE SALAD (Melitzanes Salata)

If you like the smoky, very slightly bitter taste of grilled or baked aubergines, this is another delicious recipe. When serving it to visitors, make it as part of a mixed hors d'oeuvre, in case they do not share your enthusiasm. In the eastern Mediterranean, Cyprus for instance, it is put on the table as part of the *meze*, the little dishes of cold and hot food served either with drinks, or as a meal on their own.

Serves 4–6

*2 large aubergines, about 500 g (1 lb)*
*1 clove garlic*
*3 tablespoons olive oil*
*lemon juice, salt, pepper*
*chopped parsley*

Bake the aubergines at gas 6, 200°C (400°F) until they are soft. This gives a more even result than grilling them and you do not have to watch them. Split them and scrape the pulp from the skin into a basin, in which you have crushed the garlic. Mix it well, adding the oil drop by drop until you have a thick, smooth paste; you may not need more than 2 tablespoons of oil, let taste and consistency be your guide. Season with lemon juice, salt and pepper. Stir in 1 tablespoon of chopped parsley. Serve chilled with slices of hot bread, or with tomato salad, a fish hors d'oeuvre and so on.

[*Vegetable Book*]

## FENNEL

The garden I should most like to have visited for its vegetables was made at Monticello in Virginia by Thomas Jefferson. When he returned there after his second term as President of the United States, he was free to concentrate on it and grow the seeds that were sent him from all parts of Europe. In his *Garden Book*, over ninety different kinds and varieties of vegetables are listed. Some came via an Italian friend, Philip Mazzei, who lived nearby. Some, like his fennel seeds, arrived from Italy direct. In 1824 the American consul at Leghorn, Thomas Appleton, sent him five varieties of cabbage, eleven of broccoli, three of cauliflower, and two of fennel, with an enthusiastic letter describing the superb vegetables of Italy: 'the fennel is beyond every other vegetable, delicious. It greatly resembles in appearance the largest size celery, perfectly white, and there is no vegetable equals it in flavour. It is eaten at dessert, crude, and with, or without dry salt, indeed I preferred it to every other vegetable, or to any fruit.'

Fennel, sometimes called Florentine fennel to distinguish it from the feathery herb, is eaten still in Italy as a dessert, rather as we might serve celery with cheese, except that fennel is put on as a companion – or alternative – to fruit rather than cheese. The 3rd Earl of Peterborough, one of the first people to grow fennel in this country, ate it in the same way. Presumably he brought the seeds back from his adventures in Italy, to grow them in his kitchen garden at Parsons Green in Fulham. Although his unorthodox diplomatic and military escapades dismayed William of Orange and Queen Anne, they kept sending him out on missions which invariably turned to disaster: he must have been a quick-witted and charming man. In London between-whiles he invited the liveliest people of the day to Parsons Green (Locke and Newton were two of his friends). Everyone enjoyed the Earl's conversation, and his delicious food. His fruit was extra good as it was grown against the sun-warmed garden walls – a new idea from Italy – so that one may imagine fine desserts at his table including fennel in the Italian style that Thomas Appleton described.

Fennel is often eaten with vinaigrette, or as part of a salad, a dish of *crudités*, or an *ailloli garni*. It can be cooked and served cold *à la grecque* or *à la niçoise*, i.e. in tomato flavoured sauces. You can try it with cheese instead of celery, but choose goat cheese, or a fresh Parmesan at the *grana* stage, or a creamy French cheese: Cheddars and Cheshires are not quite right. Many celery and cardoon recipes are suitable for fennel, with small adjustments: often any sauce that accompanies it can be improved with a teaspoon of Pernod, which underlines the anise flavour. And this applies, too, to recipes in which fish or chicken are being cooked with fennel; I have tried using Chinese five-spice instead, which contains a proportion of star anise, but Pernod or some other anise preparation is more successful by far.

### How to choose and prepare fennel
Recognizing fennel is easy enough: it looks like celery that has been pressed down into bulbousness by a giant hand, but instead of fretted yellowish leaves, it has feathery vivid green ones (fennel comes from the Latin for hay, fresh-cut hay I would imagine). Choosing fennel is less easy. Often it is sold in a tight wrap of plastic, but even when it isn't appearance is no guide to flavour. In this it resembles apple or celery, but as the price is high one minds more; perfect-looking fennel can be pale in flavour, battered-looking fennel can be superb. I suspect freshness and soil are the explanations. Or perhaps the commercial variety grown in Italy for export is like some of the celery we import, beautiful but dumb.

In spite of this, I buy fennel whenever I see it – not so often in

Wiltshire, more often in France where it is grown locally – because its flavour is unique in vegetables, its texture clean and crisp.

When cooking fennel, allow one head per person, as the outer layer can be stringy and has to be cut away with the hard round stalks. As the trimmings can be used for soups, fish and chicken stocks (so can any cooking water), they are not wasted. The leaves can be chopped and scattered over the dish, or kept to add to a mixture of *fines herbes* for omelettes and stuffings. For most cooked recipes, the heads are halved, then quartered.

When fennel is to be eaten raw like celery, or in salads, four heads or less for six people should be plenty. After trimming the heads of the tough parts, slice them across thinly. The slices can be separated into thin strips if you like. If sliced fennel has to wait around, or seems less crisp than it should be, put it into a covered bowl of water with ice cubes, and leave in the fridge for an hour or a little longer.

[*Vegetable Book*]

## FENNEL *À LA NIÇOISE*

The Nice style usually means tomatoes and tiny black olives. This is a good recipe, too, for celery or cardoons.

Serves 6–8

> *6 fennel, quartered*
> *3 medium onions, chopped*
> *1 large clove garlic, finely chopped*
> *olive oil*
> *500 g (1 lb) tomatoes, skinned, chopped, or medium can tomatoes*
> bouquet garni
> *100 ml (3–4 fl oz) dry white wine*
> *salt, pepper, sugar*
> *100 g (3–4 oz) black olives, stoned if they are large*
> *60 g (2 oz) grated Gruyère*

Cook the fennel in salted water. Meanwhile make a tomato sauce by softening the onion and garlic in a little olive oil for a few minutes, then raising the heat to brown them slightly. Add the tomatoes and *bouquet*. When the mixture stews to a pulp, after about 15 minutes, pour in the white wine. Season with salt, plenty of pepper, and sugar to taste.

Put the drained fennel into a gratin dish and dot the olives about.

Pour over the tomato sauce, and sprinkle with the cheese. Bake in the oven, or put under the grill, until the cheese browns slightly.

[*Vegetable Book*]


## UMBRIAN FENNEL STUFFING

Fish from Lake Trasimene in Umbria are sometimes filled with ham, garlic and fennel and then spit roasted. You can do the same thing with our fresh-water fish, and then bake them in the oven or grill them over charcoal. There is no reason, either, why the mixture should not be used for salt-water fish – it is particularly good with mackerel, for instance, as well as the more usual red mullet or bass.

> *2–3 slices* prosciutto crudo di Parma, *or other raw ham from*
> *Germany or France, or lean bacon as a last resort*
> *1 large clove garlic*
> *1 head of fennel, trimmed, quartered*
> *olive oil or butter*
> *60–90 g (2–3 oz) breadcrumbs (optional)*
> *1 egg (optional)*
> *salt, pepper*

Take a large chopping board and put on it the first three ingredients. Chop them all together with a heavy knife, until they are reduced to a crumbly mass: this is what the Italians call a *battuto*. Heat enough olive oil in a frying pan to cover the base and stew the *battuto* in it, until the fennel softens. It should not brown at all, so cover the pan if you cannot keep the heat really low.

The mixture is now ready for use. Or it can be augmented with breadcrumbs and bound with an egg. Season, using plenty of pepper.

[*Vegetable Book*]


## LEEKS *À LA GRECQUE*

Serves 4

> *3 or 4 medium leeks*
> *300 ml (½ pt) water*
> *150 ml (¼ pt) olive oil*
> *1 heaped tablespoon tomato concentrate*

*1 heaped teaspoon sugar*
*60 g (2 oz) rice*
*12 small black olives*
*chopped parsley*
*lemon juice and 3 or 4 slices of lemon*

Prepare the leeks in the usual way, cutting them into 4-cm (1½-inch) slices. Bring to the boil in a heavy pan with the water, oil, tomato paste and sugar. Season with salt and pepper, then cook, covered, for 5 minutes. Add the rice. Boil, covered, for another 8 minutes – the liquid should be almost entirely absorbed by the rice. Turn off the heat, but leave the pan covered for another 10 or 15 minutes. The rice should be cooked but firm, in agreeable contrast to the moist leeks. Add lemon juice to taste. Serve chilled, with olives, parsley and lemon slices arranged on top.

[*Good Things*]

## STUFFED LEEKS WITH APRICOTS

Serves 6, or 10 as part of a mixed first course (*meze*)

*2 fat leeks, washed, trimmed and halved*
*175 g (6 oz) dried apricots*
*250 g (½ lb) minced lean beef or lamb*
*1 large onion, chopped*
*1 large tomato, skinned and chopped*
*90 g (3 oz) long grain rice*
*2 tablespoons chopped parsley*
*2 level teaspoons dried mint*
*½ teaspoon ground cinnamon or allspice*
*salt and pepper*
*6 tablespoons olive oil*
*juice of 1 large lemon*
*pitta bread*
*sprigs of mint*

Slit each piece of leek lengthwise, but only half-way through. Rinse well and gently separate all the layers, to obtain about 24 slit tubes.

Pour plenty of boiling water over the apricots and leave to soak for 10 minutes.

Mix the meat, onion, tomato, rice, herbs and spice, and season.

Put the stuffing into the leek tubes, leaving room for the rice to swell. When you get to the smaller tubes, use two pieces together, the second one fitting over the slit to make a closed roll. Fry the rolls lightly in half the olive oil.

Put the soaked apricots in the base of a large, heavy pan and arrange the leek rolls on top. Pour in the rest of the olive oil, together with the frying juices if they are not burned, the lemon juice and 300 ml (½ pt) of the apricot soaking liquid. Cover and simmer for about 1 hour, adding extra water as necessary to prevent burning. The final result should be moist, not scorched or swilling.

Lift the leek rolls and apricots from the pan and arrange on a plate with strips of pitta bread. Garnish with mint sprigs.

[*À La Carte*]

## OKRA AND TOMATOES

When you see the long, green, tapering pods of okra, you can understand why they are sometimes called 'lady's fingers'. They should look soft and fresh, always velvety: avoid dry-looking brown ones. To prepare them, cut off any stalks and pare the cones lightly. Do not pierce the pods. Some will burst in cooking inevitably, and add their creamy seeds and juicy smooth liquor to the sauce, but the dish will look and taste better if most of the pods remain whole.

> Serves 4–8
>
> *250 g ( ½ lb) onion, or onion and leek, chopped*
> *4 tablespoons olive oil*
> *500 g (1 lb) okra, prepared*
> *500 g (1 lb) tomatoes, skinned, de-seeded and chopped*
> *1–2 fat cloves of garlic, chopped finely*
> *2 tablespoons lemon juice*
> *salt, pepper and sugar, for seasoning*
> *chopped parsley, to garnish*

Soften the onion, or onion and leek if used, in the oil in a shallow pan that will take the okra in a single layer. Keep the heat low. Push to one side of the pan and put in the okra. Raise the heat and turn the okra carefully, so that it acquires a few patches of golden brown. Put the tomato on top with the garlic and the lemon juice. Season lightly, using sugar if the tomatoes are not very strongly flavoured. Lower the heat again so that the pan simmers, cover and leave until the tomato begins to collapse into a sauce, about 10 minutes.

Remove the lid, turn the okra carefully again, and leave to cook until it is tender. This will depend on the freshness of the okra – allow 10–15 minutes. The sauce should reduce to a small quantity. With watery tomatoes, you may need to remove the cooked okra to a serving dish and boil the sauce down hard. Finally, check for seasoning and scatter generously with parsley.

Serve okra in its sauce, hot, tepid or cold, as a first course on its own with bread or with other dishes, as part of a *meze*, or as a vegetable with grilled or roast meat. Any left over can be added to meat or vegetable stews, towards the end: it gives a jellied smoothness to the sauce.

[*Dishes of the Mediterranean*]


## SWEET-SOUR COURGETTES (Zucchini in Agrodolce)

I think that recipes like this and *sarde a beccafico* are the closest we get to medieval cooking, with its air of the Middle East and Saracen tastes.

Serves 3 as a first course, 4–5 as an accompanying vegetable

*500 g (1 lb) small courgettes*
*a large clove of garlic, chopped finely*
*3 tablespoons olive oil*
*3 tablespoons wine vinegar*
*3 tablespoons water*
*6–8 anchovy fillets, salted or tinned in oil*
*3 tablespoons pine kernels or chopped almonds*
*30 g (1 oz) sultanas or raisins*
*salt and pepper*

Cut the courgettes into slices lengthways, so that they end up as strips. Simmer the garlic in the oil gently for 2 minutes, and then put in the courgettes. Keep them moving about until coated and beginning to colour lightly. Pour in the vinegar and water and cover with foil, or a lid. Simmer for 10 minutes.

Meanwhile, rinse the anchovy fillets if salted, or drain the oil from tinned ones, and crush them to a paste. Add the crushed anchovy, nuts and dried fruit to the courgettes, raise the heat and cook without covering until the courgettes are bathed in a little sauce and cooked. Keep stirring. If you like your courgettes crisp, reduce the simmering time and do not cover the pan.

Serve hot, warm or cool (when it seems to have the best flavour).

[*Dishes of the Mediterranean*]

## TOMATOES

Tomatoes, what has happened to our tomatoes? Chefs and cookery writers and concerned cooks at home have been in despair about tomatoes for the last thirty-five years. Earlier than that we were not much bothered; tomatoes were cut up into salads, served with grills, and that was the end of it. Anxiety about tomatoes came with the publication of *Mediterranean Cooking* by Elizabeth David, with our first trips to Italy after the war, with the new appeal of a very different diet from the one we had all grown up on. You needed to make a good tomato sauce for the long packets of spaghetti that became so fashionable a presence in the Fifties' kitchen. Whatever you did, it never tasted very much like the sauce that was served up in the cheapest, humblest of Florentine restaurants. I remember converting my husband to tripe on our first visit together to Florence by making him eat a bowl of *trippa alla fiorentina*, bubbling richly with tomato sauce and Parmesan. When we returned home, he suggested I make it myself. It was not at all the same.

I was still wrestling with the problem thirteen years later when I started writing for the *Observer Magazine* in 1968. By that time I had been completely seduced by the Marmande tomatoes of France. The photographer had to fly one in specially for the picture that accompanied my recipes. Of the several letters that ensued, one was from a rueful tomato grower who sent me a copy of the Ministry of Agriculture's pamphlet on the subject. All it was concerned with was measurement and regularity. The glorious tomato in the photograph was an illegal immigrant as far as commerce was concerned (the grower confessed he had a couple of rows of decent tomato varieties for family consumption – the rest of his acreage was devoted to the famous Moneymaker).

I am sure that every reputable cookery writer in those years wrote his or her threnody to the tomato, proposed solutions more or less workable. Marmande! was the battle cry. Eventually the big battalions of the food business made their genuflection and about five years ago, perhaps less, Marmande craggy tomatoes began to appear extensively in supermarkets (or else they were the American 'beef' variety). Invariably they were grown in Holland. And of course we were fooled – those huge tomatoes were and still are pumped full of water. They are nearly as tasteless as the old eight to the pound Moneymaker, though firmer, slightly less watery. *Timeo Danoas et dona ferentes.*

The trouble is simple enough to understand. Visit the flat polders of Holland. Then take a plane to Bordeaux and drive down to

Marmande, an agreeable little town with the shiniest and most exciting of markets, and surrounded by market gardens. It lies hot and dusty in the sun, quite unaware that its name has been proclaimed in every cookery column in Britain a thousand times. It's the sun that makes the difference. Northern tomatoes are swaddled in plastic and this can never have the same effect as that brutal glare that burns tomato leaves in the field and bronzes the fruit to richness. If you still feel like a journey to convince yourself, try the south of Italy in August, where people are spreading out their tomatoes in the sun to dry to a tasty red leather.

Of course, you are not convinced. If what tomatoes need is sun, you may say, why is it that tomatoes we get from Israel, Spain and the Canaries are tasteless too? In those far-off countries there comes a period in the year when the plastic shades are off and the tomatoes are open to the sun, so why don't we import as good tomatoes in August and September in Britain as we have just been eating on holiday in the Mediterranean? And by good tomatoes, everyone means tomatoes so red-flavoured, so sharply sweet, that they need no more than olive oil as a dressing and plenty of pepper, tomatoes that need no vinegar or lemon juice since they carry their own acidity, just as good radishes carry their own pepper.

There I am indeed stumped for an answer, though I do have an explanation. In a party visiting Israel we were taken with pride to vast plastic huts where tomatoes were being grown for the British market (i.e. the British supermarket). They were red, round and eight to the pound. They weren't Moneymakers but they might have been. Across the lane, tomatoes were being picked in a huge open field for the local market. They were huge and variable in size and shape, striped with scars, sometimes striped with green. They were good to eat. We embarrassed our kind hosts by taking boxes back to London. The 'housewife's choice', the specially tasteless variety being grown for export to Britain, was ignored. 'But supermarket managers say . . .' we were told.

Perhaps with the enlargement of the Common Market these irregular, glorious tomatoes will turn up at least for one period of the year. Greeks bearing gifts of tomatoes, perhaps, will no longer need to be feared. Meanwhile I suggest you plan to invest in a gro-bag and some tomato plants next year because one thing is sure: tomatoes grown in a sunny corner outside in Britain in a good summer can be a revelation of delight. I asked Joy Larkcom, author of *The Salad Garden*, what her favourite varieties were: she said Supermarmande $F_1$, Ronoclave $F_1$, with Gardener's Delight for the cherry type of tomato and Jubilee for the yellow varieties. I have the impression that yellow tomatoes taste better usually than similar red tomatoes, but that may just have been coincidence. Incidentally Mrs Larkcom has a gardener's warning against the word Marmande on a packet – some new varieties in this particular type are smoother looking but have less flavour. However, the Supermarmande seems to be all right.

ROME, ITALIA TOMATOES: plum-shaped varieties used for canning. Fresh, they are popular for salads in France.

CHERRY AND CURRANT TOMATOES: smaller varieties, very pretty for salads, and surprisingly well-flavoured. Some chefs bake quail eggs in cherry tomatoes – a delicious fancy as long as the tomatoes don't burst.

DRIED TOMATOES: a new smart ingredient of modern cooking, but well worth buying. Carapelli do good ones in oil. Eat in small strips with soft cheeses, mozzarella, fontina, havarti, on bread. Use as a relish or to make sauces – see recipe.

PASSATA: cans of sieved tomatoes. Useful for winter soups and sauces, along with canned tomatoes and tomato concentrate.

TREE TOMATOES, TAMARILLOS (*Cyphomandra betacea*): good in that, like tomatoes, they belong to the potato family, the *Solanaceae*, but there is also a relationship of flavour – see recipe.

GREEN TOMATOES OR TIMATILLOS OR JAMBERRY (*Physalis ixocarpa*): another relation, with a lacy husk like Cape gooseberries. They need husking and simmering for 3–6 minutes to bring out their flavour. Much used in sauces in Mexico – see recipe. Canned ones are available and can be used directly.

## Salsa

On a visit to California a few years ago I noticed one particular word they seemed to be using all the time – in rather a knowing way. It was *salsa*. It means no more than sauce, and why use Spanish? Soon somebody put me straight: salsa is short for the Mexican *salsa cruda* or *salsa de jitomate* (and didn't I know that Spanish was the second language in the States?). It's put on the table with tacos, beans, chicken and fish: grilled tunny with *salsa* is one of the smart dishes on today's Californian menus. Personally I prefer grilled swordfish to tunny, and *salsa* goes equally well with both. When chilled, it can also be served with very hot egg noodles.

Start making the sauce no more than 1 hour before the meal. Skin and chop 2 large, very well-flavoured tomatoes or 500 g (1 lb) smaller ones or cooked green tomatoes. Chop finely a small onion with at least 2 fresh or canned, seeded serrano or jalapeño chillis, or such chillis as you can buy. Add this to the tomato. Season with sugar and salt to taste and a good chopping of coriander leaves. Adjust the quantities to your own taste.

## Fresh Tomato Sauce

This is a half-way sauce between *salsa cruda* and Italian tomato sauces of the classic kind.

Skin, seed and chop 2 large tomatoes or 500 g (1 lb) of well-flavoured smaller tomatoes. Cook a small chopped onion and 2 chopped cloves of garlic in a little olive oil. Stir in the tomato, raise the heat. If you want a Latin-American accent, add a chopped, seeded chilli and a final seasoning of coriander. If you prefer the Italian style, omit the chilli and use basil as the final herb. Salt, pepper, sugar as necessary. Cook as briefly as possible so that you concentrate the flavour without losing freshness and texture.

## Dried Tomato Sauce

The Italian style in pasta is to add the sauce sparingly. Which means, of course, that it must be full of flavour, a relish if you like, rather than a sauce. This particular recipe from *Pasta Italian Style*, a small book written for Sainsbury's by Pat Lousada, shows exactly the austere elegance of Mediterranean eating. Any dried tomatoes can be used. If they were packed in oil, some of that can be substituted for the olive oil below. Pieces vary in size, but it it not difficult to make up the equivalent of 12 tomatoes.

Serves 4

*12 dried tomatoes, cut in strips*
*2 cloves garlic, finely chopped*
*6 tablespoons best olive oil*
*3 tablespoons parsley*
*salt, pepper*

Soak the tomato strips in 3 tablespoons of hot water for 1 hour. Soften the garlic, without colouring it, in the oil. Add the tomatoes and their juice, with the parsley, and stir over the heat for a few minutes. Season. Enough for 350 g (12 oz) tagliolini or thin egg noodles. Mix into the drained pasta, and serve 125 g (4 oz) grated Parmesan separately.

## Tomatoes and Bread

There are few things better than a thick slice of tomato on a slice of good bread, scattered with pepper and coriander or basil, especially if you have a hard-boiled egg in the other hand. The past masters of the combination must be the Italians.

They make a glorious gratin of tomato slices layered with breadcrumbs and seasonings, top it with a layer of crumbs and butter and bake it in the oven. A lovely dish with meat or fish, or on its own for supper.

Another example of the marriage is a salad of tomato with cubes of bread fried in oil and cooled (you can rub the bread first with garlic). The whole thing is then dressed with an olive oil and basil mixture. They like it left for several hours. I think there is something to be said for eating it straight away when the bread is still crisp.

The slices of Marmande or beef tomatoes can be dipped in egg and breadcrumbs before being fried. Or just in yellow cornmeal. Use butter or bacon fat for frying.

## Tomato and Pepper Salad

The flavours of this salad are light and sweet, set off by salty anchovies – and, if you like, slivers of dried tomato. For this reason it makes an excellent first course. Follow it up with well-flavoured, unmessy food – say a confit of duck's legs with new potatoes and celery, and a lime sorbet to finish.

Serves 6

*2 red peppers, quartered, seeded*
*1 yellow pepper, quartered, seeded*
*3 large Marmande or 'beef' tomatoes, skinned*
*50 g (1½–2 oz) tin of anchovies*
*about 8 pieces of dried tomato (optional)*
*plenty of chives, parsley, and basil or coriander*
*olive oil*
*wine vinegar, salt, pepper*

Range the peppers, skin side up, on the rack of the grill pan. Slide them under a preheated grill and leave until well blistered. Remove pan, put a cloth over the top and leave 20 minutes, then peel off the fine skins and cut the pepper into strips lengthways.

Halve the tomatoes round the middle and cut out the hard cores carefully. Slice each half thinly, keeping it in shape, and sprinkle with salt. With a palette knife, press down gently so that the slices flatten in a staggered line.

Transfer to a large round serving dish, sliding the line of tomato into place like the spoke of a wheel. Repeat with the other tomato halves.

Slit the anchovy fillets in half lengthways and cut the dried tomatoes, if used, into strips. Strew them between the tomatoes, with the pieces of pepper.

Chop a small bowlful of the green herbs, add olive oil and a light seasoning of wine vinegar, salt and pepper. The mixture should be very thick. With a dessertspoon put a line of herbs down the centre of each tomato spoke – oil from them will run down the tomato pieces, just enough to dress them. Chill and serve with a little bunch of basil or parsley leaves in the centre, or chive flowers.

## Tomato Charlotte with Tamarillo

Tomato and tamarillo belong to the same family, the *Solanaceae*, and they go well together – even better than the classic New Zealand partnership of tamarillo and kiwi fruit. They make a good sauce for duck, pork or ham: skin, slice and cook 2–3 tamarillos in a barely buttered, non-stick pan; when tender, add 2 or 3 large chopped tomatoes, a hint of sugar and pepper, cook briefly and finish with a little coriander. With more sugar, less pepper and no coriander, the sauce can be served hot with vanilla ice cream or cold with *coeur à la crème*.

Here, though, is a delightful pudding, simple to make, for a Sunday lunch.

Serves 6

*750 g (1½ lb) good firm tomatoes*
*3 tamarillos*
*60–90 g (2–3 oz) caster sugar*
*6 thick slices of white or light brown bread*
*melted butter*
*a little nutmeg*

Choose 6 small pots, measuring 10 cm (4 inches) across and 3 cm (1¼ inches) deep, and rub them with a butter paper. Switch on the oven to gas 6, 200°C (400°F).

Pour boiling water over the tomatoes and tamarillos. After about 20 seconds, the tomatoes will be ready for skinning: leave the tamarillos longer as their skin is thicker and more tenacious. Slice the tomatoes and cut them in wedges. Slice and chop the tamarillos coarsely. Divide them between the pots, sprinkling them with 2 teaspoons of sugar each. Cut the bread into circles that will just fit into the pots. Dip one side in melted butter, and push them into the pots, butter side up. Sprinkle with a little nutmeg.

Put the pots on a baking sheet and slide into the oven. Leave until the tops are crisp and golden brown, the fruit bubbling beneath. If they colour too soon, lower the heat and protect the tops with butter papers. Serve with Jersey cream, if you like.

[*Observer Magazine*]

## BASIC TOMATO SAUCE

When we return from staying in France or Italy, I spend a despairing fortnight trying to recreate hot and vivid noonday flavours. A hopeless pastime. It's bound to be. But I persevere with this tomato sauce, made from canned tomatoes, which produce a better flavoured result than fresh ones sold in shops. As you will find, this sauce has many uses.

> *1 tablespoon each butter and olive oil*
> *250 g (8 oz) chopped onion*
> *1 outer stalk celery, chopped*
> *90 g (3 oz) chopped carrot*
> *2 rashers bacon, diced (optional)*
> *2 large cloves garlic, finely chopped*
> *900 g (1 lb 14 oz) can Italian tomatoes*
> *1 heaped tablespoon sugar*
> *1 dessertspoon wine vinegar*
> *150 ml (¼ pt) red wine*
> *1 good teaspoon sea salt*
> *black pepper, dried origano, basil, fresh parsley*

Sweat the onion, celery, carrot, bacon if used, and garlic in the butter and oil for 10 minutes, then turn the heat up so that they brown lightly. Add the rest of the ingredients, and bring to the boil. Don't cover the pan, but keep the sauce bubbling and busy for at least 15 minutes. It will reduce to a rich stew. No need to stir.

This sauce can be stored in the fridge for a day or two.

[*Good Things*]

## DATE KICKSHAWS

Kickshaws, as their name implies, should be served in small quantity. They are light, short and fattening. They make a delightful snack with coffee, when everyone is sitting round in the kitchen and talking, and can be eaten straight from the pan. If you have an electric deep-frier so that you can fry the kickshaws at the last moment with the minimum of fuss and the maximum of safety, they are a good way to end a dinner party.

Allow three dates – enough for three fritters – for each person. Use fresh dates if possible. Stone and chop them coarsely. Add the finely-grated zest of an orange for each nine dates, and some chopped nuts if you like.

I use shortcrust pastry, as it fries to an unusual sandy texture. Puff pastry gives a less friable result. Roll out the pastry thinly and cut two circles for each fritter, using a large scone cutter of about 6-cm (2½-inches) diameter. Brush the rim of half the circles with water, and put a teaspoonful of filling in each centre. Put on the remaining circles, pressing and twisting the edges together to make a firm seal. Chill until required for cooking, then deep-fry at gas 4, 180°C (350°F) or a little higher, until a light golden-brown. Keep warm on a thick layer of kitchen paper, and serve as quickly as possible.

*Note:* of course you can use a fila pastry, brushed with melted butter and cut into strips: put some filling at one end, fold a corner down over it, then continue to turn the filling over and over until you end with a triangular cushion. Repeat with more strips.

[*Fruit Book*]

## LEMON AND LIME

A pleasure northerners never forget is a first proof that lemons (and oranges) actually grow on trees – a first sight, somewhere round the Mediterranean, of actual lemons hanging from actual lemon trees, in a lemon orchard. I add to that a second pleasure, sitting out of doors at Limone, on Lake Garda, drinking in hot sunshine a first ice-cold *limone spremuta*, squeezed from lemons grown around the village, so improbably near the chill and the snow of the Alps.

Every romantic German sipping his *limone spremuta* at Limone and getting his watercolours ready surely – and quite rightly – remembers the best, if most hackneyed poem of his honeymoon with Italy and citrus fruits – Goethe's poem from *Wilhelm Meister*, which begins –

*Kennst du das Land, wo die Zitronen blühn,*
*Im dunkeln Laub die Gold-Orangen glühn*
*Ein sanfter Wind vom blauen Himmel weht.*

*Do you know that country where the lemon-trees flower,*
*And oranges of gold glow in the dark leaves,*
*And a gentle breeze blows from blue heaven.*

That cold *limone spremuta*, with sugar collecting at the bottom of the glass, will be so lemonish, so pleasurably acid that it may make your throat a little sore, for a while.

Lemons do not do well in the full tropics, limes do not do well round the Mediterranean. English housewives or French housewives who settle in West Africa, fall back on limes, and quickly discover that they are very much stronger. So be warned, when you try limes from the supermarket. I came across a recipe in a French cookery magazine, for a Senegalese dish *poulet yassa*. Ingredients listed 1 kg (2 lb) of limes to go with 1 chicken. Obviously a mistake. Equally obviously the limes were intended to be important so I used four. The dish was uneatable, I would have thought by anyone's standards, or however hot the climate which might have made the sharpness agreeable. It was indeed a question of 'the piercing lime'. Two was the right number, the word 'kilo' had slipped in from the line below. Later I came across the right version in *La cuisine sénégalaise* by Monique Biarnès. Many recipes are of course interchangeable, which is to say that the method works for both – though I repeat, always be on the alert to use less lime if it is a lemon recipe – but the taste will be different.

The similarity of the names of the two fruit is no accident. Both come from the Arabic word *limah*. No connection, though, between lime fruit and lime tree which should really be lime tree as in Linden.

Everyone knows the anti-scorbutic virtues of both fruit. Older people will recall the lemonade given to them in February and March – presumably when the first lemons of the new season came in – to 'cleanse the blood'. That was in the days of fewer vegetables and scarce winter fruit, when our diet was stuffier altogether. Sailors were given lime or lemon juice, after ten days of salt provisions, and as rum had been added to the juice to preserve it, the occasion was a happy one.

## How to choose and prepare lemons and limes

As these fruit are priced individually, pick out the largest and freshest you can find. Avoid dry wrinkled specimens. If you have no use for the thin outer rind, the zest, pour boiling water over the fruit and leave it to stand for 5 minutes before squeezing it: you will get more juice.

Generally speaking, though, the zest should never be wasted. Put it in a jar with sugar, if you cannot use it immediately. To remove the outer peel really thinly, there is nothing to beat a lemon zester. It removes the finest of shreds which will disappear into the cooked dish leaving only delicate traces and their flavour behind. If you need julienne shreds, you can try a canelle knife, but I find it quicker and better to peel off strips with a potato peeler, trim them and cut them with a small sharp knife. Soften the peel always in plain boiling water before cooking it in anything sweet, as sugar has a hardening effect.

There are many ways of squeezing juice from lemons, and many gadgets. I have a heavy juice press over forty years old, which is a delight if there is a lot of fruit to be squeezed. Most of the time, I use the traditional beechwood juicer or reamer, or my hands – squeezing the half with one hand through the fingers of the other, which are kept slightly apart to hold back the pips. The other kinds of small lemon squeezer are fiddly to wash up and difficult to keep absolutely clean.

The acidity of lemon or lime is required with most other fruit, once you begin to cook or use it with other ingredients, not so much as a flavouring but as a flavour enhancer, to emphasize the virtues of the main fruit. With some tropical fruit, it is essential: papaya, guava, avocado. It is also used to prevent discolouration – a tablespoon of juice added to the water into which apple slices are cut will keep them white. Cut up pears on to a plate containing lemon juice: turn the pieces over and they will not go brown. Moreover, their flavour will be much improved.

Light syrup simmered with thinly cut strips of peel from lemon or lime makes the ideal liquid for poaching many fruits. Extra flavour can be added by squeezing in the juice. Pay attention, though, and taste the syrup from time to time. Fish out the peel strips before they add any bitterness.

Both fruit go admirably with fish and light meats, such as chicken and veal. A wedge of one or the other is essential with fried food, to counteract the richness. Lemon or lime juice sharpens hollandaise and mayonnaise sauces, gives a lighter vinaigrette or a more fragrant *beurre blanc* when used instead of vinegar.

If you need lemon slices and lemon juice for a dish, cut the slices from the centre of the fruit, then use the tricky ends for squeezing. The same of course with lime (or oranges).

Do not discard the squeezed-out fruit. Rub it over copper pans and basins with a little coarse salt to shine them up, or whiten your elbows by sitting and reading with them resting each in a lemon half. I remember girls at school trying to bleach away freckles with lemon juice, but it was not – happily – very successful.

[*Fruit Book*]

## QUINCE PASTE

As you go further south in France, the quince trees which we treasure one by one north of the Loire and in this country, become far more common. Their fruit is larger, though not as large as the quinces I saw in Chania market in Crete, and as golden as any apple of the Hesperides can have been against the blue autumn sky. In her book on the customs and cookery of the Périgord and Quercy, Anne Penton remarks that 'in the Périgord Agenais, quince trees were formerly used instead of fences to mark off the limits of each property in the same manner as laburnum trees were used further north in the Dordogne towards the Charente'.

Then she gives a recipe for quince preserve. Cored and quartered quinces are cooked with an equal weight of sugar, plus water to cover: the cores are tied in a little bag to dangle in the liquid as orange pips do in marmalade. They take seven hours apparently to cook to tenderness, a state which is held back, I suppose, by the hardening presence of sugar. The fruit is put into pots, the syrup boiled to setting point and poured over them. This kind of preserve is excellent with mixtures of *fromage frais* and curd cheese, such as *coeur à la crème*.

We find quince paste more useful, being disinclined to jam and runny preserves. It can be served as a sweetmeat with coffee, or laid on grilled pork chops, or mixed into apple pies and sauces as a flavouring. If kept dry, it lasts for at least two years, probably longer, but ours has always disappeared by that time – however well I hide it.

This kind of cookery is very much a family enterprise, one of the first of the preparations for Christmas. The stirring can be laborious unless there is someone to help. And the pleasure is doubled if people come in and out, sniffing the wonderful smell that reaches even the furthest rooms of the house by the time you have finished.

If you have plenty of quinces, weigh out about 2 kg (4 lb). If not, make up the weight with apples, or apples and no more than 225 g (7 oz) peeled, sliced oranges. Windfall cookers in reasonably good condition are perfectly acceptable.

Wash and cut up the quinces (and apples). Put them into a heavy pan with 300 ml (½ pt) water. Bring to the boil and simmer until the fruit is tender. Towards the end, mash it down with a potato masher or beetle. The purée should be very soft and easy to push through a drum sieve. Weigh the purée, and put it back into the rinsed out pan with an equal weight of sugar. Stir over a low heat until the sugar has dissolved, then raise the heat and boil until the mixture thickens and candies, leaving the sides of the pan and turning dark red. It will explode and pop with an occasional fat burp. Only by stirring and constant attention can you prevent the paste burning once it begins to start this thickening process. Wrap your hand in a cloth and use a wooden spoon. Eventually you will barely be able to push the spoon through the paste.

Now you can remove it and spread it out in 1-cm (small ½-inch) layers in baking trays lined with Bakewell or greaseproof paper. Push it out as evenly as you can; then, when it cools down slightly, wet your hands and press it smooth, as if you were making *gnocchi*. Put the trays in the airing cupboard, on the rack over an oil or solid fuel cooker or in its plate-warming oven. You can also put it into a gas or electric oven switched on at its lowest point. The time required to dry the paste is about 12 hours, but try cutting a square occasionally to see how the paste is getting on. When it can be cut with a hot knife into firm squares, it is ready.

Dip the squares in granulated sugar (mixed with cinnamon if you like). Pack them in layers – with rice paper in between and 2 or 3 bay leaves – in a box or an air-tight container if there is any risk of humidity. Another way is to keep them in a great deal of granulated sugar in a plastic box. As the quince paste is eaten, the flavoured sugar can be used for apple or pear dishes, as you might use sugar from the vanilla pod jar.

[*Fruit Book*]


## SEVILLE ORANGES

When Andrew Marvell wrote, in *The Bermudas*, of God hanging . . .

> '. . . in shades the orange bright,
> Like golden lamps in a green night,'

that wonderful image owed more to his religious fervour than to the facts of historical botany. It was man, Spanish man, who first hung oranges on the New World, and very late in time, too. Citrus fruits came originally from China, but by a slow route along the western road, marking the progress of Arab conquerors on their warlike journey round the north coast of Africa into Spain in the ninth and tenth centuries. In classical times there were no orange groves in Cyprus and Sicily (and no lemon groves either).

The first orange to arrive in the West from China, and to settle down in the warmer climates of Europe, was the kind we call the Seville. Elsewhere it is known just as the bitter orange, or in France as the bigarade (the original name for duck with orange sauce was *caneton à la bigarade*).

I cannot imagine why the British, of all the Europeans, and subsequently of all the European colonizations in America, have been the most faithful to this first orange. Of course it is used in Spanish and Latin American cooking, but only in this country does it dominate our kitchens for six solid weeks, just after Christmas. Everywhere you go, Sevilles are being boiled and sliced, de-pipped and sugared and cooked into marmalade. Even in households where no other jam is made, marmalade is essential. We will put up with the low standard of other jams on sale, but bought marmalade is despised by comparison with the real thing, made to the family's particular taste, to the family's recipe.

What we have rather lost, however, is our habit of using Sevilles for other things. A pity, since their season is so short.

Perhaps this is because we seem to have only a limited appreciation of the pleasures of bitterness. We don't use the bitter gourd in spite of our centuries in India. We rarely snip green coriander leaves over our meat, poultry and fish, although coriander grows easily in northern gardens. Bitters belong to gin, to marmalade and that's that.

Since it has sharpness, acidity, it's easy to see that a Seville orange can be a substitute for a lemon. More than sharpness, though, it contributes an aromatic bitterness that can become, as green coriander does, addictive. If you consider its variable and bumpy shape, its embossed skin, the pertinacity of its oil on one's fingers, you begin to understand that it may have a more magical character than the sweet orange that we now take for granted. Even if you have never seen an orange tree growing, you can believe – of *this* orange – that it has the strange and glorious habit of producing flowers and fruit at the same time. And that its blossom can scent the tattiest of Cypriot towns with an evening richness that obliterates the grime. For this reason alone it's worth making a trip to Cyprus or Sicily at the end of February and the beginning of March.

It is this orange that the Medici took as their symbol. Their painters put its glossy leaves, flowers and fruit by the bay where Aphrodite was born. Primavera dances forward with her flowers from an orange grove. Oranges still grow in the courtyard of the Laurentian Library in Florence.

By the time of the orangeries, the sweet orange had arrived in Portugal and was being grown there and sent to London. Subsequently more varieties of sweet orange arrived, and from being called Portugals, they became known as China oranges. Such names being necessary to distinguish the sweet newcomers from the useful culinary orange, the Seville, which flavoured punches and gave extra zest to veal, or to an egg custard, and provided a basis for candying into sweets and purées. Marmalade, as we know it, belongs to the later eighteenth century. Before then there were plenty of marmalades, or marmelades, about, but they were thickish purées of all kinds of fruit. The texture was runnier than, say, a damson cheese, but there was no careful contrast of strips of peel and sweet supple jamminess. The fruit embedded in the word marmalade is the quince, going back via Latin and Greek (melimelon, meaning honey apple) to the ancient Accadian word *marmalu*, or quince.

The Scots are credited with the final development of the orange preserves that we think of as marmalade, and it is in a recent publication by a Scottish cook that I found the best collection of recipes using Seville oranges (including an unusual variation of marmalade). This is Claire Macdonald's *More Seasonal Cooking*, her second book of the dishes she makes for visitors to the family hotel on the Isle of Skye.

[*À La Carte*]


## WATER-MELON FRUIT SALADS

In Tuscany, especially in Florence, in the high summer, cafés put huge water-melon halves in their windows, packed with fruit. As well as the pink-fleshed melon, the salads contain strawberries, blackberries, grapes, the fruit in season. They tempt customers in from the pavement and the dust that swirls round their knees in the afternoon heat.

For extra refreshment, the fruit is layered with crushed ice like a Persian *paludeh*, or the sherbet described by Sei Shonagon in tenth-century Japan, one of her Elegant Things:

*A white coat worn over a violet waistcoat.*
*Duck eggs.*
*Shaved ice mixed with liana syrup and put in a new silver bowl.*
*A rosary of rock crystal.*
*Snow on wistaria or plum blossoms.*
*A pretty child eating strawberries.*

Incidentally the syrup that comes from sugaring the fruit is sparked with alcohol, sometimes with gin which comes as a surprise.

You will find our smaller water-melons adequate for a party of 10–12 people. Slice off a top lid. Or, if you are good at this kind of thing, cut away a lid in Vandyke points. Some people go so far as to draw a scalloped line round the melon with the aid of a tenpenny piece, to make a guide for the knife. I do not. I do take the precaution of cutting a small nick in fruit and lid so that they can be fitted together exactly for serving.

Scoop out the flesh, remove the seeds and trim the pieces into reasonable cubes. Or use a potato-ball cutter, and keep trimmings for a sorbet or milk sherbet.

Put the pieces into a large bowl, and add
*either* the Florentine mixture as above
*or* a diced fresh pineapple and 1 kg (2 lb) strawberries, garden or wood strawberries, or the two mixed
*or* the cubed, seeded pulp of a green- and an orange-fleshed melon, plus seeded or seedless grapes.

Sprinkle the fruit with caster sugar and leave for 1–2 hours, until the juice is drawn. Add alcohol – gin, vodka, kirsch, maraschino, fruit brandy – to taste.

Pack the fruit into the water-melon shell, and pour on the syrup – fortified if need be, with extra sugar and alcohol. Replace the lid. Tie into a plastic carrier to prevent the smell pervading the refrigerator, and chill until required.

*Note:* the shell can be stored in the freezer and re-used. Wrap it in cling film, and place it in a box so that it does not get damaged by other packages.

[*Fruit Book*]

# CAKES AND PUDDINGS

## COFFEE ICE WITH CREAM (Granita al Caffè con Panna)

On holiday in Italy in the heat, one rapidly discovers two surprising things – that *caffè espresso* is far more refreshing than water, or even a pink slice of water-melon, and that bought ices can taste deliciously clear and subtle. (The second discovery can be quite a shock after experiences of raspberry ripple, choc bars and iced lollies.) These two bits of wisdom soon lead one to the finest of all water ices, *granita al caffè*, which combines the stimulus of black coffee with the refreshment of intense cold. And do not forget the important words *'con panna'* – with cream – because whipped cream sets off perfectly the bitter-sweet granules of blackish brown ice.

Use finely ground espresso coffee if you can buy it, otherwise a continental, after-dinner roast.

> *12 slightly rounded tablespoons coffee*
> *1¼ litres (2 pt) water*
> *60–90 g (2–3 oz) sugar*

Warm a stoneware jug, put in the coffee and then the water which should be boiling. Stir well and leave in a warm place for 10 minutes to brew. Strain off and sweeten with 60 g (2 oz) sugar. When cold, pour twice through a piece of sheeting or doubled muslin. Add more sugar if required. Freeze in the usual way, stirring every 30 minutes until the mixture is a mush of granules. Serve in tall glasses with a generous swirl of whipped cream on top.

*[Good Things]*

## HALVA BUTTER CREAM

An Israeli cream used to sandwich and cover plain or coffee sponge cakes. You can also use it to spread between layers of boudoir biscuits, dipped in a 50–50 mixture of rum and water, and then to cover the build-up of biscuits.

Break up 125 g (4 oz) halva into a small, heavy pan. Add 3 tablespoons strong coffee and 150 g (5 oz) sugar. Stir to a thick cream over a low heat for about 30 seconds. Remove the pan from the stove, cut 175 g (6 oz) unsalted or barely salted butter into cubes and whisk them into the tepid halva. Add 1 tablespoon of rum, if you like.

*[Dishes of the Mediterranean]*

## MALTESE CHEESECAKE TARTS (Pastizzi)

Every country that uses milk products has at least one form of cheesecake. These *pastizzi* filled with ricotta cheese are a favourite mid-morning snack in Malta: you eat them with your coffee or tea, and dip them in sugar or salt as you feel inclined. I sometimes serve them as a pudding, with a little cream, or at a weekend tea-time.

Makes approx. 24

PASTRY
*200 g (7 oz) plain flour*
*a generous pinch of salt*
*30 g (1 oz) each of soft lard and butter*

FILLING
*200 g (7 oz) ricotta cheese, or mixed full fat and cottage cheese*
*2 eggs*
*a generous pinch of salt*
*fat for greasing*

The pastry is made with little fat, but the method gives it flakiness. Mix the flour with the salt and enough water to give a soft, slightly bubbly dough (use an electric mixer if possible). Chill and then roll out into a rectangle. Spread it all over with the lard. Roll up like a swiss roll, chill again and repeat, this time spreading the dough with the butter. Roll up, chill and roll out again. Cut out 24 circles with a large cutter and line greased tartlet tins. You may get a couple more circles, depending on the rolling of the dough. Chill.

Preheat the oven to gas 6, 200°C (400°F). Mix the filling ingredients together. When the oven temperature is set, distribute the filling among the tartlet cases and slip into the oven, above the centre. After 15–20 minutes check the *pastizzi*: remove them if they are golden brown, leave them a little longer if they are still pale. Serve straightaway or while they are still warm.

[*Dishes of the Mediterranean*]

## ORANGE HALVA CAKE

I cut this recipe out of a newspaper years ago, and find that it gives a better result than versions found in current books of Greek cookery. Make the cake two days in advance, so that the syrup can soak right in.

175 g (6 oz) caster sugar
175 g (6 oz) butter
2 teaspoons grated orange rind
5 tablespoons orange juice
3 eggs, beaten
275 g (9 oz) fine semolina
3 level teaspoons baking powder
125 g (4 oz) ground almonds

SYRUP
275 g (9 oz) caster sugar
8 tablespoons water
5-cm (2-inch) piece of cinnamon stick
3 tablespoons lemon juice
6 tablespoons orange juice
2 heaped tablespoons chopped candied orange peel

Cream sugar and butter together, add rind, juice and eggs. Then mix in the semolina with the baking powder, and the ground almonds. Put into a large buttered ring mould – there should be plenty of room for the mixture to rise. If you do not possess a ring mould, use a large cake tin with a small jam jar stuck in the middle (butter the jar as well as the mould).

Bake for 10 minutes at gas 7, 220°C (425°F), then lower the heat to gas 4, 180°C (350°F) for a further 30 minutes. Test the cake in the usual way.

When the cake is nearly cooked, make the syrup. Simmer the first three ingredients together for 5 minutes, add the juices and peel.

Turn the cake out carefully – ease it first – on to a warm plate. Reheat the syrup to boiling point, and after a couple of bubblings, pour it slowly over the cake. It will slowly be absorbed. Cover the whole thing with foil and leave in a cool place for two days. If the cake seems on the dry side, make up some more syrup in half quantities. Serve with clotted cream and a scatter of toasted almonds.

[*Fruit Book*]


## PRUNES STUFFED WITH WALNUTS

A dish to remind us that the eastern end of the Mediterranean is famous for nuts and dried fruit, and that we have been importing both since the Middle Ages.

Serves 8

*500 g (1–1¼ lb) large prunes*
*a pot of freshly made, weak Indian tea*
*as many walnut halves as prunes (about 40)*
*2–3 tablespoons granulated sugar*
*1 tablespoon lemon juice*
*2 tablespoons caster or icing sugar*
*300 ml (½ pt) whipping cream*
*extra walnuts, chopped, to garnish (optional)*

Put the prunes in a bowl and strain the tea over them; it should come about 3 cm (1 inch) above them. Leave overnight.

The next day, bring the prunes to the boil in the tea, reduce the heat and simmer until they are just cooked enough for their stones to be removed neatly (about 5 minutes). Replace the stones with the walnut halves. Close the prunes and range them in a single layer in a large pan. Sprinkle with the granulated sugar and add the lemon juice, any soaking liquor that remains and extra tea or water to cover them. Simmer for 20 minutes.

Remove the pan from the heat and leave to cool. Transfer to a glass bowl. Add the caster or icing sugar to the cream and whip until bulky and thick but spreadable. Spread in a layer over the prunes and chill well before serving.

A light chopping of walnuts can be scattered over the top, if you like.

*[Dishes of the Mediterranean]*

## SIENESE FRUIT-CAKE (Panforte)

The Christmas fruit-cake of Siena, white with icing sugar on top and rice paper round the sides. It's easy to make and very good, though you will miss the attractive flowery box in which it is sold at Italian groceries.

*100 g (3½ oz) hazelnuts, toasted, skinned, chopped*
*100 g (3½ oz) almonds, blanched, toasted, chopped*
*100 g (3½ oz) candied orange peel, chopped*
*100 g (3½ oz) candied lemon peel, chopped*
*100 g (3½ oz) candied fruit, chopped*
*3 teaspoons cinnamon*
*½ teaspoon mixed spice*

*100 g (3½ oz) plain flour, sifted*
*125 g (4 oz) honey*
*125 g (4 oz) sugar*
*rice paper*
*icing sugar*

Mix nuts, peel, fruit, spices and flour thoroughly with your hands (best way to get an even mix). Bring honey and sugar to boiling point, then mix into the nuts, etc. to make a sticky cohering mass.

Line two tart tins or rings 18–20 cm (7–8 inches) in diameter with rice paper. Divide mixture between the two, pressing it down evenly but not too heavily.

Bake at gas 2, 150°C (300°F), for 30–35 minutes. Cool, then remove from the tins. If the rice paper base and edging are torn, add new ones, using dabs of egg white as glue. Sprinkle top with icing sugar.

To keep, wrap in foil. To serve, cut in small wedges. It is very much a medieval style of cake, like early gingerbread stuck together with honey and not expected to rise. I suppose that the modern descendant of these antique cakes is the impacted fruit bars that are sold in vegetarian shops.

[*Fruit Book*]

# THE EUROPEANS

THERE IS NO QUESTION that the axis of Jane's life had one end firmly anchored in Wiltshire, passed southwards through Trôo and through Provence to the olive groves of Tuscany. England, France and Italy – these were the lands she knew and loved best, and which provided constant themes for her work. She did not, however, ignore the rest of Europe and her characteristic curiosity and depth of research illuminate her writing on the foods of other countries, from the *caldo verde* of Portugal to the *gravad lax* of Scandinavia.

Her books give a remarkable insight into the food and cooking of the Continental countries, and yield a collection of fascinating and rewarding recipes. Much of the region this chapter deals with has a harsh and unforgiving winter climate. Many of the recipes therefore are for dishes that have helped the inhabitant to withstand the cold and gloom, making the very best use of the restricted ingredients available, transforming them into meals that are refined and civilized. The following piece from Jane's *European Cookery* shows that life is not only pickled herrings and snow is not always on one's boots.

Those supremely grand cities, Vienna and Budapest, were the centres of what was once the great Austro-Hungarian Empire, set down in Europe's heartlands. Surrounded by Teutons and Turks, Slavs and Italians, the Empire channelled many good things, not least a cuisine, into the Western world through its two capital cities.

Development in Austrian food took place in the eighteenth century, under French influence. With great families such as the Esterházys, Haydn's patrons, and the benevolent tyranny of Empress Maria Theresa, this style became the rule for the well-off in Hungary, too. Refinement of specifically Hungarian dishes and their acceptance into the Austrian repertoire reached a high point with the setting up of the

Dual Monarchy in 1867, when Emperor Franz Joseph I of Austria also became King of Hungary and so ruled over two joined but separate countries. Both capital cities spread with new industry and wealth. Vienna stretched out beyond the new Ringstrasse, and in 1872, Buda and Óbuda joined with the new flat suburbs of Pest on the other side of the Danube to form Budapest. Restaurant and café baroquery of twisted pillars, looking-glasses, gold leaf and round globes of light, belong to this period which ended with the 1914–18 war and the collapse of the Austro-Hungarian Empire.

Although many dishes are common to both countries' menus, they are given a different accent. One must admit and enjoy the fact that Hungarian eating is rumbustious.

For a start everything is red: curtains, tableclothes, napkins, the little embroidered jackets of gypsy musicians, the skirts of the dancing girls, the food itself – red beef, red with paprika and tomatoes, red veal and chickens, pancakes with a rosy sauce. Fogas, the pike-perch special to Lake Balaton, comes golden and rampant on a red-patterned dish. In the Nagycsarnok market in Budapest, one end of the iron building is red from floor to roof with a cascade of peppers, the fall patterned with white garlic.

I drove south one autumn through the paprika harvest – pickers bent double – on the way to the paprika factory at Kalocsa. Fringe after fringe of red peppers hung thick from the eaves of the houses, following the line of gable and porch. Red, everywhere red. I was caught up in this vigour, dreaming of Magyar horsemen and Turks in bright turbans galloping over the distances of the Great Plain. 'You know,' said the girl who was organizing the trip, 'that *puszta* only means field!' But what a field!

Hungarian food also means excellent *foie gras* which we do not get here, and excellent salami which we do. Nineteenth-century Italian refugees, who were also salami-makers, spotted the old mangalica race of pigs, and saw the similarity to pigs they used back home. Now Hungarian salami has the quality of Italian salami – the best – and is a fraction cheaper.

The delectable cakes of Budapest are for eating on the spot, either at Ruszwurm's, the charming little tea room in Buda, or at grander Vörösmarty's across the Danube in Pest. In Vienna, you can send Sachertorte, Pischingertorte (hazelnut and chocolate wafer) and Mozartkugeln (almond balls) to your friends back home, or boxes of sweets from Demel's. Demel's windows are a fantasy of almond paste sculpture – a pink church, a man in overalls holding a factory tucked under his arm, the Beatles, and coloured desserts that recall an old cookery book.

From such sugar skill, or from the hearty window opposite, a metre deep in roasted calf's knuckles, it is obvious that Austrian cooking has come a long way since the first Austrian hausfrau we know about. She is the Venus of Willdendorf, near Krems, forever in a glass case in Vienna's Natural History Museum. She ate well, obviously, mammoth steak, reindeer, Danube salmon, mountain trout, partridges from the steppes. Her descendants are about still, tidy curls under green hats with little feathers, totting up the price of a crayfish and beer party, in front of a neat round crayfish tank, or tucking into a plump dumpling in the Kärntnerstrasse.

Austria, everywhere, has places to sit down and take a little something. Walks are detours on the way to the pub. Or to the enormous beer cellars that have taken over ancient monastic undercrofts (the most beautiful and famous being Peterskeller, at Salzburg). Every lake has waterside restaurants; great parks like the Prater are dotted with beer gardens. Wine-drinkers will find a 'heuriger' to suit their taste, a pretty decorative sort of place or a few wooden tables and chairs outside a country wine cave. In Tyrol every village has a light, pinewood café, with girls in dirndls to bring you anything from an excellent cup of coffee to smoked pork and sauerkraut. Everywhere an easy willingness to serve refreshments all day (and often in English) makes one realize how sad and grudging and grimy we are here with our public eating-places.

Some people sneer at Austrian 'gemütlichkeit' – genial cosiness – and in the past it must have been stuffy, but in the freer style of today, Austrians manage to get it exactly right. Relaxed comfort is apparent, too, in their home cookery, their *hausmannskost*, which is simple yet pleasing.

My own complaint in both countries is the difficulty of having a leisurely restaurant meal where you can talk. Music is an obsession. With Mozart, Schubert, Strauss, Haydn, Liszt, Bartók and Kodály, who can blame them?

[*European Cookery*]

# SOUPS AND STARTERS

## COLD BEETROOT SOUP (Svekol'nik Kholodnyi)

This is a very popular cold soup, usually served in summer when vegetables and fresh herbs are plentiful.

Serves 6

*1 kg (2 lb) beetroot*
*2 litres (3½ pt) water*
*3 tablespoons lemon juice*
*2 tablespoons sugar*
*6 hard-boiled eggs, whites only, chopped*
*4–6 lettuce leaves, shredded*
*3 spring onions, trimmed and cut into rounds*
*½ long English cucumber, finely diced*
*2 medium potatoes, peeled, boiled and finely diced*
*6 tablespoons soured cream*
*3 tablespoons chopped parsley*
*3 tablespoons chopped dill*

Wash the beetroot thoroughly, and cook them in the water, with the lemon juice. When the beetroot are tender, remove them from the liquid, peel them, then cut them up into small cubes. Strain the beetroot liquid into a clean saucepan. Chill the chopped beetroot, sugar, chopped egg whites, lettuce, spring onions, cucumber, and the potatoes. Finish with the cream as for borscht and sprinkle with plenty of parsley and dill.

[*European Cookery*]

## DANISH CELERY AND CHEESE SOUP

A number of good soups can be made with celery, but this is the most delicious of them all. The creamed blue cheese gives a savoury yet tactful richness to the light flavour of celery. If you are using a milder blue cheese than the Danish kind, be prepared to add a little extra.

Serves 4–6

*1 medium head celery, chopped fairly small*
*2 medium onions, chopped*
*50 g (scant 2 oz) lightly salted butter*
*30 g (1 oz) plain flour*

*1 litre (2 pt) chicken stock*
*salt, pepper*
*60 g (2 oz) Danish blue cheese*
*chopped parsley*

Cook the vegetables in the butter for 10 minutes in a covered pan without browning them. Stir in the flour thoroughly, then moisten with the stock. Season. Cover and simmer for 40 minutes, until the celery is really tender. Mash the cheese to a cream and whisk it gradually into the soup just before serving it; once you start doing this, lower the heat to make sure the soup remains well below boiling point. Correct the seasoning, add parsley, and serve with croûtons.

*[Vegetable Book]*

## MUSHROOM BARLEY SOUP

Another recipe from Michael Field's *All Manner of Food*, quite different from the usual cream of mushroom soup. Mr Field does not specify the exact variety of dried mushroom to be used, but I find that ceps give by far the best flavour. Sometimes one can buy Polish dried ceps, which are good and not too expensive. Otherwise look for an Italian brand; a good one comes from Vicfungo of Costabissara in a bright orange packet labelled *funghi porcini* – you will need two to make up the quantity, as they contain only a ½ oz.

Serves 6–8

*30 g (1 oz) dried mushrooms*
*scant 2 litres (3¼ pt) chicken stock*
*60 g (2 oz) butter*
*1 small onion, finely chopped*
*½ medium carrot, finely chopped*
*½ stalk celery, finely chopped*
*125 g (4 oz) pearl barley*
*1 rounded tablespoon flour*
*salt, freshly ground pepper*
*fresh dill or parsley, chopped*

Put the mushrooms into a small bowl. Heat a ladleful of the stock, and pour it over them. After 20 minutes, or when the mushrooms are pliable, remove and chop them. Reserve their soaking liquid.

Meanwhile, melt half the butter in a large pan. Add the onion, carrot and celery and cook them gently for about 10 minutes. They should not brown. Pour in the stock, add the pearl barley, and the mushrooms and their soaking stock when they are ready. Simmer for 1 hour, or until the pearl barley is cooked.

Melt the remaining butter in another pan, stir in the flour, and cook until it turns a delicate golden brown. Add enough stock from the soup to make a smooth sauce, then tip it into the pan of soup, stirring well until everything is amalgamated. Simmer 20 minutes. If the soup becomes too thick, dilute it with more stock or water. Correct the seasoning. Sprinkle with a few tablespoons of dill or parsley, and have some more in a bowl for people to add extra if they like.

[*The Mushroom Feast*]

## SOUR CHERRY SOUP (Meggyleves)

Wonderful cherries – and other fruit – are grown in Hungary. You need dark tart Morellos, or at a pinch Dukes, to make this best-of-all cold summer soups. There are a number of versions, some with red wine, but this one with white wine, seems the best to me: it comes from Victor Sassie, owner of the Gay Hussar restaurant in London's Soho.

Serves 6–8

*500 g (1 lb) Morello cherries*
*750 ml (1¼ pt) Riesling*
*60 g (2 oz) sugar*
*5-cm (2-inch) cinnamon stick*
*grated rind of 1 lemon*
*juice of 2 lemons*
*100 ml (3–4 fl oz) brandy, optional*
*600 ml (1 pt) cream, half soured, half whipping*

Put the cherry stalks into a pan. Stone the cherries and add the cracked stones to the stalks. You can crack the stones completely and extract the kernels, which is even better but more laborious. Add the wine, sugar, cinnamon, rind and juice of the lemons. Bring to the boil slowly, simmer for 5 minutes, cover and turn off the heat. Infuse for 15 minutes. Strain into a clean pan, bring to the boil again and add the cherries with any juice. Take the pan immediately from the stove and cool. Liquidize or process some of the cherries if you want to give the soup consistency. Stir in the brandy, if using, and adjust flavourings to taste.

Put the cream into a tureen; stir in the soup. Serve well chilled.

[*European Cookery*]

## YELLOW PEA SOUP (Gulärtsoppa/Arter Med Fläsk)

Yellow pea soup is claimed as a national dish by both Denmark and Sweden. It is their equivalent to the *olla podrida* of Spain for example, with pulses and meat cooked together, then served separately but in close conjunction. There is no one correct recipe – a Swedish friend said to me briskly, 'The poor add sausage to their yellow peas, the rich smoked bacon and pork.' So take your choice, a smoked pork item of some kind is all that you need.

Danes serve dark rye bread, lager and schnapps with their pea soup (*gule aerter*). The Swedes drink a glass of hot Punsch, their sweet rum-based liqueur, with their pea soup and follow up with pancakes and waffles. Ginger rather than thyme can be the flavouring, with more or less of the other vegetables than the peas, which may or may not be sieved.

Serves 8

*300 g (10 oz) yellow split peas, soaked*
*2½ litres (4½ pt) water*
*500 g (1 lb) of smoked or green streaky bacon, or salt pork*
*small celeriac, peeled and diced, or 4 stalks of celery, chopped*
*3 leeks, trimmed and sliced, or 2 bunches of spring onions, trimmed and cut up*
*250 g (8 oz) peeled, diced carrots*
*500 g (1 lb) peeled, diced potatoes*
*6–8 small onions, peeled*
*6–8 gammon chops, green or smoked*
*bouquet of thyme sprigs, or 1 level teaspoon powdered ginger*
*boiling sausage and/or 4 frankfurters*

Cook the peas slowly in 1 litre (2 pt) water, without salt, until very tender (about 1½–2 hours). Sieve or process if you like, then season. Meanwhile, simmer the piece of bacon or pork in the remaining water for 2 hours, adding the vegetables after 1 hour, and the chops, thyme or ginger and boiling sausage, if using, after 1¼ hours.

Remove the bacon or pork, the chops and boiling sausage, cut them as appropriate and keep warm. Stir the pea purée into the bacon pan, and add extra water if the soup is too thick for your taste. Correct the seasoning. Heat, adding frankfurters 5 minutes before serving the soup.

Ladle out the soup, then, as people finish, bring in the meat to eat on side plates, with a second helping of soup.

[*European Cookery*]

## ANCHOVY AND MUSHROOM EGGS

A Scandinavian recipe which first led me to the delicious combination of mushrooms with anchovy. The sauce described here makes a piquant filling for *vol-au-vent*, or large puffs of chou pastry: it is also a great help to the plainer white fish such as cod and halibut, and a good filling for omelettes.

Serves 6

*375 g (¾ lb) mushrooms, sliced*
*60–90 g (2–3 oz) butter*
*150 ml (¼ pt) each single and double cream,*
*or 300 ml (½ pt) béchamel sauce*
*1 tin anchovies, drained, chopped*
*freshly ground black pepper*
*6 eggs*
*salt*
*dill or parsley, chopped*

Cook mushrooms in butter. Pour on cream or béchamel: simmer until thick. Add anchovies gradually, stopping when the flavour is piquant to your taste. Season with freshly ground black pepper. Spread out in a greased fireproof dish. Make six hollows in it with the back of a tablespoon, and break an egg into each. Sprinkle with salt and pepper. Bake at gas 6, 200°C (400°F), until the egg whites are just set. Sprinkle with dill or parsley, and serve immediately with toast.

[*The Mushroom Feast*]

## DANISH CUCUMBER SALAD (Agurkesalat)

In Denmark, as in Cyprus, a cucumber salad will be served often with hot meat, grills, roast lamb or pork, chicken, or with hamburgers.

Serves 4

*1 large cucumber*
*1 level tablespoon salt*
*1 rounded tablespoon sugar*
*150 ml (¼ pt) wine or cider vinegar*
*pepper*
*chopped parsley or dill leaves*

Score the cucumber down with a fork, slice thinly on the wide grater blade and salt the slices. Then squeeze them dry in a clean cloth and spread them out in a dish. Mix the sugar and vinegar and pour it over them. Pepper well. Leave for 1–2 hours in the refrigerator. Taste some and see if the seasonings need adjustment. Drain off the liquor and serve the cucumber sprinkled with parsley or dill.

[*Vegetable Book*]

## FRANKFURT GREEN SAUCE (Frankfurter Grüne Sosse)

This famous herb sauce is one of the summer triumphs of Frankfurt cookery. There are a number of versions – this one comes from a reader who grew up in Frankfurt – but they all contain 7 or 8 different herbs.

Serves 6

*15 g (½ oz) each borage, salad burnet, parsley and sorrel*
*20 g (⅔ oz) each chives and cress or watercress*
*10 g (⅓ oz) each tarragon and chervil*
*150 ml (¼ pt) mayonnaise*
*1 level teaspoon German mustard*
*2 hard-boiled eggs, chopped*
*1 small pickled gherkin, with dill, chopped*
*1 small onion or shallot, chopped*
*½ clove of garlic, chopped*
*salt and pepper*
*grated lemon rind and lemon juice*
*2 tablespoons soured cream or yoghurt, optional*
*1 egg yolk*

Chop the herbs very finely together. Add the remaining ingredients in the order given, seasoning to taste, and beating in the egg yolk last of all. Serve with fried or poached fish, or cold fish, with hard-boiled eggs, with cold meats, or use as a sandwich filling.

One simpler version is made by mixing the herbs above with a little vinaigrette, and then stirring in 300 ml (½ pt) soured cream, salt, chopped shallot or onions, and 2 mashed hard-boiled eggs.

[*European Cookery*]

## MUSHROOM CAVIARE FROM RUSSIA

The Russians are great mushroom gatherers – think of the mushroom parties in *Anna Karenina* – and have many delicious ways of cooking them. Here is one that is simple and particularly good. It can be served on its own, or as part of a mixed hors d'oeuvre. The finer you chop the mushrooms, the more the greenish-grey speckled mixture will *look* like the finest-flavoured Osetr caviare: of course it won't taste the same. Use ceps if you possibly can, otherwise cultivated mushrooms.

Serves 4

*1 medium onion, finely chopped*
*1 tablespoon olive oil*
*250 g (½ lb) firm mushrooms*
*salt, freshly ground black pepper*
*juice of ½ lemon*
*1 generous tablespoon sour cream*
*chives, chopped*

Cook onion gently in the oil until almost cooked, without allowing it to brown. Meanwhile chop the mushrooms, stalks and all. Add to the pan and cook for 8 to 12 minutes – if the mushrooms exude a lot of juice turn up the heat; the final result should be moist but not wet, the mushrooms cooked but not too soft. Season, remove from the heat, and add lemon juice, sour cream and chives to taste. Serve well chilled, sprinkled with more chives. Toast should be served as well.

[*The Mushroom Feast*]

## RUSSIAN PANCAKES (Bliny)

Bliny have traditionally had a strong association with the holiday known as *maslenitsa* in Russia. *Maslenitsa* (from *maslo*, meaning butter in Russian), originally a pagan festival celebrating the passing of winter and the coming of spring, was incorporated by the Russian Orthodox church into its religious calendar, and *maslenitsa* became a week-long holiday before the beginning of the long Lenten fast. *Maslenitsa* (like Shrove Tuesday or Mardi Gras) was the last opportunity to indulge in an orgy of eating, and bliny with butter, soured cream, salted fish and many other delicacies were served throughout the week.

Today, few Russians celebrate *maslenitsa* in its religious sense, but many use it as a good excuse for eating a lot of bliny in the company of family and friends. Needless to say, bliny are eaten all the year round as well.

Bliny can be made from different types of flour – wheat (this makes the lightest bliny), buckwheat, rye, or a combination of these. The batter is made with yeast, and must be allowed to rise twice before the bliny are fried. So allow about 6 hours to prepare bliny before eating them.

Serves 6–8

*1 litre (1½ pt) milk*
*30 g (1 oz) fresh yeast or 15 g (½ oz) dried yeast*
*500 g (1 lb) flour*
*40 g (1½ oz) butter, melted*
*1 teaspoon salt*
*1 tablespoon sugar*
*1 egg, beaten*
*sunflower oil for frying*
*15-cm (6-inch) heavy frying pan*

Heat 200 ml (7 fl oz) milk until it is warm but not boiling. Stir in the yeast till dissolved, add half the flour, and mix well. Cover with a cloth and leave in a warm place to rise for 2–3 hours.

When the batter has risen, add the melted butter, the salt, sugar and beaten egg, and the remaining flour. Mix well to a stiff batter. Then heat the remaining milk till warm and stir it very carefully into the batter till completely smooth. Cover with a cloth and put aside in a warm place for another 2 hours to rise once more. It should be the consistency of thick cream.

Heat the frying pan and smear it with sunflower oil. Many Russians use half a peeled potato, speared on a fork, to do this because it gives an even coating of oil. Pour just enough batter into the pan to cover the surface. When little bubbles begin to appear on the surface of the blin, it is ready for turning. The first blin is often unsuccessful; it takes a little practice to get the pan to the right heat and use just the right amount of oil. There is, in fact, a Russian proverb to this effect – '*pervyi blin komom*', literally meaning that the first blin is always lumpy – used to encourage people after a first failure. 'Practice makes perfect' or 'better luck next time' are possible English equivalents.

Have a deep round buttered dish by the side of the stove and put each blin into this dish as it is ready; butter the blin, and place the next blin on top. When all the bliny are cooked, cover the dish with a cloth; it is not essential to serve them immediately.

The bliny will be soft, spongy and very light. Serve them piled high on a plate in the middle of the table, surrounded by dishes of accompaniments, e.g. a sauceboat of melted butter, a bowl of soured cream, fine slices of salted herring or smoked salmon, bowls of red or black caviare. Each guest will take a blin, put it on their plate, add an accompaniment, roll the blin into a sausage shape and cut off mouthfuls of blin and filling at a time.

For a light supper in the evening, bliny can be served with a dish of jam, and followed by tea.

[*European Cookery*]

# FISH

## HOME-PICKLED HERRING, SALMON, MACKEREL OR TROUT

The high pleasure of holidays in Denmark – Tollund man, amber and archaeology apart – is working one's way through the pickled fish. In hotels or friends' houses, one never seems to eat the same kind twice. And I suppose this to be the case in Sweden and Norway as well.

An English schoolfriend, now married to a Dane in Kolding, first introduced me to this recipe – and to sweet-pickled herrings. Both are common Scandinavian dishes, and I cannot think why they are not common here as well.

Pickled salmon is much cheaper than smoked salmon. Everyone enjoys the unfamiliar flavour. Pickled herrings are almost as good, and make a wonderful standby in the refrigerator. Don't be put off, though, by the unfamiliarity of dillweed. Dill is easy to grow for the future, and for the present freeze-dried leaves of dill – known as dillweed as opposed to dillseed – can be bought in small jars from good grocers and delicatessen stores. In desperation, one could substitute fennel leaves, or chopped fresh tarragon, but dillweed is what gives the unmistakably right note.

Incidentally this is an excellent recipe for frozen Canadian salmon. Buy a tailpiece – bargaining is advisable – and ask the fishmonger to remove the bone, so that you have two kite-shaped pieces. With smaller fish, slit them along the belly and remove the innards; and the head, if you like. Press them, cut side down, firmly on to a board and press steadily along the back. Turn the fish over and you will be able to pick out the backbone quite easily, with the small bones which adhere to it.

The pickle recipe is enough for a 750 g–1 kg (1½–2 lb) piece of salmon, or for two, even three pairs of small fish.

Mix together in a bowl:

*1 heaped tablespoon sea salt*
*1 rounded tablespoon sugar*
*1 teaspoon crushed black or white peppercorn*
*1 tablespoon brandy (optional)*

Have a quantity of dillweed to hand, a good tablespoon should be enough.

Put some of the mixture, and some dillweed, into a dish. Put in the first piece of salmon, or the first whole fish, skinside down. Spread some more of the pickle on the cut side, with some more dillweed. Put in the second piece of salmon, or the second whole fish, cut side down. (Repeat this with the rest of the small fish.) Finally put the last of the pickle and dillweed on top, then some kitchen foil, and a couple of tins to press the fish together so that it is permeated by the pickle and dillweed; in fact, I use a Roman brick which we picked up in France, at the fortress of Jublains, because it is a good shape for the fish.

Leave it for at least 12 hours, and not more than 5 days. To serve, slice off the flesh – well drained – in thinnish slivers and arrange on plates or on buttered rye bread: a sweet/sour mustard and dill mayonnaise is usually served with this dish. The pickled fish can also be heated in a little butter, and served with baked potatoes and the mustard and dill sauce.

[*Fish Cookery*]

## KIPPER OR MATJES HERRING SALAD WITH MUSHROOMS

A good hors d'oeuvre if served really cold.

Serves 4

*3 large kippers (not frozen fillets), or 6 nice matjes fillets*
*125 g (¼ lb) young, fresh mushrooms*
*chopped onions, or thin onion rings*

DRESSING
*a well-sweetened vinaigrette made with corn oil and wine vinegar*
or *an olive oil and lemon dressing with a little sugar*
or *sour cream*
or *double cream, seasoned with lemon juice*

Kippers can be used without further cooking, if they are of high quality: discard the skin and bones with the aid of a sharp knife, and cut the fillets into 1-cm (½-inch) slices. The alternative is to put the kippers tail down in a large container and pour boiling water over them: remove after 2 or 3 minutes before they soften too much, then discard skin and bone. Matjes fillets may need soaking. Taste a tiny corner to see. (If you can get hold of a packet of French *harengs saurs* fillets, they are the best of all: they don't usually need soaking.)

Place the fish pieces in a serving dish, and slice the mushrooms, then fit them between the fish pieces. Pour over whichever dressing you have chosen – keep vinaigrette to a minimum or else the dish will be too wet and lose crispness. Top with chives or onion rings. Chill well.

[*The Mushroom Feast*]

## KIPPERS OR SALT HERRING FILLETS WITH DILL SALAD

Dill is an under-used herb in this country – which is a pity. It is easy to grow, and its subtle flavour of caraway goes well with fish and all kinds of vegetable dishes. Dillweed, i.e. the leaves as opposed to the seeds, which are also used as flavouring, can be bought in the McCormick range of herbs and spices. An alternative is the stronger, slightly liquorice-flavoured fennel, which is grown as a garden herb and can also be found wild on many cliffs of England and Wales.

Serves 4

*6–8 kipper fillets, or soaked salt herring fillets*
*250 g (½ lb) waxy potatoes, boiled and diced*
*175 g (6 oz) beetroot, boiled and diced*
*250 g (½ lb) eating apples, diced*
*1 small mild onion, chopped*

DRESSING
*6 tablespoons olive oil*
*1½ tablespoons wine vinegar*
*1 good teaspoon French or German mustard*
*1 scant teaspoon sugar*
*salt, black pepper*
*1 heaped tablespoon chopped dillweed*

Cut the fish fillets into strips 2 or 3 hours before the meal, prepare the dressing and mix it into each of the main ingredients, in separate bowls. Before serving, arrange the drained ingredients on a serving dish (or on pieces of bread and butter as open sandwiches), and chill.

Alternative dressings are sour cream beaten with a little lemon juice to taste, or mayonnaise, plus dill.

[*Good Things*]

## POACHED TURBOT WITH HORSERADISH

At Krogs Restaurant in Copenhagen, they serve the freshest and finest turbot you are ever likely to eat. It is first seasoned and left for a while to absorb the flavour, then it is poached in a well-flavoured *court-bouillon*. If you suspect that your fish – turbot is the ideal, but other firm white fish will do very well – is not as fresh as it should be, bake it in buttered foil (2½-cm (1-inch) thick steaks will take 20 minutes at gas 5, 190°C (375°F)).

While the fish is cooking, grate a bowl of fresh horseradish from the outside of the root (the central core is the hot part), and melt 250 g (8 oz) of butter in another bowl.

When the fish is served, everyone helps themselves to the horse-radish, sprinkling it over the fish. The melted butter is poured over the top. This is really excellent, the horseradish is sweetly piquant, and the butter adds the richness that poached fish requires. A few boiled new potatoes go well with the turbot, too.

[*Fish Cookery*]

## SCANDINAVIAN BEETROOT AND HERRING SALAD (Sildesalat)

*Sildesalat* is a favourite around the Baltic Sea and in Norway. The quantities of each ingredient can be varied, according to your taste and what is available.

Serves 4–6

*3 salt herring fillets, or matjes herring, or bloaters or kippers, filleted*
*500 g (1 lb) boiled beetroot, diced*
*vinaigrette*
*250–375 g (8–12 oz) cooked potato, diced*
*2 Cox's Orange Pippins, unpeeled, cored, diced*
*1 medium onion, cut into thin rings*
*2 hard-boiled eggs, quartered*
*chopped parsley*

Cut the fillets so that you have six nice strips, and if they are on the strong side soak them. Bloater and kipper, English alternatives, need no soaking or cooking. Put the beetroot in a bowl, and pour over a little vinaigrette. Mix the potato and apple in another bowl and add vinaigrette. Leave for 1–2 hours.

About 1 hour before the meal, arrange the beetroot on a dish after draining it. Surround it with the drained potato and apple, or *vice versa*. Place the herring strips on top. Scatter with onion, arrange the eggs and finish with a good layer of parsley. Chill.

You might prefer to use a Scandinavian cream dressing. Arrange the beetroot, potato and apple on the dish, without soaking them in vinaigrette. Mix together 1 teaspoon each of German mustard and sugar, with 1 dessertspoon of wine vinegar, salt and pepper. Whip 175 ml (6 fl oz) double cream, and fold in the vinegar mixture thoroughly. Pour over the vegetables. Top with herrings, onion, egg and parsley. Chill.

[*Vegetable Book*]

## SCANDINAVIAN PICKLED SALMON

Cheaper Canadian salmon may be used for this delicious preparation. It is easy, and it makes a much cheaper start to a meal than smoked salmon. Everyone enjoys its fresh, unfamiliar flavour:

> *750 g–1 kg (1½–2 lb) tailpiece salmon*
> *1 large tablespoon sea salt*
> *1 rounded tablespoon sugar*
> *1 teaspoon coarsely ground black pepper*
> *1 tablespoon brandy (optional)*
> *plenty of dillweed*

Slice the piece of salmon in half, carefully, and remove the backbone and any little bones, but leave the skin. Rinse very quickly, dry well and put the first piece, skin side up, in a dish. Mix salt, sugar, pepper and brandy together. Rub about a quarter of this into the skin of the first piece, turn it filleted side up and rub in half the mixture; sprinkle liberally with dillweed (sold in the McCormick range of herbs) and put the second piece on top, filleted side down. Rub the rest of the mixture into the skin, and sprinkle with more dillweed. Put a piece of foil on top, then a couple of tins as weights. Leave for at least 12 hours, and at most 4 days, in the refrigerator or in a very cool place.

To serve, drain the pieces and slice them diagonally or horizontally starting at the tail end. Serve with thinly cut wholemeal or rye bread, and butter, with lemon quarters. In Scandinavia this mustard sauce usually accompanies pickled salmon – and very good it is:

*1 heaped tablespoon French or German mustard*
*½ tablespoon sugar*
*1 tablespoon wine vinegar*
*4 tablespoons olive or salad oil*
*dillweed to taste*

Mix all the ingredients together to a thick, smooth yellow sauce. A crushed clove of garlic, a small one, may also be added.

Mackerel or trout can be used instead of salmon.

[*Good Things*]

# MEAT, GAME AND POULTRY

## GOULASH (Gulyás)

*Gulyás*, or goulash if you prefer an anglicized spelling, is flavoured with paprika – i.e. peppers ground to a powder – but here is a version that includes peppers as well. You will find it worth making a visit to a good delicatessen for Hungarian paprika to flavour this and other dishes in the book: it has a richer, darker flavour than the Spanish kind often sold in supermarkets, though it is not necessarily any hotter.

Serves 6

*1½ kg (3 lb) chuck or rump steak, cubed*
*4–5 rashers streaky bacon, cut into strips*
*4 large onions, chopped*
*3 tablespoons Hungarian paprika*
*2 green peppers, seeded, roughly chopped*
*salt*

Sear the beef in its own fat in a heavy iron frying pan. Put it into a casserole. Deglaze the pan with 300 ml (½ pt) water, and pour it over the beef when it is bubbling hot. Fry the bacon in the pan, adding the onions when the fat begins to run. Brown everything lightly, then stir in the paprika. Cook for a further 2–3 minutes, then tip it over the beef. Add the peppers. Cover closely and stew until the beef is tender. Add salt, stew a further 5 minutes, then correct the seasoning if necessary. Serve with separately cooked ribbon noodles, and plenty of green salad.

[*Vegetable Book*]


## LAMB HUNGARIAN STYLE

Alexandre Dumas, of *The Three Musketeers*, who also compiled the *Grand Dictionnaire de Cuisine*, was unusual among French lovers of good food in his open mind. He was able to conclude that lamb cooked desert-style by Arabs – complete with fleece, which was stripped off before the feast began – tasted better than any roast gigot he had eaten at home. Of this economical recipe he says, 'one of the best dishes which I have eaten in Hungary'.

The quantity of onion seems enormous, but it softens and reduces considerably. I use more paprika than Dumas suggests, though no doubt a pinch from those large fingers was nearer a tablespoon. For 6–8 people buy 1½–2 kg (3 lb) of the meatiest breast of lamb you can find. Ask the butcher to cut it into 'pieces the size of tablets of chocolate' – small tablets of 50 g (2 oz).

> Serves 6–8
>
> *1½ kg (3 lb) Spanish onions*
> *butter*
> *sugar, salt, pepper*
> *1 heaped tablespoon flour*
> *1 rounded tablespoon Hungarian paprika*
> bouquet garni
> *up to 1 litre (1½ pt) consommé or beef stock*

In a large heavy pan, cook onions in 3 tablespoons of butter, slowly at first until they soften. Sprinkle on a level tablespoon of sugar, raise heat and stir until the onions are lightly caramelized to an appetizing brown. In another pan at the same time, brown the pieces of lamb in butter. When the onion is right, stir in flour, paprika and *bouquet*. Cook 1–2 minutes, then add enough consommé or stock to make a creamy sauce. Put in the meat and cover. Simmer for at least 1¼ hours, or until the meat falls from the bones. Every 5 minutes check on the liquid level and thickness, adding a tumbler more of stock when necessary. This way of cooking means that you have a good concentrated flavour; it helps if you remove the lid of the pan after 30 minutes' cooking, so that the sauce reduces, and you top it up. Check the seasoning, skim or blot away surface fat, and serve with noodles.

[*Observer Magazine*]

## PEAS IN CREAM

Do you ever try cooking peas with any other flavouring than mint? With savoury, for instance, or young green fennel leaves? Or with spices? This old recipe using nutmeg and mace is a good starting point for experiment.

Serves 6

*scant 150 ml (¼ pt) water*
*60 g (2 oz) butter*
*500 g (1 lb) shelled peas*
*1 dessertspoon chopped parsley*
*1 teaspoon sugar*
*salt, black pepper*
*¼ teaspoon each nutmeg and mace*
*1 heaped teaspoon flour*
*120–175 ml (4–6 fl oz) double cream*
*lemon juice*

Bring water and butter to the boil. Put in peas, parsley, sugar, salt and spices. Simmer until the peas are nearly tender. Put the flour into a basin and stir in some of the cooking liquor, until you have a smooth paste. Stir in the cream and return to the pan. Cook gently until the liquor thickens and the peas are done. Taste and add more nutmeg and mace if necessary. Sharpen with a little lemon juice.

Serve as a separate course, with a dozen triangles of bread, fried in butter, tucked round the peas at the last moment before serving.

As a variation, cook a bunch of tiny young carrots separately, and add them to the peas before turning them into the serving dish.

[*Good Things*]

## PEAS STROGANOFF

Every cook hopes, perhaps against reason, to find dishes which are particularly good to eat, quick to prepare, and if not cheap, at least not outrageously expensive. There aren't many. An obvious one is boeuf Stroganoff (rapidly becoming our national dish, to judge by reports in *The Good Food Guide*). It is a recipe which is easily adapted to other lean, i.e. expensive, cuts of meat – veal, for instance, or lamb chops:

> Serves 6
>
> *peas in cream (page 291)*
> *10-cm (4-inch) thick lamb chops*
> *125 g (4 oz) butter*
> *salt, pepper, lemon juice*

Strip the lean meat from the chops, discarding fat and bone. Cut into small slices about 3 mm (⅛ inch) thick; season them well with salt and pepper. Next prepare the peas in cream, and keep them hot. Also prepare 6 slices of toast (better with lamb than fried bread), cut the crusts off, and divide each piece into two triangles. Last of all, when everything else is ready, fry the lamb quickly in foaming butter for 4 or 5 minutes. Mix meat and pan juices with the peas. Correct the seasoning with more salt, pepper and lemon juice if necessary. The flavour should be both rich and piquant. Serve immediately, not giving the lamb a chance to become tough, with the toast round the edge of the dish.

*[Good Things]*

## HIGGLER'S POT (Hökarepanna)

I had the recipe for this old dish from a Swedish friend, who lives in England. She makes it for the main course at Sunday lunch very often. First come little round open sandwiches, very fresh tasting, with shrimps and golden caviare and egg.

After the higgler's pot, we have a buttery Swedish cheese, cut in thin slices, and as pudding, vanilla ice-cream with hot Punsch (a Swedish liqueur) to pour over it and more Punsch to drink.

The only problem you may encounter with *hökarepanna* is finding the veal kidney. Order it in advance from your local veal butcher; it is a great delicacy.

Serves 8

*1–1½ kg (2–3 lb) potatoes, fairly thickly sliced*
*2 pork tenderloins, sliced 1 cm (½ inch) thick*
*2 veal kidneys, sliced 1 cm (½ inch) thick*
*500–750 g (1–1½ lb) onions, sliced*
*salt and pepper*
*300 ml (½ pt) lager*
*glass of sherry*

Cook the potatoes for 3 minutes in boiling salted water. Drain them well. Grease a deep flameproof pot with a butter paper, then put in a layer of potatoes, then some tenderloin, kidney and onions with seasoning. Repeat, and finish with a top layer of potatoes. Pour over the lager. Cover tightly and cook gently until the meat is tender, either on top of the stove or in a low oven, gas 2, 150°C (300°F). Maintain a simmer with the occasional bubble, by lowering the heat after a while. Since neither tenderloin nor kidneys are tough, this dish takes 1½ hours, but test earlier.

Taste the liquid, add extra seasoning if necessary, and pour in the sherry. Cook gently for another 5 minutes.

[*European Cookery*]


## RED CABBAGE WITH SMOKED MEAT

A complete one-pot main course, excellent midday food in wintertime. Although the origin and general method is German, the idea of including smoked poultry came from a friend in France. There *poulet fumé* is sold in most supermarkets (and rather despised). In this country it is rare; for us it turns the dish into something specially enjoyable. If you like frankfurters, they can be added as well. Indeed any of the smoked sausages are suitable, or even fried uncured sausages of quality. But whatever smoked meats you choose, the essential is a piece of smoked belly bacon with a strong, genuine flavour. There is nothing to beat the German *geräuchter bauchspeck* sold in good delicatessens. It permeates the cabbage in an irresistible way, whereas most smoked bacon on general sale, the kind in plastic packets, is far too genteel to make a proper contribution.

Serves 6–8

*1 red cabbage, sliced*
*500 g (1 lb) piece smoked belly bacon, sliced (include rind and bones)*
*500 g (1 lb) sour apples, peeled, cored, sliced*
*375 g (12 oz) sliced onion*
*60 g (2 oz) dark brown sugar*
*salt, pepper*
*1 teaspoon ground cloves*
*'4 tablespoons malt vinegar*
*150 ml (¼ pt) water*
*175 ml (6 fl oz) red wine*
*smoked pork boiling sausage or rings*
*slices of garlic sausage, thickly cut*
*frankfurters*
*fried fresh sausages*
*smoked chicken or other poultry*
*smoked ham*

Layer the cabbage, bacon, apple and onion into a commodious pot, sprinkling each layer with sugar, seasonings and cloves. Pour on vinegar and water. Cover and cook for upwards of 3 hours in the oven at gas 2, 150°C (300°F), or all day at a lower temperature if this suits you better and you have a solid fuel or oil-fired stove. The cabbage can also be cooked on top of the stove as in the previous recipe. If the cabbage is very liquid by this time, remove the lid and boil off the surplus. At this point, you can set the whole thing aside for later reheating with the meats.

Forty minutes before the meal, have the cabbage boiling and add the wine and smoked pork boiling sausage or rings. Fifteen minutes before serving, arrange garlic sausage, frankfurters, fresh sausage, poultry, ham – some or all of them – on top, to heat through properly.

Finally, check the seasonings and adjust them to taste.

Serve in the cooking pot with potatoes boiled in their jackets.

[*Vegetable Book*]


## POOR MAN'S GAME

To cheer people without much access to game, pork can be transformed into 'wild boar' and lamb into 'venison'. The strong wine marinade completely penetrates the meat to deepen the flavour towards gaminess: this means that red wine gives the most convincing result, though white wine or cider can also be used for the recipe.

Serves 4–6

*leg of pork or lamb*

MARINADE
*150 g (5 oz) each chopped onion and carrot*
*60 g (2 oz) chopped celery*
*2–3 tablespoons oil*
bouquet garni *with double thyme and parsley*
*3 cloves garlic, finely chopped*
*2 small sprigs of rosemary*
*8 juniper berries, crushed*
*10 peppercorns, slightly crushed*
*3 teaspoons salt*
*600 ml (1 pt) wine or cider*
*150 ml (¼ pt) red or white wine vinegar*

*2 onions, 2 carrots, sliced*
*2 celery stalks, chopped*
*2 leeks, sliced*
*200–250 g (7–8 oz) unsmoked streaky bacon, diced*
*60 g (2 oz) butter*
*veal or light beef stock*

Skin the meat and score the fat in diamonds. Put the meat into a deep, close-fitting pot. Brown the marinade vegetables in oil. Lightly pour off surplus fat, add the rest of the ingredients and bring to a vigorous boil. Cool, then pour over and cover the pot with foil. Leave for 4 days, turning the meat at least twice a day. Store in a cool place (not necessarily the fridge).

To cook the meat, drain it and remove any clinging bits and pieces. Strain the marinade. Rinse out the pot. Brown the cooking vegetables with the bacon, in butter. Put into the pot with the meat on top. Pour on the marinade and add stock to come two-thirds of the way up. Bring slowly to the boil, cover and leave to simmer for 2 hours, or until the meat is done. Turn it over after an hour. Shortly before the meat is due to come out, pour off most of the liquid through a strainer into a wide shallow pan. Spoon off or blot away any fat. Boil down hard to a good concentrated flavour. Put the meat into a shallow roasting pan. Give it about 20 minutes in a hot oven gas 7, 220°C (425°F) to glaze, basting it frequently with the reduced stock.

Serve the meat with green beans, redcurrant jelly, lattice or straw potatoes and either the pan juices or gravy made from them. You can whisk in butter or cream if you like a richer sauce.

*[Observer Magazine]*


## HARE WITH CREAM

Only the saddle is needed in this German recipe; the rest can be used up in a civet. Be careful to remove the pearly skin. The saddle should be larded to keep it moist during the cooking. This is not at all difficult to do – buy a fat end of bacon, or a piece of hard back pork fat, and chill it well. Cut into strips about 5 cm (2 inches) long and 6 mm (¼ inch) wide. Thread the first strip into the open end of a larding needle, and take a stitch into the meat, parallel to the backbone, as if you were sewing. The ends of fat will protrude. With a little practice, one can do this quite elegantly so that the slices of meat are neatly patterned with the bits of fat. This excellent and decorative way of making dry meats such as pigeon, fillet steak, venison and hare more succulent, certainly justifies the money spent on a larding needle.

Serves 4

*saddle of hare, larded*
*60 g (2 oz) chopped mild onion*
*60 g (2 oz) chopped carrot*
*300 ml ( ½ pt) double cream*
*150 ml ( ¼ pt) sour cream*
*2 teaspoons wine vinegar*
*redcurrant jelly*
*100–200 ml (1–2 glasses) red wine or port*

Choose an ovenproof cooking pot that just accommodates the hare. First put in the vegetables, then lay the saddle on top. Pour over cream and vinegar, which should ideally come well up the saddle of hare. Roast in a moderate oven, gas 4, 180°C (350°F), for about 45 minutes or until the hare is cooked. Baste frequently with the juices. Remove hare to serving dish and keep warm. Strain cooking liquid into a heavy pan. Boil gently, adding jelly and wine to taste. This dish is often served with chestnut purée, but I prefer whole boiled chestnuts mixed with Brussels sprouts.

*[Good Things]*

## PHEASANT IN THE GEORGIAN STYLE

This lovely and unusual dish takes time to prepare, but it's worth the trouble. Make it above all in autumn, in November, when walnuts are still fresh and juicy and the first good grapes and oranges arrive. The version here is French, coming by way of Escoffier from *La gastronomie en Russie*, by A. Petit, published in 1860. Georgia sounds like paradise: walnuts, oranges, grapes, tea and pheasants all flourish there.

Keep any vegetables you may think of serving as a separate course. This is a dish on its own.

Serves 4–5

*30 walnuts, or 250 g (8 oz) shelled walnuts*
*1 kg (2 lb) grapes*
*4 oranges, preferably blood oranges*
*1 tea bag, preferably containing green tea*
*1 pheasant*
*150 ml (¼ pt) sweet muscatel wine, e.g. Frontignan*
*90 g (3 oz) butter*
*salt, pepper*
*30 g (1 oz) flour*

Pour boiling water over the shelled walnuts, leave for 3 or 4 minutes and then remove the skin surrounding the nuts themselves (a pointed knife helps). This removes the bitter part of the walnuts. Put the grapes through a *mouli-légumes* (or liquidize and sieve), to obtain a thick juice. Squeeze the oranges. Pour 150 ml (¼ pt) boiling water over the tea bag, brew for 5 minutes, then strain off the tea. Put all these ingredients, with the pheasant, the wine and half the butter, into a casserole; ideally, it should be of a size only a little larger than the bird, so that the other ingredients almost cover it. Season with salt and pepper, and cover. Bake in a moderate oven, gas 4–5, 180–190°C (350–375°F), for 50 minutes or until the pheasant is just cooked. Cut it into four, or carve it as appropriate; arrange the pieces on a hot serving dish, and put the strained walnuts around them. Measure the cooking juices (there will be about 1–1¼ litres (1½–2 pt) and reduce to half the quantity by boiling hard. Meanwhile keep the pheasant warm in the oven (protect with buttered paper), and fork the flour into the remaining butter. When the reducing is completed, add the flour and butter to the sauce in little pieces, stirring them in well. The sauce will thicken, and acquire an appetizing glaze. Pour a little of it over the pheasant, and serve the rest in a sauceboat.

[*Good Things*]

## SADDLE OF VENISON OR HARE WITH RED WINE
## SAUCE (Rehrücken or Hasenrücken mit Rotweinsosse)

The two meats can be treated in exactly the same way, but with differences of cooking time and quantity. A saddle of venison is enough for 6 to 8 people, a saddle of hare enough for 2 or 3 (keep the legs to make a civet). With the increase in venison farming, we should gradually see more of it in our shops, though much is exported, especially to Germany. It is cheaper than beef and should remain so.

Marinading and larding are good ideas for both venison and hare, though not absolutely essential. Use a strong, large larding needle, the length of a carving knife. These are available here in England, but if you go to Paris you will have an excellent excuse to visit the splendid kitchen shop of Dehillerin by Les Halles and the Forum.

The use of fruit with dark gamey meat is something Germans understand even better than we do. They have a way of cooking game that is very appealing to our taste, which is not really surprising since we owed much to this German practice in the past.

Serves 6–8

*2½ kg (5 lb) saddle of venison or 2–3 saddles of hare, well hung and skinned*
*thick sheet of pork back fat, chilled till firm, then cut into thin strips to fit larding needle*
*salt and pepper*

MARINADE
*750 ml (1¼ pt) red wine*
bouquet garni
*1 teaspoon each juniper berries and peppercorns, lightly crushed*
*1 carrot and onion, sliced*
*1 tablespoon sherry vinegar, or 2 tablespoons red wine vinegar*
*750 ml (1¼ pt) water*

SAUCE
*150 g (5 oz) carrot, cut into sticks*
*125 g (4 oz) onion, sliced*
*white part of 1 small leek, sliced*
*2 celery stalks, sliced*
*60 g (2 oz) lard or bacon fat*
*3 tablespoons port*
*1 level tablespoon redcurrant jelly*
*100 ml (3½ fl oz) whipping or double cream*

*lemon juice*
*1 teaspoon horseradish*
*salt and pepper*

GARNISH
*4 pears, peeled, cored, halved and poached, for venison*
*lingonberry sauce or redcurrent jelly, for venison*
*fried slices of apples or pears, for hare (optional)*

Lard the meat with seasoned strips of pork back fat, taking up small 'stitches' if you have a thin larding needle, or pushing the needle right through and drawing back long strips if you have a large needle. Put the meat, fleshy side down, in a close-fitting flameproof pot. Bring marinade ingredients to the boil in a pan, simmer for 5 minutes, then cool and pour over the meat. Cover and leave for two days or leave overnight, according to the age of the meat, in a cool place. Then drain and dry the meat. Strain the marinade, reserving *bouquet garni* and spices.

Set oven at hot, gas 8, 230°C (450°F). Brown the sauce vegetables in hot fat, then put in a large cooking pot. There should be enough to make a layer in the base of the pot; if not, add more in roughly the same proportions. Brown the meat and put it on top. Pour in enough of the marinade to come just over half-way up the meat, add the *bouquet garni* and spices. Cover and put into the heated oven: after 15 minutes, lower the heat to gas 4, 180°C (350°F), and cook 30 minutes for hare, and 50–60 minutes for venison, which should, ideally, be pink.

Put the meat on a hot serving dish, carve and reassemble on the dish, and keep warm. Strain the juices into a wide shallow pan, skimming or blotting away the fat. Add any marinade left over as well. Bring to the boil and boil hard to reduce the liquid to end up with no more than 500 ml (generous ¾ pt). Add the port and boil again. Be guided by your taste rather than exact measurement, remembering that cream will be added and that the sauce should taste on the strong side, as it is to be used sparingly with the meat.

To finish the sauce, whisk in the redcurrant jelly, then the cream: when well amalgamated, sharpen slightly with lemon juice. Finally season with just enough horseradish to give a hint of it in the sauce, plus salt and plenty of pepper.

Surround the venison with halved pears, and drop a spoonful of lingonberry sauce or redcurrent jelly into the cavities of each one. With hare, omit the pears and add fried slices of apples or pears, if you like, which go better with its smaller size. Pour a little hot sauce over and round the meat, put the rest in a jug. Serve the venison with green beans or red cabbage, the hare with potato dumplings or noodles.

[*European Cookery*]

# VENISON

Venison, as far as our general diet is concerned, is a new meat. A meat of the future, and – because it is, in a sense, unnecessary – a meat whose increasing production we should, as consumers, be able to influence. As one deer farmer said, 'Let's get it right this time! We don't want venison to be the battery chickens of AD 2000.' In the past, noble lords and rich men – when they could get a licence from the Crown – built themselves a living larder in the shape of a deer park with high fences and walls. They went out and formally hunted the deer inside. Then they pigged on the venison. Now some of them are glad to sell the venison to the people, you and me, who used to poach it – if we could. The reason deer became less important as a meat was because once turnips became the answer to winter feeding, it was possible to overwinter cattle and sheep in large numbers. The ancient virtue of deer in this respect is their much reduced winter appetite. What people then preferred was the fatter meat of beef and mutton: once they were assured of year-long supplies, they dropped the leaner venison. This, of course, is precisely what makes venison a desirable meat to us now. It is naturally lean. And, for the green-minded, the whole point of deer farming is that they are efficient at converting grass (a natural foodstuff, not to mention potatoes, carrots, etc.) into lean meat.

## Venison Stroganoff

Serves 6

Cut lean meat from 6 venison chops (or 750 g (1¾ lb) lean venison) into strips. Season. Slice and cook 375 g (¾ lb) onion in butter and oil, without browning it. Raise heat, add the same weight of sliced mushrooms. When cooked, the mixture should be moist not wet. Meanwhile mix 1 teaspoon each of dry mustard and sugar with 2 pots of soured cream (300 ml (½ pt)). In a separate pan cook venison strips over high heat in butter until brown, but not overdone. Add mushrooms and cream; bring to just under boiling point, stirring.

Correct seasoning. Sprinkle with parsley and surround with straw potatoes. Serve immediately.

[*Observer Magazine*]


## CHICKEN PAPRIKA (Csirkepaprikás)

A good recipe for showing how the *paprikás* method works, the chicken being cooked with small quantities of liquid which are absorbed and concentrated, and continually replenished. This way the sauce is an integral part of the dish. Sometimes *lecsó* is added to the chicken towards the end. Or you can add bacon, peppers and tomato, the basic *lecsó* ingredients, to those below: put them in when the onion has softened, adding the bacon first for a few minutes, then the vegetables, chicken and so on.

> Serves 4
>
> *fresh chicken, jointed*
> *lard*
> *250 g (8 oz) chopped onion*
> *1 rounded tablespoon paprika*
> *cayenne (optional)*
> *chicken stock*
> *300 ml (½ pt) mixed soured and whipping cream*
> *salt and pepper*

Lightly brown the chicken pieces in lard in a sauté pan. Remove the pieces, while you put in the onion, lowering the heat so that the onion dissolves to a golden purée.

Take the pan from the stove and stir in the paprika, plus a shake of cayenne, if you like, to add liveliness. Put back and cook for another 2 minutes. Replace the chicken and pour in 125 ml (4 fl oz) stock. Cover and cook until tender. Every so often, turn the chicken and replenish the stock.

Transfer the cooked chicken to a serving dish and keep warm. Bubble the juices in the pan vigorously to concentrate the flavour. Blot away or spoon off surplus fat. Whisk in the cream, bubble slowly for 1 minute and correct the seasoning. This sauce should be a beautiful creamy pink. Strain some over the chicken and put the rest into a serving jug. Serve with egg noodles (fresh ones, if possible) and a cucumber salad.

[*European Cookery*]

## CHICKEN PÖRKÖLT

The four pillars of Hungarian cooking are *gulyás, pörkölt, paprikás* and *tokány*. *Paprikás* and some *tokány* variations include cream, but *gulyás* and *pörkölt* do not. Because *pörkölt* is cooked almost dry – the word means 'singed' – it is most appetizing in summer.

Serves 5–6

*3 medium onions, diced*
*1 tablespoon lard*
*1 tablespoon sweet Hungarian paprika*
*1¾ kg (4 lb) corn-fed chicken, jointed*
*1 tablespoon tomato purée*
*garlic clove crushed with salt*
*2 medium-sized ripe tomatoes, skinned, seeded, chopped*
*2 green peppers, seeded, diced*

Cook onion slowly in the lard in a heavy sauté pan until transparent. Raise heat and brown it evenly, stir in the paprika and add 100 ml (4 fl oz) water. Cover and stew for 20 minutes. Put in chicken, tomato purée, garlic and an extra teaspoon of salt. Cover and leave for 15 minutes. Turn chicken, add tomato and peppers. Cook until chicken is tender. It should steam in its own juice and fat. Whether you cover the pan or not in the last stage should depend entirely on the consistency of the sauce.

You can serve the dish with egg noodles, but the proper thing is *galuska*, made from a soft dough of 225 g (7–8 oz) flour mixed with an egg, 1 tablespoon lard, 1 teaspoon salt and 4 tablespoons water. Rest the dough 10 minutes. Bring 3 litres (5 pt) of water with 1 tablespoon of salt to the boil. Dip a tablespoon into the dough and tear off a small dumpling into the water. Repeat dipping and tearing. When all dumplings float to the top, switch off heat, remove them with a spoon and rinse with cold water. Drain, then reheat in lard, or chicken or goose fat.

[*Observer Magazine*]

## POZHARSKY CHICKEN RISSOLES (Kotlety Pozharskie)

The word *kotleta* in Russian can either mean a piece of meat on the bone – a cutlet – or, more commonly today, a *rissole* made of minced meat, chicken or fish. Some Russian authorities on Russian national cuisine will not tolerate references to *kotlety* in this second sense; in their view the *kotleta* which was introduced from abroad into Russian cookery in the nineteenth century does not deserve a mention alongside truly native Russian dishes. However, the fact remains that *kotlety*, made of minced beef, pork, chicken or fish, in all shapes and sizes, are one of the most ubiquitous dishes in Russia today.

These *rissoles* are the invention of a nineteenth-century cook, Pozharsky, the owner of a restaurant near Moscow. Pushkin ate Pozharsky's *rissoles* on his way from Moscow to Novgorod and immortalized them in his verse.

Serves 4–6

*1 kg (2 lb) fresh chicken, undressed weight*
*100 g (3½ oz) white bread*
*125 ml (4 fl oz) milk*
*75 g (3 oz) butter*
*salt*
*2–3 tablespoons toasted breadcrumbs*

Remove the giblets and wash the bird thoroughly. Remove the skin and the flesh from the bones (use the bones and the giblets for stock). Mince or process the chicken skin and flesh. Soak the bread in the milk, combine it with the minced chicken, and put this mixture through the mincer or processor once more. Then add 2 tablespoons of the butter, melted, some salt, and mix well.

Form the chicken mixture into oval *rissoles*; roll them in the toasted breadcrumbs. Melt half of the remaining butter in a frying pan, and fry the *rissoles*, a few at a time, in the butter lightly on both sides for 4–5 minutes until they begin to turn brown on the outside. Then put them into a preheated moderate oven, gas 4, 180°C (350°F), or cover them with a lid and leave them on the top of the stove over a low heat for another 5–10 minutes until cooked. (Russian frying pans are heavy and round, without a handle; one all-purpose handle is kept handy for gripping frying pans for easy carrying.)

Serve the *rissoles* with fried potatoes and boiled peas. Pour the rest of the butter, hot from the pan, over them.

[*European Cookery*]

# VEGETABLES AND FRUIT

## DUMPLINGS

One of the pleasures of eating in Austria and Hungary is dumplings. They are not heavy at all, but full of invention and fantasy, and used in many different ways – as snacks, soup or stew garnishes, accompaniments to main courses, and desserts. From the two bread dumpling recipes and from the potato paste given for fruit dumplings, you can improvise your own. Often little cubes of fried bread are added to such mixtures, to give a crisp contrast and a surprise.

**Bread Dumplings I** (Semmelknödel)

> *3 bread rolls*
> *1 egg*
> *100 ml (3½ fl oz) milk*
> *1 small onion, chopped*
> *3 tablespoons chopped parsley*
> *30 g (1 oz) butter*
> *flour or breadcrumbs*

Cube rolls and dry in a cool oven. Beat the egg and milk together. Soften the onion with the parsley in the butter. Mix all together, adding flour or breadcrumbs if the dough is too sloppy to handle. Run your hands under the tap, then form the mixture into little round dumplings. Slip them into a large pan half-full of boiling salted water, cover and cook for about 10 minutes. Taste one, and if cooked, remove the rest.

Left-over dumplings are turned into a homely speciality, *Knödel mit Ei*, which is a great gasthaus favourite. Cut the dumplings in slices and brown them nicely in lard, oil or butter, on both sides. Beat an appropriate number of eggs lightly, with seasoning, and scramble them in the pan with the dumpling pieces. Be sure not to overcook, but serve on the runny side, with a salad.

**Bread Dumplings II** (Serviettenknödel)

> *4 soft white rolls or baps*
> *50 g (2 oz) melted butter*
> *200 ml (7 fl oz) milk*
> *salt, grated nutmeg*

*3 egg yolks*
*1 tablespoon chopped parsley*
*4 rashers of rindless smoked streaky bacon (optional)*
*3 egg whites, stiffly whisked*

Cut the dark crusts thinly from the rolls, if using. Cube and mix the bread with butter, milk, seasonings, egg yolks and parsley. Chop the bacon into bits and fry until crisp in their own fat. Add bits, with their fat, to the bread mixture. Leave for 30 minutes. The texture should be moistly spongy – add more crumbs if it is sloppy. Fold in whites.

Butter a cloth in the centre part. Tip the mixture on to it. Fold over the long edges of cloth loosely and secure with safety pins. Tie two ends like a cracker, and then tie the strings round the handle of a wooden spoon. Suspend the dumpling in a pan half-full of boiling salted water, resting the spoon handle across the top. Simmer, covered, for 1 hour. Cool slightly, cut the strings and unwrap; slice the dumpling. (Austrians use a thread: just like a wire for cutting cheese.) Fry in butter until golden on both sides.

## Flour Dumplings

Makes 6–8

PINCHED DUMPLINGS (*CSIPETKE*): knead enough white bread flour with a pinch of salt into a beaten egg, to make a firm dough. Form into a flattish roll and place on a board. Flour your fingers and pinch off little bits into simmering soup or salted water. Give them 10 minutes to cook.

BITE-SIZED DUMPLINGS (*GALUSKA*): mix 3 level tablespoons strong bread flour with a large egg and a pinch of salt. Drop small quantities from a teaspoon into simmering soup or salted water: they cook in 4 minutes.

*TARHONYA*: pasta dough dried in little knobbly pieces that is said to have been carried by Magyar horsemen in the days of the Great Migrations, along with dried beef. All they then needed was water to make a nourishing meal. It is cooked like a *risotto*, and ends up unmistakably like pasta but with a rice-like nubbliness. These days it is rarely made at home, but bought in packages.

Cook an onion in butter until golden brown, stir in 250 g (8 oz) *tarhonya* and when it begins to brown, pour in a ½ litre (¾ pt) water. Simmer uncovered, and when the *tarhonya* absorbs all the liquid, add a little more, and again, and again, until the *tarhonya* is tender but *al dente*. Serve with *gulyás* and *paprikás* dishes, or on its own with butter and grated cheese.

[*European Cookery*]

## JANSSON'S TEMPTATION (Jansson's Frestelse)

My favourite potato gratin, which makes a good Saturday lunch. The name, I think, means no more than 'Smith's Temptation', i.e. everyone's temptation. Which it certainly is. You should make it with Swedish anchovies, which are really spiced cured sprats. I have tried them, but – to Swedish disgust – prefer the true anchovies that come in little tins, in oil, or salted. Salted, pickled anchovies of all kinds need to be filleted and soaked in water for 30 minutes before using, but for this dish Swedish anchovies and anchovies in oil can be used directly.

Serves 6

*8 Swedish anchovies, filleted or 3 tins anchovies*
*3 large onions, sliced*
*1 kg (2 lb) potatoes, cut into matchstick lengths*
*pepper and salt*
*250 ml (8 fl oz) each single and whipping cream*
*90 g (3 oz) butter*
*1 large gratin dish*

Grease the large dish with a butter paper. Fillet the anchovies if necessary, split each fillet in half and keep the liquor or oil. You can soften the onions and potatoes in butter, but it is unnecessary. Set at hot, gas 7, 220°C (425°F).

Put half the potato sticks into the dish, then half the onions. Make a criss-cross of anchovy strips all over, cover with the remaining onions and the remaining potato sticks last of all. Pepper the layers and add a *little* salt (remember anchovies are very salty). Pour over the anchovy liquor or oil, if you have it, then the single cream and dot with butter. Bake in the heated oven for 15 minutes. Then reduce the heat to gas 5, 190°C (375°F). When the dish looks nicely brown and the potatoes are tender, pour over the rest of the cream and keep at a low heat until required.

When you first check the dish, you will notice that the liquid of the gratin looks curdled. This is why you hold back some cream for the very end. I find that gratins improve if they have a chance to mellow in a very low oven, but this is not essential. In any case, Jansson's temptation is good to eat.

[*European Cookery*]


## KOHLRABI

The long, low Naschmarkt in Vienna, a double alley in the centre of a great boulevard defined by three rows of shop stalls, was originally for dairy produce. Now it is devoted to fruit and vegetables, with an occasional butcher, baker, grocer, pickle merchant and flower seller. In the autumn sun it shone like a never-ending harvest festival. A vegetable in abundance was *kohlrabi*, which I always associate with the Austrian friend who showed me the best ways to cook it.

### Method I

Peel, halve and slice into semi-circles 500 g (1 lb) *kohlrabi*. Melt 2 tablespoons each butter and oil, sprinkle in 1 level tablespoon sugar and caramelize it. Put in the *kohlrabi*, stirring until the pieces are coated. Cover, lower the heat and leave to cook till tender: there should not be much liquid. Sprinkle on 1 level teaspoon flour and stir in just enough stock or water to make a binding sauce, then cook 3–4 minutes more. Scatter with chopped parsley. Serve with roast or grilled meat.

### Method II

Trim 12 *kohlrabi* of their stalks, keeping the best stalks. Peel and hollow out the *kohlrabi*. Simmer the shells for 15 minutes in salted water. Add the reserved stalks for the last 2 minutes. Make a meat (beef/pork/veal/chicken/brains) and breadcrumb stuffing and fill *kohlrabi*. Chop inside parts of *kohlrabi* and blanched stalks; put in a buttered gratin dish, and place *kohlrabi* on top. Put a dab of butter on top of each *kohlrabi* and add enough water to cover stalks, etc. Bake at gas 4, 180°C (350°F), until the *kohlrabi* are tender – about 30 minutes. Pour on cream, fresh or soured, to make a little sauce with the juices in the dish.

[*European Cookery*]

## POTATO PANCAKES (Kartoffelpuffer)

German potato pancakes are a delicious indulgence, best eaten on their own, an ideal family dish for the weekends. The friend who supervised my first efforts assured me that the odd bluish tinge of the raw potato batter is all part of the charm and that the pancakes should be soft in the centre to contrast with the crisp brown edges.

Serves 3–4

*750 g (1½ lb) peeled potatoes*
*100 g (3½ oz) grated onion*
*2 eggs*
*175 g (6 oz) plain flour*
*a good pinch of salt*
*lard*

Shred the potatoes on the coarse side of the grater into a bowl. Mix in the onion, eggs, flour and salt, one by one, and stir smoothly and thoroughly into the potato shreds. Heat enough lard in a heavy frying pan to make ½ cm (¼ inch) depth. Put in 4 tablespoons of the mixture in a heap, then flatten it down with the back of the spoon to make a pancake about 12 cm (5 inches) or so across. If you use a large enough pan, 2 or 3 *kartoffelpuffer* can be cooked at once. When the whiskery edges are golden-brown and crisp, turn the pancakes and cook the other side. The centre will have a smooth, paler look, more like pancakes. Drain well and serve with apple or cranberry sauce, or with slices of Cox's Orange Pippins cooked in butter, and scattered with sugar.

*[Vegetable Book]*

## AN ORANGE PORT IN RUSSIA

At that time – in the early Twenties – Batum was visited by a great number of feluccas with oranges and tangerines from near-by Turkey – from Rizeh and Trapezund (in Batum they said Trebizond). These aromatic fruit were stacked in pyramids on the decks of feluccas which were as multi-coloured as Easter eggs.

I often saw one and the same scene: old Turks reclining on mat-covered oranges, drinking thick, aromatic coffee and smacking their lips.

The smell of coffee spread not only from feluccas, but also from the shingle on the beach. It was edged with coffee-grounds. Torn yellow shreds of tangerine peel were strewn conspicuously among them.

In the evening the sailors on the feluccas prayed sitting on their heaps of oranges, turned to the south-east, in the direction of Mecca, occasionally lifting up their hands or pressing their foreheads against the cold oranges . . . .

On the morning of my arrival . . . Lucienna fried a plaice. We ate the plaice served up with tangerines, washed it down with Rukhadze's vodka and felt happy.

Konstantin Paustovksy, *Southern Adventure*

Une orange sur la table,
Ta robe sur le tapis
et toi dans mon lit.
Doux présent du présent,
Fraîcheur de la nuit,
Chaleur de la vie.
Jacques Prévert

[*Fruit Book*]

# CAKES AND PUDDINGS

## APPLE STRUDEL (Apfelstrudel)

It is not as tricky to make a passable apple strudel as you might think. A really fine one is, of course, another matter, needing skill and regular practice, a developed *tour de main*. I have an Austrian friend whose mother is a dab hand at strudel pastry but she herself is not, and I can understand that such skills may skip a generation. If mother can do it well, why bother, why take her on? This friend was visiting a bread factory in preparation for a broadcast, and was surprised to find that the strudel pastry they sold was hand-made. Women in white coats threw the dough over their shoulders to get it thinner and thinner and thinner. She found it puzzling and admirable, this skill raised to art, those people in their white coats throwing pastry over their shoulders, and again, and again, day after day.

The practice of layering thin sheets of pastry with melted

butter belongs very much to the Middle East and North Africa, and to Eastern Europe as well. Their fila dough is plainer and thinner than strudel, but it can be used instead and is to be found here in some delicatessens. Frozen puff pastry can also be rolled out and then stretched. I saw fila pastry being made one day in a small shop at the back of the Chania market in Crete. The boy making it did not throw the paste over his shoulder. He pulled it out over a great tump of pastry layers, covered every so often with canvas cloths, presumably to prevent them drying out. The baker would throw a lump of dough on top of the pile, then the floury boy would walk round and round, pulling the dough out rapidly until it covered the whole thing. He was completely relaxed, he knew where exactly to pull, how fast to pull, how to coax the delicate cloth of dough to muslin transparency. Obediently the dough stretched, stretched without any obstinacy, without breaking into holes. Customers came and went, made jokes, the boy went on pulling and walking as he answered them. The baker wrapped things up, took money, without the rhythm of that shop being in the least disturbed. I stood and watched. Both men enjoyed their small drama, showmen conniving in an exhibition of skill, enjoying the sunny day, the chat and, all the time, this steady walk round the tump that grew higher by millimetres, yet what speedy millimetres.

To make a beginning with strudel dough, choose a day when you have time, peace and a companion. Clear the kitchen table, or one end of it – enough to accommodate eventually and with ease an oblong of roughly 50 × 60 cm (20 × 24 inches). Make the dough first, and prepare the filling as it rests. My Austrian friend suggests substituting roasted chopped walnuts and other nuts instead of breadcrumbs – I use both and always leave out the sultanas as I cannot bear them with apples, or cooked in that kind of way.

Serves 10

DOUGH
*125 g (4 oz) plain flour*
*½ large beaten egg*
*30 g (1 oz) melted butter or appropriate nut oil*
*a generous pinch of salt*

FILLING
*100 g (3½ oz) fresh breadcrumbs*
*butter*
*250 g (½ lb) sharp cooking apples*
*100 g (3½ oz) caster sugar*

*60 g (2 oz) sultanas (optional)*
*100 g (3½ oz) chopped walnuts, almonds, hazelnuts, etc,*
   *toasted if you like*
*caster sugar to finish*
*melted butter for basting*

To make the dough, use an electric beater or the processor for quick and even mixing. Use warm water to mix the ingredients to a soft and supple dough, with a waxy look. Put it on to a board in a warm place. Rinse out the mixing bowl with hot water, dry it and turn it upside down over the dough. Leave for 30 minutes.

For the filling, fry the breadcrumbs lightly in 100 g (3½ oz) butter until golden rather than brown. Peel, core and slice the apples thinly. Mix sugar, sultanas if used, and nuts. The nuts should be blanched to get rid of their skins, and all or some can be toasted in a low oven or under the grill. There is no law about strudel fillings: Austrians make their own variations – so can we.

Spread a cloth over the table where you intend to work. Sprinkle it with plain flour to stop the dough sticking. Place the dough in the centre and roll it out into a fairly thin oblong. If there are two of you, oil your hands and stand either side of the table. Slip your hands underneath the dough, raising it and stretching it partly by its own weight, partly by the gentle pulling movement of your hands. I find that it is best to use the back of the hand, so that you work palms down. This prevents the dough being broken by an involuntary movement of the fingers. Gradually it becomes so transparent that you can see the pattern of the cloth through it. Eventually, you may be able to read the newspaper through it – text, not headlines: this is the counsel of perfection.

You will have noticed that when making this pastry, warmth is the thing. Warm dough, warm hands, as if you were making bread.

When you first experiment, the dough is bound to develop a few holes. These can be patched at the end, if they are large, or close together, with bits of dough cut from the edge and rolled or pulled thin. When you have stretched the dough as far as you dare, trim off the thick edges (they can be dried, grated into soup as pasta). Do not worry about making a neat oblong. Only the final edge needs to be cut straight.

To fill the pastry, brush it over first with melted butter. Then spread the breadcrumbs over it, leaving a wide rim at the straightened edge and a narrower rim at the opposite edge and the sides. Put the apple on top of the breadcrumbs, then the sugar, sultanas and nuts.

Flip the long edge opposite to the straightened edge over the filling, then fold over the sides (this is why you left rims free). Start rolling carefully, using the cloth to turn the dough over into a roll. When you come to the end, brush the edge with water, so that it will stick to the dough, then flip the whole thing on to a piece of Bakewell paper and slide it on to a baking sheet. If the roll is on the long side, bend it gently to fit the tray.

Melt 60 g (2 oz) butter and brush it over the strudel. Bake at gas 4, 180°C (350°F) for about 35 minutes until beautifully browned and crisp. Baste from time to time with butter. Sprinkle with caster sugar before serving, and provide cream.

Although strudels can be eaten cold, they are at their very best when hot or warm straight from the oven. Any left over can be reheated. The quantity above is enough for 10 people.

*Note*: other fruit can be used; all the northern favourites, plums, apricots, gooseberries, rhubarb, blackcurrants, bilberries.

[*Fruit Book*]

## EMPEROR'S PANCAKE (Kaiserschmarrn)

A fluffy pancake inspired by Emperor Franz Joseph I, and a great Viennese speciality. If you prefer, you can bake the pancake in the oven at gas 6, 200°C (400°F).

Serves 4

*200 g (7 oz) flour*
*a pinch of salt*
*60 g (2 oz) caster sugar*
*4 large egg yolks*
*3 tablespoons butter, melted*
*60 g (2 oz) sultanas*
*scant 500 ml (good ¾ pt) milk*
*4 large egg whites*
*a little butter*
*extra caster sugar*

Mix the first six ingredients, then beat in the milk. Whisk the whites stiffly and fold them in. Melt butter in two pans. Divide the mixture between them – it should be about 2 cm (¾ inch) thick. When golden brown, turn and cook on the other side. Pull apart with two forks in the pan, making rough little pieces, and cook briefly, turning them about. Divide between four hot plates and sprinkle with sugar. Serve immediately with *Zwetschkenröster*:

> *1 kg (2 lb) Zwetschke (Quetsche) plums, or other dark plums*
> *150 g (5 oz) sugar*
> *2 cloves*
> *a small cinnamon stick*
> *juice and rind of a lemon*

Zwetschke plums can be gently torn apart and the stone picked out, other varieties may need more effort. Simmer remaining ingredients with 125 ml (4 fl oz) water for 5 minutes, then put in the plum halves and stir until thick. The plums should fall into lumpy pieces, the final result being somewhere between a compote and a jam. This mixture can be used for fruit dumplings, too.

Do not give up hope of finding Zwetschke plums in England. I heard of some in Cambridge market two years ago and the friend who bought them wrote to me that 'Austrians do not think of it as just another plum – like Kraut (smooth cabbage) and Kohl (crinkly cabbage), there is the Pflaume (plum) and the Zwetschke.'

*[European Cookery]*

## GUNDEL'S WALNUT PANCAKES (Palacsinta Gundel Módra)

Gundel's restaurant, with its wrought-iron gate, stands solidly on the edge of Budapest's City Park. Károly Gundel took the City Park restaurant over in 1910, and turned a good one into a great one, Hungary's best. Everyone went there: the great, the notorious, the smart, students and middle-class families. The poor who came to his kitchen were fed with an open hand. Gundel wrote several books. Corvina, the state publishing house, keeps a revised edition of one of them in print, the little *Hungarian Cookery Book*. In his introduction, he acknowledges the refining influence of French chefs in the nineteenth century – 'Hungarian cooking became lighter without losing its originality'.

Gundel's has recently been restored, though not I think to its original decor, but the old specialities remain on the menu, like these splendid pancakes.

Serves 4

*12–16 pancakes*

WALNUT FILLING
*250 g (8 oz) walnuts*
*125 g (4 oz) sugar*
*125 g (4 oz) chopped raisins*
*grated rind of 1 orange*
*6 tablespoons double cream*
*4 tablespoons rum*

CHOCOLATE SAUCE
*30 g (1 oz) cocoa*
*30 g (1 oz) sugar*
*3 egg yolks*
*200 ml (7 fl oz) milk*
*100 ml (3½ fl oz) whipping cream*
*125 g (4 oz) dark chocolate, broken up or grated*
*4 tablespoons rum*

TO FINISH
*60 g (2 oz) butter*
*6 tablespoons rum*

To make the filling, chop about one-third of the walnuts to pinhead size and grate the rest. Mix the two together. Add the other filling ingredients. Put a spoonful in each pancake and fold it in four. Repeat with remaining pancakes.

For the sauce, beat the cocoa, sugar and egg yolks together. Bring the milk and cream to boiling point, then beat into the cocoa mixture. Return to the heat, and cook gently until the custard thickens slightly. Do not overheat, and keep stirring. Then remove from the heat and mix in the chocolate and the rum. Pour into a jug and keep warm.

To serve, melt the butter in a large frying pan and put in the pancakes. Fry them lightly on both sides. Warm the rum in a ladle and set it alight as you pour it over the pancakes. Turn them again, and serve bubbling, with the chocolate sauce.

*Note*: you can omit the flaming if you like, but this is the way they serve them at the restaurant.

[*European Cookery*]

## REDCURRANT CAKE (Ribiselkuchen)

The best of redcurrent desserts, and this is an Austrian speciality in the version given to me by a friend who lived many years in Vienna. She makes it now for her dinner parties in Paris, cutting it into smallish squares. The combination of almond pastry, soft and crisp meringue, sharp red freshness, makes it the ideal end to a meal.

*160 g (5 oz) butter*
*375 g (12 oz) caster sugar*
*4 egg yolks*
*100 g (3 oz) ground almonds*
*300 g (10 oz) flour*
*500 g (1 lb) redcurrants, free of stalks*
*4 egg whites*

Cream butter and one-third of the sugar, add yolks, almonds and flour. Or else mix to a dough in the processor. Roll out into a circle to fit a 23-cm (9-inch) tart tin, preferably one with a removable base. Bake at gas 5–6, 190–200°C (375–400°F) for 30 minutes or until cooked.

Meanwhile mix redcurrants with half the remaining caster sugar (some people like to cook them gently, then strain off and reduce the liquor, to make a jammy mixture, but this is not necessary except in wet summers). Whip egg whites until stiff, again add half the remaining sugar and whip once more until thick and soft. Finally fold in the last of the sugar.

Take the almond base from the oven. Raise the heat to gas 7, 220°C (425°F). Spread redcurrants and sugar (or their thick syrup) over the pastry, leaving a narrow rim of cake free. Pile on the meringue, right to the edge of the cake. Fork it up and put into the oven for 15–20 minutes until the meringue is nicely caught with brown. Be guided entirely by appearance, rather than precise timing. Serve warm or cold.

*Note*: if you want to get ahead, make the whole thing earlier in the day. Or just make the base the day before and complete with redcurrants and meringue nearer the time of serving.

You can use other sharp fruit, raspberries, gooseberries – use young green ones and cook them first – or in winter a purée of dried apricots cooked in orange juice.

*[Fruit Book]*

# THE AMERICAS

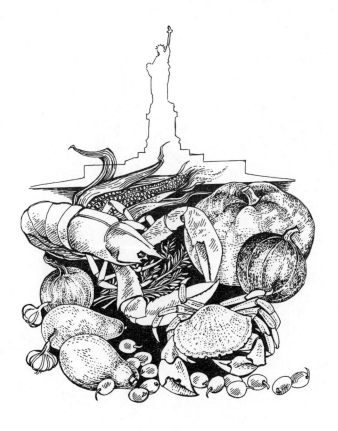

JANE'S FIRST TRIP across the Atlantic was made in her early fifties. She returned thrilled and delighted by her discovery of New York, and made up for lost time by returning frequently to America. She was intrigued both by the paradox of the American diet, the co-existence of the truly dire and the remarkably high quality, and by a national cuisine so firmly rooted in the cooking of its European immigrants. She contemplated, and indeed began to work on a series on American cooking for the *Observer*, but sadly it fell by the wayside.

Nonetheless, she found occasion to explore to some extent the cooking of this huge continent, developing particular sympathy for the cooking of the southern states, and the simple but often elegant dishes of the Shakers. Nor did she dismiss the potential of the commonplace and obvious. Her last series for the *Observer*, 'Slow Down Fast Food', included articles on both hamburgers and baked beans. The recipes in this section are, therefore, as diverse and wide-ranging as the continent from which Jane drew them.

## THOMAS JEFFERSON (1743–1826)

'I am an Epicurean,' wrote Thomas Jefferson. 'I consider the genuine (not the imputed) doctrines of Epicurus as containing everything rational in moral philosophy which Greece and Rome have left us.

> *Happiness the aim of life*
> *Virtue the foundation of happiness*
> *Utility the test of virtue*
> *Pleasure active and In-do-lent*
> *In-do-lence is the absence of pain, the true felicity*

*Active, consists in agreeable motion: it is not happiness,*
  *but the means to produce it.*
*Thus the absence of hunger is an article of felicity;*
  *eating the means to obtain it.'*

Unlike many people in power, Jefferson felt that such felicity was for everyone. This great and attractive man, author of the Declaration of Independence, third President of the United States from 1800 to 1809, and founder and designer of the University of Virginia, saw that his new country could be an earthly paradise, if its natural wealth were to be exploited according to the best of European civilization. As one writer has pointed out, in 1743, the year Jefferson was born, the English in America were a fringe of Europe on the seaboard, focussed on London, the interior was viewed more as a barrier than a treasure house; by 1826 when Jefferson died, there was a population of ten million Americans, the hinterland was being explored and inexhaustible raw materials were being found.

Jefferson's ideas were advanced when he went as Minister Plenipotentiary of the new country to France in the 1780s. He determined to discover the most successful aspects of European life, so that America might benefit and avoid European mistakes. He travelled to Holland (where he bought a waffle iron), Germany, Italy, England (he was ravished by our gardens, but thought the architecture wretched), with the aim of discovering how our agriculture might be adapted to American circumstances. He sent seeds, plants, trees to the States, and had American seeds, plants and trees sent to friends in Europe.

On a journey into Italy, he bribed a porter to take out rice from Piedmont; then fearing that he might not succeed, filled his own pockets with rice – the penalty, had either been caught, was death, so jealously guarded was the export of rice from the Po valley. Many people thought Italian rice superior to Carolina on account of a special machine used to husk and clean it. Jefferson discovered that although quality control was severe, the superiority lay in the variety. Later in life he said that one of his greatest benefactions to America was the introduction of 'dry' rice that could be grown without unhealthily swamped fields. He would be pleased now, I think, to see the packets of Carolina rice on sale in every French supermarket.

At his ingeniously designed house of Monticello in Virginia, then at the White House, a French steward, Petit, and two French chefs, Julien and Lemaire, were employed to supervise and train his staff.

Jefferson's elder daughter, Martha, acted as hostess – her mother had died when she was a child – and in 1791 he gave her for Christmas a recent augmented edition of a cookery book published in 1746, *La Cuisinière bourgeoise*, by Menon, one of the best and most popular books of the day. Martha had accompanied Jefferson to Paris, had been educated there, so understood well what the highest standards of cookery should be.

Jefferson deplored English guzzling, just as Sydney Smith did a generation later. He praised the French: 'In the pleasures of the table they are far before us, because, with good taste, they unite temperance. They do not terminate the most social meals by transforming themselves into brutes.' What would he say about American steaks these days, and 'doggy bags'? At the White House and Monticello, he banned the habit of drinking healths at dinner. The health was bound to be returned, and that set up a chain of health-drinking that had half the guests under the table before the meal was through. This prevented conversation, and conversation round a well-supplied table was Jefferson's idea of a civilized dinner.

Jefferson is sometimes criticized from hindsight by modern commentators for not being a more passionate reformer, especially in the matters of slavery and women's rights. He treated his own slaves as well and better than other people treated their white servants, and phrases indicating his concern with the lot of all poor people, whatever colour they were, thread through his letters. He well understood that improvement was not to be effected by flannel and charitable bowls of soup, but by the increase in national prosperity that the energetic and powerful could achieve for the country. He did not regard poverty as immutable, or the just reward of idleness.

From a famous passage in a letter to Lafayette, his attitude is clear: he urges Lafayette first to get to know the condition of the provinces – a matter in which French governments have not excelled – 'you must ferret the people out of their hovels as I have done, look into their kettles, eat their bread, loll on their beds under pretence of resting yourself, but in fact to find out if they are soft. You will feel a sublime pleasure in the course of this investigation, and a sublimer one hereafter, when you shall be able to apply your knowledge to the softening of their beds, or the throwing a morsel of meat into their kettle of vegetables.'

[*Food with the Famous*]

# SOUPS AND STARTERS

## CARROT SOUP WITH CHERVIL CREAM

Serves 6–8

*4 large shallots, finely chopped*
*45 g (1½ oz) unsalted butter*
*1¼ kg (2½ lb) good carrots*
*1¾–2 litres (3–3½ pt) chicken stock*
*salt and freshly ground black pepper*
*125 ml (4 fl oz) whipping cream*
*2–3 tablespoons chopped chervil*

Sweat the shallots in the butter over a low heat. Scrape or peel and dice the carrots. Add them to the shallots and stir thoroughly. Continue to cook gently for about 10 minutes, stirring from time to time. Add stock to barely cover the carrots and simmer until tender. Put through a *mouli*, dilute further to taste and season.

Whip the cream until thick but not stiff. Season and add the chervil to taste.

Reheat the soup without boiling and divide between very hot bowls. Float spoonfuls of the chervil cream on top.

[*À La Carte*]

## EAST CRAFTSBURY PUMPKIN OR SQUASH SOUP

A recipe from Evan Jones's magnificent and informative book, *American Food.*

Serves 4

*1 pumpkin or other winter squash, about 20 cm (8 inches)*
*    in diameter and 18–20 cm (7–8 inches) high*
*2 tablespoons very soft butter*
*sea salt, pepper*
*1 medium onion, sliced thinly*
*60 g (2 oz) long grain rice*
*generous ¾ litre (1½ pt) chicken stock*
*freshly grated nutmeg*

GARNISH
either *4 bacon rashers, crisply fried, crumbled*
*2 tablespoons grated Mozzarella cheese*
or *125 ml (4 fl oz) double cream*
*1 heaped teaspoon chopped chives*

Cut a lid from the stalk end of the pumpkin or squash, then remove the
seeds and cottony fibres (it is easier to do this with your hand rather
than a spoon). Rub inside the walls with the butter, then sprinkle them
with salt and pepper. Put in the onion and rice. Set the pumpkin in a
pan or ovenproof dish. Bring the stock to boiling point, pour it into the
pumpkin and replace the lid. Bake for 2 hours at gas 5, 190°C (375°F).
Remove the pumpkin – or squash – from the oven, and with a pointed
spoon scrape some of the pumpkin flesh from the walls into the soup.
Taste and correct the seasoning. Add the nutmeg to your liking – a good
pinch will probably be about right. Either scatter the bacon and cheese
on top, or heat the cream and pour that in with the chives. Replace the
lid and bring to the table. As you serve out the soup, be careful to scrape
in more of the pumpkin so that everyone has a good share.

Like baked pumpkin and *carbonada criolla*, this makes a most
attractive dish if you are careful to pick out a perfectly-formed and
unblemished squash or pumpkin. If you want to prepare this soup for
a large party, it is prudent to make it with several pumpkins rather
than one huge one, which will certainly crack with the weight of the
stock before it is ready.

[*Vegetable Book*]


## MUSSEL OR SCALLOP CHOWDER

Chowder sounds uncompromisingly North American to us –
Newfoundland chowder, Manhattan chowder, New England chowder.
In fact this old one-pot meal of fish, potato, onion and salt pork was
taken across the Atlantic by Breton sailors searching for cod. Like
their wives at home they made it in a huge iron *chaudière* (in other
words, a hotpot or cauldron, anglicized in the eighteenth century to
'chowder'). Circumstances demanded the substitution of ship's biscuit
for potatoes; but once the dish settled down on the eastern seaboard of
Nova Scotia and New England, potatoes went back into the pot. In
time a new local ingredient, milk, was added to enhance the stew,
where a Breton cook would have used, and still uses, cider or wine.

I like these satisfying dishes of the pre-oven age. Like Lancashire
hotpot or Irish stew or Welsh cawl, fish chowders are easy to prepare

and very easy on cost (what could be cheaper than this recipe?), yet they make the most of the simple ingredients. They have a basic goodness which pleases everyone.

Serves 4

*1 kg (2 lb) fish bones and trimmings*
*¾ litre (1¼ pt) water*
*125 g (4 oz) salt pork, or green streaky bacon, diced*
*250 g (8 oz) chopped onion*
*1 tablespoon flour*
*600 ml (1 pt) scalded milk*
*1 teaspoon sugar*
*500 g (1 lb) potatoes, cubed*
*1 kg (2 lb) mussels or 4–6 scallops*
*salt, cayenne pepper*
*chopped parsley*
*4 dessertspoons double cream, or 90 ml (3 fl oz) single cream*

Most fishmongers will give you a free handful of fish bones and trimmings, or will charge you at most a few pence for them. Put them into a heavy large pan with 600 ml (1 pt) of water and simmer for 40 minutes without seasoning, while preparing the vegetables. Put salt pork or bacon pieces into a heavy pan on a low heat. When the fat begins to run, put in the onion and brown lightly. Stir in the flour, then, bit by bit, the strained fish stock and hot milk. Add seasoning, sugar and potato. Cook until the potato is just done, but not in the least mushy.

Meanwhile open the mussels in 150 ml (¼ pt) water, remove from their shells and keep warm. Strain the mussel liquor into the chowder, correct the seasoning with salt and cayenne pepper, and simmer for a moment or two. Just before serving add the chopped parsley, mussels and cream.

If scallops are used, remove the coral. Slice the white part and add to the chowder when the potatoes are almost done. Simmer for 5 minutes, correct seasoning and add coral. Simmer for another 3 minutes, then add parsley and cream and serve.

Toast and hot water biscuits are usually served with fish chowders.

[*Good Things*]

## SHAKER TOMATO CUSTARD

A recipe from a cookery book of the American Shakers, that puritanical sect born of the Quaker movement two centuries ago. The collection of favourite dishes is the serene opposite of what might have been expected from these Shaking Quakers, with their ecstatic song and dancing rituals, their gift of tongues, their strong Puritanism.

The first great leader, Mother Ann Lee, had worked as cook in the new Manchester Infirmary before taking a group to America in 1774. I suspect her experiences in the kitchens there must have been happy, because she and her followers developed a tradition of good food lovingly prepared from first class ingredients in clean, well-ordered surroundings. Plenty of eggs, cream, wholemeal bread, fruit, vegetables, honey, poultry, maple syrup, puddings flavoured with rose water, all their own produce, gave Shaker mealtimes an air of cheerful comfort – even if men and women sat at separate tables.

'If we find a good thing, we stick to it' was another Shaker principle. So they were still using European eighteenth-century recipes when they had been forgotten in their original countries. Sometimes a European recipe was adapted to a New World ingredient, as with this tomato custard, a living fossil of the kind one often comes across in American food.

Serves 6

*1 kg (2 lb) ripe tomatoes*
*4 large eggs, beaten*
*125 ml (4 fl oz) milk*
*about 3 tablespoons sugar*
*salt, grated nutmeg*

Quarter, stew and sieve the tomatoes – add no water. Cool and add the remaining ingredients, adjusting the last three to taste. Pour into 6 buttered pots. Stand them in a pan of hot water and bake at gas 4, 180°C (350°F) until the centre is barely firm (it continues to cook as it cools). Serve warm or chilled, with or without cream.

[*Vegetable Book*]

## AMERICAN THREE-BEAN SALAD

Serve as part of a salad meal, or on its own or with a hot spicy *chilli con carne* (page 342). You can vary this salad as you like; I often put in some black beans as well, or as a substitute if I am out of haricot beans. The salad can be made the day before you need it. If you do this, do not put in the parsley and chives until the day you eat it. An important point is to put the beans hot into the vinaigrette dressing, so that they absorb the flavour.

Serves 4–6

*100 g (3–4 oz) each chick-peas, haricot beans and dark red kidney*
   *beans, all soaked separately*
*8 tablespoons chopped spring onion or onion*
*2 cloves garlic, finely chopped*
*plenty of chopped parsley and chives*
*5–6 tablespoons olive oil*
*1 tablespoon wine vinegar or lemon juice*
*salt, pepper, sugar*

Cook the chick-peas for 2 hours, adding the haricot beans after
1 hour. Keep an eye on the pot, so that the haricot beans are not
overcooked to bursting point. Cook the kidney beans separately for
1½ hours, as they dye the water and anything cooked with them (or
use canned red kidney beans instead). Mix the remaining ingredients
in a bowl, adjusting the seasonings to your taste. Put in the drained
hot vegetables, turning them over well. Leave to cool down, then put
in the refrigerator to chill. Scatter some extra parsley and chives over
the top before serving.

This is a good and most beautiful dish, the colours and shapes of
the beans are like a painting.

[*Vegetable Book*]

## AVOCADO DIP (Guacamole)

A spiced creamy sauce from Mexico, the avocado's homeland. It can
be used as a dip, with toast, biscuits, pieces of raw vegetable, potato
crisps. It can be served as a sauce with fish or chicken. Mexicans eat it
with tortillas rolled round a well seasoned meat filling. The proportions of the various ingredients can be altered to suit your taste; the
quantities below were given me by Elizabeth Lambert Ortiz, the
expert in Mexican cookery. She often uses canned jalapeño or serrano
chillis, rather than a fresh one: their flavour is milder and more
aromatic from the canning liquid. Mix together:

*2 large avocados, peeled, mashed*
*1 rounded tablespoon finely chopped onion*
*2 medium tomatoes peeled, seeded, drained and chopped*
*1 fresh green chilli, seeded and chopped (or chilli powder to taste)*
*1 clove garlic, finely chopped*
*1 tablespoon fresh chopped green coriander, or 2 tablespoons chopped parsley*

*lemon juice, salt, pepper, sugar to taste*

Put into a bowl, cover with plastic film if you wish to keep it overnight, and serve well chilled, with drinks or as a first course.

[*Vegetable Book*]


## CAESAR SALAD

So many stories and versions of America's Caesar Salad seem to be in circulation, that one might think it was a dish of Roman antiquity. In fact it was invented half a century ago, in 1924, by Caesar Cardini, who ran a popular restaurant at Tijuana, just south of the American-Mexico border. The following ingredients and method came from his daughter, Rosa, and were given in *Julia Child's Kitchen*.

> *2 large cos lettuces*
> *2 large cloves garlic*
> *salt*
> *175 ml (6 fl oz) olive oil*
> *3 slices white bread, cubed*
> *2 large fresh eggs*
> *juice of 1 lemon*
> *30 g (1 oz) freshly grated Parmesan*
> *pepper*
> *Worcester sauce*

The basis of the salad is prepared in advance, but the dressing and mixing are done at the table. If you can think of it in time, crush the garlic and salt into the oil for the croûtons, several days in advance. It is important that all the ingredients should be of first class quality.

Separate the lettuces. Pick out 6–8 leaves for each person, nicely shaped, unblemished leaves 8–18 cm (3–7 inches) long. Wash and dry them tenderly so that they do not break, then roll them in a cloth and put them in the refrigerator until you have completed the other preparations.

Next crush the garlic with ¼ teaspoon of salt and mix it with 3 tablespoons of oil. Put the bread cubes on a baking sheet and put them into a cool to warm oven to dry out; baste them from time to time with the garlic-flavoured oil, so that they become crisp all through but nicely browned. When they are ready, put them in a bowl on a tray. Julia Child gives a quicker method of preparing the croûtons. First toast the bread, then cut the croûtons and fry them for a minute in the strained garlic oil. So long as they end up rich and crisp all through and a nice brown, it doesn't matter which method you choose.

Next put the eggs into quite a large pan of vigorously boiling water – it should not go off the boil so take the eggs from the fridge, if you keep them there, in good time. Boil the eggs for 1 minute only, then remove them to a bowl and put that on the tray with the croûtons.

Pour the lemon juice into a little jug. Put the cheese into a small bowl. Arrange them on the tray as well, along with the pepper mill, the salt cellar, the Worcester sauce and the rest of the oil in a second jug. You will need spoons, too.

Lastly unwrap the cos leaves and put them in a really large bowl so that there is plenty of room for turning them. You are also supposed to chill the plates for the salad.

### To prepare the salad at table
If you are given to baroque flourishes in the dining room and take chafing and flaming in your stride, this is your moment. If you find such performances nauseating rather than fun, just go at it quietly while everyone is talking and with luck they will not notice what you are up to. The salad will taste the same.

First scoop under the salad with the salad servers. Then pour 4 tablespoons of oil over it. Move the servers to the back of the bowl, opposite to you, then bring all the salad over and up in a wave. Be careful you do not misjudge the movement and end up with the wave in your lap. This is why you need a big bowl and why you may find it easier to stand, rather than sit. Sprinkle on ¼ teaspoon of salt. Grind the pepper mill over it eight times, pour on 2 tablespoons of oil and turn the salad over again in the same way. Julia Child uses the word 'toss' – this puts me in mind of hay-making and cabers; I think it is more prudent to turn.

Pour on the lemon juice and six drops of Worcester sauce. Now break in the eggs, praying the thin shells do not crush to pieces in your hands or over the salad. Turn again twice, so that the lettuce is covered in the creamy egg and oil mixture. Sprinkle on the cheese. Turn again. Scatter the croûtons over all and turn twice.

Do not sit down yet. You have not finished. You now have to arrange the salad 'rapidly but stylishly' leaf by leaf on the chilled plates (which by now are unchilled, so there is little point in bothering in the first place, unless you are a speedy operator). At the side of the leaves put a few croûtons.

The approved manner of eating Caesar salad is to pick up the leaves with your fingers, asparagus style, then eat the croûtons with a knife and fork. Cloth napkins and small bowls of water for the fingers are essential, as the dressed stems of the lettuce are far more messy than asparagus. Serve it on its own as a first course.

[*Vegetable Book*]

## CREAMED CORN PUDDING

The most delicious of all fresh corn recipes, even better than corn-on-the-cob. It provides just the right amount of moisture and richness and buttery flavour. Try to use corn scraped from the cob. If you have to use the whole canned or frozen grains, break them down slightly in the blender or electric chopper. Do not overdo this: they should not be turned into a purée, but have a thick, clotted look when mixed with the cream.

Serves 6

*approx. 4 corn cobs, or 500 g (1 lb) corn grains*
*150 ml (¼ pt) each whipping and double cream, or 300 ml (½ pt)*
   *whipping cream*
*1 level dessertspoon sugar*
*salt, pepper*
*60–90 g (2–3 oz) butter*

Mix the corn with the cream, sugar and enough salt to bring out the flavour. Add a little pepper. Rub a gratin dish, or six small pots, with half the butter. Put in the corn cream and dot the remaining butter over the top. Bake in a warm oven, at gas 3, 160°C (325°F) for 30–45 minutes, until the sides and top are nicely crusted with golden-brown. Serve as a first course.

[*Vegetable Book*]

# FISH

## ANTOINE'S POMPANO *EN PAPILLOTE*

If you cannot buy pompano, do not despair. Use fillets of any good firm fish instead – John Dory, turbot or brill, salmon trout, rainbow trout, or bass. The rich crab sauce is excellent with this type of fish.

Serves 6

*6 fillets pompano*
*skin, bones and head for stock*
*750 ml (1¼ pt) water*
*1 shallot, chopped, or 1 heaped tablespoon onion, chopped*
*90 g (3 oz) butter*
*600 ml (1 pt) dry white wine*
*250 g (½ lb) crab meat*
*250 g (½ lb) shelled prawns*
*½ clove garlic, chopped*
*250 g (½ lb) onion, chopped*
*sprig of thyme*
*bay leaf*
*1 heaped tablespoon flour*
*2 egg yolks*
*salt, pepper*

Season the fish. Simmer skin, bones etc., in the water for 30 minutes, strain into a measuring jug (there should be about ½ litre (¾ pt) of stock). Cook shallot in 30 g (1 oz) butter until it begins to soften; add fillets. When they are lightly coloured on both sides, pour in the wine and simmer until the fish is just cooked and no more. Strain off the wine and set it aside. Leave the fish to cool.

Meanwhile, lightly fry crab, prawns or shrimps, and half the crushed garlic in another 30 g (1 oz) of butter. Add the onions and the remaining garlic. Cook gently for 10 minutes, covered. Add herbs and 300 ml (½ pt) of the fish stock. Make a thick sauce in the usual way with the remaining butter, the flour and the stock. Incorporate the white wine in which the fish was cooked, and the crab and onion mixture. Thicken further with the egg yolks. Correct seasoning. Remove the thyme stalks and bay leaf.

If you want to present the pompano properly, cut six paper or foil hearts large enough to contain the fillets. (Otherwise cut six oblongs, about 23 × 30 cm (9 × 12 inches).) Brush them lightly with oil. Put a layer of sauce on one half of each heart, then the fish and more sauce. Fold over the other side and twist the edges tightly together to make a close seal. Put these parcels on a baking sheet; place them in a very hot oven (gas 8, 230°C (450°F)) for about 10 minutes.

*Note:* this is said, by Marion Brown in *The Southern Cook Book*, to be the genuine recipe from Antoine's. I have seen variations elsewhere in which crab meat alone was used, with no prawns, and 125 g (¼ lb) of sliced mushrooms added to the onions.

There is no reason why such a delicious sauce should not be served with pompano, and other fish, which have been poached in white wine, without the *en papillote* finish.

[*Fish Cookery*]

## BAKED AVOCADO WITH SHRIMPS, PRAWNS, OR CRAB

Here is the most successful way of serving avocados hot. The flavour is not lost in the brief cooking and blends deliciously with the shellfish and cheese sauce.

Serves 6

*3 large avocados*
*lemon juice*
*300 ml (½ pt) thick béchamel sauce*
*2 heaped tablespoons grated Cheddar*
*1 heaped tablespoon grated Parmesan*
*3 tablespoons double cream*
*175 g (6 oz) peeled shrimps or prawns or crab meat*
*salt, pepper*
*breadcrumbs, melted butter*

Halve the avocados and remove the stones. Enlarge the cavities, but leave a good firm shell behind. Cube the avocado you have cut away. Sprinkle it with lemon juice, and brush more lemon juice over the avocado halves, to prevent discoloration.

Heat two-thirds of the sauce, which should be very thick indeed as it is a binding sauce. Keep it well below boiling point. Leave the pan on the stove while you stir in the cheeses, gradually, to taste. The flavour should be lively, but not too strong. Mix in the cream and shellfish, with seasoning, and the avocado cubes. If the mixture is very solid, add the remaining sauce. You need to strike a balance between firmness and sloppiness; in the final baking the sauce should not run about all over the place, but keep the shellfish and avocado cubes nicely positioned.

Put the avocado halves into a baking dish. Divide the stuffing between the cavities, mounding it up. Scatter on the breadcrumbs and pour a little butter over them. Bake for 15 minutes at gas 6, 200°C (400°F) and complete the browning under the grill if necessary. Do not keep the avocados in the oven any longer than this, as they do not improve with prolonged heating.

[*Vegetable Book*]

## LOBSTER NEWBERG

This is one of the best of all lobster dishes, expensive, easy to prepare and easy to eat. It's credited to America, and it was first served at Delmonico's restaurant in New York in the early 1890s. But, like *crème vichyssoise glacée*, it was the invention of a French chef, and it's in the purest French tradition. The proprietor first called the dish after one of his wealthy clients, Mr Ben Wenberg, in particular because he had popularized the use of the chafing dish, i.e. cooking done at the table instead of in the kitchen, as in this recipe. Either Mr Wenberg did not appreciate the delectable compliment, or he fell out with the proprietor for some other reason, because the name was soon altered simply but unrecognizably from lobster Wenberg to lobster Newberg or Newburg.

### Original Style

Serves 4

*150 ml (¼ pt) double cream*
*150 ml (¼ pt) single cream*
*3 egg yolks*
*150 ml (¼ pt) Madeira or sherry*
*450–600 ml (¾–1 pt) cooked lobster meat, diced*
*salt, pepper*

Using a shallow pan on a table cooker, heat the double cream to just under boiling point. Add the single cream beaten up with the egg yolks. When the sauce is thick (*it must on no account boil once the egg yolks are added*), pour in the Madeira, and stir in the lobster to reheat. Serve with rice.

### With Boiled Lobster

*ingredients as above, plus 120 g (4 oz) butter*

Heat lobster with 60 g (2 oz) of butter in a large pan. Pour in the wine and rapidly boil it down to half; draw the lobster to the side so that it doesn't overcook. Stir in the double, then the single cream beaten with the egg yolks. Thicken over a low heat. Just before serving add the extra 60 g (2 oz) of butter cut into little pieces: they should melt into the sauce without cooking, to give it a glaze and extra flavour.

This makes a finer flavoured dish than the original chafing-dish recipe.


## With Live Lobster

*ingredients as above, plus glass brandy*

Pound the coral with 60 g (2 oz) of butter, and set it aside. Cook the lobster, cut in pieces, in 60 g (2 oz) of butter until it turns red. Warm brandy, set it alight and pour over lobster in the pan. When flames have died away, add the Madeira. Finish the sauce as above, adding the coral butter at the end.

Best version of all. Brandy seems to have a special affinity with lobster. This recipe can be used for scallops.

[*Good Things*]


## LOUISIANA COURT-BOUILLON

Serves 6

*1 kg (2 lb) cod fillet*
*salt*
*freshly ground black pepper*
*170 g (6 oz) red or white onions, chopped*
*1 celery stalk, chopped*
*3 spring onions, chopped*
*1 small green pepper, seeded and chopped*
*2 cloves of garlic, chopped*
*125 g (4 oz) lard, or 125 ml (4 fl oz) sunflower oil*
*60 g (2 oz) flour*
*250 g (½ lb) tomatoes, skinned, seeded and chopped*
*90 g (3 oz) tomato paste, or 2–3 tablespoons concentrated tomato purée*
*  plus some chopped dried tomato*
*150 ml (¼ pt) red wine*
*¼ teaspoon ground allspice*
*2 teaspoons Tabasco or cayenne pepper to taste (optional)*
*a few fresh basil leaves (optional)*

FISH STOCK:
*1 kg (2 lb) cod heads, bones, filleting debris, plus shellfish
   debris if available*
*2 large cloves of garlic, unskinned, crushed*
*250 g (½ lb) red or white onions, unskinned*
*1 can of passata, plum tomatoes, or 500 g (1 lb) fresh tomatoes,
   quartered*
*6 sprigs of parsley*
*1 bay leaf*
*the leaves of a head of celery, or 1 large stalk, sliced*
*½ teaspoon thyme leaves*
*½ teaspoon marjoram*
*1 small hot chilli or cayenne pepper*

*plain rice, boiled*
*slices of bread*

First make the fish stock by putting all the ingredients into a large
pan and adding 2½ litres (4 pt) of water. Bring to the boil, then
lower the heat to maintain a gentle simmer for around 30 minutes.
Taste occasionally, remove the chilli when the brew is fiery enough
for your taste, and strain the stock.

Meanwhile, cut the fish into wide strips and season them. Mix the
chopped onions, celery, spring onions, green pepper and garlic in a bowl.

Your next operation is to make a roux. You may think you know
how to do this, since a roux is the standard basis for a number of
classic sauces, but a roux is a different matter altogether in Louisiana,
and a major flavouring item. It can be tricky, and should it turn a
speckled burnt colour you have to throw it away and start again. The
point is that by careful cooking and unremitting steadiness, you can
progress from a light yellowish roux, to a golden brown one, and from
that to a rich, almost mahogany, brown colour. There you stop for
this particular recipe.

Set a small, heavy, iron frying pan on the heat with the fat or oil.
With larger pans, make a bigger quantity of roux and set what you
do not need aside in the refrigerator. When the oil is very hot, stir in
the flour and keep stirring. Raise the pan from the heat often.
Gradually you will achieve a deepening colour. When you have a rich
brown, remove and mix in the bowl of chopped vegetables – this has
the effect of lowering the temperature and preventing deeper colour.
The roux stiffens as it cools. Put the pan back on a low heat and cook
until the vegetables begin to soften. It helps to add some of the
tomatoes to slacken the mixture.

When the vegetables are ready, transfer them to a large pot, add the remaining tomatoes and tomato paste and 1 litre (1½ pt) of the fish stock, the wine and the allspice. Simmer for 1 hour, stirring to prevent any risk of sticking, and adding extra stock to prevent over-thickening. Taste towards the end, season, and add the Tabasco or cayenne pepper if extra heat is required. All this can be done in advance, indeed the deep red sauce with its special flavour from the dark roux seems to improve with standing for a few hours.

Just before serving, bring the sauce – perhaps more of a soup than a sauce – to boiling point. Put in the fish, stir the pieces about and remove from the heat after about a minute. The fish cooks surprisingly quickly. It is better to stir it about in the very hot liquid off the stove to complete the cooking, rather than risk it being overdone and becoming mushy.

Check for seasoning for the last time, and if you wish, tear up the basil leaves into the *court-bouillon* and serve.

To serve: heap the boiled rice into bowls, pour over the *court-bouillon* and serve with the same wine that was used in the cooking and plenty of bread.

[*À La Carte*]

## MARION JONES'S GREEN FISH SOUP

A fish soup that can be made by anyone, anywhere.

> ½ large onion, thinly sliced
> 1 small leek, thinly sliced
> 30 g (1 oz) unsalted butter
> 30 g (1 oz) flour
> 1 litre (1¾ pt) fish stock, flavoured with fennel, salt, pepper, nutmeg
> 500 g (1 lb) skinned, filleted haddock, whiting, hake, ling or conger eel, cut up
> 375 g (¾ lb) sprouting broccoli or calabrese
> about 6 tablespoons cream (optional)

Sweat onion and leek in the butter until soft: do not brown them. Off the heat, stir in the flour with a wooden spoon. Cook gently for a few minutes, stirring. Remove from the heat again and pour in most of the stock. Simmer for 10 minutes, season with pepper and salt and add fish. Cook for just 1 minute and leave to cool. Blend at top speed until smooth, or process and sieve.

Meanwhile, peel broccoli or calabrese stalks, cut off some flowering heads for a final garnish and chop the rest. Cook the chopped part in just enough lightly salted water to cover. Drain, keeping the liquor, and refresh under cold water (to set the bright colour). Mix with some of the liquor and sieve into the fish soup, blending again if necessary. Dilute to taste with remaining fish stock and broccoli liquor. Reheat until just below boiling point, add cream, check seasoning and garnish with steamed broccoli flowers.

[*Observer Magazine*]

## RED SNAPPER CRÉOLE

Serves 6

*6 red snappers (about 1½ kg (3½ lb)), cleaned*
*seasoned flour*
*1 lemon*

SAUCE
*375 g (12 oz) chopped onion*
*3 stalks celery, chopped*
*1 chopped green pepper 175 g (6 oz)*
*60 g (2 oz) butter*
*2 cloves*
*grated rind of the lemon*
*60 g (2 oz) chopped parsley*
*½ teaspoon each rosemary and thyme*
*1 bay leaf*
*2 cloves garlic, finely chopped*
*2 × 400-g (14-oz) cans tomatoes*
*1 tablespoon Worcester sauce*
*Tabasco*
*salt, freshly ground black pepper, sugar*

Make the sauce first, taking trouble to get the reduction and seasonings to your taste before baking the fish. It's an elaborated version of the *sauce créole*.

Put onion, celery and pepper into a frying pan with the butter. Cook gently until soft. Add cloves, lemon rind and herbs, including garlic. Quickly drain the tomatoes and add them (keep the juice for another recipe). Leave this mixture to boil down busily for about 20 minutes, or until it has lost its wateriness and become a liquid purée. Stir in the Worcester sauce, then add the rest of the seasonings to taste.

Sprinkle the fish with seasoned flour and place them in an ovenproof baking dish. Arrange slices of lemon on top, two to each fish, and pour the sauce round and between them.

Bake in a moderate oven gas 4, 180°C (350°F) for about 20 minutes until the fish is done. Baste occasionally.

*Note:* one large red snapper can be used instead of six little ones; it will take longer to cook: 35–45 minutes.

Some recipes suggest making the sauce above in half-quantity, and adding enough breadcrumbs and egg to bind it to a stuffing. Chopped shrimps and prawns are sometimes mixed in as well. Filled with this mixture, the fish are then baked in the juice from the tomatoes, plus a little water and lemon juice, or simply in a well-buttered dish.

[*Fish Cookery*]


## SOFT-SHELL CRABS

A speciality of Venice, and of the southern coast of North America. They are not a separate species, but crabs which are 'moulting' – i.e. they have shed their shells, and the new one is still fragile. This sudden loss of weight means that they rise to the surface and can easily be caught. The Venetian *molecchie*, a May delicacy, are tiny, about 3–5 cm (1–2 inches) across. They are washed, then soaked for a while in beaten egg (which they largely absorb). Just before the meal, they are drained, shaken in flour and deep-fried. One eats the whole thing, shell, claws, the lot, and it tastes like a crisp delicious biscuit.

In America the crabs are larger – 2 or 3 are a reasonable portion – but they are treated in much the same way. Sometimes they are grilled and brushed with melted butter. Tartare sauce or a similarly flavoured mayonnaise is served with them. Here is a more elaborate recipe from *New Orleans Cuisine*, by Mary Land:


### Crabs Seasoned in Rum

'Select six soft crabs – female are best. Rinse live crabs gently in lemon water. Place in a crock with enough Myers rum (three-fourths), milk (one-fourth), whole cinnamon and nutmeg to cover. Let crabs stay in liquid two or three hours. If they show evidence of dying remove at once. Clean crabs by removing "dead man" and feelers. Rinse gently in cold water. Place crabs back in milk-rum liquid for half hour. Dry gently and dip in egg batter, then in rolled Corn Flakes. Sauté about ten minutes in sweet butter.'

[*Fish Cookery*]

# MEAT AND POULTRY

## THERE'S THE BEEF

The St Louis World's Fair and 1904 are the place and date Americans give for the birth of the hamburger. It seems to make sense – vast crowds to be fed as rapidly as possible – but, in fact, it is wrong. The hamburger was already an item of popular eating nearly two decades earlier, at least in Washington State. There, at Walla Walla, a country town over 200 miles south-east of Seattle, in the 5 January edition of *The Union* of 1889, the hamburger makes its first printed appearance – 'You are asked if you will have "porkchopbeefsteakhamandegghamburgersteak or liverandbacon".' This breathless swoosh of an entry suggests familiarity, and so an even earlier origin.

Why the name? It means, of course, 'from Hamburg', one of the main ports of emigration from Germany to the States (it gave its name to no less than seven different settlements in the new country). But why Hamburg in Germany, since almost every other European country that sent emigrants to America had developed meat balls and patties, to make less tender cuts of beef more palatable and quicker to cook?

I would suggest, but this is pure guesswork, that it was a compliment to the German community which in the States – as in nineteenth-century Britain – was pre-eminent for its high-quality butchers' shops, its delicatessens and resourceful cooked-food shops. Perhaps it was some German butcher, homesick for Hamburg, who had the idea of putting a beef patty into a toasted bun, thereby transforming it from a main-course-with-vegetables into a convenient sandwich for selling at markets and fairs and the fast-food diners required by the growing industrial towns. Anyway the hamburger took off, and in the 1920s chains of hamburger bars got going.

Incidentally, the sandwich, the first modern fast food, we owe to John Montagu, the charming but corrupt Fourth Earl of Sandwich. Sometimes in the early 1770s his passion for gambling kept him at the card table for twenty-four hours. To keep going, he shouted for slices of cold beef to be put between slices of toast. The convenience of the idea caught on and until recent times the sandwich was primarily filled with some kind of meat. The hamburger seems to have been the first hot sandwich.

Another point of success for the American hamburger was, I suspect, the mincing machine. Chopping meat with a sharp knife can – for an expert – be quite a speedy business, but most cooks aren't experts and special chopping knives and machines were invented as early as the seventeenth century in Britain. The really foolproof chopper was the sausage machine of the mid-nineteenth century, with a handle and barrel that contained rotating blades. This could be operated by the most inexperienced butcher's boy or scullery maid and was soon developed into the meat-mincing machine that we all know. In a Spong catalogue of the early 1860s, such machines are catalogued with testimonials from grand kitchens, including one from the head chef of Buckingham Palace. As many of our labour-saving machines were much improved at this period in the States – egg-whisks for instance – perhaps they were first with these mincing and sausage-making machines?

The third point of success with the American hamburger is the fine quality of the beef used. At butchery counters you can buy hamburger meat, sirloin, round or chump steak, to make burgers at home. And there are diners and inns and bars and joints where the grillman prides himself and feels 'some of the exhilaration of the soloist as he goes about his chores. The performance of the chef at the local diner,' writes Ralph Gardner Jnr in *Roadside Food*, 'is in stark contrast to what goes on at those multinational burger machines where the act of creation is invisible; there's something sinister and totalitarian about a bushel of Styrofoam-encapsulated Big Macs sitting under a heat lamp . . . orders filled even before they are placed. In the act of the grillman moulding a burger to plump perfection, we see the modern world's equivalent of the medieval artisan.'

How I agree. Our children once ganged up on me; my eating habits were too rarefied. Sophie was deputed to educate me in life's realities. She took me off to a caff in Brighton, where she was living at the time, made me park the car and wait while she bought a couple of hamburgers for our lunch. As she handed mine over – it smelled of stale oil – cheap ketchup dripped on the gear lever. The bun turned woolly soft in my mouth. The meat was gristly and overcooked. Recently a nephew and his American wife were kinder. One Sunday they drove me out of New York to see the wonderful Mercer tile museum at Doylestown. We stopped for lunch at the old inn in the centre of town and they ordered cheeseburgers. A real treat. They were plump and pink in the centre. The bun was toasted and encircled with the correct embellishments: tomato, onion, lettuce, impeccable French fries. There was a jar of pickled gherkins, too. I didn't see the grillman but I'm sure he was just as Ralph Gardner described. Even more delicious were the hamburgers we made at Broad Town for the purposes of this article, following a blend of my

American niece's instructions and Julia Child's. It was one of the best lunches we ever had.

## Hamburgers

Go for the best organically produced beef you can find, or for Aberdeen Angus or Hereford or Red Devon beef – not just because of the good rearing, but because more trouble will have been taken in handling and hanging the carcase. Be choosy. A home-made hamburger should be a treat, bearing no resemblance whatsoever to a frozen beefburger or a Big Mac. Some people buy sirloin, rump or round, but chuck steak has an excellent flavour and a reasonable proportion of fat. As Julia Child says in her book *The Way to Cook*, a hamburger steak is not diet meat: it should consist of 80 per cent lean meat, 20 per cent fat. Although no seasoning is needed beyond salt and pepper, I agree with my niece that thyme makes a wonderful addition, and the other optional extras add to the succulence.

> Serves 4–6
>
> *1 kg (2 lb) chuck steak*
> *salt, pepper*
> *flour for dredging*
> *groundnut or sunflower oil*
> Optional extras: *2 teaspoons fresh thyme*
> *2 tablespoons grated raw onion*
> *2 tablespoons soured cream*
> *1 egg, beaten*

Chill steak until just firm in the freezer. It will then be easy to remove surplus fat and – very important – the connective gristle that might clog the mincer. Cut the meat and 20 per cent fat into 4-cm (1½-inch) strips. Feed them through the mincer with a medium to large plate. You will end up with just about 700 g (1 lb 7 oz) of hamburger meat.

For a basic hamburger, all you now need is a flavouring of salt and pepper. However, optional extras give an extra delicious result, even if you only add the thyme. Stir it in, adding onion and cream if you like. Use 2–3 tablespoons of egg to make mixture soft rather than sloppy. Taste and check seasoning.

To form hamburger steaks: Julia Child favours the 150 g (5 oz) hamburger (which means you will get 4 or 5 from the quantities above), but I find it better to divide the mixture into 6. Use moistened hands to form loose plump patties of a size to fit into the buns or muffins; they should be about 2 cm (¾ inch) thick. The meat should not be firmly impacted into a sharp-edged disc. Chill until required. Just before cooking, turn lightly in flour.

To cook hamburgers: have all the garnishings and sauces ready, the buns toasted. Brush a stove-top ridged iron grill pan, or a heavy cast-iron frying pan (e.g., Dutch oven lid, or skillet), with a thin layer of oil, and heat it up. Give the hamburgers 2–3 minutes a side.

If they are soft to the touch, they will be rare. If just springy, medium-rare. If you must have them well done, catch them before they are like rubber balls. In summer, the barbecue is ideal for cooking hamburgers. In winter, you will do better to follow the method above rather than use the domestic grill, which is never quite hot enough to get a juicy brown outside with a pink inside.

To serve hamburgers: this is where you need extra hands. On each warm plate arrange a slice of beef or Marmande tomato to one side, with a slice cut across a sweet white onion and half a large pickled gherkin cut – if you like – into a fan. Slit and toast the bun and put the base in the centre of the plate with a nice bit of greenery beside it, or on top. Then place the hamburger on the bun and position the top of the bun so that it tilts from the centre of the hamburger to the plate. If you are serving French fries or hash browns, put them on the opposite side to the tomato and onion. Serve ketchup, mustard or salsa separately.

## Cheeseburgers

'Occasionally a misguided grillman will place the cheese on the bun instead of the burger and brown it under the broiler' – Ralph Gardner Jnr again – 'This is a crime in my book and probably warrants some form of community restitution. Cheese and burger must have time to get acquainted and to synergize in such a way that the cheese melts and runs down the side of the burger like lava down the slopes of Vesuvius.'

Make the hamburgers as above, but provide yourself with one square slice of Gruyère or Cheddar or Gouda per hamburger, just a little larger than the burger's surface. When the hamburgers are cooked, lay the cheese on top of the hotter side so that it melts slightly and runs down the side. A moment under the grill or in a hot oven helps the melting. Garnish as above, adding coleslaw if liked.

Mr Gardner is also insistent on Coke with cheeseburgers. 'Perhaps it's because between bun and burger, fries, pickle and slaw you're wedging so much food into your mouth at one time that only an industrial-strength soft drink can wash it all down and cleanse the palate for the next bite.' I confess to preferring wine.

[*Observer Magazine*]

## CHILLI CON CARNE

Buy stewing meat for this dish, beef, veal, mutton or pork, rather than the finest cuts. Underdone left-overs can be used, as well. Avoid minced beef. You can use tinned red kidney beans, they are delicious, but it is far cheaper to buy them loose and uncooked at a good grocery or delicatessen. Another alternative is to omit the kidney beans from the stew and serve them separately in a salad, or as part of three-bean salad (page 325).

Serves 4–6

*500–725 g (1–1½ lb) meat, cubed*
*olive oil*
*1 large onion, chopped*
*2–3 cloves garlic, crushed*
*1 small green pepper, seeded, sliced*
*Colorado sauce (below)*
*1 tablespoon tomato concentrate (optional)*
*1 teaspoon ground cumin*
*125–250 g (4–8 oz) red kidney beans, cooked*
*salt, brown sugar*

Trim the meat where necessary and brown it in olive oil. Transfer to a casserole. Brown the onion and garlic lightly in the same oil, and scrape on to the meat. Add the pepper, sauce and just enough water to cover the ingredients. Cover tightly and leave to stew until cooked, keeping the heat low. Check the liquid level occasionally. By the end of the cooking time it should have reduced to a brownish red thick sauce. If it reduces too soon because the lid of the pan is not a tight fit, or you had the heat too high, top it up with water.

Last of all add the tomato if used, the cumin, the kidney beans if you are not serving them separately as a salad, with salt and brown sugar to taste. Simmer a further 15 minutes, correct the seasoning and serve with rice and a green salad.

[*Vegetable Book*]

### Colorado Sauce

A delicious sauce to use when making *chilli con carne*, rather than the chilli powder sold in small bottles. It can also be used as a marinading mixture.

*6–7 small dried red chillis, or 4–5 large fresh ones*
*1 large red pepper*
*1 large onion, chopped*
*1 large clove garlic*
*salt*

If the chillis are dried, soak them in a little water for 1 hour, then slit them and wash out the seeds. Discard the stalks. Do the same with the large pepper. Purée with the other ingredients, using the soaking water if necessary to moisten the vegetables. If you use fresh chillis, you might need 1–2 tablespoons of cold water. Season with salt. You can keep this sauce in a covered container in the fridge for two days, or you can freeze it.

*[Vegetable Book]*


## SWEETBREADS WITH OYSTER

This American recipe is in the old European tradition of oysters with meat, from the days when oysters were a poor man's food and able to be used as a seasoning.

Serves 4

*500 g (1 lb) prepared sweetbreads*
*2 tablespoons flour*
*½ teaspoon paprika*
*30 g (1 oz) butter*
*150 ml (¼ pt) double cream*
*2–3 dozen oysters with their liquor*
*salt and mace to taste*
*3 tablespoons dry sherry*

Divide the sweetbreads into small pieces. Roll them in the flour and paprika mixed together, then fry them in the butter until they are a nice golden brown. Pour in the cream and make a sauce by stirring it well into the pan juices. Add the oysters and their liquor; when the edges begin to curl up the dish is ready. Season with salt, mace and sherry to taste.

Serve with triangles of bread fried in butter.

*[Good Things]*

## FRIED CHICKEN MARYLAND WITH CORN FRITTERS

This dish has lost its charm by over-exposure in cheap restaurants. At home, it tastes quite different and is a delicious way of serving chicken. The classic accompaniments are fried bacon and sweetcorn fritters. Sometimes I have had fried banana with it, too, which is not at all correct but popular with the children. Fried chicken Maryland is an ideal family dish.

Serves 4–6

*1 large or 2 small farm chickens, jointed*
*milk*
*seasoned flour*
*bacon fat or lard*
*2 tablespoons plain flour*
*½ litre (¾ pt) milk*
*4 tablespoons double cream*
*2 egg yolks*
*salt, pepper*
*1–2 streaky bacon rashers per person*

CORN FRITTERS
*60 g (2 oz) plain flour*
*2 tablespoons milk*
*a good pinch of paprika*
*a good pinch of cayenne*
*1 large egg yolk*
*¼ teaspoon salt*
*175 g (6 oz) drained canned or cooked corn*
*1 large egg white, stiffly whipped*

Dip the chicken pieces in milk, then turn in seasoned flour. Brown them all over in bacon fat or lard. Transfer them from the pan to an oven dish. Cover it tightly and put into the oven at gas 4–5, 180–190°C (350–375°F) for 30 minutes, or until cooked. Add no liquid. With the pan juices make a sauce: stir the plain flour into them, cook for a moment or two, then pour in the milk and cream. Simmer gently for 15 minutes. Just before serving, when everything is ready, beat in the egg yolks and thicken without boiling over a low heat. Season. Grill the bacon rashers.

While the chicken is in the oven and the sauce simmering, make the corn fritters. Mix the ingredients in the order given, then drop tablespoons of thick batter into hot butter and fry until golden-brown both sides.

Arrange the cooked chicken, bacon rashers and corn fritters on a large hot serving dish. Put the sauce into a jug.

If you like the idea of banana as well, peel, halve and quarter three large ones, and fry the pieces gently in butter. The snag about this is that you have too many things to take care of at the last minute, unless you can call on some help for frying the bananas.

*[Vegetable Book]*

## GUMBO

The difference between this recipe and the Mediterranean type of stew is the inclusion of peppers and chillis or cayenne, and a substantial piece of country ham (substitute smoked gamon or bacon, bought in a piece).

Serves 4–6

*250 g (8 oz) country ham, cubed*
*175 g (6 oz) chopped onion*
*175 g (6 oz) chopped celery*
*1 red or green sweet pepper, chopped, minus seeds*
*lard*
*up to one tablespoon tomato concentrate*
*500 g (1 lb) tomatoes, peeled, chopped*
*500 g (1 lb) okra, trimmed*
*salt, pepper*
*cayenne, or 1 dried chilli, chopped, with seeds*

Stew the ham, onion, celery and sweet pepper in a little lard. When they are beginning to soften, raise the heat so that they colour lightly. Put in 1 teaspoon of tomato concentrate and the tomatoes. Stir for a moment or two, until the tomatoes begin to subside into a stew, then put in the okra and seasonings. Cover and simmer slowly until cooked, checking from time to time in case a little water is required. The okra should not be left high and dry, neither should they be completely covered with liquid. Taste and adjust the seasonings, adding extra tomato concentrate if it seems a good idea.

*[Vegetable Book]*

## CHICKEN GUMBO

Serves 4–6

*250 g (8 oz) gammon rasher, cubed*
*1 farm chicken, jointed*
*125 g (4 oz) chopped onion*
*1 clove garlic, chopped*
*1 red pepper, chopped, minus seeds, or 1 dried chilli chopped, with seeds*
*375 g (12 oz) okra, trimmed, sliced*
*lard and any fat from the chicken above*
*1 tablespoon flour*
*250 g (8 oz) chopped tomato*
*1 tablespoon tomato concentrate*
*chicken stock or water*
bouquet garni
*salt, pepper, cayenne or Tabasco sauce*
*1–2 dozen oysters (optional)*
*parsley*

Brown the gammon and chicken, onion, garlic, red pepper or chilli and okra in the lard and chicken fat. You will have to do this in batches, transferring each item as it colours to a large pot and adding more lard as necessary; start with the meat and colour it over a sharpish heat, then lower the temperature for the vegetables, so that they soften and do not become too brown. When the last batch is ready, stir in the flour, cook for a couple of minutes, then add the tomato, concentrate and enough stock or water to make a slightly thickened sauce. Tip this over the contents in the large pot, adding extra liquid if need be, barely to cover the meat and vegetables. Put in the *bouquet* and seasoning (if you use chilli rather than red peppers, go lightly with the cayenne or Tabasco). Simmer, with the pot covered, until the chicken is tender – about 1 hour or longer. Meanwhile, open the oysters, being careful to save all their juice. Ten minutes before serving the gumbo, mix in the oysters and their liquor to heat through. Taste and adjust the seasoning. Remove the *bouquet*, and add a good chopping of parsley. Serve with boiled rice.

If you cannot afford oysters, use mussels instead. This is better than having no shellfish flavour at all.

*[Vegetable Book]*

## TURKEY OR CHICKEN WITH GRAPEFRUIT

This dish is best made with pink grapefruit. I approached it with caution as the mixture of poultry and grapefruit seemed an odd one, but it works well. The better the poultry, the better the result.

Serves 6

*turkey or chicken joints for 6 people*
*salt, pepper, 1 level teaspoon thyme*
*butter*
*3 tablespoons brandy*
*250 ml (8 fl oz) dry white wine*
*juice of 1 grapefruit*
*2 whole grapefruit*

Season the joints with salt, pepper and the thyme. Leave for several hours or overnight.

Brown the joints in butter to a light golden brown, then flame with the brandy. Turn the pieces over in the flames. Now; *Either:* transfer the meat to a buttered ovenproof dish, dot it with butter and pour in the wine and grapefruit juice. Bake for about 1 hour at gas 5, 190°C (375°F), turning occasionally and removing breast joints when cooked. *Or:* add the wine and juice to the sauté pan, cover and leave until tender, turning the pieces over twice.

Meanwhile, peel thin strips from one of the grapefruit. Cut them into shreds and simmer 3 or 4 minutes in water: set aside for garnishing. Strip remaining pith and peel from both grapefruit, and cut the wedges of flesh out, freeing them of thin white skin and pips. Do this over a plate to catch the juice, which should be added to the liquid in the poultry pan.

When the poultry is tender, arrange it on a warm serving dish. Heat through the grapefruit segments in the pan juices and place them round the joints. Taste the juices, boil down slightly and add seasoning. Beat in a couple of tablespoons of butter, in little bits, and pour over the joints just before serving. Scatter the peel strips on top.

Cauliflower finished with butter and a chopped hot chilli goes well with this dish.

*[Fruit Book]*

# VEGETABLES AND FRUIT

## BASIC CRANBERRY SAUCE

Weigh a packet of cranberries if the measure is not given on the wrapping, then tip them into a saucepan. Add water or orange juice to come almost to the top but not quite. The liquid should show through the berries without floating them from the base of the pan.

Simmer without a lid until the berries start to pop open – this takes place quite rapidly. The more berries burst, the softer and thicker the sauce will be. Four minutes gives the consistency we like.

Remove from the heat and stir in half the cranberries' weight in sugar. Most people will find this sweet enough; too much sugar brings out the bitterness.

I find that a 175 g (6 oz) packet of cranberries makes enough sauce for 6 to 8 people. If you make more, it can be kept in covered jars in the refrigerator.

[*Fruit Book*]

## BEANS VILLAGE STYLE

This is the easiest recipe for beans I know. It's a good one, and cheap. All you need are two or three homely ingredients, an ovenproof pot (the Italian *fagiolara* does well, or a French storage jar, or stoneware jug), and a collection of open-air appetites.

Beans village style are the antique basis from which cooks evolved *cassoulet* in the Languedoc and Boston baked beans in north America. Locally produced French additions were tomatoes, onions, garlic, sausage, preserved goose and occasionally a *ragoût* of mutton. American additions reflected their trade – molasses, soft brown sugar and rum from the West Indies. People in the circumstances of those days, a century or two or three ago, could not consult books of international cookery for inspiration: they consulted their store-cupboards and kitchen gardens and cellars instead.

Serves 6

*500 g (1 lb) haricot beans*
*180–250 g (6–8 oz) streaky bacon in a piece*
*bay leaf, sprig thyme, sprig parsley*
*salt, pepper*

Soak the beans in the usual way. Tie the herbs together. Put all ingredients, except salt, into the cooking pot and add just enough cold water to cover. Add a lid of double foil, firmly secured to prevent steam escaping. Simmer in a slow oven, gas 2, 150°C (300°F) until the beans are cooked (1½–2 hours). Season with salt, at the end, as required.

### Baked Beans Southern Style

Nearer the home of the kidney-bean, cooks make use of other Southern ingredients – peppers, molasses and tomatoes. Being a hot substantial dish, these baked beans are best followed by fruit, say a chilled pear, or chilled melon.

Follow the ingredients and method for beans village style, but remove them from the oven when they are half-cooked. Take out the herbs, and mix in:

> *1 green pepper, deseeded and chopped*
> *1 large onion, chopped*
> *2 large tomatoes, chopped*
> *molasses (black treacle), salt and pepper to taste*

Remove the bacon and slice it. Turn the beans, etc., into a large wide dish, put the slices of bacon on top and finish cooking in the oven without a lid. Beans and bacon will develop a rich brown glaze, almost a crust.

*[Good Things]*

## MRS RANDOLPH'S OCHRA, CIMLIN OR CUSTARD MARROW, AND TOMATOES

*The Virginia Housewife*, written by Mary Randolph and published in 1825, was the first regional American cookery book. It contains many standard European recipes of course, but there are plenty of ways of dealing with the vegetables characteristic of Virginian gardens such as Monticello, Jefferson was unusual for his time in preferring vegetable dishes to the high protein diet that most people enjoyed (he felt that too much 'animal food' is what makes the English character so gross, rendering it 'insusceptible of civilisation'). He described himself as eating little meat, 'and that not as an aliment so much as a condiment for the vegetables which constitute my principal diet'.

Here are three of Mrs Randolph's recipes, all simple to follow, in her own words:

### 'To Make Ochra Soup

Get two double handfuls of young ochra, wash and slice it thin, add two onions chopped fine, put it into a gallon [4 litres – the American pint being closer the half-litre than to the Imperial pint] of water at a very early hour in an earthen pipkin, or very nice iron pot. It must be kept steadily simmering but not boiling: put in pepper and salt.

At twelve o'clock, put in a handful of lima beans: at half passed one o'clock, add three cimlins [custard marrows] cleaned and cut into small pieces, a fowl, or knuckle of veal, a bit of bacon or pork that has been boiled and six tomatoes, with skin taken off. When nearly done, thicken with a spoonful of butter, mixed with one of flour. Have rice boiled to eat with it.'

*Note:* okra came from Africa with the slaves, but was soon valued by their masters as well for its flavour, and for the sticky juice which gives a jellied smoothness to sauces, stews and soups. It can also be cooked with onion and tomato: leave it whole, just removing the hard outer skin from the cone at the stalk end – do not pierce through, as the juices should stay in when okra is to be served as a vegetable on its own.

### 'To Cook Squash or Cimlin

Gather young squashes, peel and cut them in two. Take out the seeds, and boil them till tender. Put them into a colander, drain off the water, and rub them with a wooden spoon through the colander. Then put them into a stew pan, with a cup full of cream, a small piece of butter, some pepper and salt – stew them stirring very frequently until dry. This is the most delicate way of preparing squashes.'

*Note:* a recipe that can be used for every kind of squash, although it is at its best with custard marrow (cimlin). Pumpkin, cucumber, courgettes, chayote all do well, though with the more watery kinds, it is essential first to drain the purée, and then to dry it out over a moderate heat, before adding cream etc.

### 'To Scallop Tomatoes

Peel the skin from very large, full ripe tomatoes – put a layer in the bottom of a deep dish, cover it well with bread grated fine; sprinkle on pepper and salt, and lay some bits of butter over them – put another layer of each, till the dish is full – let the top be covered with crumbs and butter – bake it a nice brown.'

*Note:* tomatoes were treated with caution by the English and northern French until modern times, but Jefferson loved them. One variety he grew, Spanish tomatoes, were especially fine and large – what the trade nowadays calls 'beefy'. Marmande and Eshkol are similar in style, firm flesh, no wateriness, and ideal for cooking as for salad. Avoid sloshy tomatoes from the supermarket; not only do they have no flavour, but they will ruin this dish with their moisture.

*[Food with the Famous]*


## OKRA (Hibiscus Esculentus)

Lady's fingers is our English name for the soft tapering pods known as okra elsewhere. It reminds me of a description I once read by a French traveller of Créole ladies in the Antilles eating with their fingers. They picked up their food with such lazy but skilful grace that not a drop fell on to their pale dresses. Their white hands remained clean.

In fact the name is shortened from Our Lady's fingers, by analogy with Lady's mantle or Lady's bedstraw, an image of a grander, less indolent softness. The general idea, though, is worth remembering as a market guide, since the pods should be young and tender. Once the angle lines are brown and dark patches appear, they are not worth buying. They will cook to a kind of stringiness that winds round your teeth and sticks in the throat.

Practicality apart, I go for the name of okra because it reminds me of the plant's native land. And of its history, which is not soft or pretty at all. Okra comes from *nkurama*, its name in the Twi language of the Gold Coast. Slaves took okra with them to the Caribbean and the southern states of America. The name that sticks there is another African word, gumbo, of Angolan origin. And gumbo is the name given to American dishes in which it appears, even in small quantities, because the pods contain a clear gummy liquid which smooths the sauce. It thickens it too in a jellied way which makes you lick your lips. So you may get shrimp gumbo or chicken gumbo, stews and soups which have this characteristic texture, even though the sliced green pods have disappeared from view into the general *mélange*.

### To prepare

Nip off any stalks. Trim round the tiny cone at the stalk end to pare off the hardness. Be careful not to pierce this cone if you intend to keep the okra whole, seeds and juice inside. Should there be dark lines down the angle of the okra, slice them carefully away using a potato peeler for a shallow, even cut.

[*Exotic Fruits and Vegetables*]

## PAWPAW (Carica Papaya)

In Mexican markets I was puzzled by stall after stall of vast objects, an orange-toned green, varying greatly in size. Some of them looked as if they might weigh 5 kg (10 lb) or even more. When I asked about them, I was told they were pawpaws, and that pawpaws (often called papaya) do vary enormously, except for one or two varieties bred especially for commercial orchards – the solo from Hawaii and the papino from South Africa being the best-known examples. As their names suggest the fruit are small enough for one person to manage: they are the kind we see in our greengrocers and supermarkets.

The pawpaw is a giant plant rather than a tree. Its juicy green stem grows straight and tall, with a plume of leaves branching out from the top. When the fruit is formed it grows close under the leaves down the stem in a great cluster, the whole thing looking like an exotic Brussels sprout. James Grainger described it well in his poem on *Sugar Cane* (1764), writing of the 'quick pawpaw, whose top is necklaced round/With numerous rows of parti-coloured fruit'. The name pawpaw and its various pronunciations and spellings derive from the Carib word *ababai*: one gets more than a hint of this in the babaco fruit that are sometimes on sale in London – these are mountain pawpaws, and the fruit has to be cooked before you eat it.

The fruit makes a perfect breakfast in the tropics: you will be presented with beautifully cut apricot-pink slices and a wedge or two of lime – lime being the essential partner, as it is of a number of other mild-tasting tropical fruits.

Pawpaws can be used when green in soups, stews, chutneys and jams, when they begin to turn yellow (this is the stage when they are transported, since the skin becomes more tender as the fruit ripens and extra susceptible to damage) and when they are ripe. In general treat green pawpaws like squashes and marrows, and the pink-fleshed fruit like melon – with ginger, for instance, pepper, or in slices with thin slices of Parma, Westphalian, Bayonne or country hams, or with lettuce and in salads to go with smoked chicken or cooked ham or salted duck. Ripe pawpaw halves can be scooped out a little, filled with spicy beef and rice mixtures (include the flesh you remove, chopped) and baked in the oven; the cool, tempered sweetness sets off well the heat and zip of such dishes.

### To prepare

Halve the fruit and you will see that the cavity is full of deep grey seeds, the size of best caviare. They have a distinctive mustard taste, a greenish taste, and are not eaten. Scrape them out, then sprinkle the flesh with lime or lemon juice, if you are going to dig in with a spoon. Or slice and peel and season with lime juice, if this is appropriate, and a little sugar.

[*Exotic Fruits and Vegetables*]


## POTATO CAKES

It is important to use freshly cooked potatoes if you want potato cakes to taste as they should. I was delighted and surprised to come across a version of our familiar potato scones and cakes, in a pastrycook's shop in Orléans, and even more delighted to find the recipe, which is very close to ours.

Whatever kind of potato cake you want to end up with, you start with a basic mixture:

> 250 g (½ lb) potatoes, scrubbed
> 30–60 g (1–2 oz) butter
> salt, pepper
> about 60 g (2 oz) plain flour

Boil, peel and sieve the potatoes. Mix in the butter while they are still warm, then season well. Gradually add the flour until you have a firm dough that you can roll out – the best way of doing this is to mix everything together with your hands.

### Thin Potato Cakes

Roll out the dough into a circle about ½ cm (¼ inch) thick or a little more. Cut it across into triangles and prick them with a fork. Cook them on a greased griddle or frying pan or hot plate, turning them so that they brown on both sides. Eat with butter, while they are still hot.

## Thick Potato Cakes

Shape the dough into a roll about 4 cm (1½ inches) in diameter. Cut it into slices a good 1 cm (½ inch) thick. Cook as above, only rather more slowly. Good with bacon and egg.

*[Vegetable Book]*

# FRIED AND BAKED PARSNIPS

Parsnips need richness, as I have said; this need not come only from butter and cream, but from dripping or from the neutral agency of a deep-frying oil.

## *Variations*

SARATOGA CHIPS: cut the parsnips into wedges downwards. Remove any woody core. Parboil them until they are almost tender. Drain them, then deep-fry them until golden-brown.

Peel, and slice the parsnips. Cut out the core when necessary, to turn the slices into rings. Parboil them until almost tender and drain. Dip them in egg, roll them in breadcrumbs and fry them in clarified butter until golden.

Boil, peel and sieve 1 kg (2 lb) parsnips. Mix with 2 large eggs, 1 tablespoon of flour, 100 g (3½ oz) melted butter, 125 g (4 oz) chopped walnuts and enough milk to make a soft but coherent mixture. Deep-fry tablespoons of the mixture. Serve with fish, or on their own.

Peel and cut parsnips into pieces a good 1 cm (½ inch) thick. Boil for 5 minutes, drain well. Bake them in a tine of dripping − along with potatoes, if you like − on a top shelf in the oven when you are roasting beef. Or put them round the beef to cook more slowly in the juices.

*[Vegetable Book]*

# CAKES AND PUDDINGS

## CARROT AND GINGER CAKE

Serves 6–8

*125 (4 oz) lightly salted butter, softened*
*90 g (3 oz) caster or soft pale brown sugar*
*125 g (4 oz) self-raising flour sifted with 1 level teaspoon baking powder*
*2 eggs*
*2 tablespoons syrup from the ginger jar*
*3 knobs of stem ginger, drained and chopped*
*125 g (¼ lb) carrots, coarsely grated or shredded*
*2 level tablespoons ground almonds*

Preheat the oven to gas 4, 180°C (350°F). This cake can be made by the all-in-one method: whizz the butter, sugar, flour, baking powder, eggs and syrup together in a food processor, or with an electric beater. Alternately beat them to a smooth mixture with a wooden spoon.

Mix the ginger, carrots and almonds and add to the cake dough.

Line a 20–23-cm (8–9-inch) long loaf tin with Bakewell paper and add the dough. Smooth the top, hollowing it down in the centre with the back of a spoon. Bake for 55 minutes.

You can ice the cake using icing sugar mixed with ginger syrup, serve it as a teabread in buttered slices or blend cream cheese with half its weight in butter, sweeten slightly, and leave people to help themselves.

[*À La Carte*]


## JEFFERSON DAVIS TART

Jefferson Davis was head of the Confederacy of the Southern States of America, until defeat in 1865 by the North at the end of the Civil War. It seems inappropriate that anyone who shared in that experience of carnage should have a sweet frothy-topped tart named after him – Pavlova cake, yes, but gâteau Petain, Montgomery sponge, Rommelstrudel, Haig fairy cakes? I think not.

Like a number of other English dishes, transparent pie or tart has survived in America when it has disappeared here. The holding mixture of eggs, butter and sugar – in other words, a custard with melted butter taking the place of cream or milk – sets to a semi-transparent firmness. Flavouring items differentiate one version from another. Two favourites here were sweetmeat pudding and Duke of Cambridge pudding and I reckon they are due for revival. In the States, especially in the South, chess tarts, Kentucky pie, pecan or black walnut pie and this date and nut tart are still very much alive.

For me, the tart is improved by using all dates, rather than half dates, half raisins, and I halve the quantity of sugar to the amount listed below (it is still very sweet). A good pudding for a family lunch party.

For a 23-cm (9-inch) tart tin, lined with plain shortcrust pastry, mix together the following ingredients in the order given:

> 125 g (4 oz) softened butter
> 150 g (5 oz) light brown sugar
> 3 large egg yolks
> 250 ml (8 fl oz) whipping cream
> 1 level teaspoon cinnamon
> ½ teaspoon allspice
> ⅓ nutmeg finely grated
> 6–8 stoned, chopped dates
> 100 g (3½ oz) raisins
> 60 g (2 oz) roughly broken pecans, or walnuts

Bake at gas 6, 200°C (400°F) for 10–15 minutes, then down to gas 3, 160°C (325°F) for a further 20 minutes.

Top with 3 large egg whites, whisked and sweetened with 125 g (4 oz) caster sugar, to make a meringue. Put back into the oven until nicely browned.

*Note:* Kentucky pie has no nuts or spices; chess tarts are made small with raisins and nuts, no dates or spices.

[*Fruit Book*]


## KEY LIME PIES

On the low coral islands – the keys – of Florida, semi-wild limes grow on thick and thorny trees. Nobody bothers with them much by way of cultivation, and the fruit remains small and very acid. This key lime pie is a local speciality, made in many versions with condensed milk and lime juice. Not as revolting as it sounds. By adding eggs, you can head off the sweet-sharp excesses of the partnership. The second version comes from Even Jones's *American Food.* 'It uses neither evaporated milk nor the gelatin common to most Florida lime pies: it is as fresh as any fruit ice cream.'

## *Variations*

For a 23-cm (9-inch) shortcrust pastry case, baked blind, beat – electrically if possible – 5 egg yolks until they are thick. Slowly add a 400 g (14 oz) can of sweetened condensed milk, then the grated peel of 3 limes and 150 ml (¼ pt) lime juice. Beat 3 of the whites separately to soft peaks, then fold into the yolk mixture. Bake at gas 3, 160°C (325°F) until the filling is firm, 15–25 minutes. Serve cool, or chilled, with whipped cream.

Line a 23-cm (9-inch) tart tin or pie plate with Graham cracker (digestive biscuit) crust. Bake 10 minutes at gas 4, 180°C (350°F). Cool.
   Beat (electrically, if possible) 5 egg yolks over simmering water until very thick. Gradually beat in 125 g (4 oz) caster sugar, and go on beating until the mixture is pale and falling off the beater in threads. Remove basin from heat. Add 2 teaspoons grated lime zest and 150 ml (¼ pt) lime juice. Whisk 4 egg whites and a pinch of salt until thick and soft, add 60 g (2 oz) sugar gradually, beating all the time. Fold a third into the lime custard, then the rest. Pile into the crust and bake for 15 minutes at gas 4, 180°C (350°F). Cool, then chill and freeze. Take from the freezer 10 minutes before required. Top with whipped cream and thin slices of lime, or fresh strawberries dipped in caster sugar.

[*Fruit Book*]

## PEACH AND ORANGE ICE

Don't despise this American recipe because the fruit is canned – the combination of flavours is most successful. Use white peaches if you can, they are more finely piquant than the yellow ones.

> *300 ml (½ pt) sieved canned peaches*
> *300 ml (½ pt) orange juice*
> *125 g (4 oz) sugar*
> *1 dessertspoon lemon juice*

Mix together until the sugar is dissolved. Freeze to a granita, stirring every 30 minutes. Fresh strawberry pulp, or canned apricot pulp may be substituted for peaches – they all combine well with orange juice.

[*Good Things*]

# INDIA AND THE
# FAR EAST

J ANE'S ENDLESS FASCINATION with the things people ate and the way they prepared them found fertile ground in the world beyond Europe. To have written a scholarly, informative and practical book on exotic fruits and vegetables on the sole inspiration of someone's portfolio of drawings indicated this well, as did her masterly descriptions of the place of the mushroom in Chinese and Japanese cooking. She knew that the Gorgeous East, with its ancient civilizations, was bound to contain a gastronomy that had been refined over the centuries. In several of her books she acted as an ambassador for the East, introducing a Western audience to foreign dishes ranging from the exotic to the everyday with the same enthusiasm and enlightening voice with which she wrote of things much nearer home, and more familiar.

> *A mushroom: stuck*
> *To it a leaf*
> *From a tree somewhere.*

Anyone who has ever picked over a basket of wild mushrooms will understand the quiet delight of this seventeenth-century haiku by the great Japanese master Basho.

The mushroom with its leaf, Basho's mushroom, is the matsutake (*Tricholoma matsutake*), the great delicacy of Japanese mushrooms, on a par with our finest cep, *Boletus edulis*. 'The arrival in early October' – this is Joan and Peter Martin in *Japanese Cooking* – 'of the matsutake mushrooms, flatly nestling in their beds of fern, is one of the first signs that autumn is truly here.' The high prices paid for this prized mushroom from the red pine forests (*matsu* means pine; *take*, mushroom) are not regretted, because it is 'superb, with an aroma and flavour quite unlike any other mushroom.' If you are lucky you may find canned matsutake. Or you might try substituting one of our *Tricholoma* species, the wood blewit. Certainly they work well in the Japanese recipes for undried mushrooms, with their unusually fresh flavour, a kind of light earthiness. Equally good, perhaps even better, are the edible ceps. And cultivated mushrooms can be used, though their flavour is a little on the weak side.

The great mushroom, though, of Chinese and Japanese cooking, with a role equivalent to our own cultivated mushrooms, is the shiitake. This is the most common dried mushroom on sale in oriental shops (and in many delicatessens). If you ask for dried Chinese or Japanese mushrooms, this is what you will be given. It's a tree fungus growing on the trunk of the shiia and other hardwood trees – hence the name. Which means that its cultivation is quite different from our own indoor mushroom-producing industry, being a sideline of forestry. The point is that the 'bed' on which the shiitake will grow must be a log of wood, not the elaborately prepared mattress of compost which is compacted into huge oblong trays for the comfort of our European cultivated mushroom. In other words, it's an outdoor industry with all the problems of weather and situation.

This type of mushroom-growing may not seem so odd to us in the future. We may one day find the corners of our state forests bristling with yard-long pieces of wood neatly stacked in inclining rows. The list of mushrooms which it might be possible to cultivate successfully consists mainly of woodland species, some of them like the oyster mushroom growing on, rather than under, trees. There is also talk of growing shiitake in Europe. It's a matter of convincing forestry commissions that further varieties of mushroom are worth their trouble and attention. I hope these moves are successful. We are far too tied, particularly in England, to the one mushroom, whch is by no means the finest in flavour.

A primitive form of cultivation of shiitake has been practised first in China, then in Japan, for well over a thousand years. It was a question of helping the natural processes along, of simulating natural conditions, and then of hoping for the best. As in Europe, the reproduction and growth of mushrooms was not properly understood until the nineteenth century, and the latter part of the century at that. At last, in the Twenties, scientists discovered how to prepare the spawn, and mushroom growing could be expanded to a profitable industry.

While Philip Miller was describing in his *Gardener's Dictionary* of 1741 the methods by which gardeners around London were managing to produce mushrooms, Japanese growers were beginning to look systematically for trees on which the shiitake had started to grow. They would cut off the branch, and place it alongside new logs, hoping that the spawn would spread naturally to them.

It sounds simple enough, and the method is basically the same today. I suspect it was more successful than Hannah Glasse's rough and ready method of boiling up mushrooms and throwing them and their water on to manure-covered hotbeds, which is described in her *Art of Cookery* (1758). But it involves more heavy labour in the dragging about of the logs. It needs skill and knowledge, too, as the right wood must be chosen for the logs, and the logs must be cut at the right time.

The scientists have refined but not altered the old method. No one goes looking for a tree on which the shiitake is already growing nowadays. Spore emulsions are prepared in the laboratory, then they are injected into or brushed over the bruised and moistened logs. The logs are then propped up at a low angle from the ground, in a good situation. This cannot be created artificially, in the way that our mushroom grower can prepare huts or caves to receive the mushroom trays. A place must be found at the edge of a wood, where there is the right amount of wind. And it must be above the fogs of the valley. The ground must be moist, but well drained, never soggy. Then one needs the right mixture of dampness and warmth in the weather.

Several months later, the logs are moved to a 'raising yard'. This time they are propped up more steeply, in serried ranks like an army's row upon row of defensive stakes. There they stay until the shiitake are ready for picking. The whole process takes longer than our three-month cycle. On the other hand, the bed logs last for several years, whereas our mushroom compost has to be renewed after each batch of mushrooms.

The shiitake grower has another advantage, because his mushroom is tough, and stands up well to handling and delays (though it is best eaten within a couple of days of being picked). It can be dried quickly, too, either in specially heated sheds or, as far as the smaller grower is concerned, in the sun. In other words, the grower has a double product – the fresh shiitake, which must go reasonably fast to the markets of Japan, and the dried shiitake, which make such a successful export. He can also send them to factories where they will be canned or pickled in vinegar, along with wild mushrooms.

As I have said, both Japanese and Chinese cooks make great use of the shiitake, but the Chinese have a speciality of their own which can be bought in some oriental shops. This is a crunchy, gelatinous textured relation of the 'Jew's ear' (*Auricularia auricula*), another tree fungus. The Chinese call it wood ear, or cloud ear, or silver ear. Our Jew's ear is edible but not highly regarded among mushrooms, and according to Hsiang Ju Lin and Tsuifeng Lin in *Chinese Gastronomy*, the popularity of the wood ear in China has a certain element of perversity. They group it with other texture foods such as shark's fin, bird's nest and *bêche-de-mer*, observing that they are 'absurdities' unless prepared with the right sauces and stocks. On their own they are 'as appetizing as a piece of paper.' An element in their high reputation is the chance they give the cook to show off his taste and skill: 'Perhaps in their ultimate artificiality, they are the most sophisticated of food.'

Another mushroom which is popular in southern China, south-east Asia and Madagascar is the padi-straw mushroom (*Volvariella volvacea*). It is grown out of doors, on rice straw as the name suggests, and is marketed fresh or dried. I have never seen it on sale in England, but judging by a note and recipe in Gloria Bley Miller's *The Thousand Recipe Chinese Cookbook*, it is available in America. There are two edible species of *Volvariella* in northern Europe, but they are both rare. One interesting thing: the oldest mushroom picture in existence, from a market in north Africa in Roman times, is of a *Volvariella*, though a different species from the padi-straw mushroom. This, like most of the scientific information in the section, comes from *Mushrooms and Truffles*, by R. Singer, a book for anyone who is interested in the present and future cultivation of mushrooms.

I hope your illusions will not be spoilt, or your sense of what is fitting in the realms of *chinoiserie*, when I add that the cultivation of *Agaricus bisporus*, our own familiar supermarket mushroom, is big business in the East as well – particularly in Korea and Taiwan. So you need not feel regretfully unauthentic if you use them when making Chinese and Japanese dishes. Indeed some recipes stipulate 'fresh' mushrooms or even 'champignons'. The word 'fresh' might include a number of mushrooms, wild as well as cultivated, but 'champignons' is unmistakably our cultivated western mushroom.

[*The Mushroom Feast*]

# SOUPS AND STARTERS

## CLEAR CLAM SOUP (Hamaguri Ushiojitate)

The *kombu* listed in the ingredients is a processed Japanese seaweed which comes in dark greenish-black sheets. It is used as a flavouring for soups and stock, as we might use a *bouquet garni*.

Serves 6

*12 sprigs watercress, or young spinach leaves*
*1 teaspoon salt*
*24 clams or cockles*
*7½-cm (3-inch) square* kombu
*6 slices lime or lemon peel*
*6 large fresh mushrooms*
*1 dessertspoon soya sauce*
*monosodium glutamate (optional)*
*saké (optional)*

Blanch the watercress or spinach in a little water with half the salt for 1 minute. Drain, and set aside. Scrub the clams or cockles, then put them into a large pan with 1½ litres (2½ pt) of water. Add the *kombu*. Bring to the boil, then remove the *kombu*. Leave for 2 minutes or until the clams or cockles open. Strain off the stock into a clean pan, discard all the shells but six, arrange the clams or cockles in them, and place in six bowls with the reserved watercress or spinach, and lime or lemon peel.

Now bring the strained liquor to the boil with the mushrooms, soya sauce and remaining salt, and add a seasoning of monosodium glutamate, if you like, but not very much. A dash of saké is also a good idea, if you can get it. Boil for a few moments. Put a mushroom into each bowl, then carefully pour in the soup down the side so that the arrangement is disturbed as little as possible.

[*The Mushroom Feast*]

## WINTER MELON SOUP (Tung Kua T'ang)

This is a lovely soup, beautiful to look at, varied and clear to the taste. It has the further merit of being simple to make. Do not worry too much about finding the correct Chinese ingredients, apart from the mushrooms, which are essential. Substitutes for other items work successfully. In fact the success of the soup depends on using a good chicken stock: in other words, make it when you have been cooking a boiling fowl (or have been able to buy giblets).

Serves 4

*750 ml (1¼ pt) chicken stock*
*500 g (1 lb) winter melon or cucumber, peeled*
*4 dried mushrooms, at least 2½ cm (1 inch) across, soaked*
*45 g (1½ oz) tinned Yunnan ham, or* lachschinken, *or Danish smoked
 bacon, cut into 2½-cm (1-inch) squares*

Put the stock into a pan. Cut the melon or cucumber into 6-mm (¼-inch) thick pieces, about 2½ cm (1 inch) across, and add to the stock. Drain the mushrooms, discard the hard stalks, quarter mushrooms, and add to stock. Bring to the boil and cook gently for 15 minutes, pressing the mushroom pieces once or twice to extract the maximum amount of juice into the soup. Place the ham or *lachschinken* or bacon into the soup bowls, and pour the contents of the pan over it.

[*The Mushroom Feast*]

## CHIRASHI-ZUSHI WITH SWEET BEANS

The Japanese are famous for their bean cakes and buns, which are often sold in the most exquisite wrappings and boxes. They also cook beans in syrup and serve them with savoury rice dishes. Beans prepared this way are so good that I sometimes serve an anglicized version of *chirashi-zushi* as an hors d'oeuvre, to give us an excuse for eating them. People who are fortunate enough to live near an oriental foodstore might like to substitute the Japanese ingredients (in brackets) for capers, etc.

Choose a plain beautiful serving dish for *chirashi-zushi*, and take extra time to arrange the items elegantly. There are six of them to prepare, each serves 4–6.

*125 g (¼ lb) haricot or butter beans*
*90 g (3 oz) sugar*
*75 ml (½ gill) water*
*½ teaspoon soya sauce (preferably Japanese)*

Soak and simmer the beans in the usual way, adding a little salt at the end. Drain well. Make a syrup of the sugar and 75 ml (½ gill) of water by bringing to the boil, and stirring until the sugar has dissolved. Add the beans and keep them below boiling point for 10 minutes. Stir in the soya sauce and leave to cool.

> 250 g (8 oz) rice
> 2 tablespoons wine vinegar
> 1 teaspoon sugar
> soya sauce to taste (or 2–3 tablespoons dashi)
> 60 g (2 oz) cooked carrots, chopped small
> 1–2 tablespoons capers (or 60 g (2 oz) chirasu-boshi)

Boil the rice in the usual way. Rinse well under the hot tap, then mix in the other ingredients. More sugar or vinegar or soya sauce – or less – may be added to taste.

> 125 g (¼ lb) mushrooms (or 45 g (1½ oz) dried Japanese mushrooms)
> 1 tablespoon soya sauce (preferably Japanese)
> 1 tablespoon sugar

Remove the stems of the mushrooms, and cut them in strips (dried mushrooms must be soaked in tepid water for about 20 minutes, before slicing). Simmer until cooked in soya sauce and sugar. Cool. Mix in with the rice.

> 125 g (¼ lb) green beans, preferably haricots verts
> 1 teaspoon each soya sauce and wine vinegar (or 2 tablespoons dashi,
>    ⅛ teaspoon salt)

Mix the ingredients together and leave to soak for 1 hour.

> 125 g (4 oz) cooked, peeled shrimps
> 2 tablespoons wine vinegar
> 1½ tablespoons sugar

Mix together, leave for 30 minutes, then drain.

> 2 eggs
> a pinch of salt
> 1 teaspoon sugar
> 1 teaspoon soya sauce (or 2 teaspoons dashi)
> corn oil

Beat the eggs well, add salt, sugar and soya sauce or *dashi*. Brush a heavy frying pan with a thin coating of oil, place over a moderate heat for a few moments, then pour in a thin layer of beaten egg. It will cook quickly, and should not be moved about but left in an even layer. Remove with a palette knife or fish slice. Repeat until the egg is finished and you have three or four pancakes. Roll them up, then slice them downwards into thin shreds: they will look like tiny slices of jam roll.

Serve with warm saké. Bowls of clear Japanese soup (with bean curd and mushrooms) can accompany the dish – the soup is easily prepared from dehydrated packages sold in oriental food shops.

[*Good Things*]

## STIR-FRIED CHINESE CABBAGE WITH MUSHROOMS AND BAMBOO SHOOTS

I notice that Chinese cabbage, celery cabbage or Chinese leaf (*pe-ts'ai* and *pai-ts'ai* to the Chinese themselves) is creeping quietly but steadily into good greengroceries all over. It is by far the best of the Brassicas, and simple to grow. Indeed, whenever I see gardens full of the usual rank-smelling cabbage, I wonder why we still bother with such things when this pleasurable relation is in all the seed catalogues.

Stir-fried, as in this recipe, Chinese cabbage keeps its fresh taste and crunch, but benefits from the heavier crispness of bamboo shoots and the chewiness of mushrooms. A fine vegetable dish, on its own, or with a Western meal.

Serves 4

*500 g (1 lb) Chinese cabbage (or Savoy, if you must)*
*125 g(4 oz) tinned bamboo shoots*
*6 dried mushrooms, soaked*
*oil*
*about 1 teaspoon salt*
*about ¼ teaspoon sugar*

Slice cabbage so that it falls into strips about 6-mm (¼-inch) wide, across the leaves. Rinse and slice the bamboo shoots. Reserve a few tablespoons of the mushroom soaking water, then quarter the mushrooms, discarding the stems. Heat the frying pan, and pour in just enough oil to cover the base thinly. Stir-fry the cabbage for 1 minute, keeping it moving and turning the whole time, so that all the strips are coated thinly with oil. Add bamboo shoots, mushrooms, salt, sugar and reserved mushroom soaking liquor. Bring to a sharp boil, cover, and cook for 5 minutes, or until the cabbage is cooked but still crisp. Correct seasoning. Serve immediately.

[*The Mushroom Feast*]

# FISH

## FISH BAKED IN SALT

This recipe, which can also be used for chicken, pork or beef, puzzles me. I find it in books on Lyonnais cookery, even the great-grandmotherly *Ethnocuisine du Lyonnais*, always without explanation. It cannot be an old recipe, as salt was so precious a commodity in the past that no one would have dreamt of using 2½ kg (5½ lb) of it for a family joint.

In fact, I first encountered the idea in Chinese cookery books, and variations of it in Japanese fish recipes. Could it be an import from the Far East by one of the nouvelle cuisine chefs who are clustered in and around the Lyonnais?

The salt can be re-used for compatible meat, or for seasoning compatible soups, stews and grills. I store it in plastic bags in the freezer, weeding out any lumps where the juices have caught a little, and not keeping it very long. But then I buy my salt in sacks in France where it is cheap. For a first attempt, cook a small whole fish and see if you agree with me that the method gives a lively fresh flavour, not very salty, which is surprising, and the impression that you have the pure, true taste of the ingredient.

This is what you do. Choose a pot into which the chicken, meat or fish fits with about 3 cm (1½ inches) to spare all round. Line with heavy or doubled foil. Put 3 cm (1½ inches) of salt in the bottom and put in the chicken, breast down, with other meat or with fish. Pour in enough salt to bury the victim completely, with a 2-cm (1-inch) layer on top. Put into a preheated oven, gas 8–9, 230–240°C (450–475°F), and leave for 1–1½ hours for a 1–2 kg (3–4½ lb) chicken, 1½ hours for 1½ kg (3 lb) pork or beef (boned loin or fillet), and 30 minutes for a larger mackerel, or other fish weighing 500 g (1 lb).

Turn out on to large baking sheet. It will emerge as a fairly solid block. Tap it with a hammer, but carefully, as the salt spreads enthusiastically to reveal a golden-skinned chicken or joint (fish skin tends to peel off with the salt). Brush off the salt and serve with simple accompaniments such as potatoes baked in their jackets.

[*À La Carte*]

## JAPANESE-STYLE FISH (Sashimi)

Serves 6

*750 g (1½ lb) sea bass, sea bream, sole or plaice*
*250-g (½-lb) slice of pink tuna fish or 350 g (¾ lb) mackerel*
*7½-cm (3-in) length of white radish*
*1 level tablespoon* wasabi *(green horseradish powder),*
*  or 2 level tablespoons finely grated fresh ginger*
*6 spring onions cut into curled shreds*
shoyu *(Japanese soya sauce)*
*lime juice (optional)*

Scale and fillet the fish, leaving the skin intact. Wrap in greaseproof paper and chill in the freezer until firm (about 1–2 hours). Peel and finely shred the radish.

No more than 1 hour before it is needed, mix the *wasabi* to a thick paste with a little water. Let it stand for about 20 minutes. If you use ginger, shape it into 6 little mounds.

Remove the fish from the freezer and cut diagonally into paper-thin slices. If this is not possible, cut into 6-mm (¼-inch) slices or, with flat fish, into strips. Pick out any tiny bones with tweezers.

To serve: arrange the fish on 6 chilled plates with a blob of *wasabi* (or a mound of ginger) and some shredded radish. Garnish each with a spring onion and serve bowls of *shoyu* sauce, or a mixture of half *shoyu* sauce and half lime juice, separately.

To eat: mix the *wasabi* or ginger into the *shoyu* according to taste with a little radish. Dip slices of fish into this mixture with chopsticks.

[*À La Carte*]


## MANGO PRAWNS

'I was a long way from the sea when I heard about this one,' wrote Alan Davidson in the *Seafood of South-East Asia*, 'precisely, at Ban Houei Sai, the enchanting village which stands on soil studded with sapphires in the Golden Triangle area of Laos. I was on the trail of *Pangasianodon gigas*, the giant catfish of the Mekong. Peter Law, a narcotics expert from Hong Kong, was following other trails of his own; but he is also a gastronome and was moved by some turn in the conversation to impart this recipe to me ... may be used for crab instead of prawns. Whichever you use, the amount of crustacean and the amount of mango should be about equal. The quantities given are right for 4 people.'

Use the large cooked Mediterranean prawns that a number of fishmongers have taken to selling, otherwise go for crab.

Serves 4

*8 prawns*
*4 mangoes*

DRESSING
*300 ml ( ½ pt) mayonnaise or thick cream*
*2 tablespoons freshly grated horseradish*
*a squeeze of lemon or lime juice*
*1 teaspoonful sugar*
*a little freshly ground pepper*
*a little single cream or creamy milk to thin dressing, if necessary*

Peel the prawns, and cut up into chunks. Prepare the mangoes so that you are left with the empty skins and the flesh cubed.

Mix prawns and mango. Mix the dressing ingredients, then stir it gradually into the prawn and mango. Stop when the mixture is nicely bound and not in the least liquid. Divide between the empty mango skins, and arrange on a dish. Garnish with strips of sweet red or green pepper and mint leaves. Serve chilled.

[*Fruit Book*]


# TEMPURA

In other words, fritters, because the European fritter is thought to have been the origin of this popular Japanese food. When the Jesuit missionaries arrived with Saint Francis Xavier in sixteenth-century Japan, they ate the dish on Ember Days, fast days occurring at four periods of the year – the *quattuor tempora* – when ordinations could take place. The first Tokugawa ruler, Ieyasu, died about sixty years later from a surfeit of *tai tempura*, fritters of sea bream or *tai*, the most prized of Japanese fish. Some at least of the missionaries' works had made devoted converts.

If you have an electric deep frier, you will find tempura easy to organize on the *fondue bourguignonne* principle – which is to say that all the separate ingredients that go to make up a tempura are prepared beforehand, and the cooking is done last of all at table with no loss of sociability for the cook. This is the ideal, because these rather delicate fritters should be eaten immediately, straight from the pan, each person dipping his piece into a small bowl of sauce the moment it's ready.

In Japan, chopsticks are used for both cooking and eating tempura. But unless you are very skilful with them, you will find it easier, when cooking, to make use of a perforated spoon in the normal way. Fondue forks are the obvious solution, if you have them.

Prepare the three elements of the dish – sauce, seafood and vegetables, batter – in the following order:

Serves 4

SAUCE
2 tablespoons saké ⎫
1 tablespoon mirin ⎬ or 3 tablespoons mirin or dry sherry with some sugar
2 tablespoons sugar
150 ml (¼ pt) dashi or stock

Simmer together for 2 minutes. Pour into a bowl, or individual bowls, and leave to cool.

FISH AND VEGETABLES
16 mushrooms or shiitake
24 large prawns in their shells
24 mussels, scrubbed and scraped
2 aubergines
4 spring onions

Cut stalks of fresh mushrooms level with the caps, or soak the shiitake until soft, drain them, and discard stems. Shell the prawns. Open the mussels in a large pan, covered, over a very high heat: remove them from their shells (keep the cooking liquor for another dish). Cut the aubergines into 8 or 12 pieces each, according to their size. Trim roots and damaged outer skin from the spring onions. Arrange elegantly on a dish. (Other ingredients can be added – e.g., cubes of firm white fish fillets, pieces of young carrot, red and green pepper and so on.)

BATTER
The master of a tempura restaurant in Tokyo, the famous Tenichi restaurant, has written a small book on the special foods of the capital. In it he gives this recipe for the correct, very light batter. He observes that the old way of reading the characters of the word *tempura* gives you 'flour' and 'silk-gauze'. 'The whole word could mean to wear light stuff of flour, as a woman wears silk-gauze that desire may be stimulated in the beholder by glimpses of the beauty underneath.' This gives you a good idea of what the fritters should look like when they are ready to eat.

Break an egg into a measuring container, and whisk it smooth. Add four times its bulk of water, then five times its bulk of flour. In other words, if your egg occupies 30 ml (1 fl oz) you should end up with 300 ml (½ pt) of batter. Whisk well.

Heat a pan of deep oil to between 180°C (350°F) and 185°C (360°F). Dip the individual pieces of food into the batter, shake off the surplus, and deep-fry for a few minutes until the coating is crisp and a rather whitish brown. With the spring onions, you will find it easier to use your fingers for dipping them into the batter rather than a perforated spoon. If you are not handing out the cooked fritters straight from the pan, arrange them on an elegantly folded napkin on a serving plate and keep them warm in the oven. Obviously the cooking has to be done in batches, so that there is no risk of the oil losing heat.

*Note*: half the quantity can be used to make the first course of an otherwise Western dinner.

[*The Mushroom Feast*]

## POACHED COD WITH SHELLFISH (Vatapa)

Serves 6

*1 small whole cod, or a tailpiece of 1½ kg (3 lb)*
*salt*
*freshly ground black pepper*
*500 g (1 lb) large prawns in their shells*
*300 ml (½ pt) fish or chicken stock*
*2 tablespoons groundnut or sunflower oil*
*125 g (¼ lb) onion, chopped*
*2 large cloves of garlic, chopped*
*2 fresh green chillis, chopped, seeds included*
*400 g (14 oz) can of tomatoes or fresh tomatoes, skinned and chopped*
*2 tablespoons finely chopped ginger*
*60 g (2 oz) dried shrimps (available from oriental stores)*
*100g (3½ oz) lightly toasted cashew nuts*
*100 g (3½ oz) lightly toasted, blanched, split almonds*
*600 ml (1 pt) coconut milk made with half milk, half water, from fresh, desiccated or creamed coconut; or a can of coconut milk plus milk and water*
*6 tablespoons chopped coriander or parsley*
*250 g (½ lb) Italian rice*
*125 ml (4 fl oz) coconut milk*
*4 tablespoons palm oil (optional)*
*250 g (½ lb) small cooked prawns*
*sprigs of coriander or parsley (optional)*

Season the cod and set aside. Reserving two for the garnish, shell and, if necessary, devein the prawns, then boil up their shells with the fish or chicken stock or 300 ml (½ pt) water for 15 minutes. Strain and discard the debris.

Heat up the oil and cook the onion, garlic and chilli slowly until the onion begins to soften. Add the tomato and simmer. Meanwhile, whizz the ginger, dried shrimps and nuts in a processor or blender. Add the tomato mixture. You will not get the purée completely smooth, as nuts and dried shrimps always keep a certain graininess.

Put the tomato mixture into a pan large enough to contain the cod, add the coconut milk and simmer for 15–20 minutes, adding the coriander or parsley after 10 minutes. Add the prawn shell stock as required if the sauce becomes too thick.

Lay the fish in the pan and simmer for 10 minutes, occasionally spooning the sauce over it. Turn the fish and complete the cooking. Lift out the cod on to a hot serving dish and keep it warm.

Meanwhile cook the Italian rice in 1½ times its volume of water. As the liquid is absorbed, add the coconut milk equal to half its volume and simmer until the rice is tender. Season with salt.

Taste and reflect on the sauce in the pan. It may need more stock, or more seasoning. Stir in the large prawns and, if you wish, the palm oil, which adds a glorious colour. Give the prawns 4 minutes to heat through (or a little longer if uncooked) and boil the reserved prawns for 2–3 minutes. Pour the sauce round the fish, serve with the Italian rice and garnish with the two reserved large prawns, the small prawns and coriander or parsley if you wish.

[*À La Carte*]

# MEAT AND POULTRY

## STUFFED PAPAYAS WITH *LASSI*

If papayas are plentiful where you live, or if ever they become cheap and abundant, this is a good way of presenting them for a change. It is not the pinnacle of high eating, but for summer lunch when hot foods need to be slightly piquant and dry yet juicy, it is a good dish, especially if you put a jug of *lassi* on the table as well.

Although raw meat is given in the ingredients, you could use the pink part of left-over veal or beef. It may seem a nuisance to chop it, but with a heavy sharp knife, it is quickly done and it tastes much better. Getting this kind of mixture right, dry but moist and meltingly spicy, is not too easy: you need to give yourself every help you can, and chopping rather than mincing the meat makes the right start.

Serves 6

*6 ripe papayas*
*2 limes, or 1 lime and 1 lemon*
*1 large onion, finely chopped*
*oil*
*2 large cloves garlic*
*1 small seeded red chilli*
*2½-cm (1-inch) piece ginger root, peeled*
*500 g (1 lb) veal or beef, chopped*
*2 pinches turmeric*
*60 g (2 oz) blanched, slivered almonds*
*150 ml (¼ pt) veal or beef or chicken stock*
*salt*
*6 rounded tablespoons cooked rice*
*2 level teaspoons* garam masala
*1 tablespoon each chopped green coriander and parsley*
*3 heaped tablespoons fresh breadcrumbs*
*2 spring onions, sliced*
*melted butter*

Halve and seed the papayas. Remove most but not quite all of their flesh, so that the skins have a nice pink lining. Chop the flesh into rough dice and put into a bowl with the finely-grated zest of the limes or lime and lemon. Squeeze in the juice. Range the papaya shells on a buttered baking dish.

Cook the onion slowly in 3 tablespoons of oil until it begins to soften. Raise heat to brown it nicely, stirring to get as even a colour as possible.

Meanwhile chop together garlic, chilli and ginger. Add to onion, and fry for 2 more minutes. Then put in the meat, turmeric and almonds. Raise the heat to brown the meat rapidly. Pour in the stock, lower the heat and cover. Simmer for about 15 minutes until the meat is tender and the liquid more or less vanished, with just a little juice remaining. Season. Stir in the rice and *garam* and add to the papaya dice. Taste and correct the seasoning. Add the herbs and taste again.

Stuff the papayas. Sprinkle them with breadcrumbs and pour on some melted butter. Bake in a fast oven, gas 6–7, 200–220°C (400–425°F) for about 20 minutes until the top has a golden crusty look. Sprinkle with the spring onion just before serving.

To make the *lassi*, put equal quantities of yoghurt and iced water – 600 ml (1 pt) of each is about right for six people – into a liquidizer or processor. Add some cream, if you like, and also six ice cubes. Whizz together until the mixture has a head of foam. Taste and add salt, then whizz again. Pour into a jug and stand in the refrigerator until required: the foam lasts for several hours. Put a pinch of cumin in the centre just before you serve, if you like, by way of decoration.

With a salad and some cheese to follow, this makes an agreeable meal. The *bonne bouche* is coming to the end of the spiced meat and rice, and finding the tender pink layer of papaya underneath.

[*Fruit Book*]


## MONGOLIAN FIRE POT (Shua Yang Jou)

Mongolian fire pot is a one-pot dish of a kind to be found all over the world from Japanese *nabé-mono* to French, Swiss and Dutch *fondues* (or Lancashire hot-pot though it does not need a table burner). They make relaxing and sociable meals, an entertainment as well as food. They all require the same equipment, one large pot and a source of heat. The Chinese have a specially designed metal pot and burner in one that can be bought in this country, but the dish can be perfectly well cooked with fondue equipment, and fondue forks may well be easier for your visitors than chopsticks.

The meat must be cut into thin slices, paper thin, or 'flying thin' as Mrs Chao calls them in *How to cook and eat in Chinese*. For this you do not need Peking skill with the cleaver. Put the lamb to chill in the coldest part of the refrigerator until it is firm. Then you can easily cut fine, thin, nicely shaped slices. As with many other Chinese dishes, everything happens at the last minute, so it is wise to have someone to help.

Serves 6

> *1½ kg (3 lb) boned lamb from leg or shoulder*
> *125 g (4 oz) transparent Chinese noodles*
> *250 g (½ lb) fresh leaf spinach*
> *500 g (1 lb) Chinese leaf*
> *12 part-cooked rolls, or home-made bread dough*
> *2 litres (3½ pt) stock made from chicken and lamb bones*
> *2 large spring onions or small leeks*
> *1 large clove garlic, chopped*
> *2 good teaspoons chopped fresh ginger*
> *60 g (2 oz) green coriander or parsley chopped*

SAUCE
*12 tablespoons soya sauce*
*2 tablespoons pale dry sherry*
*2 tablespoons sesame oil*
*1 rounded tablespoon soft brown sugar mixed with 1 tablespoon very hot water*
*½ teaspoon cayenne*
*5 teaspoons canned fermented red bean curd*

Cut the chilled meat into thin slices. Divide between six plates and put into the refrigerator (cover them with film wrap if you need to stack plates). Pour ½ litre (a good ¾ pt) of very hot water over the noodles, leave for 30 minutes, drain and put to one side of a large serving dish. Wash, trim and dry the spinach leaves. Slice and blanch the Chinese leaf for 3 minutes in boiling salted water, drain and put with the spinach on the noodle dish. Put the rolls in a steamer, set over boiling water, cover and leave for 20 minutes; if you are using home-made dough, leave it to rise for 1 hour in a warm place while you are coping with the above preparations, then form it into rolls, prove for 15 minutes, then steam for up to 30 minutes – they should end up white and puffy and light. Mix the remaining ingredients together and bring them slowly to the boil. Mix the sauce ingredients; put some into six bowls and the rest into one bowl to be kept as a seasoning for the final stew.

Set the table by putting a plate of meat, a small bowl of sauce, chopsticks or fondue forks, and a porcelain Chinese soup spoon or dessertspoon in each place, with a napkin. Put the table burner in the centre, so that everyone can reach it. Place the noodles and vegetables on one side, the hot rolls on the other and keep the extra bowl of sauce somewhere near you so that it doesn't get used too soon. Also provide yourself with a soup ladle.

When all your visitors are seated, bring in the boiling stock and set it over the burner. Aim to keep it at a steady boil. Each person picks up a slice or two of meat with chopsticks or fork, and 'rinses' it in the stock. After a few seconds, the meat will have changed colour and be ready to eat; different people may like it cooked for different lengths of time. Dip the meat in the sauce before eating it, and take an occasional mouthful of hot roll.

When the meat is all finished up, ladle a little stock into each person's sauce bowl to make some soup for them to drink, while you put the noodles and vegetables into the stock to cook for a few minutes. The stock by this time will have a delicious flavour from the meat. Share this vegetable stew round the table, adding extra sauce from the spare bowl as seasoning.

Finish the meal with a huge basket of tangerines or grapes or both. Or with peeled oranges, the traditional end to many Peking meals.

[*Vegetable Book*]

## AUBERGINES *À LA CHINOISE*

Chinoiserie is one of the joys of European civilization, and I see no reason to apologize when it breaks out in cooking. Authenticity is not its aim (I should like to take a visitor from Peking into the eighteenth-century rococo Chinese room at Claydon House in Buckinghamshire and watch his face), but pleasure. Or perhaps delight is the word, delight in the exotic, that 'bright world of the imagination, where we take our true holidays', as Edward H. Schafer says in *The Golden Peaches of Samarkand*.

Serves 4

*500 g (1 lb) aubergines, peeled, diced, salted*
*cooking oil*
*30 g (1 oz) dried mushrooms, soaked, stemmed, quartered*
*175 g (6 oz) lean smoked Danish bacon, cut in squares*
*175 g (6 oz) cooked chicken, diced*
*125 g (4 oz) chopped walnuts*
*4 tablespoons soya sauce*
*3 tablespoons Madeira*
*1 tablespoon sugar*
*a pinch of monosodium glutamate (optional)*

Fry the well-drained aubergines in oil, and when they are half-cooked, add the mushrooms, bacon, and chicken. Mix remaining ingredients in a bowl. When the aubergines are cooked and the other ingredients well heated, pour in the contents of the bowl. Stir the whole thing together, and serve when really hot.

[*The Mushroom Feast*]

## FRIED RICE (Nasi Goreng)

If you like Indian and Chinese food, you will certainly enjoy this dish from Indonesia (*nasi* means rice, and *goreng* fried). The pleasure of eastern dishes is the way that the different elements are kept separate and retain their identity, while combining into one delicious whole.

As with Chinese fried rice, the important thing is to pre-cook the rice, either the day before or several hours in advance. This is of course no problem in countries where rice is the staple food. Here it needs mild forethought.

Measure out 300 ml (½ pt) basmati rice and cook it with 600 ml (1 pt) water. When done, fork it up lightly and spread on a plate to cool.

Assemble the following ingredients. Prepare the side dishes first, then the omelette strips, then the fried rice and finally the fried eggs. If you have a *guo* (*wok*), this is the best utensil for frying the rice: the ingredients fall back into the centre of the pan while you stir, so that everything is kept in an ordered perpetual motion.

Serves 6

SIDE DISHES
*cucumber cut into 5-cm (2-inch) strips*
*125 g (4 oz) salted peanuts*
*6 bananas*
*60 g (2 oz) butter*
*juice of ½ lemon*

OMELETTE
*4 eggs*
*salt, pepper*
*butter*

FRIED RICE
*150 g (5 oz) chopped onion*
*2 large cloves garlic, chopped*
*½ teaspoon dried chilli flakes, or a chopped fresh chilli minus seeds*
*5 anchovy fillets (or ½ teaspoon* trasi)
*1 teaspoon salt*
*groundnut or sunflower oil*
*1 tablespoon soya sauce*
*250–375 g (8–12 oz) roast pork/ham, diced*
*6 eggs (optional)*

Put cucumber and peanuts into separate bowls. Peel and slice bananas in half lengthways, place them in a greased ovenproof dish, dot with butter and sprinkle with lemon juice. Bake at gas 7–8, 220–230°C (425–450°F), for 10–12 minutes, turning the pieces over after 5 minutes. Put them in another bowl.

To make the omelette strips, beat the four eggs with a little salt and pepper, and cook three or four thin omelettes in the usual way, keeping them slightly moist. Roll them up and slice across, so that they fall into a tumble of strips. Keep them warm.

For the fried rice, reduce the first five ingredients on the list to a paste in the blender with 5 or 6 tablespoons of oil. Scrape the mixture out into a *guo* or frying pan and cook steadily until the paste begins to bubble and brown. If you do not have a blender, chop the five ingredients as finely as possible, then fry them.

Stir in the cooked rice and fry until lightly browned, adding more oil if required. Keep stirring. Now add the soya sauce and cubes of meat, and cook for another 5 minutes, still stirring, until everything is well heated through.

Spread the rice over a large serving dish and put the omelette strips on top. Quickly fry the six eggs and put them among the omelette strips.

Place all the dishes in the centre of the table, for preference on a dumb waiter. Give each person a spoon and fork, a shallow bowl and lager or beer to drink.

[*Fruit Book*]


## CHICKEN STUFFED WITH DRIED MUSHROOMS AND CHESTNUTS

Chestnuts are a great favourite with the Chinese, as they are with us. This is a most sympathetic dish to our Western idea of things. The point of hanging the chicken up in a blast of cold air is to dry out its skin, which will then become particularly crisp and succulent as it roasts: this is the method used to make the skin of Peking duck such a pleasure to eat. In Peking, though, the dry cold air is supplied by the Gobi desert and not by an electric fan.

Serves 8

2–2½ kg (4–5 lb) roasting chicken
14 shiitake mushrooms
250 g (½ lb) chestnuts
125 g (4 oz) chopped onion
3 tablespoons soya sauce
salt
pepper
1 tablespoon sherry
1 tablespoon peanut or corn oil

Hang the chicken up by a piece of string in front of an electric fan, or the cool air from an electric fan heater. Leave it for 2 hours.

Meanwhile soak, then slice, the mushrooms, discarding stems. Peel and chop the chestnuts. Mix mushrooms and chestnuts with onion, two-thirds of the soya sauce, ½ teaspoon of salt and a dash of pepper. Stuff the dried chicken with the mixture and truss securely.

Mix sherry with remaining soya sauce and rub it over the bird. Then brush it over with oil. Put on to a rack over a roasting pan with a good 2½ cm (1 inch) of water in it, and put into a gas 5, 190°C (375°F), oven for 20 minutes. Reduce the heat to gas 3, 160°C (325°F) for another 40 minutes or until the bird is cooked. Baste from time to time, and add more water to the pan if necessary. Serve in the Western style; or cut up and arrange on a warm dish in the Chinese manner.

[*The Mushroom Feast*]


## FROGS' LEGS/CHICKEN BREASTS/SWEETBREADS WITH BANANA *RAITA*

*Kela* – i.e. banana – *raita* is one of those delectable yoghurt salads that cool and set off well-spiced Indian dishes, pilaffs, *tandoori* foods, and Mughal braised dishes. While I occasionally enjoy assembling and cooking Indian food, I do not see why certain embellishments such as the various *raita* should not be served with European meals, or eaten in European ways. This particular version makes a fine summer breakfast dish, and it sets off certain mild meats that we often serve with fruit in some form or another. The recipe below is based on Julie Sahni's recipe in *Classic Indian Cooking*, a book of careful instructions and good dishes, published in New York.

An important thing is not to add the banana to the *raita* more than 1 hour or 1½ hours before the meal. The banana loses its bite, and the *raita* becomes very wet with its juice.

Frogs' legs in this country – and very often in France, too – are bought deep-frozen. They taste like chicken, but have a delicacy and small size that makes them more appetizing. If you do use chicken – or turkey – breasts, cut the whole breast into its two parts then slice them through into escalopes and remove the skin: this means that three chicken breasts give you a dozen escalopes. Sweetbreads should be blanched, pressed and sliced in the usual way: soak them in salted water for 1 hour, drain and simmer them in light stock with lemon juice until they lose their pink raw look, drain again and remove knobbly skin and gristle, then press between two plates in the refrigerator for several hours or overnight. Although veal and lamb sweetbreads taste much the same, veal is far superior from the point of view of size and succulence, the consistency is better, too.

RAITA
2 heaped tablespoons sultanas or seedless raisins
30 g (1 oz) blanched, slivered almonds
200 ml (7 fl oz) natural yoghurt
100 ml (3½ fl oz) each soured and whipping cream
1 heaped tablespoon honey
1 medium-sized ripe but firm banana
a pinch of salt
6 cardamom pods


RICE
375 ml (12 fl oz) brown rice
1 tablespoon oil
1 heaped tablespoon butter


MEAT
30–36 frogs' legs
or 1 kg (2 lb) sweetbreads, prepared
or 3 whole chicken breasts, sliced through into 12 escalopes
4 level tablespoons flour
2 level teaspoons salt
1 level teaspoon cayenne pepper
1 level teaspoon curry powder, own mixture or good brand
clarified butter
chopped coriander, parsley, chives

To make the *raita*, pour boiling water over the sultanas or raisins and two-thirds of the almonds: leave for 10 minutes. Toast the remaining almonds. Mix yoghurt and creams with the honey. Taste and add more honey if you like, but do not oversweeten. Stir in drained raisins and almonds. Slice the banana thinly and add that, with the salt. Take cardamom seeds from the pods and crush them. Add a little at a time to the *raita* – you may find that half is enough for your taste. Turn into a serving dish and scatter with the toasted almonds. Chill for 1 hour.

Cook the brown rice in a large pan of salted boiling water, with the oil which prevents the pan boiling over. Simmer for 30 or 40 minutes until tender, drain and rinse with hot water. Mix with the butter and pile up on a warm serving dish. Cover lightly with butter papers and keep warm in the oven.

Pat the meat dry with kitchen paper. Mix flour, salt, pepper and curry powder, and turn the pieces of meat in it. Fry them in clarified butter, not too fast; they should end up a pinkish-gold colour. Frogs' legs and chicken escalopes do not take long – turn after 3 or 4 minutes, then test after 7 minutes' cooking time. Sweetbreads can stand a slightly hotter temperature, and longer cooking – time will depend on the state they are in after blanching.

Arrange the pieces up against the pile of rice and round it. Scatter with a little coriander, not everyone likes the taste so go carefully, and then with parsley and chives. Serve with the *kela raita*.

[*Fruit Book*]

## STEAMED EGG CUSTARD WITH CHICKEN AND FISH (Chawan-mushi)

An excellent supper dish. The unusual – to our way of thinking – collection of nicely seasoned bits and pieces is distributed among individual pots, then the egg and stock mixture is poured over the top. The ideal pots to use are china or glass egg coddlers, with well-fitting lids, but any small pots will do so long as they are covered with foil.

Serves 4

CUSTARD
*4 eggs*
*225 ml (1½ gills)* dashi *(see below) or chicken stock*
*1 teaspoon salt*
*1 teaspoon* mirin *(see below) or dry sherry with some sugar*
*½ teaspoon soya sauce*
*¼ teaspoon monosodium glutamate*

CHICKEN
*125 g (¼ lb) chicken breast, thinly sliced*
*1 teaspoon* mirin, *or dry sherry with some sugar*
*1 teaspoon soya sauce*

SEAFOOD
*4 large prawns in their shells*
*125 g (¼ lb) good white fish*
*½ teaspoon saké*
*salt*

VEGETABLES
*4 dried mushrooms, soaked*
*4 French beans*

Mix custard ingredients, and strain. Mix chicken ingredients and leave for at least 5 minutes. Shell the prawns and split them in half with a sharp knife: cut the fish into julienne strips and sprinkle with saké and a little salt. Quarter the mushrooms, and discard their stems. Blanch the beans in boiling salted water until barely cooked; drain and slice diagonally. Divide chicken, seafood and vegetables among four pots (see above), pour the custard over them, cover them, and steam in a large pan of water for 20 minutes – a self-basting roaster works well. Or cook them in a moderate oven in a *bain-marie* until just set, without being brown on top – 30 minutes. Serve immediately.

*Dashi*, made from seaweed and dried *bonito*, is the basic Japanese soup stock, their *court-bouillon*. A packet of instant *dashi* powder, to be mixed with water, is perfectly satisfactory for this recipe: chicken stock or plain water can be used instead. Dried gourd strips will have to come from an oriental supplier, but you may find sheets of *asakusa-nori* at some health food shops. *Mirin*, the sweet Japanese rice wine, has a flavour entirely of its own; the only substitute is dry sherry with extra sugar.

[*The Mushroom Feast*]

## STIR-FRIED CHICKEN WITH MUSHROOMS

One of the easiest dishes to include in a Western meal. As you can substitute fresh for Chinese fried mushrooms, the only ingredient likely to cause a little difficulty is the ginger.

Serves 4 as a main dish

*500 g (1 lb) boned chicken breast*
*4 teaspoons cornflour*
*1 egg white*
*2 tablespoons Chinese rice wine, or dry sherry*
*salt*
*4 tablespoons oil*
*2 slices fresh ginger root, peeled*
*2 heaped tablespoons finely chopped onion*
*12 large Chinese mushrooms, soaked, quartered, stems removed,*
*    or 250 g (½ lb) fresh mushrooms, sliced*
*1 tablespoon soya sauce*
*90 ml (3 oz) chicken stock*

Chill the chicken, then slice it as thinly as possible and cut each slice into strips about 12 mm (½ inch) wide and 2½ cm (1 inch) long.

Mix them with half the starch in a bowl until they are coated; add egg white, wine, and a teaspoon of salt, and mix well. Heat half the oil in a frying pan, and stir-fry the ginger and onion for a few seconds, until they begin to have a whitish appearance, then put in the chicken. Stir it about for 1 minute, until chicken is opaque and just cooked. Remove to a dish and keep warm. Pour remaining oil into the pan and fry the mushrooms for 1½ minutes, scraping the pan well. Put chicken back in pan, and add soya sauce. Quickly mix remaining starch with chicken stock, tip into the pan (keep stirring), and cook for a moment or two until the meat and mushrooms are glazed with a clear brown sauce. Correct seasoning if necessary.

## Variations

This simple stir-fried chicken with mushrooms recipe, from *The Thousand Recipe Chinese Cookbook*, by Gloria Bley Miller, can be varied by substituting one of the mixtures below for the mushrooms mentioned in the master list of ingredients:

*125 g (¼ lb) fresh mushrooms, sliced*
*6 shiitake, soaked, stemmed, quartered*

*250 g (½ lb) fresh mushrooms, sliced*
*250 g (½ lb) Chinese leaf (celery cabbage), sliced*

*125 g (¼ lb) fresh mushrooms, sliced*
*2 stalks of celery, sliced*
*125 g (4 oz) shelled walnuts, roughly chopped*

*125 g (¼ lb) fresh mushrooms, sliced*
*125 g (¼ lb) bamboo shoots, sliced*

*6 shiitake, soaked, stemmed, quartered*
*125 g (¼ lb) bamboo shoots, sliced*
*125 g (¼ lb) shelled walnuts, roughly chopped*

*1 cucumber, peeled, sliced*
*125 g (¼ lb) fresh mushrooms, sliced*
*6 water chestnuts, sliced*
*4 stalks celery, sliced*

[*The Mushroom Feast*]

## DUCK WITH PINEAPPLE (Vit Nâù Thom)

In France, Chinese cookery has become popular, as you would
expect, via Vietnam and returned settlers as well as Vietnamese who
wisely left before the Americans took over. This duck recipe has the
South-East Asian accent of pineapple that we also know from the
Cantonese cookery of many of our Chinese restaurants. I have adjusted
it slightly from a little book I bought at the splendid oriental shop
near the station at Tours, *Petit Livre de Recettes de cuisine Sino-
Vietnamiennes et exotiques*. Use a can of unsweetened pineapple rings,
better still a fresh pineapple peeled and cut into six rings and
simmered in a little water until tender.

It is worth making the effort to find cloud ears (or wood ears as
they are sometimes called). Their crisp jellied texture adds a lot to
this dish. Most oriental stores have them, although they are not so
much in demand as the shiitake.

> Serves 6
>
> *1 large duck with giblets*
> *1 large onion, sliced*
> *2 large cloves garlic, halved*
> bouquet garni
> *10 g (⅓ oz) dried Chinese mushrooms (shiitake)*
> *10 g (⅓ oz) dried cloud ear mushrooms*
> *60 g (2 oz) butter*
> *1 large onion, chopped*
> *1 large clove garlic, chopped*
> *1 rounded tablespoon flour*
> *flour*
> *1 can pineapple rings*
> *1 teaspoon tomato concentrate*
> *salt, pepper, cayenne, soya sauce*
> *250–500 g (½–1 lb) string beans, half-cooked*

First bone the duck and cut it into pieces about 3 cm (good inch)
square. Break up carcase and put with giblets, sliced onion, halved
garlic cloves and *bouquet garni* into a large pan. Cover generously with
water and simmer for 2–3 hours. This can be done in advance.

Reduce stock to ½ litre (¾ pt). Put rinsed mushrooms into
separate bowls and pour very warm water over them, to cover. Leave
to soak and swell, about 20 minutes. Cut them into 3 or 4 pieces
each. Discard the stalks of the Chinese mushrooms. Keep and strain
the liquor.

The duck can take 1½ hours to cook, so give yourself plenty of time (the dish can always be reheated, but keep fruit and beans for adding at this stage to preserve their freshness). Brown it in half the butter, putting it skin side down first: you will need to do it in two pans, or two batches. As you turn the pieces over, add the chopped onion and garlic. When the duck is nicely coloured, pour off the surplus oil. Amalgamate the duck in one pan. Sprinkle with flour and turn the pieces again for 3 minutes.

Pour in the pineapple juice, tomato concentrate, mushroom liquor and enough of the stock to come most of the way up the duck. You will need more or less according to the quantity of pineapple juice. Add the mushrooms, stirring them in. Cover and simmer until the duck is almost cooked, then remove the lid and allow the sauce to reduce.

Taste for seasoning when the duck is tender, adding soya sauce if you like it, 1–2 tablespoons. Put in the pineapple cut into cubes, and the beans. Simmer a further 10 minutes. Serve with boiled rice.

[*Fruit Book*]

# VEGETABLES AND FRUIT

## THE AMAH'S PEAS

When a friend of mine was a little girl in Peking, her *amah* used to cook peas this way as a special treat. It's a messy dish, but not as messy as asparagus. There are people who might think it a little noisy (the Chinese are less inhibited than we are over good food), so choose your guests with care. Be sure to provide them with large cloth napkins; paper ones disintegrate.

Serves 6

*scant 1½ kg (3 lb) peas*
*salted water*

Peas of early middle-age benefit most from this method of cooking. Pick them over, discarding leaves, stalks, and any pods which are broken or blemished. Rinse and then cook them in a large pan of boiling salted water. Drain them well and serve in individual bowls as a first course (or as a separate vegetable course). The idea is to put a pod into your mouth, and suck out the steamed peas and the small amount of delicious juice inside the pod. The outer green part of the pod tastes good too.

You may have noticed that the cook does not shell the peas.

[*Good Things*]

## STIR-FRIED BEAN SPROUTS

Unless you have a Chinese *guo* (*wok*), you will need to cook the bean sprouts in two batches if you are using a whole bag at once.

Serves 4–6

*1 bag bean sprouts*
*oil, preferably groundnut oil*
*1 clove garlic, crushed*
*250 ml (8 fl oz) chicken stock*
*pepper, salt, sugar*
*1 dessertspoon soya sauce*
*1 heaped teaspoon cornflour*
*2–3 spring onions, cut in 2-cm (¾-inch) lengths*

Drain the rinsed sprouts well. Cover the base of the pan with a thin layer of oil, add the garlic and heat up. Stir in the sprouts and keep them moving about, over a high heat, for 1 minute. Add the stock and cook hard for a further minute, still stirring. Season to taste and add the soya sauce, plus the cornflour slaked in 3 tablespoons water, and the spring onions. Cook for 1 minute more, there should not be much liquid, just a binding creamy juice to set off the cooked, but still crisp, sprouts. Eat with rice or as a pancake filling.

This recipe can be varied in many ways. Reduce the stock by half, and put in 250 g (8 oz) skinned, chopped tomato with it. The whole thing can be turned into a light main course by frying 200–250 g (7–8 oz) thinly sliced lean pork or chicken, with or without an equal weight of peeled shrimps (avoid frozen ones, they are too watery), for 1 minute before putting in the sprouts.

[*Vegetable Book*]

## STIR-FRIED FOUR SEASON BEANS (Ch'ao Ssu Chi Tou)

In other words, French beans with water chestnuts. It is a pity that water chestnuts have to be bought in cans, since their flavour is much diminished. Still their crispness remains. If you cannot find them locally, substitute blanched almonds.

Serves 4–6

*500 g (1 lb) French beans*
*6 teaspoons oil*
*1 scant teaspoon sugar*
*10 water chestnuts, sliced, or 60 g (2 oz) blanched almonds*

*4 tablespoons chicken stock*
*1 teaspoon cornflour mixed with 3 extra teaspoons chicken stock*

Cut the beans into 5-cm (2-inch) pieces. Heat a heavy frying pan. Add the oil, then the beans. Do not overheat, as the beans should not brown. Keep them moving over the heat for 3 minutes. Add the sugar, water chestnuts or almonds and the stock, stirring all the time. Cover and leave to simmer for 2 minutes. Taste and add a little salt. Mix up the cornflour liquid and add it to the pan. Stir until the beans are lightly glazed. Serve at once.

In winter this is a good way of cooking frozen beans, the long whole kind not sliced runner beans. Be prepared to adjust the times according to the tenderness of the beans. They should be cooked but still slightly crisp. Serve with rice.

*Note*: 'four season' refers to the long growing period of French beans like *quartre-saisons* roses and strawberries in France.

[*Vegetable Book*]


## STIR-FRIED MANGE-TOUT PEAS

After all I have said about the delicacy of these peas, the Chinese stir-fry method may seem a shocking way to cook them. Soya sauce? Sherry? Strong chicken stock? Desecration. So it should be, but it isn't. Remember that this dish, like many other Chinese dishes, should be eaten with rice. The strong ingredients, used by the spoonful rather than in quantity, help keep the flavour of the peas on top, prevent it being drowned by the blandness of the rice.

Prepare the rice before you start cooking the peas. Allow 175–200 g (6–7 oz), if you are serving the two dishes together as a first course or a course on their own.

Serves 4–6

*500 g (1 lb) mange-tout peas, prepared*
*4 tablespoons corn or groundnut oil*
*5 tablespoons strong chicken stock, or clear vegetable broth*
*3 tablespoons butter*
*1 tablespoon soya sauce*
*1 rounded teaspoon cornflour*
*1 rounded teaspoon sugar*
*2 tablespoons sherry*
*½ tablespoon hoisin sauce (if possible)*
*salt*

Make sure the peas are dry or they will spit dangerously in the oil. Heat the oil in a large *guo* or frying pan (for this kind of cookery thin metal pans are better than thick ones). Add the peas and stir them over a medium heat for 2 minutes, or a shade longer. Quickly tip in the stock or broth, butter and soya sauce and continue to stir until the peas are just tender. Bring the smaller thinner ones up to the top, so that the larger ones cook more quickly. Mix the cornflour, sugar and sherry with 3 tablespoons of water and the hoisin sauce if used. Mix into the peas, stirring all the time, until the sauce is a shiny coating – about 1 minute. Taste and add salt.

*[Vegetable Book]*


## AMBAKALAYA

A sweet green mango relish from *101 Parsi Recipes* by Jeroo Mehta, to serve with lentil dishes, especially the lamb and lentil dish called *dhansak*.

Peel and slice 1 kg (2 lb) soft ripe green mango into six pieces each. Cook without water over a medium heat for 5 minutes. Boil 6 tablespoons water with 500 g (1 lb) jaggery or pale soft brown sugar, to make a syrup. Add with a 5-cm (2-inch) piece of cinnamon to the mangos. Cook for 15 minutes, uncovered, until the liquid is a medium thick syrup. Cool.

*[Fruit Book]*


## LEMON GRASS (*Cymbopogon citratus*)

Lemon grass is easily recognized from its tufts of long grass-like leaves. When you encounter it at the market it has been trimmed at the top, like a head of celery, and the coarsest outer leaves removed. Some recipes will specify the white inner part of lemon grass, others the green part. Or you will just be required to use two stalks or leaves, which should then be crushed slightly and chopped. The outer leaves can be used as flavouring then, like bay leaves, removed before the dish is served. You may find it easier to get dried lemon grass, or lemon grass powder, which should be used by the pinch.

Lemon grass is one of the flavourings that seem to be gaining popularity in the West with young chefs working in the new style. I recall one particularly delicate fish soup at Hubert's restaurant in New York, and being told that the chef – originally from the Philippines – had used lemon grass in the stock.

*[Exotic Fruits and Vegetables]*

## MANGO (*Mangifera indica*)

Of all exotic fruit, perhaps of all fruit, the mango is the finest. Not every mango all the time, but the mango at its best. 'The mango is the pride of the garden,' wrote one great poet of the thirteenth century, 'the choicest fruit of Hindustan.' In the sixteenth century Akbar, the Mogul Emperor, who was a contemporary of Elizabeth I, loved mangoes so much that he had a great orchard planted entirely with them, the Lakh Bagh near Darbhanga, a hundred thousand trees.

Mangoes appear to have been cultivated for over 4,000 years, and in their natural state are little better than 'a ball of tow soaked in turpentine'. Reducing the fibre and bringing the turpentine down to an enticing breath that adds character to the richness of the fruit was the work of generation after generation of gardeners. By the time of the Buddha it was reckoned a fine enough fruit for a mango grove to have been given to him for meditation. The Portuguese took to it enthusiastically, judging by some of the names associated with the fruit, which they called *mangas* from the Tamil (it seems that mango came to us via the Dutch, from the same source). The finest type of mango for high dependable quality is the Alphonse, from Affonso d'Albuquerque, an early Governor of Portuguese territories in western India. The finest group of mangoes is the Mulgoba, meaning 'makes the mouth water', while the Sandersha ('parrot beak' from the sharper oval shape) is best for cooking.

But how are we to judge their quality when we regard a tray of mangoes in the fruit department of a supermarket? I do not understand why they have escaped the labelling regulations of variety and origin. Only when we know these things will we be able to discriminate among the many varieties and learn, as it were, to know the Cox's Orange Pippin from the Bramley and Golden Delicious. If only the early years of the introduction of this fruit could be better handled – and why not a Mango Council to look after this? – the mango could make a permanent part of our most delightful eating, could become the pride of our table. No longer just an embellishment as Dryden described it in talking of an unripe poet:

> There's sweet and sour: and one side good at least
> Mango's and Limes, whose nourishment is little,
> Tho' not for food, are yet preserv'd for Pickle.

### To choose
Choosing good mangoes is not easy. However carefully you consider them, you will find that they vary as much and more than any other

fruit. The perfect mango, like the perfect peach, is an experience that may occur rarely and quite unexpectedly. Thanks to imports we can now buy them for most of the year – something that people living in India and Pakistan will envy us, since the mango season is a short one there. Families with mango trees in their gardens rarely get the chance of ripe fruit, since children start their secret thefts when the mangoes are green and acid. I confess I like mangoes with this fresh sharpness, when they are just right for jams and chutneys, for savoury dishes and for cooking lightly with some sugar. At this stage, as a rule, you will only find them in Indian stores and markets.

The mangoes found in supermarkets and general greengrocers are intended to be eaten ripe. If they are a little hard, keep them in a warm place for a few days until they begin to give when you cradle them in your hand and squeeze gently. Colour is nothing to go by. There are many varieties with differing appearances. Some are deep green with a red flush in places, some are plain green, some are yellow and some are that glorious sunburst of yellow and pinkish orange which seems to announce the perfect fruit.

### To prepare

At first preparing a mango can seem tricky. Stand near the sink so that you can rinse your hands and arms easily. First you should understand that the stone, though wide, is narrow in depth. This means that if you stand the mango upright, narrow side towards you, you can slice down a little distance from the stalk on either side – this gives you two shallow boats of mango, plus the stone with a ring of pulp and skin round it.

Once you get used to the mango's anatomy, you can slice in directly with a small sharp knife held at the right kind of angle to free the flesh from the stone, without making too messy a job of it. This gives you larger 'boats' with a concave top in which you can pour cream or coconut cream, or arrange pieces of lime. If the intention is to eat the mangoes out of hand, score the pulp of the 'boats' in a diamond pattern just down to the skin; the eater then picks up the piece and bends the skin back, pushing the centre part up so that the diamond opens like a flower, which makes it easier to eat – in theory at any rate. Mangoes can also be peeled like a peach: score the skin down, spear the mango with a fork and strip away the sections. If the mango is soft and juicy, I would not advise this course of action. It would be better to slice in to the stone so that the pieces fall out in wedge-shaped sections, then remove the skin, or remove and eat the flesh from the skin with a knife and fork.

All in all, there is something splendid about eating a mango which is not for the prim and the pernickety; as the greengrocer realized when he put up a poster saying, 'Share a mango in the bath with your loved one.'

[*Exotic Fruits and Vegetables*]

## MANGOSTEEN (*Garcinia mangostana*)

I went into Fauchon's in the Place Madeleine in Paris one day via the fruit department. I always go in by that door because the moment you push it open paradise wafts towards you. No need for blue sea, palm trees, since the exquisite blend of guava and passion-fruit smells, pineapple, oranges, mango, cantaloup and charentais melons, figs, apples and perfect pears with tiny wood strawberries, provide an incomparable sweetness of distant places. The next move is to check on all the trays and punnets to see if there is anything I've never encountered before. There always is. On one visit it was a heap of purple-brown fruit, rounder than apples, but about the same size. They might have been carved from some dark unknown wood, each one finished with a top ruff of firm, rounded petal shapes. They had no scent at all. They played no part in the wafts of scent around them. I took advice – 'Mangoustans, Madame!' – and bought three for the family supper.

Away from the splendours of Fauchon, they looked drab. Sniffs all round. I said firmly, 'They are the most delicious fruit in the world!' The family thought I had been robbed.

With a sharp knife I cut into the firm shape, which was not as hard as it looked, and moved it round until a cap came off with those winged petal shapes. Inside was a jewel of plump, white, sectioned translucency, set in a case of glorious pink. As we admired it, the pink faded into a deeper deader tone, and I lifted out the small sections. Even thousands of miles from Malaysia, they tasted fragrant, unlike anything else except that the flesh had the consistency of lychees.

The most delicious fruit in the world? Yes, perhaps, in Malaysia – at any rate, off the tree, or from a market-seller's plaited tray in Thailand. To someone living in the British Isles I would judge the most delicious fruit would be a yellow raspberry direct from the cane on a warm day, or a William pear at the exact moment of perfection. But most of us have as much chance of these two experiences, or perhaps less chance, as of going one day to south-east Asia and eating a mangosteen in its perfection.

If such fruit, like others in this book, is to be savoured on its own, how should it be presented? Such things are not for casual eating. The dessert stage of a meal is, I suppose, the obvious occasion, the time for surprises and sheer pleasure when people are no longer hungry. Or it might go well in the late afternoon with wine, when friends call, and you can sit round a table talking.

[*Exotic Fruits and Vegetables*]

# TREATS AND
# CELEBRATIONS

ANYTHING JANE GRIGSON PUBLISHED was compulsive reading, the sort of prose that is enough on its own to create the faithful newspaper subscriber, no matter what might be thought of the rest of that week's edition, or to stimulate the special journey to the bookshop in the first week of publication. The reason for her great popularity and for the affection in which all her readers held her must lie in the fact that she never forgot, and her writing never concealed, her joy in friendship and companionship and the pleasures of the table that contribute to their enjoyment.

So when an occasion came round for a celebration, it was seized on; it did not always have to revolve around a formal holiday such as Christmas. There could be much more personal and incidental reasons for spontaneous rejoicing.

The upbringing that helped make Jane ever conscious of the need for value and for the economical use of ingredients did not in any way diminish her delight in the best, not to say the luxurious. The treats, Lucullan recipes and dishes for special occasions in this chapter round off the picture of someone whose actively enquiring mind and catholic tastes have their memorial in her marvellous range of articles and books.

# STARTERS

## CAVIARE AND OTHER HARD ROES

Caviare is a grand and painful subject. It is one of the most delicious, most simple things to eat in the world (and one of the most nutritious, too, but that's an academic point). It is also one of the most expensive. It has an air of mythical luxury – mythical to our modern experience at any rate. The food of Czars, of those incredible tyrants who cherished fine fat fleas and Fabergé knick-knacks, while most of their subjects lived in a poverty of indescribable squalor. The mainstay, along with champagne and oysters, of *La Belle Époque*. Odd that the caviare trade should never have been so efficiently organized as now, under the Soviets and their pupils in the business, the Iranians.

Another odd thing: caviare isn't a Russian word at all (it's called *ikra* in the USSR). It seems to be a word of Turkish–Italian origin, derived perhaps from the port of Kaffa, on the south-east coast of the Crimea, which had been important even in classical times. Under the Genoese, from the mid-thirteenth century, to the mid-fifteenth century when it fell to the Turks, Kaffa was a vast international port, a depot on the trade route to China.

The origins of caviare must be as difficult to trace as the word itself. Aristotle remarked that the sturgeon was prized for its caviare. The Chinese had developed methods of treating and trading in caviare as early as the tenth century A.D. Probably earlier, as they had long used refrigeration to protect delicate foods on journeys across China to the Emperor's court. Edward H. Schafer, Professor of Chinese* at Berkeley University, California, sent me this reference from the *T'ai pin huan yü chi*, a tenth-century official gazetteer, which says: '. . . at Pa-ling, where the Yangtze river flows out from Lake Tung-t'ing, an area also noted for its tea, the natives catch sturgeon, simmer the roe in an infusion of Gleditschia sinensis seeds (an acacia-like plant, normally used as a black dye), then pickle it in brine . . . extremely delicious!' It sounds like an early form of pasteurization.

I think, though, that one has to look much further back for the origins of caviare. Consider the reality, the basic nature of the product – really no more than the salted hard roe of a sturgeon. Once man came to the skill of being able to trap and catch fish, and to organize a supply of salt, he could not avoid the experience of caviare. Imagine

---

* Author of *The Golden Peaches of Samarkand*, a study of exotics imported into China in the T'ang dynasty; recommended to anyone who's interested in food, wine, spices etc.

him, squatting over a sturgeon by the mouth of some great grey river on the Baltic or North Sea, slitting up the belly and diving into the incredible mass of eggs – up to 20 per cent of the total weight – with a handful of salt. I'm sure he reflected gratefully that this part at least he could not smoke or dry for winter stores: it must have been a bonus in the hard realities of mesolithic survival. A crude affair by comparison with the finest *malossol* Beluga perhaps but still caviare.

Caviare today is a pampered product compared with those mesolithic feasts. It has to be, because of the problem of conveying a food, which should be eaten immediately, to the far-off societies that can afford it. We've killed our own sturgeon population, and have to look to the Caspian Sea, the only place where these vast creatures survive in any quantity. Even there they are in danger from Russian oil drilling, from hydro-electric stations and from the sinking level of the sea itself. There's also the problem of human greed, politely described as 'over-fishing'. Now, the Caspian sturgeon seek the southern rivers of the sea, the ones flowing down to the Iranian coast, for their spawning. The Iranians produce 210 tons of caviare a year, in consequence, which is not so far behind the Russians with 320 tons. They have learned everything they can, from Soviet technicians, about processing caviare, and about farming the fish, and with state control produce caviare of the highest standard. (The Rumanians produce tiny amounts – comparatively speaking – from Black Sea sturgeon; so do the Turks.)

The three main kinds of caviare are called after the species of sturgeon which provide them. The largest-grained and therefore most expensive (the price is based on appearance and not flavour) is taken from the Beluga, *Huso huso*, a giant sturgeon 4 metres (12 feet) long which can live to a 100 years, and which reaches maturity at the same age as a human being. It may – with luck – contain 59 kg (130 lb) of eggs, from deep grey to a soft moon-white. Next largest are the eggs of the Osetr, *Acipenser gueldenstaedtii*; they are sometimes golden-brown, sometimes greenish, or grey, and are first in flavour with people who know about caviare. The smallest-grained, and therefore the cheapest, comes from the Sevruga, *Acipenser stellatus*: it's the one most widely on sale, and the most reliably steady in flavour.

With these three divisions, caviare is graded. The finest is *malossol*, which means slightly salted. Any of the caviares are best eaten fresh, which is only possible in the largest towns: for the provinces, where trade is not brisk and conditions of storage less ideal, it must be pasteurized. The difference in quality is comparable with the difference between fresh and potted *foie gras* – or between fresh and pasteurized milk and cheese. To me pasteurization spoils the pleasure of eating these foods, because the elusive, vital flavour has been killed.

Caviare is exported fresh in 2-kg (4-lb) tins, which have been piled up with salted eggs. Sliding lids are placed on top, then gently pressed down at intervals so that all surplus brine is excluded. A rubber band is stretched round to make an air-tight seal. The tins travel in ice in refrigerated containers, to keep the caviare at the correct temperature of −1°C (30°F); one pamphlet observes that it is fatal to put caviare in the deep-freeze: 'it is reduced straightaway to a somewhat expensive soup!' An importer − such as W. G. White Ltd. on Churchfield Road in Acton − will re-pack it, sending fresh caviare twice a week to London's best hotels and grocers, and putting smaller amounts of pasteurized caviare into little pots, for distribution to delicatessen stores all over the country.

At their offices I was shown the most beautiful of gastronomic spectacles: a tray with three of these tins on it, opened, with a little bowl of Osetr caviare, and a pot of salmon caviare, often known by its Russian name of *keta*. The Beluga in one tin was silky in texture, and lightly delicious. The Sevruga in another tin had a more pronounced and sea-like flavour. The Osetr in the bowl had been pasteurized, so it was difficult to judge if it really was the finest of all: again, the taste was different. The salmon eggs were enormous, and a translucent vermilion. They were certainly the visual stars of the tray by comparison with the Quaker-greys and sombre greens of the caviare, but after the others they tasted bitter. The third tin contained a tacky seaweed-coloured substance, in which the form of the eggs could hardly be seen. This was pressed caviare, made from the damaged eggs of the various species of sturgeon, salted and impacted together. I liked the taste very much, and the slightly toffee-ish substance. Considering that the price is less than half the Sevruga, I recommend it as an ideal candidate for a first sampling of caviare. Everyone needs a celebration occasionally and I think it's worth saving up for caviare: the pressed kind is a possible extravagance for people whose incomes do not quite come up to their appreciation of food. Which, I think, means most of us.

Red caviare is so different. It's delicious enough, like a superior smoked cod's roe, but it's not in the same class as caviare proper. Neither is lumpfish caviare from Iceland or Denmark, which is dyed black like those tenth-century roes from the sturgeon of Lake Tung-t'ing (though not with *Gleditschia sinensis* seeds). They are not to be despised, but keep them for lesser occasions.

### To serve caviare
First of all, the amount − allow 30 g (1 oz) per person as a decent minimum, 45 g (1½ oz) is luxurious. Keep the pot in the refrigerator

until required, then place it on a dish and surround with ice. As nothing should impair the delicate flavour of this greatest of all luxuries, avoid wine and vodka. And do not be tempted to mix in some cream cheese to make it go further. All that is required is toast, or water biscuits, or rye bread, or – best of all – the buckwheat *bliny* on page 282.

So much for the finest quality. With lesser grades or pressed caviare, you could add unsalted butter for the toast or rye bread, or melted butter for *bliny*. Perhaps some sour cream as well, or lemon juice. Pressed caviare is delicious spread on small split potatoes, baked in their jackets and not larger than duck's eggs (unless you can afford a great deal of caviare).

When it comes to the 'caviare' of other fish, chopped spring onions, hard-boiled eggs, or cream cheese which has not been too processed, can all be added to make a large hors d'oeuvre. And when it's a question of following a recipe for home-made 'caviare', you can experiment as much as you like. Personally I like it quite on its own, too. It's very good, but I won't pretend that it compares with the finest Russian and Iranian product, which has transformed the slightly porridgey quality of hard roe into a most poetic texture.

[*Fish Cookery*]

## SWEETBREAD *VOL-AU-VENTS* (Bouchées à la Reine)

If you have to stretch a few sweetbreads (or use some left over from another meal), make these *bouchées à la reine*, which have no hint of frugality about them. Cold chicken is the meat often used, but I've noticed that sweetbreads are usually included. Sometimes they're the only meat used. These *bouchées*, these queenly mouthfuls, were named for Marie Leszczinska, gourmet daughter of Stanislaus Leszczinsky, King of Poland, and wife of Louis XV of France.

Should you feel disinclined to make puff pastry, bake shortcrust tartlets instead, or one large pastry case. Alternatively 5 cm (2 inch) thick slices of bread can be deep-fried (cut the crusts off, and hollow out the middle part to contain the sweetbreads first). The filling can be put into scallop shells or small pots, covered with buttered crumbs and set in a hot oven, or under the grill, until browned and bubbling. None of these will be *bouchées à la reine*, but they'll be appetizing all the same.

Serves 6

*12 baked* vol-au-vent *cases, or 1 large puff pastry case baked blind*
*300 g (10 oz) diced, prepared sweetbreads, or mixed sweetbreads and*
   *chicken*
*30 g (1 oz) butter*
*1 heaped tablespoon flour*
*300 ml (½ pt) sweetbread cooking liquor, hot*
*150 ml (¼ pt) hot milk*
*175 g (6 oz) mushrooms, sliced thinly*
*150 ml (¼ pt) double cream*
*salt, pepper, lemon juice*

Melt butter, stir in flour and cook for 2 minutes. Gradually
incorporate sweetbread liquor and milk. Simmer this sauce until it's
reduced to a thick consistency. Add the mushrooms, and cook for
another 10 minutes, then add the cream. Simmer again until the
sauce is thick without being gluey. Season well with salt, pepper and
lemon juice. Reheat the sweetbreads, or sweetbreads and chicken, in
the sauce carefully so that they don't disintegrate. Be sure to bring it
to the boil, then simmer for 5 minutes.

Meanwhile, put the *vol-au-vent* cases into the oven to heat up.
Arrange them on a serving dish and pour in the filling. Replace the
lids and serve immediately.

[*Good Things*]


## THREE KINGS SALAD

I make this salad after Christmas to go with cold ham, turkey and
spiced beef. It was first made in desperation when the salad greenery
had been finished and the shops were still closed. Now it is part of the
festival for us.

Serves 6

*4–5 slices Chinese cabbage*
*1 ripe avocado*
*½ a lemon*
*2 Chinese gooseberries (kiwi)*
*1 dessertspoon cider vinegar*
*4 dessertspoons hazelnut or sunflower oil*
*salt, pepper*
*60 g (2 oz) toasted hazelnuts or almonds*

*4–5 lychees*
*1 purple Italian onion or sweet Spanish onion*

Cut the cabbage about ½ cm (¼ inch) thick across the wide end. Rinse, drain and dry in a cloth. Put in the bottom of a salad bowl or deep dish.

Not too long before the meal, peel, stone and cube the avocado. Squeeze the lemon over it to prevent discoloration, then arrange in the centre of the cabbage. Peel and slice the Chinese gooseberries, putting the slices round the avocado. Pour on the vinegar and oil. Scatter lightly with salt, more generously with black pepper. Put on the nuts, then peel and cut up the lychees discarding the stones and arrange them on top. Finally cut a few very thin onion rings and put them between the lychees. Be careful not to overdo the onion.

Serve cool rather than chilled.

[*Fruit Book*]

# FISH

## LOBSTER WITH GRILLED OYSTERS (Aragosta Luculliana)

This grand recipe has been sent to me from Italy. At least I think it's grand, but I've a suspicion Lucullus would have thought it sadly simple. This Roman gourmet had a series of dining rooms, of increasing splendour. If he ordered dinner for ten friends in, say, the blue room, his slaves knew without further instruction that the meal was to cost £100. Other rooms meant far more. One day Lucullus was, exceptionally, dining at home without guests. The slave asked which room he would like the meal to be served in, expecting a £10 answer. Lucullus named the most expensive room of all.

After that, it may come as a surprise to you that the only ingredients demanded by this recipe are:

Serves 4

*2 lobsters*
*1–2 dozen oysters*
*12 tablespoons breadcrumbs*
*milk*
*8 tinned anchovy fillets*
*125 g (4 oz) butter*
*mustard powder, cayenne pepper, salt*

Split the boiled lobsters in half down the middle. Now ease the flesh, without removing it from the shell, as if you were cutting a grapefruit. (If the lobsters are alive, split them down the middle, dot them with butter and bake in a hot oven, gas 6, 200°C (400°F).)

Arrange the raw oysters, removed from their shells, along the cut sides of the lobsters; pour in the oyster juice. Moisten the breadcrumbs slightly with a little milk, squeezing out the surplus. Chop the anchovy fillets finely, mix into the bread and put this mixture over the oysters. Melt the butter, season it with mustard, cayenne pepper and salt. Brush this evenly over the breadcrumbs. Heat for 10 minutes under the grill, or in a very hot oven, to brown the crumbs and heat the lobster.

*Note:* I suspect this recipe was intended for crawfish, which lack the large claws of the lobster. For this reason, I usually remove all the lobster meat from claws and body and throw away the inedible bits. This leaves room in the shells for all or most of the lobster meat; if there is too much keep it for another dish.

[*Good Things*]


## SMOKED HADDOCK *KULEBIAKA*

This recipe, based on the Russian *kulebiaka*, makes a fine main course for a luncheon party. It's a rich, magnificent affair, so the rest of the meal should be light.

Serves 8–10

PASTRY
*500 g (1 lb) plain flour*
*250 g (8 oz) unsalted butter, chilled*
*90 g (3 oz) lard, chilled*
*1 teaspoon sea salt*
*iced water*

Put flour in a bowl, cut butter in small pieces, and put with lard into the flour. Add salt. Rub to a crumbly mixture, then bind with iced water. Divide in two, one part a little larger than the other, and refrigerate for at least 2 hours. Meanwhile prepare the filling.

FILLING
*750 g–1 kg (1½–2 lb) smoked haddock*
*½ litre (¾ pt) milk*
*150 ml (¼ pt) water*

*125 g (4 oz) long-grain rice or* kasha
*300 ml (½ pt) chicken stock*
*250 g (½ lb) mushrooms, sliced*
*125 g (4 oz) butter*
*lemon juice, salt, pepper*
*250 g (½ lb) onion, chopped*
*3 teaspoons dried dill, or 2 teaspoons curry powder*
*3 large hard-boiled eggs, chopped*

GLAZE
*1 egg yolk*
*1 tablespoon cream*

TO FINISH
*125 ml (4 fl oz) soured cream*
*250 g (8 oz) butter*
*lemon juice*

Cut haddock into several large pieces, and place in a saucepan. Bring milk and water to the boil, and pour over the fish. Stand it over a very low heat for 10 minutes: the liquid should not even simmer, just keep very hot. Remove skin and bone from drained, cooked fish and separate into large flakes (use cooking liquid for making a fish soup).

Cook rice or *kasha* (i.e. buckwheat, obtainable from health food shops – this is the correct cereal for *kulebiaka*, but I find the flavour a little strong and prefer rice) in the chicken stock and drain it.

Fry mushrooms in 30 g (1 oz) of the butter. Season with lemon juice, salt and pepper. In a separate pan, cook onion until tender in 60 g (2 oz) of butter: keep the lid on the pan, and the heat low, so that the onion does not brown. Season.

To assemble the pie, roll out the smaller piece of pastry to an oblong approximately 20 × 40 cm (8 × 16 inches). Place it on a baking sheet which has been buttered or lined with paper. Place half the rice on top, leaving a 2½-cm (1-inch) border free, and sprinkle half the dill or curry powder over it. Mix the glaze ingredients together and brush the free rim of pastry with it. On top of the rice put half the mushrooms, half the onions, half the hard-boiled eggs, and all the haddock. Then use up the remaining filling ingredients in reverse order, so that you finish with rice. Melt the remaining 30 g (1 oz) of butter and pour over.

Roll out the second sheet of pastry and drape it over the whole thing, pressing it down at the edges. Trim, then roll the edge into a piping effect, so that the whole *kulebiaka* looks like a pillow. Make a central hole, decorate top with leaves cut from the trimmings, and brush over to glaze with the egg yolk and cream. Bake 45 minutes, starting at gas 7, 220°C (425°F), then at gas 6, 200°C (400°F), as the pastry begins to brown.

Just before serving, bring sour cream to the boil and pour into the pie through a funnel placed in the central hole. Melt the butter, flavour it with lemon juice, and pour into a heated sauceboat. Have everything – serving dish, plates, and sauce – very hot.

*Note:* if you can lay your hand on some ceps, use them instead of mushrooms, allowing 375 g (¾ lb). The flavour will be even better.

### Salmon *Kulebiaka*

Serves 8–10

Substitute a generous pound of salmon for the smoked haddock in the preceding recipe. Slice it fairly thinly, and firm the slices in a little butter, but do not cook them right through.

Turbot (or sole) can also be used. The point is to have a fish of good texture and fine flavour.

[*The Mushroom Feast*]

# MEAT, GAME AND POULTRY

## BOEUF STROGANOFF

Originally the Stroganoffs were a family of tough and enterprising Russian merchants. After the conquest of Kazan in 1552, the Czar gave them huge grants of land in the Urals, which they colonized and exploited ruthlessly. Salt mines, iron and copper works, as well as the profits from trading and land, brought them riches and power until they became one of the great families of Imperial Russia. This recipe, from the end of the nineteenth century, was invented by the family's French chef and named in their honour.

It's a fine combination of French method and Russian ingredients. It also has the advantage of being quick and simple to prepare. Some versions of the dish, which has become so popular in Europe and America in the last few years, include tomato, and flour to thicken the sauce. I have even seen a suggestion that minced meat should be used. Such things are an insult.

Serves 6

*750 g (1½ lb) well-trimmed fillet steak*
*salt, freshly ground black pepper*
*125 g (4 oz) butter*
*2 tablespoons oil*
*500 g (1 lb) onions, sliced*
*500 g (1 lb) mushrooms, sliced*
*2½ teaspoons mustard powder*
*2 teaspoons sugar*
*600 ml (1 pt) soured cream*
*parsley, chopped*

Cut the meat into 6 mm (¼-inch) thick slices, then cut each slice into strips about 6 cm (2½ inches) long and 6 mm (¼ inch) wide. Season and set aside while the vegetables are cooked. Melt half the butter with the oil in a large frying pan, and cook the onions gently until they begin to soften without browning. Now raise the heat and add the mushrooms. By the time they are cooked without being too soft, the juices should have evaporated almost entirely, leaving the mixture moistened but not wet to the point of swilling. Keep mixture warm over a low heat. Mix the mustard and half the sugar to a paste with a very little hot water, and keep it by the stove. Now quickly fry the beef strips in another pan in the remaining butter (in two batches if necessary). They should brown in a few seconds, and not be allowed to overcook. Add them to the mushroom mixture, and stir in the mustard paste, then the sour cream. Correct the seasoning, and bring to just below boiling point. Turn into a dish and sprinkle with parsley.

The Russians serve *kartoplia solimkoi* with *boeuf Stroganoff*, in other words matchstick potatoes made in exactly the same way as chips – the only difference is that the potatoes are cut into thin pieces about 5 cm (2 inches) long and 3 mm (⅛ inch) wide and thick. Their crispness enhances the piquant creaminess of the beef in its mushroom and sour cream sauce.

[*Dishes of the Mediterranean*]

## LAMB EN CROÛTE WITH FRESH FIGS AND GINGER

Serves 4–6

*1 large loin of lamb, about 1¼ kg (2½ lb) before boning*
*1 stick of celery, roughly chopped*
*1 carrot, sliced*
*1 onion, unpeeled and roughly chopped*
*30 g (1 oz) butter*
*1 small leek, trimmed and chopped*
*5 fresh figs, finely chopped*
*2½-cm (1-inch) length of fresh ginger, peeled and finely chopped*
*30 g (1 oz) brazil nuts, chopped*
*15 g (½ oz) breadcrumbs*
*1 tablespoon fresh chopped parsley*
*salt*
*freshly ground black pepper*
*370 g (13 oz) packet of puff pastry*
*beaten egg to glaze*
*1 tablespoon sesame seeds*
*90 ml (3 fl oz) ginger wine*
*90 ml (3 fl oz) double cream*
*2–3 fresh figs*

Get your butcher to bone the lamb and ask for the bones. Preheat the oven at gas 7, 220°C (425°F) and brown the bones for 15 minutes. Place in a pan with the celery, carrot, onion and scant 1 litre (1½ pt) of water. Bring to the boil, reduce the heat and simmer for 2–3 hours, skimming off fat and scum when necessary. Strain, return to the saucepan and boil to reduce to 150 ml (¼ pt).

Melt the butter in a frying pan, add the leek. Fry for 5 minutes, then stir in the figs, ginger, brazil nuts, breadcrumbs, parsley and seasoning.

Place the lamb, skin side down, on a board. Spread the stuffing down the centre and roll up the meat, securing at 2½-cm (1-inch) intervals with string. Place in a roasting tin and cook at gas 7, 220°C (425°F) for 15 minutes. Drain off all but 1 tablespoon of the juices and set aside the roasting tin. Leave the meat to cool then remove the string.

Roll out the pastry thinly and brush the edges with beaten egg. Place the meat in the centre of the pastry and bring the pastry over the meat to enclose it completely, trimming off excess pastry at the ends. Transfer to a dampened baking tray with the join underneath.

Score a diamond pattern on the pastry, brush with beaten egg and sprinkle with sesame seeds. Cook for 15 minutes at gas 7, 220°C (425°F). Reduce the heat to gas 4, 180°C (350°F) and cook for a further 40 minutes for rare or 1 hour for medium, covering with foil if the pastry gets brown.

Towards the end of the cooking time, add the reduced stock, ginger wine and cream to the roasting juices in the tin and cook until the mixture thinly coats the back of a wooden spoon.

Slice the lamb and serve with a little of the sauce. Garnish each plate with half a fresh fig, cut in a fan shape.

[*À La Carte*]

## GAME FOR A CHANGE

Since the downfall of turkey into the freezing cabinet over the last couple of decades, many people have turned to alternatives at Christmas. Beef was the first obvious choice, a fine large piece of Aberdeen Angus that has been well hung being one of the best of life's edible experiences. Then poultry farmers turned to geese and alternative breeds of turkey that were closer to pre-war or much earlier birds. This year the alternative seems to be game – and I suspect that this has something to do with the lively British Deer Farmers' Association, as well as with the health lobby's discovery that game meat, being lean, is better for us.

There are people who enjoy the clear, rich, clean flavours of game, who have been eating it for years whenever they could afford it and who are happy that it is now easier to come by. Its new virtuous status is a bonus.

There must be a certain unease about game farming. It is inevitable when one tastes what has been done to trout, chicken and turkey, and quite a lot of salmon. Let us hope that the Association, and any other game-farming bodies, will be organized tightly enough to keep out the cowboys so that the results of game farming will be properly fed, decently slaughtered and wisely hung. Inevitably the result of a tamer life will be a tamer flavour, which of course will suit some tastes, perhaps even the majority at first. Let us hope that the general desire for blandness will not drive out the true wild game flavour that for many of us is a passion.

If you are not in the habit of buying game, the first thing to do is to find a proper game dealer (who may well be the fishmonger rather than the butcher). Buy game from someone who knows its history, who has an interest in selling you the real thing. And if by some ill luck you choose a tough bird, or the game given you was inadequate don't hesitate to go back. Make a polite but firm complaint, show willingness to try again.

Butchers are very much on the defensive these days – and so they should be. In this country we are badly served. Supermarkets have more than 50 per cent of the meat trade and vegetarians are increasing in number. No wonder when one sees the messy shops, tatty plastic trays, bloody overalls, badly hacked meat. Such reflections should give you the confidence to complain. Stand your ground. Cooking game is as simple as cooking any other form of meat. If you can manage that, you have no reason to let the butcher browbeat you by impugning your culinary skills in the matter of game. Per contra, when you are sold a particularly successful pheasant or haunch of venison, be ready with the compliments when you visit the shop next time.

The most obvious disadvantage of buying wild game is that some creatures survive more successfully in the wild than others. In the cossetted conditions of the deer or wild boar farm, they have an easier life and may often be in better shape (that, after all, is part of the point of domestication). Older and tougher game can be braised or stewed into wonderful dishes – all you need is full information on the right way to cook what you are buying. Prudence dictates, too, that you have a dummy run before Christmas lunch is upon you. You should also get your order in good time and choose a slack moment to discuss the matter with the supplier. Balance up beforehand whether you want to go for the clear intensity of wild game with its slight aura of risk, or the blander tranquillity of farmed deer or wild boar. I must add that my own experiences of farmed pheasant and partridge have not been happy; a Gressingham duck (a cross between mallard and a domestic breed) is a good half-way measure and more likely to appeal to a large family party than, say, mallard, teal or widgeon.

Books worth consulting: *Classic Game Cookery* by Julia Drysdale; *Game for All* by Nicola Fletcher; *The Game Cookbook* by Colin Brown.

[*Observer Magazine*]

## BREASTS OF WOOD PIGEON WITH LENTILS AND WILD RICE PANCAKES

A winner of a dish from Mark Slater, who is the young chef at Cromlix House, Dunblane, north-west of Edinburgh. They specialize in game there and this lovely earthy and smooth combination of flavours sets off pretty well any type of game, whether feathered or furred, roasted or pan-cooked in the magret style (try it too with domesticated or Gressingham duck magrets). The operations are straightforward and the effect unpretentious.

Serves 4

*4 wood pigeons, trussed, seasoned*
*oil*
*600 ml (1 pt) game or chicken stock*
*1 glass red wine*
*1 good sprig of thyme*
*5 crushed juniper berries*
*2 teaspoons redcurrant jelly*
*about 2 teaspoons arrowroot*
*salt, pepper*

LENTILS
*250 g (8 oz) dark brown or green lentils, soaked 12 hours*
*60 g (2 oz) lard*
*1 carrot, ½ onion, ½ leek, all cut in small dice*
*½ large clove garlic, finely chopped*
*2 teaspoons granulated sugar*
*300 ml (½ pt) chicken stock*

PANCAKES
*125 ml (4 fl oz) each double cream and milk*
*130 g (4½ oz) flour*
*2 eggs and 1 egg yolk*
*1 egg white, beaten until stiff*
*125 g (4 oz) wild rice, cooked*

Switch on oven to gas 6, 200°C (400°F), and preheat the grill.

Brown the pigeons on one side in a little oil for about 8 minutes, then turn them and cook the other side for 6–8 minutes. Cut off the breasts, which will be red on the inner side, and put them to one side. Chop the carcases and put with the stock, wine, thyme and juniper to simmer for 20 minutes, then increase the heat and reduce the liquid to about 300 ml (½ pt). Strain into a small saucepan, skim and stir in the redcurrant jelly over a low heat. Slake the arrowroot with a couple of tablespoons of cold water, and use it to thicken the sauce slightly. Season it with salt and pepper.

Meanwhile drain and cook the lentils for 3 minutes in boiling salted water. Tip them into a sieve, but do not refresh. Melt the lard in an ovenproof pot, stir in the diced vegetables and, when they are thoroughly coated, add the garlic, tomato, sugar and stock, then the lentils. Bring to the boil, then braise in the oven for 15–20 minutes. Taste for seasoning.

The batter for the pancakes can be made in the usual way and well in advance of the rest of the dish, but do not fold in the beaten egg white until just before cooking – which should be done immediately before serving. Brush four crumpet rings with butter inside and butter a non-stick pan. Put in the rings and heat up, then ladle a little batter into each ring. When the top begins to set and show bubbles, scatter a little wild rice on top. Range the pancakes on the rack of a grill pan. When everything else is ready and dished up, put the pancakes under the heated grill so that they puff up a little. Makes 12–16 pancakes.

While you make the pancakes, put the pigeon breasts into the oven in order to heat them through. They should be covered with a butter paper.

To serve: arrange the lentils on a hot serving dish, or on four warm plates. Slice the pigeon breasts into three pieces each, diagonally, and place them on the bed of lentils. Put the pancakes and any vegetables around the sides. Pour some of the sauce over the pigeon, and serve the rest separately.

[*Observer Magazine*]

## CIVET OF VENISON

A dish for a banquet, or at least for a meal of celebration.

Serves 8

*1½ kg (3 lb) stewing venison, diced and trimmed*

MARINADE
*375 ml (½ bottle) red wine*
*1 medium onion, sliced*
*3 tablespoons brandy*
*3 tablespoons olive oil*
*salt, black pepper*

SAUCE
*250 g (½ lb) streaky bacon in a piece*
*60 g (2 oz) butter*
*2 large onions chopped*
*1 large carrot, diced*

1 large clove garlic, crushed
2 tablespoons flour
beef or venison stock
bouquet garni
125 g (¼ lb) mushrooms, sliced

GARNISH
1 dessertspoon sugar
24 small onions (pickling size)
beef or venison stock
24 small mushrooms
8 slices of bread
chopped parsley

Mix the marinade ingredients together, seasoning them well, and soak the venison in it overnight. Next day, melt the butter (sauce ingredients) in a heavy pan, and brown the bacon in it, which you have first cut into strips about 2½ cm (1 inch) long and 6 mm (¼ inch) wide and thick. When the fat runs from the bacon, put onions and carrot and garlic into the pan to be browned lightly, then the well-drained venison. Stir the flour into the pan to take up the fat, and make a sauce by adding the strained marinade, plus enough stock to cover the ingredients (everything can be transferred to a deep casserole if this is more convenient). Add the *bouquet* and mushrooms, and simmer until the venison is cooked – about 1½ to 2 hours. Skim off any surplus fat. (The cooking up to this point may be done the day before the venison is to be eaten.)

Half an hour before the meal, prepare the garnish and reheat the civet if necessary. Melt 30 g (1 oz) of butter with the sugar in a heavy pan. Turn the small onions in this until they are well coated. Add just enough stock to cover them, and cook at a galloping boil. This will reduce the liquid to a spoonful or two of caramel. Be careful it doesn't burn, and keep shaking the onions about in it so that they are nicely glazed. Cook the mushrooms whole in 30 g (1 oz) of butter, with salt and pepper. Cut the bread into triangles, and fry in the last 60 g (2 oz) of butter.

Arrange the civet on a large hot serving dish, removing the *bouquet*, and put the mushrooms and onions on top pushing them down a little so that they look naturally part of the dish (but not too far so that they disappear). The croûtons go round the edge. Sprinkle with parsley and serve very hot.

[*Good Things*]

# CAKES AND PUDDINGS

## CHOCOLATE AND APRICOT CAKE (Rigo Jancsi)

In 1896 the young and far from innocent Princesse de Caraman Chimay ran off with a gypsy musician, Rigó Jancsi (meaning Johnny Blackbird), and set up house in Paris. No case of the raggle-taggle gypsies-O!, for the Princess Clara was the rich daughter of the richest, most illiterate landowner of north-west America (one paper described him as 'the millionaire muskrat catcher'), and there is no record that her distinguished Belgian husband ran after her. With her full lips 'like an open pomegranate', her white plump skin and her restless eyes, she had the look of a saint. Gypsy Johnny was thirty-eight. When he drove beside her through the Bois de Boulogne, her hand on his knee, he grinned 'till his strong white teeth showed under his moustache', a twirled moustache. She posed for photographs with a bicycle, like a saucy baker's boy – triangular hat pushed back, cigarette drooping from her mouth and a black velvet knickerbocker suit which showed off her legs in black silk stockings. Paris talked of little else – tut tut, my dear, did you ever? – and Toulouse Lautrec made a lithograph that exactly expressed the fair white Princess 'giving her favour and her purse to a little brown fiddler in the Hungarian band'.

The Hungarians were openly enchanted when their gypsy musician brought his princess home. Enterprising pastrycooks in Budapest made cakes in his honour. This one, with its pale plump filling, became a classic.

Makes 24 squares

CAKE
*6 egg whites*
*a pinch of salt*
*6 egg yolks*
*125 g (4 oz) sugar*
*2 level tablespoons cocoa*
*45 g (1½ oz) flour*
*melted butter, for greasing*
*½ pot apricot jam plus 1–2 tablespoons water*

GLAZE
*60 g (2 oz) dark or bitter chocolate, broken up*
*2 level tablespoons cocoa*
*100 g (3½ oz) sugar*
*4 tablespoons water*
*½ level teaspoon unsalted butter*

CHOCOLATE CREAM
*2 level teaspoons powdered gelatine*
*2 tablespoons water*
*60 g (2 oz) dark or bitter chocolate, broken up*
*300 ml (½ pt) double cream*
*300 ml (½ pt) whipping cream*
*175 g (6 oz) vanilla sugar*
*2 baking trays, about 27 × 37 cm (10½ × 14½ inches)*

To make the cake, whisk egg whites with salt and 1 tablespoon water until very thick and firm. Beat in the egg yolks one by one, beating all the time (use an electric beater if possible). Then add the sugar, beating it in thoroughly. Sift together the cocoa and flour. Sprinkle it round the sides of the egg mixture and fold it in carefully. Set the oven at moderately hot, gas 5, 190°C (375°F).

Line the baking trays with non-stick baking paper. Brush it with melted butter. Spread the cake mixture evenly in the trays and bake in the heated oven for about 15 minutes or until cooked.

Invert each tray over a clean cloth. Leave for 5 minutes, then remove the trays and peel away the paper. Warm the apricot jam with the water and, when it boils and begins to disintegrate, sieve it: brush over one cake.

Next make the glaze by melting the chocolate in a basin over simmering water (or the top of a double boiler). Remove the basin (or pan) and cool until tepid. Mix cocoa and sugar to a paste with the water, and add with the butter to the chocolate. Put back over simmering water and stir for 5 minutes. Pour over the chocolate cake without the apricot jam on it. Leave to cool until the glaze is firm. Trim the cake with a heated knife blade, then cut it carefully into 5-cm (2-inch) squares, without cutting completely through.

Make the filling. Mix the gelatine with the water. Put the chocolate, creams and sugar in a basin over simmering water (or the top of a double boiler) and heat until thick. Stir in the gelatine and remove the basin (or pan) from the heat. When the cream is almost set but just pourable, whisk it with a rotary beater until it holds a firm shape and becomes pale in colour. Use an electric beater only if you are good at controlling it: but be careful or the chocolate cream will turn to butter. Should it do this, chill the chocolate cream, then soften, and whisk in 125 g (4 oz) of unsalted butter, adding the cream gradually.

Spread this chocolate cream filling over the apricot-glazed cake. Chill until just about firm – not hard – and then carefully place the chocolate-glazed squares on top. Leave overnight – chilling again – then cut down between squares to separate the pieces.

[*European Cookery*]


## EASTER CAKE (Kulich)

This yeast cake is a little difficult to manage with the egg whites and peel and so on. I find it is best kept in a polythene bag between meals, or until you serve it, with *paskha*, so that it does not dry out too much.

The recipe below is based on the one in *Russian Cooking*, published by Mir in Moscow, 1974, and translated by F. Siegel.

*Kulich* is baked in tall, round moulds, so the dough rises and puffs up to give a 'chef's hat' effect. Use two large coffee tins if you do not have tall brioche moulds.

Serves 8–10

*600 g (1¼ lb) flour, sifted*
*1 packet Harvest Gold dried yeast*
*180 ml (6 fl oz) warm milk*
*¼ teaspoon salt*
*3 egg yolks*
*150 g (5 oz) sugar*
*3 cardamon seeds, crushed*
*150 g (5 oz) butter, softened*
*3 egg whites, stiffly whisked*
*75 g (2½ oz) raisins*
*25 g (scant 1 oz) each candied fruit and blanched almonds, chopped*
*blanched almonds, candied fruit and peel, chopped, or white glacé*
*icing (optional)*

Mix 250 g (8 oz) of the flour with the yeast in a mixing bowl, then stir in the milk. Put the mixture into a polythene bag, put in a warm place and leave till spongy and doubled in size – about 1 hour.

Then mix in the salt, 2½ egg yolks (set aside about half a yolk for gilding the *kulich* afterwards), sugar, cardamon and butter. Then add the egg whites and 250 g (8 oz) more flour. The dough will be on the wet and sticky side. Add the rest of the flour gradually until you get a dough that leaves the sides of the bowl. If it is a little sticky, do not worry too much. Put in a warm place and leave to rise again – about 2–3 hours this time.

Knock down the dough and add the fruits and almonds. Divide between two buttered and floured moulds; the dough should come half or two-thirds of the way up. Leave to prove – about 1 hour.

Set the oven at moderate, gas 4, 180°C (350°F).

Bake the *kulich* in the preheated oven for about 45 minutes. Check after 35 minutes, by inserting a cocktail stick or thin skewer, which should come out clean.

When ready, turn out and brush with remaining egg yolk and decorate, if you like, with chopped fruit and nuts, or icing, pouring it on so that it dribbles down the sides. Stick a candle in the top of each one if it is Easter.

[*European Cookery*]

# DRINKS

## BACHELOR'S JAM (Rumtopf)

This preserve which starts with strawberries is destined for Christmas and New Year parties. You need a 5-litre (9-pt) stoneware jar, or a special *rumtopf* from Austria or Germany which can sometimes be bought in this country.

Before you start, a word of warning. The method is easy, foolproof. The tricky part is the quality of the fruit. It must be of the finest, and preferably from a garden that you know has not been much subjected to sprays: in the opinion of one expert, whom I consulted after a batch had developed mould for no reason that I could see, it is difficult these days to make a *rumtopf* that you can rely on, and he is convinced that the reason is the chemical treatment that commercially grown fruit undergoes.

This poses a real dilemma with the required soft fruit. You can scrub an orange or an apple without harming it: a strawberry that becomes acquainted with water loses its virtue.

Another point to watch is the alcohol. Cheap rum and brandy sometimes means weaker rum and brandy.

If after these warnings, you decide to try your luck, this is what you do:

Prepare 1 kg (2 lb) of strawberries, removing their hulls. Sprinkle them with a ½ kg (1 lb) sugar and leave overnight. Next day, tip the whole thing, juice included, into a well-washed and dried *rumtopf*. Pour on 1 litre (1¾ pt) of rum (as in Austria and Germany) or brandy (as in France).

Put a clean plate directly on the fruit to make sure it stays below the surface. Cover the jar with plastic film and the lid. Keep in a cool dark place.

Add more soft fruit and sugar – half quantities are fine – as the summer progresses. Add more alcohol, too, from time to time to keep the liquid level up. It should clear the fruit comfortably. Remove and replace the plate each time.

Suitable fruits include:

> sweet and sour cherries (including stones), raspberries, logan-berries, boysenberries, mulberries, peaches, apricots, greengages, mirabelles (include an occasional stone), melon, pineapple (cubed), 1-2 apples and pears.

Although gooseberries, currants and blackberries can go in, they do tend to go hard and uncomfortable.

When the pot is just about full, top it up with a final dose of alcohol. Cover with fresh cling film, then the lid, and leave until Christmas, at least a month.

### To use

Serve in wine glasses with cream floated on top.

Serve as a sauce with ice creams, vanilla or honey for instance.

Mix with champagne, mostly the liquid with not too much fruit, for a cocktail.

Make a triangular build-up of boudoir biscuits, dipped in black coffee, glued together and covered with whipped cream that includes sugar and finely ground coffee – but not too much – and serve the *rumtopf* as a sauce.

[*Fruit Book*]


## CHERRY BRANDY

To make this in France, people go looking for deserted cottage gardens to find the old-fashioned *guignes*, the black and red cherries that we call geans. They make a superb liqueur, but the cherries are not much fun to eat. My grandmother, who was a great cherry brandy-maker, used Kentish Reds which are a Duke cherry; and her cherries were worth eating (except when they were twenty-five years old, by which time they were rather tasteless having given everything to the liqueur).

Whether in England or France or anywhere else, the method is the same. You fill a clean bottle or bottling jar almost to the top with cherries. Cut their stalks down to a tiny length first, then prick them several times with a darning needle and put them into the bottle as you go.

Pour in caster sugar to come about a third of the way up, then enough brandy to cover the fruit. Cork it up tightly, or close the bottling jar in the usual way.

Leave in a cool, dark place for as many years as you can bear to, or at least until Christmas. In time, the sugar dissolves. You can help it along by giving the bottle a gentle turn from time to time. Bottling jars can be turned upside down.

[*Fruit Book*]

# MENUS FOR SPECIAL OCCASIONS

## A CELEBRATION OF FRIENDSHIP

The Master of the Sunday Lunch died in 1988. Adey Horton had been much on my mind as I was preparing these articles. His life, at any rate his earlier life, was an improbable fiction, and it had an appropriate end. We had feared this winter for him, afraid he might collapse in the dark, on the gravel courtyard between the two caves where he lived. In fact he died quite suddenly at nine in the evening. Two friends were with him. This mysterious transplanted Englishman went sociably and in a more cheerful humour than one might imagine of a man with cancer of the mouth and throat.

He wrote to us about thirty years ago after reading a book of Geoffrey's, *The Painted Caves*, describing the strange village of Trôo. He found us a cave to rent there one summer, then a tiny house to buy (we were decidedly *entre deux vins* after a cheerful lunch, but never regretted the expenditure of £468). We owe him twenty-four years of that particular happiness which comes from learning to live in another country than one's own. Early on I asked him to write me a guide to charcuterie. Troubles prevented him. So I also have to thank him for a living (as I suppose my daughter Sophie does, too).

His humour was vast. He was a great story-teller, a devoted and assiduous, if occasionally exasperating friend, not gifted as a husband or father. His third wife once remarked with a wry smile, 'Adey collects people.' That indeed was his great gift, showing most splendidly in the organizing of Sunday lunch, an event that occurred almost daily in the summer months of July and August when the whole of France seems to be on holiday.

He showed us what this particular event could be, stretching its possibilities to their limit. There were introductions, matchmaking, reconciliations, the persuasion of children into civilized behaviour (keeping glasses filled, cushions at elderly backs, sticks to hand). Conversation was uninhibited, with great sky castles of fanciful specu-lation. With his wild mixture of local friends and farmers, Parisians, English, Americans, Africans, Australians, scholars, musicians and gypsies, jokes and opinions flew across the trestle tables that were set up in the courtyard, or in a small patch of woodland that he owned. Chains of friendship began with Adey's Sunday lunches.

The food was copious, contributory and mainly local. We grilled eels on a barbecue, or kebabs of miscellaneous pork. The meal began with the lavish charcuterie of the region. Salads followed the grill and cheese from the small farms of the Loir valley. To finish there was Pithiviers and *fromage frais*, or a splendid chocolate cake, peaches in wine, mirabelle and greengage tarts. Wine, marc and coffee – we never wanted it to end.

One day Geoffrey and I found a lost château in the Sarthe, at Sémur-en-Vallon. It had Rapunzel towers, green moat with sheep grazing, a ruined mill, the dusty romantic air of 'Le Grand Meaulnes'. We took Adey to see this discovery. 'When we win the pools,' said Geoffrey, who never did the pools, 'we'll buy this place and you can have a wing there and live in state – on condition that you superintend lunch on Sundays. Just the setting for the Master of the Sunday Lunch.'

From another friend in the last two years I have learnt a more urban and practical style of Sunday lunch. Theatre of a different kind. The secret is a leisurely progression of small courses, only one of which entails cooking on the day itself. Here is a menu:

Vegetable soup, say watercress
Roasted peppers in olive oil, with anchovy, dried tomatoes and basil
Duck stuffed with a guineafowl and wild rice, beans, potatoes
Green salad
Cheese, including a soft goat's cheese and preserves
Little pots of chocolate with rosemary, or a fruit salad

By the time we get to the biscuits and dessert wine, then the coffee, several hours have passed. We have laughed and argued and at no stage eaten too much. We are not allowed to wash up. Sometimes our host must grit his teeth as he smiles goodbye at seven in the evening, but he does not admit to it.

### Tartare of Salmon and Sea Bass

This has been a popular first course in France for several years now. I suspect it started off with the Minchelli brothers on the Ile de Ré where they opened a fish restaurant in 1963. Their strong suit has always been freshness, and ever since they moved to Paris early in the Seventies the quality of the fish has been the basis of their reputation at Le Duc on the Boulevard Raspail.

The first time we ate fish tartare it came in tiny heaps on minute tartlets with the aperitifs (alternating with fried quail's eggs, still warm, on toast stamped out neatly in circles). If you are not serving the almond tart later on, this is something to consider.

Another way is to serve it in well-chilled heaps on salad leaves, with very hot, rough-cut toast.

Even if you go for this latter, more generous serving, you still should keep the quantity small as the effect is very satisfying. 375 g (12–13 oz) is quite enough for 6–8 people, assuming a soup first and a main course afterwards: by this I mean trimmed weight, ready to cut up. Chill it thoroughly in the freezer to firm it up but don't let it freeze hard – this makes it easier to cut up.

Meanwhile make a mayonnaise in the usual way with a large egg yolk, 150 ml (¼ pt) light olive oil, lemon juice and pepper. To it add, according to your taste, chopped gherkin, small capers, a little anchovy fillet chopped, a splash of Tabasco and Worcester sauce.

Slice the fish ½ cm (generous ⅛ inch) thick. Then dice it. The effect should be of a coarse but well-disciplined chop. Mix in a little of the sauce tartare, say a generous teaspoon, then a second and a third. At this point you may well have added enough; the mixture should be lightly bound together with the sauce itself being obvious. Add appropriate fine chopped herbs. Chill until required, but do not keep it hanging around more than a couple of hours.

### Lindsey's Almond Tart

This tart is almost biscuit-like and goes well with fruit. For instance, peaches or nectarines poached in a light tea syrup, or, better still, Doyenné de Comice pears in a lemon and vanilla syrup, or a quince and vanilla syrup.

Serves 6–8

PASTRY
*125 g (4 oz) butter*
*150 g (5 oz) flour*
*1 tablespoon sugar*
*3 or 4 drops each almond and vanilla extracts*

FILLING
*150 g (5 oz) blanched slivered almonds*
*250 ml (8 fl oz) whipping cream*
*150 g (5 oz) sugar*
*a pinch of salt*
*1 tablespoon Grand Marnier*
*1 tablespoon Kirsch*
*2 drops almond extract*

Make the pastry well in advance. Cut up butter, let it soften to room temperature before cutting it into the flour and sugar (use a pastry blender or 2 knives). When it is a coarse meal, add the extracts and 1 tablespoon of ice-cold water. Form into a dough, then wrap in plastic film and chill for 1 hour at least. Use to line a 23-cm (9-inch) tart tin with a removable base, pressing it into place – it is a very tender dough, which makes it tricky to roll. Keep back a little for subsequent patching, and press the pastry so that it rises above the rim of the tin. Prick lightly and chill again for up to 8 hours or freeze.

Bake this shell in an oven preheated to gas 6, 200°C (400°F) for about 10 or 15 minutes, until it begins to be firm and start browning. Remove and cool. Patch any holes with the dough you kept back.

For the filling, mix all the ingredients in a pan and stir over a low heat until the sugar has dissolved and the whole thing glistens – 10–15 minutes. Cool slightly and spread over the pastry.

To bake, line the floor of the oven with foil, set the heat to gas 4, 180°C (350°F). Give the tart 25–30 minutes in mid-oven. The filling may well bubble over, then it calms down and starts to caramelize. For an even colour, turn the tart regularly during the last 15 minutes of cooking time. When baked, remove and cool to room temperature before slicing.

[*Observer Magazine*]

## PICNICS

It might be sensible to give recipes for oxtail stew and vacuum-cooked rice pudding, since we are considering picnics in May, but decency compels a certain optimism on my part. That is the convention. It is indeed odd that a nation whose weather is so unpredictable should be such ardent and accomplished picnickers.

Some of my happiest moments in childhood were spent crouching in the lee of a northern stone wall, cooking spring nettles in an old toffee tin on a reluctant fire, rain crashing down with the warm insistence of Lake District weather. Even better were the days we huddled together for warmth in the great shadow of Pavy Ark by the tarn, teeth chattering their way through sandwiches of the wartime national loaf and Lancashire cheese. We picked our dessert of bilberries as we walked on up to the Langdale Pikes. My husband remembered picnics with his brothers on the top of church towers or the platform of old pollarded willows – they hauled up a primus for making tea, and ate gingerbread from the village shop.

Indeed, my husband was a Master of Picnics. He would drive on until teatime before he found a site worthy of the feast that he knew Sophie and I would have assembled. By the time he stopped the car, we would be more than crotchety. Then, seated 2 m (6 feet) up on top of a dolmen, or settled down into nests of thrift on a sea cliff, we had to confess he had been right. Once we even cooked our *andouillettes* by a railway track beside the canal at Saint Denis, north of Paris: the writhing sculptures of dying kings and queens in the cathedral afterwards were almost an anticlimax after the hoots of friendly laughter and the roars of 'Bon appetit!' Before country journeys, we would examine maps through a magnifying glass to discover fords, wonderful but sadly disappearing places.

Our last picnic, like so many earlier ones over the years, was to the high stony Causses near the gorges of the Tarn. We were in search of those flat rosette thistles that people thereabouts nail to their doors to tell the weather (they open to the sun, close to the rain). And we found them in abundance, enough for all our doors, close to a huge rocky chaos that from the distance looked like a town. We drove up steep roads and tracks:

> *Through dandelion grasses, then rippling of fords,*
> *Climbing to a dry karst slowly; through butterflies, past*
> *Debris of picnics, stones of the executed, and through junipers.*

Geoffrey wandered off to discover flowers and pick my juniper berries, while I set up table and chairs, spread out the food in that brilliant light.

In a way, food doesn't matter a damn, so long as it is of top quality, has an edge to it rather than sloppiness, and is accompanied by an element of liquidity. This can be plenty of fruit, plus fizzy and still water with home-made fruit syrups and cordials. For an evening picnic, a chilled – or boiling hot – soup is a good idea. And wine, especially champagne or white wine and soda water. Indeed, wine is what dramatizes the occasion for me; after those wartime childhood picnics which had to depend for their glamour entirely on the landscape, wine is essential, though being the driver as a rule these days, I drink very little of it. After wine and fruit, provide good bread. Then all you need is a lively spread, which need only be unsalted butter, coarse salt and celery or fennel. Cheese and a fine salami or ham on the bone are obvious embellishments, so is asparagus at this time of year with eggs mollets or Chinese tea eggs. Anything beyond that is a bonus, and certainly once the word picnic hovers in the air as the week ends, I do make one or more of the following dishes, and work out what we might be able to pick up along the way.

Always have a picnic kit ready, so that you can concentrate on food and drink once somebody says, 'Let's have a picnic today,' viz:

cutlery, corkscrew and bottle opener in a zip pencil case
stainless steel beakers, or very firm plastic beakers
plastic plates on which you can rest paper plates (saves washing up and smells in the car)
a roll of plastic bags for rubbish, left-overs and booty (mushrooms, bilberries, blackberries, fossils)
moisturized squares, intended for wiping up babies
an attractive cloth to set the food on
matches, salt, sugar, peppermill, tea bags
insect spray and Moon Tiger coils (especially for evening picnics)
kitchen roll or tissues
Elastoplast and a cologne stick for infant hurts and fatigue
tiny folding picnic stove, slug pellets to burn and picnic pans

This all sounds cumbersome, but it packs up quite tidily.

Of course, if you go in for High Life picnicking, you will have a fitted basket of porcelain, silver and linen. And somebody, I hope, to carry it. One friend remembers picnics of this kind in the Highlands when she was a child in the Thirties. It was the chauffeur's job – how appropriate – to warm up the soup over a stove. Her grandmother sat out of the drizzle under a large umbrella, while the children kept off the midges with oil of citronella and waving ferns.

## Picnic Bread

This flat bread, in the style of *focaccia*, is particularly handy for picnics. Just slit it with a sharp knife and it is ready for people to make their own sandwiches. If the rest of the meal has a reasonably starchy element, there will be enough bread for 8.

*500 g (1 lb) bread flour*
*1 packet (2 teaspoons) Harvest Gold or easy bake yeast*
*2 teaspoons fine salt*
*2 tablespoons olive or nut oil or melted butter*
*about 250 ml (8 fl oz) water at blood heat*
either *2–3 cloves garlic, crushed, chopped*
or *½ teaspoon each aniseed, coriander seed and peppercorns, well but coarsely ground*
or *24 fine black or green olives, stoned, chopped*
or *60 g (2 oz) chopped* prosciutto crudo
or *1 medium chopped onion, sweated in oil until soft, and mixed with coarsely chopped walnuts*
*olive oil, coarse salt, thyme*

Mix half the flour with the yeast and salt. Add the oil or butter and most of the water. Mix to a thick batter. Leave 20 minutes, until fermented and bubbling, then add the remaining flour to make a soft, almost tacky consistency. The dough should be extremely malleable, on the verge of sticking. With some flours, you may need the last of the water. Knead electrically or by hand. Pick up the dough in one hand, pour a little oil into the bowl with the other. Turn the dough in this so that the bowl is oiled as well. Stretch clingfilm across the top, or tie into a plastic bag, and leave in a warm place for 1½–2 hours.

Punch the dough down, mix in one of the flavourings, or none, and put back in the bowl. Cover as before and leave in the refrigerator overnight.

In the morning, brush out a baking tray 36 × 26 × 3 cm (14½ × 10½ × 1¼ inches) deep with olive oil. Pat out the dough to fit, or roll it and put it into the tin. Snip the top in decorative rows with the scissors. Scatter with coarse salt and thyme. Tie into a plastic bag, leave to prove for at least 40 minutes. Switch on the oven to gas 9–10, 250°C (500°F). Bake the bread for 20 minutes, turn it over and give it another five. Brush the top lightly with oil for the gloss, and leave to cool. Best eaten the same day.

## Rice and Tunny Salad

One of the staple dishes of summer cookery in our Loir and Loire country in France. The food there is gentle and classic, the kind that makes one think of picnic lunches in the orchard. The proportions given by Boulestin are so close to ours that I am reminded that he came from Poitiers, in the southern part of our region. Of course they can be varied: according to taste, pocket and the rest of the meal, there will be more or less tunny and tomato to rice.

Serves 8

*250 g (8 oz) cooked long-grain rice*
*2 tins of tunny in oil, broken up with a fork*
*4 medium tomatoes, skinned, pipped, finely chopped*
*6 fillets of anchovy, chopped, or 30–50 g (1–2 oz) black olives,*
    *stoned, chopped*
*chopped parsley, chervil and tarragon to taste*

Mix the above ingredients together in a bowl. Dress with a vinaigrette consisting of ⅔ olive oil and ⅓ wine vinegar (rather more vinegar than normal), salt, pepper and a little Dijon mustard.

## Spring Salad

A fresh and delicately lively salad, a contrast to the strong and savoury pepper recipe on page 427. Particularly good with the duck legs, or with slices of ham on the bone. If you are also making the tunny salad, leave out the new potatoes.

Cook 375 g (¾ lb) new potatoes, the same weight of shelled peas and 175–250 g (6–8 oz) mange-tout or sugar snap (jacket) peas – keep the latter on the crisp side.

Meanwhile make a dressing of olive oil, wine vinegar, chopped mint, a pinch of sugar, pepper and salt. Cut up the potatoes and add them while still warm to the dressing, plus the warm peas, turning gently. Cool the mange-tout or sugar snap peas separately.

Line a bowl with salad leaves. Put in the potato and shelled pea salad, draining off any surplus dressing, and lay the mange-tout or sugar snap peas on top with chopped chives or spring onions. Crumbled crisp bacon is an alternative to the onion flavouring.

## Paul Bailey's Pepper, Anchovy and Basil Salad

When he is fed up with novels, broadcasts, reviews, Paul Bailey has
the endearing habit of making exotic preserves and lively dinners for
his friends. He is incapable of walking past a market stall of plums or
red peppers without stopping, it's his secret vice, and like a punter he
ends up with nothing as he gives it all away. This dish is a kind of
preserve as it improves with being made in advance, and has an
intense flavour. Indeed if you make it in a large enough quantity, it
could provide a picnic in itself so long as you take bread – *focaccia*, for
instance, or some other Italian bread – and wine as well.

Carapelli put up a good preparation of dried tomatoes in olive oil,
called *Le Delizie della Tavola*. Alternatively soak dried tomatoes in
water until they begin to be tender and plump: do not leave them
until they are sodden.

Serves 8

*4 large peppers, halved, seeded*
*5–6 tins anchovy fillets*
*milk*
*about 12 dried tomatoes, halved*
*olive oil, pepper*
*several good sprigs of basil*

Grill pepper halves, cut-side down, until black and blistered. Lay a
folded tea towel over the top and leave for 30 minutes, then skin and
cut into strips. Soak the drained anchovy fillets (keep the oil) in milk
for 1 hour, then drain and cut lengthways in half.

Layer peppers, anchovies and tomatoes into a deep refrigerator box
with a close-fitting lid. Pour over the anchovy oil, then enough olive
oil to cover generously. Pepper well. Cover the box, and store in the
refrigerator for 6 hours or up to 5 days.

Before setting out on the picnic, taste and add more pepper. Then
tear basil leaves over the top, and put back the lid firmly. The dark
reds and chestnut-brown colours make a beautiful sight in contrast
with the basil and it is a delight to dip bread into the rich and
appetizing oil, as you eat this lively salad.

## Duck or Chicken Legs with Apple Mayonnaise

The simplest way of transforming meat, poultry and – above all –
fish, is to season them well in advance of cooking. The effect of this

mild curing is astonishing, and savoury out of proportion to the forethought required.

Serves 8

*8 duck or chicken legs*
*2 large juicy cloves of garlic, halved, crushed*
*4 teaspoons salt*
*2 teaspoons black pepper*
*¼ teaspoon nutmeg, mace or* quatre-épices
*1 large bay leaf, cut into fragments*
*1 teaspoon thyme leaves*
*goose, duck or chicken fat or lard*
*large sprig of thyme (see recipe)*

Rub poultry all over with the garlic. Mix salt and seasonings and rub over the pieces, especially on the cut side. Cover and leave in the refrigerator overnight. Next day put into a heavy pan, cover with melted fat or lard and, in the latter case, add the thyme sprig. Include any bits and pieces of bay leaf, etc.

Bring to the boil, reduce to a simmer and leave uncovered until the legs are cooked, about 25 minutes for chicken, 45 minutes or longer for duck, depending on your interpretation of the word *simmer*. The legs should be lightly browned: should they be on the pale side, colour them by dry-frying in a non-stick pan. Drain well and serve tepid or cold. On other occasions they are delicious served hot.

*Apple mayonnaise*: mix together an equal quantity – say, 150 ml (¼ pt) each – of firm apple purée and mayonnaise made with groundnut or sunflower oil, and lemon juice, or a mild white wine vinegar. This sauce needs a slight discordance to give depth, so add a final seasoning of grated horseradish, *wasabi* or mustard.

## Meat Loaf (Polpettone)

Elizabeth David's *polpettone* – meat loaf – from *Italian Food* makes ideal picnic food. It tastes good and looks beautiful when sliced to show the centre. In Florence, where *polpettone* is a great domestic speciality, it tastes best when made with veal and beef: here veal and pork give a better result. The traditional method of cooking is to brown the roll of meat, then braise it in wine and stock either on top of the stove or in a low oven: in her gloriously illustrated and amplified new edition of *Italian Food*, Mrs David suggests baking it in a rectangular loaf tin or terrine which makes it even more practical for a picnic.

Serves 8

*500 g (1 lb) each raw minced veal and pork, or veal and beef*
*4 eggs*
*1 clove garlic, crushed and finely chopped*
*1 finely chopped onion*
*a handful of parsley, chopped*
*pepper, salt*
*2 hard-boiled eggs*
*60 g (2 oz) cooked ham*
*60 g (2 oz) Provolone or Gruyère cheese*

Mix ingredients down to and including pepper and salt, using your hands. Coarsely chop and mix together the three remaining ingredients.

Set the oven at gas 2, 150°C (300°F). Line a loaf tin or rectangular terrine with greaseproof or baking parchment, brushed with a little melted butter.

Pat out the meat mixture into a square the length of the tin or terrine, on a lightly floured board. Put the chopped mixture down the centre and bring the meat mixture up and over it, forming a big sausage shape. Lower it into the tin or terrine, lay a butter paper on top and bake for about 1½ hours, removing the paper after 1 hour for the top to brown. Serve cold for a picnic (usually this dish is eaten hot, perhaps with a sauce made from tomatoes, but it tastes even better cold).

## Chinese Tea Eggs

Boil eggs for 6 minutes, drain and tap them lightly all over with a spoon to crack them. Fragments of shell may drop off, but try to avoid this. Put back in the pan. Cover with cold water. Add 2 tablespoons orange pekoe tea, 2 teaspoons salt, 2 tablespoons dark soya sauce and, if you like, a generous pinch of aniseed. Simmer gently for 1 hour, covered. Remove and leave to soak in the water for a few hours if possible (1 hour will, in fact, do). Remove and drain the eggs. Shell them at the picnic, when people will discover to their delight the most beautifully marbled patterns on the white. Inside the eggs are creamy.

## Tomato and Oatmeal Tart

This dish, one of the few I can claim to have invented, is a particular favourite of vegetarian friends. The tomato sauce and the pastry can be made in advance.

*125 g (4 oz) each flour and rolled oats*
*125 g (4 oz) butter, or mixed butter and vegetarian fat or lard*
*1 egg*
*¼ teaspoon salt*

FILLING
*1 medium onion, chopped*
*1 clove garlic, finely chopped*
*60 g (2 oz) butter*
*500 g (1 lb) ripe tomatoes, skinned, seeded, chopped*
*tomato concentrate or cayenne or finely chopped chilli or* harissa
*1 large egg*
*half-and-half or single or soured cream*
*1 heaped tablespoon grated Parmesan*
*30–60 g (1–2 oz) grated dry Cheddar*
*thyme*

Make pastry in the usual way, line a 23-cm (9-inch) tart tin, prick the base with a fork and bake blind at gas 5, 190°C (375°F), until set firm but not coloured – approximately 10 minutes.

Meanwhile make a reduced and pulpy tomato sauce by softening the onion and garlic in the butter, then adding the tomatoes and boiling them down. Season to taste with concentrate or hot seasonings, and salt. Spread on the pastry case.

Break the egg into a measuring jug, add enough cream to bring it up to 150 ml (¼ pt), and beat in the Parmesan and 30 g (1 oz) Cheddar. Season and pour over the tomato.

Top with a lattice of twisted pastry strips, or with 30 g (1 oz) grated Cheddar and a scatter of thyme. Return to the oven for about 25 minutes until the top is firm and lightly browned.

## Dessert

There can be no better finish than a fresh goat or sheep cheese and a basket of berries to go with it. If you live in Edinburgh or the southern outskirts of Glasgow, a picnic into the gentle country below these two towns might provide you with a slice of Humphrey

Errington's Lanark Blue that goes down so well with celery or crisp salad leaves, a hunk of bread and a glass of red or white wine (Casanova had a passion for Chambertin with Roquefort which the Lanark Blue so resembles, but something less glorious will do perfectly well).

Melons stuffed with strawberries are a delightful and transportable dessert. Choose a couple of large melons for 8 people (orange-fleshed ones tend to have most flavour), buy a pound of strawberries as well and 3 or 4 passion fruit. At home, remove lids from the melons with a zigzag Vandyke cut. Scoop seeds into a sieve over a bowl. Heat the juice with 4 tablespoons sugar and the pulp of the passion fruit. Do not let it boil for more than a second. Hull and halve the strawberries and add them to the tepid syrup, turning them over and over. Leave to cool. Pack into the melons and tie them tightly into plastic bags or wrap in clingfilm. Don't forget to take a serving spoon to dislodge the melon pulp from the skin.

[*Observer Magazine*]

## THE SPIRIT OF CHRISTMAS

One of my earliest memories is of my father singing at Christmas *Adeste fideles, Laeti triumphantes*. He had a lovely tenor voice, clear, unaffected, warm and joyful. It burst from him, escaping his local government official envelope of striped grey trousers, black coat, even spats (when I was very young), with a vigour that makes me wonder what emotions were held back, deep inside, by the dam of his normal disciplined behaviour. He is ninety-two now (1988) and cannot sing anymore, but I still lack the nerve to probe this particular mystery.

He sang loudly in his (cold) bath. He sang at the weekends, taught us songs, while our mother played the piano. Above all, he sang at matins when we formed a demure, tidy row in church, about twelve rows back from the choir. Nobody else in the congregation sang very much. They were too refined. He didn't care. I suspect he didn't notice, but if we were silent, he would glance at us in a pained way, wondering if perhaps we might be coming down with something.

As a young man he had sung in church choirs and knew how to stress the psalms as they were chanted. 'My heart is inditing of a good matter ... Full of grace are thy lips ... My tongue is the pen of a ready writer ... O praise God in His Holiness, praise Him in the firmament of His power ... Let everything that hath breath prai ... ai ... ai ... aise the Lord!' And come Christmas, he taught us how to pronounce choral Latin. '*In dulci jubilo*. Now sing we all io, io ...

Our heart's joy reclineth *In praespio!*' emerged from our infant throats without a stumble or inaccuracy.

Looking back now, I see that the greatest gift he gave me was not the rules for a good life, so sweetly and earnestly instilled, but the unconscious acceptance that music and poetry, especially in combination, are the greatest of man's achievements. At every season, in every event that marks my life, that feeling is there. Words and music well up, comfort, companionship, pain and delight.

And so it is that we have always begun our Christmas in my father's way – with carol singing, which by a strange coincidence, for his character was very different, happened to be my husband's way. Our Christmas bears no relation to the old rollicking festivities of the distant past, and not even a very close relationship to the Christmas that was invented in Britain by the Victorians. Christmas tree, wreath for the front door, decorations never make an appearance until three o'clock on Christmas Eve. We switch on the radio and wait in a tense hush for that first pure note of the boy's voice in *Once In Royal David's City* from King's College Chapel.

My father was at Cambridge. So was I. So were all of my husband Geoffrey's family from the sixteenth century to his generation, when he and his brothers broke the rule and went to Oxford. As the choir comes nearer and we hear the red and white robes swishing gently to the sound, we are glad we are busy. That way we can disguise our tears as the chaplain reads the Bidding Prayer, reminding us of those who rejoice in a greater light and on a farther shore.

That is Christmas, our private but universal start. Our public start in the Wiltshire village of Broad Town is a more hilarious affair, the arrival of the local choir singing carols, greatly augmented by the children from the school, sundry parents, and cheerful hangers-on. For about ten years it was organized by a witty, literate, and musical priest, our vicar, now regrettably called to higher things in a grand parish close to Salisbury Cathedral.

One year he persuaded a farmer to clean the dung from his tractor so that a living Nativity tableau could be driven around the village from house to house. Mary sat on a bale of straw, lurching slightly. She clasped not the latest addition to the community, but a big baby doll with a wobbly halo. Joseph clenched his teeth as he tried to keep upright, clinging to a lantern. When they came to our house, everyone rushed to the door. The two protagonists were quite forgotten. It took a few unholy Wiltshire shrieks before they were helped down over the huge wheels and ushered to the front of the choir that by now was two verses into *Hark! The Herald Angels Sing*.

We stood in the open doorway, welcomed them as best we could.

The children rushed into the candlelit hall to see what this place offered to eat and drink. The grown-ups sat down. Cakes, biscuits and other treats were handed round as decorously as anyone could wish. The more daring children sipped a little mulled wine, but soon turned back to orange and lemon squash. The candles guttered, their light catching the raisins in the Christmas cake.

One memorable year our carolling was even on television, nationwide. To make a talking point – we were one small item in a food magazine programme – I had used Mrs Beeton's mincemeat for the mince pies. An excellent recipe with rump steak in it, as well as the more usual beef suet. One small neighbour, the cheekiest boy in the village, decided to tease us. The cameras homed in on him. He bit into a mince pie, wrinkled his nose, laughed at me, and said, 'dis-gus-ting'. Which gave life to what might otherwise have been a boring interlude for those inhabitants of Great Britain who did not have the good fortune to be acquainted with the 570 souls of Broad Town parish.

When everything was eaten up, and *Silent Night, Holy Night* sung, as always, at my husband's request, the BBC team began to take down their tripods and pack up their equipment. The last little girl emerged from the loo. The vicar shooshed his flock to the door. Bidding us goodbye he swung his long black coat into place, adjusted the silver clasp, and called back over his shoulder, 'Count the spoons! You never know what I may have concealed about my person!' A shame that this best of all priestly exits was uttered off camera.

General advice for entertaining carollers: keep everything as small as possible, so that it is easy to eat without crumbs everywhere. Don't try to be original. In my experience, clever food is not appreciated at Christmas. It makes the little ones cry and the old ones nervous.


## A MEDITERRANEAN CHRISTMAS

About this time of year, in 1978, we found ourselves in Crete, and for a few days under the wing of Johnny Craxton, the painter, an old friend of my husband's. On one jaunt he took us up into the hills above Chania to visit a family he knew well. After the hospitable preliminaries, we were shown round the white-walled nest of a house, a tiered dovecot of a house round a courtyard, goats and chickens, hay and sacks of provisions below, humans above, with cheeses, herbs and home-made soap drying on the ledges of every windy aperture.

The men had just come home with the new-pressed olive oil, green-gold and thick. It was, they remarked, so welcome at that time of year. Why, I asked? Advent of course, a season of fasting for them, no meat, no eggs. On oil, olives, vegetables, fruit and bread, they got themselves into physical as well as spiritual trim for Christmas. I hope they ate fish, but milk, cheese and butter were out.

In that sunny world, citrus orchards laden with fruit, sweet-smelling narcissi wild in the fields, huge quinces and apples in the market, a lean diet seemed tolerable. No wonder the Greek Orthodox Church maintains a fast that our more northerly churches have long abandoned. In recent years, though, it has become easier to eat a lean diet and many of us find ourselves doing so instinctively at this time of year. So in deference to that wise Orthodoxy, I have chosen a meal that in its ingredients is a reminder of the Eastern Mediterranean where Christmas began.

The soup is made with red onions and red wine, earthy and substantial without being heavy. The main course is lamb, the celebratory meat of the Mediterranean, quite outside our Christmas menus that have centred on goose, turkey, pork and beef. The *ragoût* combines one very antique, biblical vegetable, the leek, with the aubergine that only arrived from south-east Asia and India via the Arabs in the thirteenth century.

The dessert is a favourite of ours, an unsweetened sheep's milk junket that we first encountered in northern Spain, served in tall, 150 ml (¼ pt) pots of glazed rough earthenware. You could substitute Channel Island cow's milk, though it lacks the dazzling white richness of sheep's milk. This is eaten with alternate mouthfuls of ripe, translucent persimmon, a fruit that came to the Mediterranean this century from Japan. Sharon fruit, the milder, tannin-free variety that can be eaten when firm, may be served instead, but it cannot match the true persimmon for flavour.

To tell when a persimmon is ripe for eating, cradle it in your hand: it should feel like a jelly held in place – just – by the skin. If it is still firm, its tannin will pucker your mouth. Once at the right stage, persimmons can be stored in the lowest part of the refrigerator for a day or two.

The persimmon has become a favourite Christmas fruit of Italy, where its orange globes ripen on bare branches long after the leaves have fallen. A pity the Three Kings are not still around: its beauty and splendour would have gone well with their jewelled images.

## Red Onion and Wine Soup

Start by making a herb stock, which can be done 1–2 hours in advance. Simmer together, for 25 minutes, 1¾ litres (3¼ pt) water and 1 scant teaspoon of salt with several branches of fresh thyme or

1 teaspoon dried thyme, 8 branches parsley, 3 bay leaves, 3 cloves of garlic, all tied into a muslin. Finally, remove the bag, squeezing out the liquid, and keep until required.

Serves 8–10

*1 kg (2 lb) red onions*
*a well-flavoured olive oil*
*4 cloves garlic, chopped*
*½ teaspoon coarse salt*
*500 g (1 lb) can chopped tomatoes, plus 2 or 3 fresh tomatoes, skinned,*
*    seeded and chopped*
*250 ml (8 fl oz) Beaujolais or other full-bodied red wine*
*salt, pepper*
*2–3 slices of baguette per person, or thick slices of a more*
*    interesting bread*
*fresh thyme leaves*

If the onions are large, quarter them. If medium to small, cut them in thirds. Then slice thinly. Stir them in a large soup pot with 4–5 tablespoons olive oil over a low heat. When they are coated, leave to stew down slowly, about 30 minutes in all, stirring occasionally.

Pound the garlic with the coarse salt, then stir it into the soft onions with all the tomato and about a mugful of the herb stock. Add ½ teaspoon salt, cover and stew 15 minutes. Add the wine and boil vigorously without a lid to reduce to a slack purée. Pour in the remaining stock, half cover and leave to simmer 25 minutes. Check seasoning, adding pepper.

Brush the bread with oil and bake until nicely browned in a moderate oven. Put into 8–10 bowls, ladle on the soup. Add a little olive oil to each and sprinkle with fresh thyme. Alternatively, you could just serve the bread with the soup, or half and half. The slices should end up crisp all through, and thick.

## Aubergine and Leek *Ragoût*

One hot afternoon the Hodja, the divine fool of Islam, of whom many stories are told, sat down sleepily under a walnut tree at the edge of a field of purple aubergines. As he dozed off he wondered why God in his infinite wisdom had caused aubergines to grow at ground level and walnuts high on trees of great height: surely they would be easier to harvest the other way round? A little later he was woken by a walnut falling on his head. 'Now I understand.'

For this dish choose aubergines of a size you would not care to have landing on your head. Peel them or not as you please.

Serves 6–8

*4 medium-sized aubergines*
*salt*
*the white part of 4 leeks*
*olive oil and butter*

Dice and salt the aubergines. Leave for 1 hour, then drain, rinse if too salty, then dry. Slice leeks into matchstick shreds. In a large sauté pan, cook aubergine until meltingly tender in oil. Aim for a moist result, lightly browned in places. Add extra oil as required. In a separate pan, cook the leek in butter and its own juices, stirring all the time: aim to keep a slight crispness. Season and mix with the aubergine.

Whereas aubergine can be cooked in advance and reheated, leeks must be done at the last minute.

## Noisettes of Lamb in Two Guises

Noisettes are a good choice for a special meal, as they can be prepared in advance, then cooked at the last moment. The first recipe is Greek, from Claudia Roden. The second Provençal, from Jean-Marc Banzo, of the Clos des Voilettes at Aix.

### With vine leaves in fila pastry

Serves 8

*16 noisettes, a good cm ( ½ inch) thick*
*16 large vine leaves*
*8 sheets fila pastry*
*melted butter*
*salt*
*1 egg white*
*lemon wedges*

MARINADE
*6 tablespoons olive oil*
*2 tablespoons lemon juice*

*about 125 ml (4 fl oz) red wine*
*coarsely ground pepper*
*3 cloves garlic, crushed, chopped, plus 1–2 teaspoons* rigani, *oregano or*
*marjoram*

Mix all the marinade ingredients together.

Trim the fat from the noisettes, leaving the 'eye' of lean meat and put into the marinade for up to 1 hour.

Pour boiling water over the vine leaves, if packed in brine, and soak until palatable. (In summer use fresh leaves blanched until just limp in boiling water: always avoid using canned leaves as they are too tender.) Drain both the meat and the leaves.

Cut the sheets of fila pastry in half lengthways and brush with melted butter. Salt the noisettes, wrap each in a vine leaf and put at the narrow end of each pastry strip. Then flip over the sides, and roll up and seal the ends with a dab of egg white. Brush all the packages with melted butter.

To cook, either bake for 10 minutes on the top rack in the oven preheated to gas 6, 200°C (400°F), or – and I think this is better – deep-fry for 4–5 minutes, until golden brown, in oil at a temperature of 170°C (340°F). These timings give pink meat.

Serve with lemon wedges and the *ragoût,* or alternatively with a chicory salad containing coriander or watercress and a nut oil dressing.


## Crépinettes with creamed garlic

If you are serving the aubergine and leek *ragoût,* substitute another vegetable stew for the ratatouille, e.g. peperonata.

Serves 8

*500 g (1 lb) ratatouille*
*2 pieces of caul fat*
*8 long noisettes, each weighing 125–150 g (4–5 oz) trimmed*
*500 g (1 lb) cloves garlic, peeled*
*200 ml (7 fl oz) milk*
*200 ml (7 fl oz) crème fraîche, or mixed soured and double cream*

Chop or mill the ratatouille coarsely, to make a rough, spreadable paste. Rinse the caul fat in warm water to make it supple and cut eight squares from it, large enough to enclose the pieces of lamb. Make a bed of ratatouille in the centre of each square, put the lamb on top, season and spread with more ratatouille (you may not need it all). Wrap caul round, cutting away any lumpiness, and turn the packages over on to a plate. Chill until required.

To make the creamed garlic, stew the cloves in milk and creams in a covered pan until soft – about 20 minutes. Crush, sieve and season, adding a little water or stock if necessary to give the purée a loose rather than stiff consistency.

To cook the crépinettes, first preheat the oven to gas 8, 230°C (450°F), then brown them on both sides quickly in a non-stick pan brushed with oil. When they are a rich golden colour, put them in the oven for 10 minutes.

Pour off surplus fat from the frying pan and stir in the garlic purée to heat through and take up any meaty juices. Put a noisette on each very hot plate, on a bed of garlic. Serve with plenty of bread.

## Persimmons and Cuajada

Serves 8

*1 generous litre (2 pt) sheep's milk*
*3 teaspoons rennet or junket tablets*
*8 large ripe persimmons*
*8 lemon wedges*

Bring the milk to blood heat, quickly stir in the rennet and pour into one large bowl or eight individual pots. Leave undisturbed at room temperature to set, then chill.

Cut off the stalk ends of the persimmons, like a lid, so that people can dig in with their spoons and squeeze in drops of lemon, taking alternate dips into the junket and fruit. Pass round Jersey cream and a bowl of golden granulated or preserving sugar, or clear honey, or chopped preserved ginger (e.g. Noel's Simply Ginger). Biscuits are also a good idea, crisp ones, or something of the brandy snap type, like the following Lace biscuits:

*75 g (2½ oz) butter*
*75 g (2½ oz) rolled oats*
*125 g (4 oz) caster sugar*
*1 egg, beaten*
*1 level teaspoon each flour and baking powder, mixed*

Preheat oven to gas 4, 180°C (350°F). Grease two baking sheets with butter papers.

Melt butter over a low heat, stir in oats immediately. Remove from heat and add sugar, then egg. Stir in flour and baking powder. Drop 4 teaspoons of the mixture, well apart, on each baking sheet.

Bake until pale brown. Remove and press biscuits over a greased rolling pin to make a tuile effect. Should the biscuits stick to the sheet as they cool, put the sheet back in the oven briefly and try removing them again.

[*Observer Magazine*]


## EDIBLE GIFTS

Edible gifts between adults are, I think, something new in this country. Years ago the grocer put a little extra item into the Christmas order as a thank you for your continued and regular custom. We've all read about vicars' wives and squires' wives with beef tea. People in the country are often generous with a brace of pheasant or partridge, but this is not quite what we mean.

Until about thirty years ago, or perhaps even twenty, edible gifts were the department of the seven-year-old, who started rolling fondant the day the holidays began, colouring it pink, flavouring it lavishly with peppermint, to disguise the grey fatigue of the much-worked shapes. The lucky recipient, usually a grandmother or aunt, took them with a loving hug and a brave mouth.

Latterly, though, whether from America or Europe or from a new pride in our own culinary skill, has come a pleasant interchange of delightful things to eat, presents unique to the giver. I noticed it first in France, in the early Sixties (with some dismay as well as pleasure – what return could we make?) when friends came to lunch with a beautifully arranged basket of things from the garden, with a jar of raspberry jelly or a bottle of mirabelle liqueur tucked in as well.

Peripatetic Americans would order special boxes of sweets from the best confectioner in lieu of the cookies they would have contributed had they been at home. In the past ten years I have noticed friends in England doing the same thing. Nowadays, at Christmas, their jars and boxes of delights are a real addition to the basic repertoire of the season.

Indeed, the presents I now remember best are the edible ones. Perhaps because some of them are repeated regularly, Christmas would not be Christmas without them. All the recipes below are things the family has been particularly grateful to receive. The cynical Martial may have observed that gifts are fish-hooks. I would rather say, with Charles Lamb, that 'Presents endear Absents'.

Feasting apart, pleasure also comes from wrapping and presentation, as much an indication of the intentions of the giver as the delicious contents. Some friends make a year-long search for elegant jars. I have a niece who haunts London paper shops for special Japanese papers and a daughter who eschews holly and bells for the stark clarity of plain colour and contrasting glitter. Everyone wraps presents, but edible presents seem to receive a special treatment.

## Cheese Biscuits

Mix together, by hand or in the processor, 250 g (8 oz) each flour and grated Leicester cheese with 200 g (7 oz) lightly salted butter. A little cayenne can be mixed in at this stage if you like.

The dough will be on the tacky side. Scrape it on to two pieces of greaseproof and form into rolls. Chill until firm. Slice thinly and distribute on baking parchment-lined trays. Sprinkle with cayenne or a coarsely ground peppercorn mixture, or with sesame or poppy seeds. Bake about 10 minutes in an oven preheated to gas 4, 180°C (350°F) or until crisp – timing depends on thickness of the slices.

## Spiced Nuts

Pat Bellman, who comes to help with the cooking, has the most agreeable habit of giving us spiced nuts at Christmas. They are particularly good, and not arduous to make. Have a good mixture of nuts, blanching or skinning as appropriate, and cutting brazils into pieces. Put 750 g (1½ lb) of nuts into a bowl. Mix a heaped tablespoon *garam masala* with 2 tablespoons peanut oil and mix thoroughly into the nuts. Spread them in a single layer on a baking sheet. Sprinkle with a teaspoon of fine sea salt. Give them 20 minutes in an oven preheated to gas 4, 180°C (350°F), shaking them every so often so they toast evenly.

## Dried Tomatoes in Olive Oil

Put the tomatoes into a large bowl and pour boiling water over them to cover them generously. Leave 5 minutes, scoop out with a slotted spoon, draining them well and put them into jars.

While they are still warm, pour over a robust olive oil and add some cloves of garlic, bay leaves and branches of rosemary as well as some lightly crushed peppercorns. Cover when they are cold, topping up the oil if necessary to make sure the tomatoes are completely submerged. Leave for at least a fortnight before using.

## Salted Lemons or Limes

An attractive preserve for anyone who likes Middle-Eastern and North African food. It is used as a flavouring for certain stews, and as an accompaniment to salads, fish and so on. Jars of the Kilner type are the most practical. Sometimes you can find them with coloured wire fastenings. Wash and rinse, then dry upside down on the rack of a low oven to sterilize them.

Quarter enough lemons or limes to fill the jars, cutting across twice at right angles, but not completely through – a tulip effect. Cram 1– 1½ teaspoons coarse salt into each one and press it back into shape. Put a thin layer of salt in the base of each jar and pack in the fruit, pushing it down to get in as much as possible. Cut batons from two wooden skewers that can be fitted into the neck of the jars to hold the fruit down. Then pour in strained lemon or lime juice to cover. Alternatively use cold brine – dissolve 30 g (1 oz) coarse salt in 300 ml (½ pt) boiling water, then leave to cool.

Close the jars and store in a cool dark place for 3–4 weeks before broaching. As you remove the fruit, make sure that the remaining contents are submerged in the liquid. To use: rinse the lemons, cut completely into wedges, then scrape off and discard the pulp. If the peel is very salty, it can be soaked. For a salad or to serve as an accompanying relish, pour over olive or groundnut oil and sprinkle lightly with cayenne.

## Marinaded Mushrooms (*Funghi Sott'olio*)

The other day I happened to be passing the Neal Street Restaurant, and Antonio Carluccio gave me a jar of his pickled mushrooms. They reminded me of the quantities of ceps that I used to put up in oil when I was writing *The Mushroom Feast*. In those days the woods of our commune were full of ceps, chanterelles and hedgehog mushrooms (*Hydnum repandum*). Out of season, substitute close firm button and marron mushrooms, oyster mushrooms and fresh shiitake. Use an unfiltered olive oil, or at least one with a good flavour.

The bouillon can be used for several kilos of mushrooms, just keep the level topped up with boiling water and taste to make sure the mushrooms are not too strong.

*1 kg (2 lb) mixed firm mushrooms, prepared weight*
*juice of 2 lemons*
*fresh bay leaves and sprigs of thyme*
*a few juniper berries and peppercorns (mixed green, black and pink)*
*olive oil*

BOUILLON
*1 medium onion, quartered*
*4 halves cloves garlic*
*5 halves shallots*
*thinly cut zest of 2 lemons*
*1 teaspoon cumin seeds*
*2 teaspoons lightly crushed black peppercorns*
*2 teaspoons lightly crushed juniper berries*
*3 generous sprigs thyme, 3 bay leaves*
*7 tablespoons white wine vinegar*
*2 teaspoons salt*

Brush any earth from the mushrooms, quarter cultivated and marron mushrooms if they are 2½ cm (1 inch) across. Cut shiitake and oysters in convenient sections. Keep the two sorts of mushroom in separate bowls. Sprinkle with lemon juice, turn gently with your hands.

Tie the bouillon ingredients, down to and including bay leaves, loosely into a piece of muslin. Suspend in a large pan containing vinegar, salt and 1¼ litres (2¼ pt) water. Simmer steadily for 10 minutes, then bring to a rolling boil.

Put a small batch of mushrooms into a blanching basket and dunk in the bouillon. It should barely go off the boil. Timing from when it returns to the boil, give the mushrooms 2 minutes. Remove, draining the liquor back into the pan, and try a piece. The flavour should be very mildly sharp, just a little lemonish piquancy, and the texture quite firm. Make adjustments to the bouillon flavouring at this stage. Cook the remaining mushrooms in batches, giving the oysters and shiitake just a minute's boiling.

When the mushrooms are cool, mix and pack them into sterilized jars, pushing 1–2 bay leaves down the sides (green side out) and scattering in a few juniper berries and peppercorns. Cover with olive oil and seal.

The mushrooms can be served directly as an hors d'oeuvre or in a salad. Or they can be added to a risotto, stuffing or sauce. The oil makes a splendid vinaigrette.

*Note*: you can augment the mushrooms with small whole pickling onions, shallots and cloves of garlic, just a few to each bottle. Skin them and put into the bouillon in a separate bag from the flavouring items: they should be tender enough after 10 minutes' simmering and 2 minutes' boiling, but check anyway.

## Clementines in Armagnac

Sometimes at the beginning of December you can buy very small, almost miniature clementines. These are the best for this preserve, especially if you intend to give it away and the look is important, but larger ones can be used.

*1 kg (2 lb) clementines*
*600 g (1¼ lb) sugar*
*1–2 vanilla pods*
*Armagnac*

Prick each clementine with a darning needle five times. Make a syrup with the sugar and 1 litre (scant 2 pt) water and add 1 long or 2 short vanilla pods. Boil steadily for 4 minutes, put in the clementines and bring to simmering point. Half-cover and simmer for 1 hour. Check every so often, removing any fruit that is on the verge of cracking, which spoils the appearance though not the flavour.

Drain and fill into hot dry presentable jars. Pour in Armagnac to come three-quarters of the way up the fruit. Meanwhile, reduce the syrupy cooking liquor to concentrate the sweetness. Keep tasting and remove from heat before it becomes very bitter. Cool to warm, then use to fill the jars. Divide vanilla pod if need be, then put a piece into each jar. Close and keep for a fortnight before using. (Surplus syrup can be kept for sauces and fruit salads.)

*[Observer Magazine]*

# BIBLIOGRAPHY

## BOOKS BY JANE GRIGSON

*Charcuterie and French Pork Cookery*, Michael Joseph, 1967; Penguin, 1970

*Good Things*, Michael Joseph, 1971; Penguin 1973

*The International Wine and Food Society's Guide to Fish Cookery*, The International Wine and Food Publishing Company/ David and Charles, 1973; *Fish Cookery*, Penguin, 1973

*English Food: An Anthology*, Macmillan, 1974; Penguin, 1977

*The World Atlas of Food: A Gourmet's Guide to the Great Regional Dishes of the World*, Mitchell Beazley Publishers Ltd, 1974

*The Mushroom Feast: A Celebration of All Edible Fungi, Cultivated, Wild and Dried Varieties, With More Than 100 Recipes to Choose From*, Michael Joseph, 1975; *The Mushroom Feast*, Penguin, 1983

*Cooking Carrots*, Abson Books, 1975

*Cooking Spinach*, Abson Books, 1976

*Jane Grigson's Vegetable Book*, Michael Joseph, 1978; Penguin, 1986

*Food with the Famous*, Michael Joseph, 1979; Penguin, 1981

*Jane Grigson's Fruit Book*, Michael Joseph, 1982; Penguin, 1983

*Year of the French: Six Recipes by Jane Grigson from the BBC2 Series*, Warren Editions, 1982

*The Observer Guide to European Cookery*, Michael Joseph, 1983

*The Observer Guide to British Cookery*, Michael Joseph, 1984

*Dishes of the Mediterranean*, A Sainsbury Cookbook, 1984; *The Cooking of the Mediterranean*, A Sainsbury Cookbook, 1991

*Exotic Fruits and Vegetables*, Jonathan Cape, 1986

*The Cooking of Normandy*, A Sainsbury Cookbook, 1987

# Index